# The Dismantling of India's Democracy

# The Dismantling of India's Democracy

## 1947 to 2025

PREM SHANKAR JHA

SPEAKING TIGER

SPEAKING TIGER BOOKS LLP
125A, Ground Floor, Shahpur Jat, near Asiad Village,
New Delhi 110049

First published by Speaking Tiger Books in 2025



ISBN: 978-93-5447-750-8
eISBN: 978-93-5447-945-8

10 9 8 7 6 5 4 3 2 1

Typeset in Minion Pro by SÜRYA, New Delhi
Printed at Chaman Enterprises, New Delhi

# Contents

# Preface

This book is not a celebration of success, but a lament over failure. The failure is heart-wrenching because India almost took democracy to heights that no country had scaled before, and then failed to reach them. Our freedom movement, and our Constituent Assembly, created the most ethnically diverse, but culturally homogeneous, democracy in the world. But they failed to embed it in sufficiently durable soil to ensure that its roots would endure and grow stronger over time. Their failure to do so has extracted a price from our people that has grown higher with every passing year, and the democracy we were so proud of has begun to resemble the Fascism that devastated inter-war Europe in the twentieth century, and is raising its head again there and in parts of Asia and South America today.

India gained its independence on the 15th of August 1947, which was considerably earlier than the original date set for it, of June 30, 1948. But while Britain's rush out of India was sudden and forced by its own exhaustion after the Second World War, the shift of first administrative and then legislative power from British to Indian hands had begun much earlier.

Even at the height of its power in India, the British had left varying degrees of self-governance, under their oversight, to some 584 princely states that made up more than forty per cent of the sub-continent. In the part of British India that it ruled directly, it had begun to devolve administration to Indians through the creation of the Indian Civil Service. In 1922, the Indian component of the Indian Civil Service was substantially increased by allowing the entrance examination to be held co-terminously in India and England.

More grudgingly, the British had also begun to devolve legislative power to Indians in small doses from the beginning of the twentieth century. This had begun with the Morley–Minto reforms of 1909, was enlarged by the Montagu–Chelmsford reforms of 1919, and more decisively by the Government of India Act, 1935. But in all of these enactments, the franchise was limited to property owners. This restricted the number of voters to at most ten per cent of the adult population, who were almost entirely, if not exclusively, males.

All the above acts prescribed separate quotas for every minority community and religion in the country that the British could think of. Thus, there were seats reserved for Muslims, Christians, Sikhs, Anglo-Indians and various other minorities as well as for the princely states. The intended purpose was to limit the formation of common legislative purpose and leave effective power, even in the subjects that had been 'transferred' to Indians by the reforms of 1909 and 1919, in the hands of the Crown.

That was the fractured heritage, culminating in the partition of British India, which the constitution of free India set out to repair. It is against this mammoth task that one needs to measure what the Constituent Assembly's labours achieved, within a single decade of Independence. It is therefore all the more painful to measure the failures and disappointments that have followed.

This book is an attempt to do both. The conclusions it reaches are not reassuring: while our Constitution, and the democracy it created, unified the country to a degree never achieved before, by and large without resort to violence, those whom the people have chosen to rule have not served them equally well. As a result, after a spectacular initial success in nation building, India's democracy has increasingly failed to meet the political and economic aspirations of its people. This has opened the doors for the emergence of an alternative, authoritarian model for India's future, loosely labelled *Hindutva*.

This book seeks to understand the causes of this steady drift to the Right, and the very real threat that it could end with the replacement of a democracy that celebrates India's ethnic and religious diversity by an unstable, increasingly authoritarian autocracy—an intolerant variant of European Fascism—that will make many of India's ethno-national communities rebel, and lead to India's disintegration. To do so it first highlights India's initial success in building an extremely diverse democratic polity; and then traces its subsequent failure to capitalize upon this success and create a stable and vibrant democratic nation. It explores the causes of this failure and highlights similarities between these and the political and economic causes of the emergence of Fascism in Europe after the First World War.

It ends with a warning about the threat we face today, but also a small hope that our democracy will endure.

CHAPTER ONE

# A Brief Note on Representative Democracy

In his penultimate book, *The Third Wave: Democratization in the Late Twentieth Century*, Samuel Huntington described the near-universal acceptance, in the second half of the twentieth century, of democracy as the best form of government, as the culmination of a process that had begun with the rise of capitalism and the nation-state. His thesis, although well argued, was naïve for it considered democracy to be of relatively recent origin, and co-terminous with adult franchise and universal suffrage—i.e. one adult, one vote. But democracy is far older than capitalism and the democratic system it brought about both in form and content. It was the mode of government in several of the city states of ancient Greece, notably Athens, five hundred years before the birth of Christ. It was also the mode of governance in the Licchhavi confederation that ruled most of what is now north Bihar and Nepal's Terai, at much the same time.

In Athens, the electorate was limited to the male heads of landowning families. In the Licchhavi confederation, it was limited to the male heads of *Kshatriya* families who, by and large, were also the principal landowners. Athenians practised direct democracy—one man, one vote; the Licchhavis, indirect democracy, in which each principality elected a representative to send to a central council at Vaishali. The common feature of both these forms was a desire to limit the electorate to those who had a stake in the preservation of the society they lived in. In his immortal work, *Politics*, Aristotle had described the practice of politics as the noblest of human arts because it seeks the common good of the largest form of human society, i.e. the state. In almost the same breath he cautioned readers against being swept away by calls for 'democracy', i.e. rule through decision-making by all. His reason was that democracies define freedom badly: 'everyone lives as he wants and "toward whatever [end] he happens to crave", as Euripides says'. The purpose of government was 'the good of the whole', and this, he believed, was best achieved by a 'polity' (*politeia*), a 'virtuous popular regime' that was to be a mix of aristocracy and oligarchy.

The British had followed the same logic while ruling India when they restricted the vote to property owners, but they had done so with the purpose of maintaining the stability of their empire. Any restriction of the electorate was therefore anathema to the Congress party when the country gained its freedom. India's Constituent Assembly opted immediately for the removal of all restrictions upon the electorate and the adoption of universal suffrage instead.

It felt no qualms in doing so because by the middle of the twentieth century, democracy had come a long way, not only in form but also philosophy, since the days of the Greeks and Licchhavis. The fear of 'democracy' unleashing demagogy, and leading to 'bad freedom' had almost completely evaporated. This was because when it was resuscitated as an ideal form of government by French philosophers three centuries ago, it was to justify the revolt of an emerging commercial class against the crushing power of monarchs, backed by a landed aristocracy, who claimed a divine right to rule that was sanctified by a complaisant church.

Numbers count in any revolution. So, while this concept of democracy gained rapid acceptance, it exalted precisely what Aristotle had feared most: it claimed that *all* men (humans) were born free and equal, and had an equal right to the fruits that

God had so bountifully bestowed upon the earth. It condemned hierarchy and absolutism, and demanded that people be ruled by the laws that they themselves made through a common consensus, or a commonly agreed process of arriving at one. Jean-Jacques Rousseau called this the 'Social Contract'. The contents of this contract would be determined by a 'General Will' that would emerge through debate, and automatically serve the best interests of the largest possible number. Democracy, based on such a social contract, would therefore empower all the members of society, the rich and the poor alike.

Reality never succeeds in matching our dreams, but over the two centuries that followed, through bloody revolution and crippling, suicidal war, but also through the foresight of leaders who recognized and accepted the need for gradual change, the shift of power from monarchies to representatives of the people was achieved in Britain, the USA, France and Germany, then Scandinavia, Italy, the British 'white' colonies—Canada, Australia and New Zealand—and then in Spain and Portugal.

This vast political change coincided with, and was spurred by, the rise of industrial capitalism. Capitalism created a politicized working class, the *proletariat*, by bringing workers into continuous direct contact with their peers on the factory floor. The workers developed a consciousness of their common interest. Their employers, and political leaders, recognized that not only economic peace but also political power could be secured by conceding some of their demands. In the end, all men and women did not become equal, but all gained the right, and increasingly the means, with which to aspire to equality, through education.

These concessions empowered the poor. But the empowerment remained incomplete so long as they remained at the mercy of market forces alone. People living in tribes or villages had never lost their sense of social unity, for when all was said and done, every member of the tribe or village felt some degree of responsibility for the more unfortunate among them, right down to the village idiot. Capitalism broke this complex web of social responsibility by first shifting the workplace from the village to the town and then by replacing the two earlier forms of social exchange, Reciprocity and Redistribution, with the sole mode of Exchange.[1]

In this new world, the poor exchanged their labour for food and shelter in a contractual arrangement very different from the one that Rousseau had envisaged. When business conditions were good they earned good wages, lived well and sent money back to their families in the village, as migrant workers in India and China do today.[2] But when the factory or workshop closed, they not only lost their jobs but also their food, lodgings and support for their families. In the words of the great economic historian and anthropologist Karl Polanyi, they found themselves in a 'stark utopia', in which they could not know a moment of peace, and in which many of them could not, ultimately, survive.

Democracy's crowning achievement was the *re*-creation of social security in an urban, industrialized society. This was begun by Otto von Bismarck, chancellor of the unified German Empire, in the 1880s, taken over wholeheartedly by Britain after an epic constitutional battle in 1909, and followed with varying degrees of enthusiasm by the other European democracies, and the USA.

All of this unfolded even as a new middle class, educated in British established and administered universities in India, and in the elite universities and Inns of Court of Britain, was taking shape in India. For this Western-educated middle class, freedom and self-government—later embodied in democracy—were therefore synonymous. But India was an entirely different kind of entity from the European democracies. The latter were all small states when they began their democratization. Most of them had already gone through the violent process of nation building and had established sovereign, unitary states backed by established churches, which had legitimized the forced homogenization of diverse cultures in the name of God and the Crown. All of them were therefore fairly advanced industrial states when the democratic process reached its full flowering.

India was the exact opposite. In the middle of the eighteenth century, it was huge, rich and ethnically diverse to an extent that stupefied the European mind. But with no strong central power to hold it together, it was also ripe for plunder. The century of pillage by the British East India Company that followed reduced it from the second richest to one of the poorest countries in the world. Despite this, by 1947, it had developed a small but extremely efficient industrial structure in a few cities. Nine out of ten of its people, however, still lived in the villages where traditional cultural norms, including an inordinate respect for age and hierarchy within families, and ritualized oppression of the lower castes, was the norm. To say that turning this India into a modern, industrialized, democratic state was immensely more difficult than turning the Russia of 1918 into a modern, industrial state would be an understatement.

Despite this, to the world's amazement, while the Soviet experiment failed, ours succeeded. By the mid-nineties, we had created the most complex, but at the same time most flexible, democratic system the world had seen. And unlike Europe, where the modern nation-state was born out of war and forced ethnic homogenization, our leaders created a modern state almost entirely without resorting to war. It is this singular achievement, which the midnight's children of Partition took for granted, that is now in mortal danger of getting undone.

CHAPTER TWO

# India's Unique Achievement

The mortal danger, of losing our democracy, was far from apparent in May 1994, when Prime Minister Narasimha Rao paid his first and only state visit to the United States of America. Although it came a bare seven years after Rajiv Gandhi's visit in 1987, it far surpassed the former in importance for it took place in a world transformed by the end of the Cold War and an India transformed by its new-found economic freedom. In the US, the Democrats had returned to power after being in the wilderness for twelve years. Victory in the Cold War had released US foreign policy from its straitjacket, and revived some of the expansive generosity it had shown towards Germany, and the developing countries, in the first decades after the end of the Second World War.

The India that Narasimha Rao represented was also radically different from the one that had existed seven years earlier, for its economy was no longer hemmed in by import bans and sky-high tariffs. The integration of its large home market with that of the rest of the world was well under way, and was being watched avidly by American investors.

At the White House press conference that followed Rao's one-on-one meeting with Bill Clinton on May 19, the President paid India a tribute that few of those who heard it have forgotten. He began his statement to the assembled media by listing the subjects he had discussed with Rao from a few slips of paper in his hands—clearly *aides-memoire* from his aides. Then, with the briefest of pauses, he added, 'Along with the US, India is one of the world's great experiments in multi-cultural democracy. His people have fought for more than four decades now to keep democracy alive under the most amazing challenges.' These remarks were not scripted for he did not look down at the notes that he had been consulting earlier even once. More than what he said, it was the tone in which he said it, and the slight emphasis he put on the word 'amazing', that revealed the depth of his admiration for India's achievement.[1]

Clinton's praise in 1994 was sincere. As a Rhodes scholar and student of philosophy, politics and economics at Oxford University, he had perceived what few others had till then: that in sharp contrast to nation building in Europe and North America, India had succeeded in turning itself into a modern nation-state *without taking recourse to war*. After the end of the colonial era in the 1960s, 130 new countries had joined the United Nations. All but a few had started out as democracies. Only five had been able to sustain and stabilize it. India was by far the largest and most complex among them. So, as the leader of the world's richest and most powerful democracy, Clinton's praise for India's success was not therefore simply a diplomatic courtesy, but was born out of a genuine desire to understand how India had done it.

What made the Indian experience unique was the starting point from which it had begun. The European nation-state had been born out of protracted conflict—the hundred years of internecine struggle between feudal chieftains that preceded the formation of the northern Italian state system in 1478; the 104 years of civil strife in England that began with the War of the Roses in 1455 and ended with the assumption of ecclesiastical authority by Queen Elizabeth in 1559; the six decades Louis XIV took to create a unified, centrally ruled, France; and most devastating of all, the Thirty Years' War in continental Europe from 1618 to 1648, which cost eight million lives through battle, disease and famine. The horrific destruction of that war led to the

Treaty of Westphalia, which was Europe's first concerted effort to create the foundations of peace and proscribe war.

This was easier said than done. In the three centuries that followed its signature, the nascent nation-states of Europe had to defend their borders from attack while simultaneously suppressing upsurges of sub-regional loyalties within them. By gradual degrees they learned to minimize external threats by creating well-marked and heavily defended 'hard' frontiers with their neighbours; the internal one, from sub-nationalism, was met by fostering the growth of a single, homogeneous cultural narrative.

The rise of industrial capitalism reinforced both these tendencies by bringing a third element into this mix of motives: this was the competition to industrialize. This created the rationale for a further hardening of the boundaries between nation-states. Tariff barriers and import bans sprang up to protect the domestic market space from invasion by 'alien' industry. Capital movements were blocked to prevent accumulated profits from leaving one country in quest of better earnings in another. Finally, the free movement of labour was blocked to prevent the high wages and social benefits in the industrialized countries from attracting cheap foreign labour from their neighbours.

Thus, by degrees the nation-state became an instrument for the creation and preservation of economic autarchy. Economic autarchy further deepened cultural, political and economic divisions that nation building had already created between the people of neighbouring countries. The penultimate step in nation building was cultural homogenization. This was achieved by enforcing a common language and a single, sanitized version of history. In communities where this too did not work, nation-states played their last card. That was 'ethnic cleansing'.

By the late nineteenth and early twentieth centuries, ethnic cleansing had become the second handmaiden of a nation-state-based world order. When the Ottoman Empire began to lose its grip on the Danube-Balkans region, successive waves of Turkish Muslims were forced to leave the newly emerging nations of

Bulgaria, Serbia and Greece. The xenophobic reaction this created in Turkey, particularly as the Ottoman Empire found itself on the losing side in the First World War, culminated in the organized expulsion of Greeks from Thrace, the region around Istanbul, and of Armenians from Anatolia (Asian Turkey). The latter reached its height when a 'Young Turk' government rounded up nearly all the Armenians in Anatolia and marched them into the Syrian desert. By some estimates, 1.5 million Armenians died during that death march and in other attacks on Armenians between 1915 and 1918. There were similar pogroms of Jews in the Russian Empire, specifically in Poland and Ukraine between 1881 and 1884.

By the early twentieth century, forced homogenization and ethnic cleansing had become the defining features of the European nation-state. Its bestiality reached its nadir in the Holocaust in which Hitler's Nazis starved, worked or gassed to death six million Jews shipped into Germany and Poland from all over Europe, and took human civilization to the lowest point in its 5,000-year history of unremitting violence.

After the Second World War, the Charter of the United Nations restored the Westphalian international order and maintained a tenuous peace in the world for half a century. But the resulting peace proved short-lived. The end of the Cold War in 1986, and the upsurge of America's ambition to create a unipolar world similar to the *Pax Romana* of the first till fifth centuries AD, fatally weakened the Westphalian underpinnings of the UN charter and began its slide into irrelevance. The two developments responsible for this were the onset of economic globalization, and the resurgence of ethnicity.

## The Origins of Globalization

Globalization originated in dramatic breakthroughs in transport and information technology that occurred in the sixties and seventies. These made it possible for giant multinationals to manufacture goods in the low wage countries of Asia and Latin America and ship them back to their home markets at a lower overall cost than they would have incurred by producing them at home. That was the beginning of the internationalization of both manufacture and marketing that came to be known as Globalization. The political and economic compulsions of Global Capitalism were starkly opposed to those of Nation-state Capitalism. National capitalism had required a constant reinforcement of barriers to trade, capital movements and labour. Globalization required the removal of all three to create a large enough market for it to function with maximum efficiency. This reversal of the goals of the industrialized countries surfaced abruptly at the Tokyo round of trade talks under the General Agreement on Tariffs and Trade (GATT) in 1980. In these, and the rounds that followed under the World Trade Organization (WTO), the industrialized nations asked the developing countries to cooperate, and not compete, with them by progressively removing controls on the movement of goods, services and capital across frontiers, and to harmonize the rules and regulations that governed international business.

But the circumstances of the birth of the nation-state, in war and conquest, had left nation-states poorly equipped to cope with the simultaneous integrative pull of the global market and the divisive push of ethnicity. In their relationship with the newly decolonized countries, therefore, they are far more comfortable with a hierarchical structure than an egalitarian one. Today, therefore, when such industrialized nations promote peace because this is now an essential requirement for the success of globalization, they tend to do so in the role of authority, administering law, and not as equal parties seeking peace through accommodation.

To this type of mindset, ensuring 'global peace' has meant ensuring a monopoly of military power for the industrialized nations; 'free trade' has meant lowering or eliminating tariff barriers in the developing countries while retaining the right to put up non-tariff barriers around their own economies. This mindset is most evident in the contradiction between the ever more free movement of goods, services and capital across national boundaries and the ever more restricted movement of labour. This asymmetry is not questioned despite the fact that the industrialized countries have been its principal victims. For as wage differentials between the rich and poor nations have widened, the flight of industry from the high to the low wage countries has become more rapid, and more pronounced.

The enforced cultural homogeneity that is a key feature of the nation-state has also made it difficult for European nation-states to deal with a resurgence of ethnicity within their boundaries. In an effort to limit the flight of capital from their shores the European and American nation-states have opened their doors to immigrants from poor and war torn countries. But this has created an entirely new challenge that few have found a way of meeting. This is because the archetypal nation-state is unitary, i.e. one in which all of its citizens are directly ruled by a single central authority. Such states frown upon intermediate layers of loyalty, such as to region, race, language or religion. By the same token, the possibility of there being different laws for different, identifiable subgroups within a single legal system is unthinkable. But this is the very least that the recognition of ethnic diversity requires. As a result, there is a predisposition in all the industrialized countries to treat every demand for ethnic self-assertion as a demand for secession. This has created tensions between 'natives' and immigrants that are creating a marked shift towards the far right in more and more of them, including the USA. But growing global interdependence has made the cost of any sudden, let alone violent, economic severance well-nigh insupportable.

The information revolution has also largely ruled out their only other option—that of ethnic cleansing. With global television, mobile telephony and digital transfers of information having brought the world into people's drawing rooms, the pogroms that Turkey, Germany and Russia launched against minorities, such as the Armenians, the Jews and the Poles of Silesia, in the first half of the twentieth century, will no longer be tolerated. Today, among the industrialized countries, Israel is the only country that continues to use ethnic cleansing as an instrument of national policy, and it is by no means certain how long its neighbours, and the rest of the world, will tolerate it.

## The Indian Model of Nationhood

In sharp contrast to European nation building, the Indian state is founded upon a ready acceptance of India's ethnic, linguistic, religious and cultural diversity. India has more than 2,000 ethnic groups, and twenty-nine principal languages, of which thirteen are spoken by more than ten million people, and another sixteen that are spoken by more than a million. Twelve of the thirteen major languages belong to powerful ethno-linguistic groups that have lived in independent kingdoms for several centuries at a time over the past two millennia.

To a child travelling by train from Calcutta (now Kolkata) to Delhi in the 1940s, India was a wonderland of diverse experiences. At every station where the train stopped, not only was the language spoken on the platform different, but also its pitch and intonation. The dresses of the women, the head-dresses of the men, their colours, materials and designs, all changed every fifty or so miles. Even the food and sweetmeats sold by hawkers on the platforms changed from one station to the next. The variety encountered on a train to Madras (now Chennai) was even greater.

But India also has a long tradition of empire. From the Mauryan Empire till the British, for 850 out of 2,300 years, most of the Indian subcontinent has been ruled by a single central authority. At their height these empires spanned not only all of north and most of the south India, but also trans-Himalayan Afghanistan. Even after these perished, the memory of empire, and the hankering to restore it persisted for generations and provided the motive force for expansion and consolidation within the subcontinent.

So strong was the pull of this dream that in 1771, a decade after the Maratha Empire's defeat at the hands of the Afghan invader, Ahmad Shah Abdali, Mahadji Sindhia, one of the three pillars of its resurrection, entered Delhi with the express purpose of restoring the titular Mughal emperor, Shah Alam II, to his throne. Not content with this, he virtually destroyed the Jat kingdom based in Mathura, and the Pashtun Rohillas based in Rohilkhand, to restore the Mughal Emperor's eminent domain over its immediate neighbourhood, and protected it with Maratha troops till his death.

Another lesson of history that was ingrained in the leaders of the Congress party, formed in 1885, was that invasions of India had succeeded during periods when domestic empires had disintegrated, and failed when the invaders had encountered a strong central power in control of the plains of Hindustan. Alexander had turned back after defeating Porus, who ruled the territory between the Jhelum and Chenab rivers, because he realized that Porus, whom he had been able to defeat in large part because Porus' rival Ambhi, the ruler of Takshila, had sided with him, had only been a local ruler.

The battle against Porus had cost more lives than any they had fought till then, in part because Porus had deployed somewhere between eighty-five and 200 war elephants (the latter being the figure given by the Greek historian Arrian), which were a new and terrifying weapon that the Greeks had not encountered till then. When his generals learned that the main Nanda army—of the Nanda Empire that covered a large portion of the north Indian plains—drawn up beyond the Beas river consisted of 200,000 infantry, 80,000 cavalry, 8,000 war chariots and 6,000 war elephants against their 40,000 infantry and 7,000 cavalry, they advised Alexander to turn back.

A far more dangerous invasion, one that would possibly have destroyed the Vedic culture of India, was foiled repeatedly between 1243 and 1305 AD by two Muslim rulers of the Delhi Sultanate—Ghiyasuddin Balban and Alauddin Khilji. These were the repeated and determined attempts by the Mongols to invade and conquer northern India, after the rise of Genghis Khan in 1206. Their first invasion of India occurred in 1241 and took the

Delhi Sultanate by surprise. The Mongols were therefore able to advance all the way till Lahore, 400 kilometres north-west of Delhi, which they sacked at will.

But that changed when Ghiyasuddin Balban took control of the Delhi Sultanate first as the principal adviser to the Sultan and later as the Sultan himself. To keep the Mongols at bay, Balban built a string of forts along the north-western frontier, manned them with a standing, professional army and appointed his best generals, including Prince Muhammad Khan, his favourite son, to lead them. In a succession of battles between 1279 and 1285, Prince Muhammad inflicted a succession of defeats on the invaders, but the last of these cost him his life.

Balban died soon after his son's death, but the military base he had built endured and enabled the next powerful ruler in Delhi, Alauddin Khilji, to inflict two more crushing defeats on the Mongols in 1305 and 1306 which cost the invaders thousands of lives. Those defeats ended the Mongol threat to India and turned them towards Europe.

The third lesson ingrained in the Indian psyche is that empires in India have prospered when their rulers have respected the personal laws and practices of their subjects, and perished when they have tried to impose cultural or religious uniformity upon them.

Two oft-cited examples from recent history are the Mughal Emperor Aurangzeb's attempt to re-impose the *jizya* tax on non-Muslims and curb the growing influence of Rajput princes in his court by bringing Ajit Singh, the minor ruler of Marwar, to Delhi to be raised as a Muslim, and Lord Dalhousie's attempt to enforce the Doctrine of Lapse.

Aurangzeb's decisions alienated the Rajputs of both Mewar and Marwar who formed the bulk of the Mughal army at the time, depleted the Mughal war chest, and severely weakened his army. This sparked insurrection among the Marathas, Rajputs and the Deccan sultanates. The resulting internecine wars left the empire so critically weakened that his successors were unable to ward off the invasion by Nadir Shah, the Shah of Persia, in 1739, and eight invasions by Ahmad Shah Abdali between 1748 and 1767.[2] By the time of the last of these, the Mughal Empire remained only in name. Aurangzeb's wars had left the treasury virtually empty. The loot carried away by Nadir Shah and Ahmad Shah Abdali stripped the empire of its treasures as well, leaving the Emperor without even the 'eminent domain' that was needed to sustain the court. One by one, its provincial governors and subsidiary princes stopped paying tribute, declared themselves independent and began fighting with each other. This became the fertile ground in which European trading companies with their capital and their small but well-trained standing armies obtained the land grants that eventually flowered into colonies, and finally the British empire in India.

Till quite recently, British historians used to insist that the 1857 uprising was no more than a mutiny of British Indian sepoys against the use of new rifles that fired cartridges sealed with pig or beef tallow. But it is now clear that the prime cause was an attempt in the late 1840s by Lord Dalhousie, the Governor General who promulgated a Doctrine of Lapse, to expand British possessions by annexing the territories of Hindu rulers who had entered into 'subsidiary alliances' with Britain, if they died without a natural son. This went directly against the age-old Rajput practice of adopting a son, usually a close relative, who would succeed him when he died, and sent the entire community and much of Hindu India up in flames. The sepoy mutiny only dictated the timing of the general insurrection that followed.

Perhaps the most important but least noted example is provided by the rapid demise of the Mauryan Empire within fifty years after the death of Ashoka. Among the many possible causes of its sudden demise was his decision not only to require his subjects to change a wide range of traditional customs and practices to bring them in line with *Dhamma*—the Buddhist right path—but also to appoint *Dhamma Mahamattas*, a kind of religious police, and *Rajukas* (rural officials), to 'persuade' people onto the right path. The Dhamma Mahamattas were supposed to report directly to him, but as he became more removed from day-to-day governance in later life, they began, increasingly, to abuse the authority that he had delegated to them. This created a gathering wave of discontent that broke shortly after Ashoka's death and caused the Mauryan Empire to disintegrate.

This change is reflected in a change in the tone of the imperial edicts of Ashoka's reign. While the earliest edicts, cut into rock faces, were advisory—urging the people to choose the path of virtue in their relations with each other, stop or at least limit the killing of animals and birds, and eschew lavish festivities (i.e. ostentation and quite possibly drunkenness), later edicts—especially several issued in the 27th year of his reign and inscribed on iron pillars—show that the Dhamma Mahamattas had, by then, been given the power to 'persuade the waverers'.

As Romila Thapar, the foremost historian of ancient India notes: 'the officers have made the propagation of *Dhamma*...their sole function. The king appears to be obsessed with the idea that everyone must practise *Dhamma*. The constant repetition of the word *Dhamma* shows that his enthusiasm is no longer that of someone propagating a new idea, but something that has become part of his very being... The picture of the *Mahamattas* persuading "the waverers" is not entirely a happy one. The degree of self-responsibility that was apparent in the earlier pronunciations of *Dhamma* seems to have given way to a more ordered approach which leaves little choice to the individual. *Dhamma* seems to have acquired an organized set of rules which the *Dhamma Mahamattas* enforce, not entirely according to the will of the individual'.[3]

Ashoka ruled for thirty-seven years, and appointed the Dhamma Mahamattas in the 14th year of his reign. So, by the time he died, the Dhamma Mahamattas and Rajukas had had twenty-three years in which to create resentment against the state through their heavy-handed, and quite possibly extortionate, behaviour. What happened then has been repeated many times in the two millennia that followed: the weakening of central power that followed Ashoka's death allowed first the outlying, and then the inner, principalities to break away from the empire. Less than half a century later, the Mauryan Empire had passed into history.

These are the lessons of history that went, consciously or unconsciously, into the construction of India's modern nationhood. As a result, its founders relied from the beginning upon the accommodation of ethnic and historical claims, and used the lure of democratic participation in an independent India, and its vast market, to widen its base. Our independence movement co-opted not only liberation movements in the British administered territories such as the Vishal Andhra, the Akali, the Greater Haryana and the Tamil Eelam, but also in the larger princely states, where it co-opted democratic struggles that had been demanding greater political participation in decision-making, like the Jammu and Kashmir National Conference in Kashmir, into the grander aim of ending the rule of both their princely rulers and their British overlords to gain their freedom.

This ethno-linguistic diversity was enshrined in the Indian constitution in words whose significance has yet to be fully absorbed. The Constitution called India a 'Union of States'. The implication is clear: the areas being merged were not provinces of a single administration but states that had enjoyed a distinct political and cultural identity before the British conquered them, and therefore before independent India was created. This was not simply a recognition of the fact that 461 princely states, which had not been directly ruled by Britain in 1947, had voluntarily joined the new nation, but of a far older political and cultural heterogeneity—the fact that every part of India had a history of having been an independent state, with its own language, culture and cuisine, that long preceded the creation of the Indian union on August 15, 1947.

The wording of the Constitution was therefore an implicit commitment to preserve that heterogeneity. This commitment was met by the linguistic reorganization of state boundaries in 1957, which re-defined the borders of the Indian states on the basis of the principal language spoken within them. Proof of the success of this strategy in cementing India's unity came barely a decade later when the Dravidar Kazhagam ('Dravidian Federation'), which had been campaigning to form a separate Tamil nation—Dravida Nadu—since before Independence, changed its name to the Dravida Munnetra ('Progressive') Kazhagam, and redefined its goal as the attainment of power in Tamil Nadu within the Indian union, through the electoral process. This single act swept it from the fringes of power to its centre in a single election, in 1967. Since then, the offer of ethnicity based identity within a federation had helped quell rebellions in half a dozen smaller states, including Punjab, Nagaland, Mizoram, Assam, Mizoram, Nagaland, and autonomous territories within existing states such as the Gorkhaland territorial administration within West Bengal, and Bodoland within Assam. By 2014, it had also ended the armed rebellion that had begun in Kashmir in 1989.

India's ethnicity-based federalism has therefore not only succeeded in building a modern nation-state, but also created a model that the Western democracies can learn from as they struggle to protect their national identities in the face of the disintegrative pull of globalization. Indian federalism is similar in form but very different in content to the federalism of the USA or Australia. In the latter, with the lone exception of Quebec in Canada, federation is based on little more than administrative convenience and the fact that the federating states joined the union at different points in time. Indian federalism, by contrast, is built on the historical foundations of the empire-state in which, for hundreds of years at a time, starting from the Mauryas and ending with the British, a single paramount power ruled a host of ethnic sub-states, each of which had its own history, culture and traditions of independence. The empire-state succeeded so long as it respected the autonomy of its constituent units. The modern Indian state has also succeeded because it has enshrined the autonomy of the states in the Constitution. Indeed, it has done more than that: having inherited what Granville Austin, independent India's first constitutional historian, called a quasi-federal state, successive national governments have enlarged the autonomy of the state governments by increasing their share of revenues and Plan grants and reducing the need for central clearances in their disbursement. In conjunction with the linguistic reorganization of state boundaries, this has turned India, by degrees, into a wholly new type of democracy—a federation based not upon geographical or administrative convenience, but upon respect for the ethnic identity of the constituents of the empire-states of the past.

The principal feature of 'ethnic federalism' is that the entire nation is one economic zone in which not just capital but also labour is free to move anywhere in search of work. In practice, this freedom is constrained to varying degrees in the weaker economic states by rules that require employers to give a minimum proportion of the jobs to people from that state. Such rules are observed sketchily at the best of times but provide an important psychological reassurance to the host population in each state. In a few of the economically weaker states, there are similar restrictions upon the freedom to buy land and start a business. But here too, a wide variety of exceptions and loopholes ensure that their impact is mainly psychological.

On the other hand, there are very real safeguards for peoples' ethnic identities. The Constitution leaves education, agriculture and law and order entirely in the hands of the state governments. People thus learn their own mother tongues and their own histories in school. The laws they are governed by fully reflect their own traditional laws and customs. This is doubly safeguarded by keeping agriculture, where most of the oldest customary law is to be found, firmly under the aegis of the state governments.

There is an elaborate system of financial devolution. Certain taxes are collected by the centre and kept by it. Others, like the sales tax, are collected and retained by the states. But the main taxes, the income tax and the customs and excise duties, are collected by the centre and shared by it with the states, according to a formula revised every five years by a statutorily appointed finance commission. Overall, the share of the states in the total tax revenues of the nation has risen steadily till it has more or less stabilized at slightly more than half. The division between the states of centrally collected tax revenues, and of central assistance for the states' planned investments, has contained a strong element of redistribution, to aid the weaker states. This has not levelled the playing field completely. Private investment has continued to concentrate in a handful of industrially advanced or mineral rich states. But the psychological reassurance these enactments provide have played an important part in keeping India free from ethnic conflict and strengthening the bonds of the nation.

Two other methods used by the Indian state to harmonize the demands of ethnicity and nationhood need to be mentioned. Not long after the linguistic reorganization of India's states in 1957, it became clear that this had not completely resolved the problem of ethnicity. Several of the new states contained ethnic subgroups who found themselves if anything even more at a disadvantage in the face of a now more homogeneous majority. Initially, this problem came to light in the Northeast, where the state of Assam contained a large number of distinct tribal groups. The first solution to this problem, tried out after local agitations had outlined the need for one, was the subdivision of large states with into smaller ones. Thus, a hill states' federation was carved out of Assam and named Meghalaya in 1968, and the centrally administered border regions of the Northeast were consolidated into seven additional states of the Indian union a few years later.

But it soon became apparent that every such division would create a new minority and a fresh demand for a new state. Thus, in the early eighties, parliament decided to devolve some of the powers given to the states to a third tier of elected institutions. This was done by creating Autonomous Development Councils within a state that were self-governing in education, culture, local law and order maintenance, and development planning at the district level. The purpose of creating the ADCs was to safeguard the identity of numerous tribes within several of the states that had distinct languages and customs.

Beginning with the Gorkhaland Territorial Administration, which was carved out of West Bengal in 1988, by 2015, parliament had created twenty-five such districts. All but two of them were in Assam, Meghalaya and the north-eastern border states of Manipur, Nagaland and Arunachal Pradesh adjoining Myanmar, Tibet and China.

Finally, between 1989 and 1992, the centre created a fourth and final tier of self-governing institutions. This consisted of district, municipal and village councils (*panchayats*) which also had to be re-elected every five years. The centre gave them limited powers of taxation and devolved a sizeable part of the states' developmental allocations to them to frame and finance local development plans. The performance of these panchayats has been uneven, but they have made local administration far more responsive to local needs.

Taken in its entirety, India has the most complex and at the same time most flexible system of devolution and power sharing that the world has ever known. The measure of its success is not that there has been no ethnic conflict in India, but that there has been so little, and that accommodation has been reached in all cases but one, with little violence. Taking the Punjab, Kashmir, Nagaland, Mizoram and upper Assam insurgencies together, in all no more than forty-four million people had been affected by ethnic violence out of a population of more than 1,200 million in 2011.

In 1994, when Rao met Clinton at the White House, India's nation building through democratic devolution was more or less complete. So, it would have been surprising indeed if Clinton had not been profoundly intrigued by India's success in weaving diversity into unity without war.

Today, a quarter of a century later, there is an even more urgent need for the world to learn from India's success. For a savage nationalist reaction to globalization is setting in all over the world. In country after country, including the United

Kingdom and the USA, the nation-state is making its last stand. Governments have come to power that wish to stop, even reverse the process of globalization. In the newer nations, extremist Islam, aggressive Hindu fundamentalism, and renascent Christian and Jewish fundamentalism are on the rise. The attempt to reverse an irreversible process is pushing the world towards war. India has not been free from ethnic tension. But this has consistently failed to infect more than a small minority of the affected groups: a striking example of this is the absence of Indian Muslims from the ethno-religious conflict that raged in Syria and Iraq between 2011 and 2018. According to a US State Department assessment in 2016, from twenty-seven to thirty thousand[4] Europeans had gone by then to Syria and Iraq fight for *Daesh*—the brutal Islamic State sought to be created in the region by the oil rich Sunni Arab states of the Persian Gulf.[5] But the number who went from India, where Muslims number well over 200 million, was 106! Of these only three went directly from India. The rest were recruited from among migrant workers already in the Gulf countries.[6]

Another, to Indians even more significant, example is that while neighbouring Pakistan has been racked by Sunni–Shia strife that began within a decade of its birth, although a quarter of Indian Muslims are Shias, there has not been a single Sunni–Shia riot of any significance during the entire seventy-eight years and counting of India's existence.

CHAPTER THREE

# Where Did Disenchantment Begin?

The short answer to the question this chapter's title asks is: At the very beginning.

Democracy began to lose its shine when the governments formed under the aegis of the Constitution failed to provide India's citizens with the three requirements of good governance they needed most. These were economic security, the rule of law, and speedy, affordable justice. Over the next half century, this failure, which deepened with every passing year, opened the way for the legitimization of an alternative model of nationhood that despised ethnic diversity and religious pluralism as being products of weakness, and advocated a return to the power of the great Hindu dynasties of the past: in other words, to the transformation of India into a 'hard' Hindu nation-state similar to the unitary nation-states of Europe. The main proponent of this return to the past was Vinayak Damodar Savarkar, whose 1923 book, *Hindutva*, and several subsequent writings, became the ideological foundation of the Rashtriya Swayamsevak Sangh (RSS).

The single most serious failure of 'Nehruvian' democracy has been its inability to provide secure employment for the youth of the country. As of the date of writing, 83 per cent of the youth in the labour force—those between fifteen and thirty—have no employment whatever. There is an all-pervasive denial of elementary justice and respect for human rights; a mounting failure to maintain law and order, especially in the rural areas of northern India; rampant corruption in the bureaucracy and the police, and lax and self-indulgent legal procedures that have made any approach to a court of law for justice expensive and interminable. Taken together, these failures—of the police, the administration and the judiciary—have virtually dismantled the rule of law and thrown rural India back into the arms of feudatory local strongmen who enable them to meet their goals through terror, extortion and murder.

India's legal system has completely broken down. The arrears of cases that remain to be adjudicated has risen from year to year till it now stands at over forty million, and will take 120 years to dispose of.[1] Indian jails are crowded with undertrials who have been living in them for years because they cannot afford a lawyer, or bail. Those who do manage to get bail remain embroiled in cases that drag on for years. Even industrial disputes—the ones where the legal process moves fastest and cases are most likely to be settled out of court—take an average of 1,430 days to resolve, against, say, Singapore's 150 days. In 2015, industry spent 4,079,508 *months* of time on settling industrial disputes, and this did not include minor disputes that were settled at the state and local levels.[2]

The police is stretched to breaking point. It is poorly trained, and grossly understaffed, especially in the division that requires the largest number—crime. On the other hand, entry into it now regularly requires paying a bribe to the decision makers. Lacking the means, the staff and the training to conduct proper inquiries, police now regularly arrest those against whom complaints have been lodged, and then wring confessions out of them using 'third degree' methods. This procedure has become so widespread that magistrates now often disregard even signed confessions the moment the defence lawyer claims that they were extracted by force. With trials going on endlessly and even dangerous criminals often being let out on bail, the police has begun to take the law into their own hands and killing their prisoners in elaborately staged 'encounters', where the deceased are invariably claimed to have resisted arrest and fired upon them first. (We will discuss in greater detail in Chapter 12 the encounters in Gujarat after 2002, but this had of course become endemic long before Narendra Modi even became the chief minister of the state.)

Despite a belated spate of highway construction begun in the early 2000s, India's infrastructure of roads, power supply and power distribution lines is still poorer than that of Kenya's, and a far cry from that of Botswana, both much smaller economies. Its cities are among the most crowded and polluted in the world. Its small towns are even worse for they lack even the vestige of town planning that the city centres have managed to retain. In the vast majority of India's villages, power supply is either intermittent or simply not there.

'Pollution', a polite word for filth, is so pervasive that we have trained our eyes not to see it. Eighteen out of the twenty-five cities with the most polluted air in the world are to be found in India.[3] Our roads and railway tracks are lined with garbage for miles outside every city or railway station. Throughout the length and breadth of the country, river after river is choked with not merely sewage, which is at least bio-degradable, but with plastic, which is not. In 2018, a plan for the revival of Delhi as a city by the river Yamuna (which is what it was before 1857) prepared by the University of Virginia with funding by the government of Spain, pointed out that 153 water channels that flowed into a drainage canal that carried 70 per cent of Delhi's waste water back into the Yamuna were clogged with plastic that had piled up over the years, causing the sewage in them to back up and flood adjoining areas after heavy rains. If that is the state of India's capital, the state of its smaller cities can well be imagined.

Both the Yamuna and the Ganges, rivers considered so sacred that they are woven into the very fabric of Hindu thought and legend, have been treated with utter contempt—for they and their tributaries have been dammed and their waters so completely diverted into canals for agriculture that some of their tributaries now run dry in the hot pre-monsoon months. Landfills are no longer available, so garbage disposal has come to mean picking up the garbage inside city limits and dumping it a few kilometres beyond city limits. Today, every city and town in India is ringed by fields of garbage in which gaily coloured plastics bloom eternally like flowers from hell.

But worse than the all-pervasive failure of administration described above is the way in which India's democracy has managed to disempower the people of the country, and left them at the mercy of a political class whose need for money to fight elections has developed into an all-consuming pursuit of wealth, an extortionist petty bureaucracy and an unaccountable police force. Even today, when the digitization of citizens' transactions with the government have reached a fairly advanced stage, bribes are still regularly extracted from them at most levels of government from the village to the central and state ministries. Almost every permission, certificate or license has a price. And the more a person stands to lose from not obtaining it, the higher the 'price' becomes.

Their disenchantment with secular (now derided as Nehruvian) democracy has made more and more of the younger, post-Nehruvian generations, look for an alternative. This has led to a steady rise in support for the ideological alternative offered by 'Hindutva'. This shift came to light when the Bharatiya Janata Party's vote rose from 7.74 per cent in 1984 to 11.36 per cent in 1989. In the next two decades, it continued to rise till it reached 18.8 per cent in 2009. The jump in support that brought it to power occurred in 2014, when its vote skyrocketed to 31 per cent. This enabled it to win 282 seats out of the 543 in parliament, and form its first national government under Prime Minister Narendra Modi. In 2019, the BJP's vote share reached its peak of 37 per cent, giving it 303 seats in parliament. In these years ten years, it replaced the Congress as the dominant party in India's democracy, and therefore got its first chance to implement its Hindutva agenda under Prime Minister Modi. As is described in later chapters of this book, Modi's government has all but succeeded in destroying the independence of the four pillars upon which peoples' freedoms rest in mature democracies—the legislature, the executive, the judiciary and the media.

### 1973–75: The First Revolt

What caused this radical shift of loyalty?

Indians have been paying the price for the state's failures for almost half a century, but with growing resentment. Their disillusionment first surfaced when there was a sudden upsurge of student unrest Gujarat in December 1973. The trigger was a monsoon failure in 1972, which had caused food shortages and a sharp spurt in inflation in the following year. But the catalyst that turned this into a political protest was the widespread belief that at a time of drought and hardship, the Congress chief minister of Gujarat, Chimanbhai Patel, had manipulated edible oil prices to benefit family and friends.

Prime Minister Indira Gandhi first tried to propitiate the students by forcing Patel to resign, declaring President's Rule in the state and putting the Vidhan Sabha (the state legislative assembly) into suspension. But this turned out to be a tactical mistake for, sensing her weakness, the entire opposition, from the communists to the Jana Sangh (the earlier incarnation of the Bharatiya Janata Party) joined the students and demanded the dissolution of the assembly and the holding of a new election. When Mrs Gandhi capitulated a second time, the student movement spread rapidly to Bihar and, by June 1974, to Karnataka, UP and Punjab. In the words of P.N. Dhar, Mrs Gandhi's principal secretary at the time, 'Nobody shed a tear for the demise of the rule of law and constitutional means of changing governments.'

Matters came to a head on January 3, 1975, when, in a possibly unconnected event, L.N. Mishra, the railways minister in the Indira Gandhi government, was assassinated by means of a bomb placed under the dais at a public meeting in Bihar. Senior leaders in the Congress began to fear that the country was descending into chaos and advised Mrs Gandhi to declare a national Emergency. Mrs Gandhi again demurred, but gave in after a judgement given by the Allahabad High Court against her in June 1975, of exceeding the permitted level of spending on her election to parliament in 1971, threatened to push her out of office and leave a vacuum at the centre.[4]

The Emergency that followed saw a severe curtailment of democratic rights notably through press censorship and the imprisonment of scores of opposition MPs and MLAs. But it did restore order. However, the underlying cause of disenchantment—growing economic insecurity compounded by an increasingly predatory government—continued to grow. This gave birth to a vigorous civil society movement whose sole purpose was to use the law of the land to curb the predatory excesses of the state. This movement had impressive successes. Over five decades beginning in the 1970s, a growing number of powerful NGOs, spearheaded by the People's Union for Civil Liberties (PUCL) and the People's Union for Democratic Rights (PUDR), waged an unrelenting struggle against the abuse of executive power before the Indian judiciary. Other NGOs, notably the Association for Democratic Rights (ADR) have concentrated upon informing the voters about the antecedents of the candidates who were asking for their vote. The ADR has continued to do so, and regularly publishes details of the declared wealth, and criminal records, of candidates fighting central and state elections, highlighting the records of the winners.

Beginning in 1979, when a landmark judgement by Justice P.N. Bhagwati of the Supreme Court opened the way for public interest litigation, these and scores of other civil rights organizations have taken the battle to the higher courts of justice, campaigning to protect and enlarge the civil rights of the citizens of the country. In 2005, civic action received a further boost when a Congress government headed by Dr Manmohan Singh passed a Right to Information Act, which required the bureaucracy to provide information on actions of the administration upon receiving a specific demand from the public.

Both these had an initial positive effect upon the bureaucracy that did not last. In the late eighties, in the first action of its kind, the Karnataka High Court sentenced the chairman of the Bangalore Development Authority to six months' imprisonment for contempt of court when he failed to reinstate an employee fired for corruption, upon the reversal of the judgement against him, within the time period stipulated by the High Court. This sent a salutary shock wave through the bureaucracy across the entire country. But since then, even as the bureaucracy has become increasingly unresponsive to the people and PILs have multiplied, the higher courts' judges have been overwhelmed and begun to fight shy of giving verdicts against the state. One indication of this is that the Karnataka High Court's sentence of imprisonment has never been repeated.

Similarly, the salutary effect that the RTI had upon the bureaucracy's use of power has worn off gradually as bureaucrats have developed ways of stalling for time. One response appears to be that of murdering the applicants. By the end of 2016, the number RTI activists murdered had crossed sixty.

The only way for citizens to express their disillusionment or anger that still remains fully open is to throw the incumbent government out of power. This began happening in a small way in the months before the 1967 elections, when entire caste groups split from the Congress party and formed local parties of their own. In 1967, the Congress' share of the vote fell to a then low of 40.7 per cent. It managed to retain a majority at the centre but lost it in six state assemblies. By the early eighties, state governments were being thrown out with such regularity that scholars gave this trend a name, calling it 'the anti-incumbency factor'.

### The Second Upheaval

The worm finally turned in August 2010, only weeks before the start of the Commonwealth Games in New Delhi. A few weeks earlier, the Indian High Commission in London had reported to New Delhi that the British income tax authorities had raised questions about the transfer of £250,000, followed by £25,000 a month, by the Commonwealth Games Organising Committee in Delhi to two London-based companies owned by a single person of Indian origin, one Ash Patel. The nature of the services being rendered was unclear. The Indian government's investigation revealed that Patel had been given a contract of more than £450,000 to provide 'outdoor display services' for functions surrounding the arrival in London of the royal Baton for the Commonwealth Games. The contract had been issued without inviting tenders.

Fresh humiliation came when the British media reported that the Queen was furious and had refused to attend the traditional launching of the Olympic torch from London, and have anything else to do with the function. The cup of shame overflowed a week before the Commonwealth Games were to start, when the inspection team sent out by the Commonwealth Games Federation found that the athletes' village was not only not ready but 'filthy and unimaginable': in fact a snake crawled out of one of the rooms while they were there. This opened a Pandora's Box of complaints by the CGF's representative in Delhi against the way in which the government's organizing committee had slighted it, and excluded it from all decision-making.

With the stench of corruption strong in its nose the government launched a full-scale inquiry into the conduct of the Commonwealth Games Organising Committee. This indicted Suresh Kalmadi, a former minister who was well known for his connection with builders in the city of Pune, in Maharashtra, and two of his Organising Committee officials. But the respite it earned was brief. Only weeks later, the Comptroller and Auditor-General of India (CAG) issued a report on the award of mobile telecom licenses for the 2G spectrum in 2007, which squarely indicted the serving minister for telecommunications for having flouted laws and norms and awarding 2G spectrum licenses to no fewer than 122 companies on a first come, first served basis. The CAG concluded that if the licenses been auctioned, as is the practice in most countries, it would have fetched the exchequer between eight and forty billion dollars more in revenue.

The government protested vigorously, and to a great extent correctly, that the CAG's higher estimate, in particular, verged on fantasy, because it did not take into account the revenues that would accrue to the government from the revenue sharing agreements it would enter into with the licensees. It also pointed out that auctioning the mobile telecom bandwidth had been the initial practice, but had been given up, in favour of revenue sharing, because the resulting overbidding made the cost of telephone calls prohibitive.

However, it soon became apparent that the first come, first served process had also been 'fixed' to ensure that favoured companies got the lion's share of the auctioned bandwidth. One company, Reliance Telecom, was found to have set up 100 dummy companies with an initial capital of a paltry Rs 100,000 ($2,500, in 2010). Belatedly, Dr Manmohan Singh forced the minister, A. Raja, to resign, launched an investigation and arrested him. But by then the CAG report had triggered an avalanche of other disclosures. The most damaging of these were recordings of phone conversations between Niira Radia, a well-known lobbyist for some of the most respected telecommunication companies in the country, and politicians, well-known journalists and heads of industry associations, members of Delhi's power elite, taped by the Income Tax Department in 2008–09. All of these conversations had centred on ensuring that A. Raja, who had begun the first come, first served process before the elections, would once again be awarded the telecom portfolio in the new government.

The Niira Radia tapes tipped the country into a full-scale confrontation between civil society and the government. A civil society movement against corruption was galvanized into new life. In the preceding years, the movement had been lobbying the parliament in vain to set up an Ombudsman (locally called the *Lokpal*, Sanskrit for 'Defender of People' or 'People's Friend', but functionally the chief vigilance officer of India) with independent powers of investigation and prosecution to curb corruption and high-handedness in the legislature and the bureaucracy.

The hurricane of revelations that followed the exposure of the Commonwealth Games scam made it decide that nothing would come of gentlemanly representations, and it took to the streets. To do so it roped in one of the most respected figures of grassroots politics in India, seventy-three-year-old Kisan Baburao Hazare, known across the country as 'Anna' (father) Hazare, who had as far back as 1991 set up the Bhrashtachar Virodhi Jan Andolan ('People's Movement against Corruption').

Hazare had begun life as a flower seller in Mumbai and prospered sufficiently to open two shops by 1962 when, in response to India's humiliating setbacks in the border war against the Chinese, he decided to enlist in the rapidly expanding Indian army. Hazare served as a truck driver for nine years through two wars with Pakistan and came literally within an inch of losing his life when he was the only survivor of an aerial attack by the Pakistan Air Force on his convoy during the 1965 war. In 1971, he left the army and went back to his parched, drought prone village of Ralegan Siddhi, near the city of Ahmednagar in Maharashtra, a village where agriculture was so uncertain that much of its population had taken to selling home-brewed moonshine to make ends meet.

Hazare persuaded the bootleggers—not always peacefully—to close down their stills, and began a programme of watershed management to prevent soil erosion and conserve the monsoon rains. The resulting rise in the water table and adoption of advanced practices like drip irrigation allowed a fivefold increase in the cropped area. Villagers began to grow two crops and shifted to cash crops including fruits, vegetables and chillies. More fodder allowed them to bring in hybrid cattle and increase the yield of milk by thirteen times.

Anna Hazare had made his village affluent and self-reliant, but continued to live in Spartan simplicity in a single room of his ancestral home. When the government issued a draft Lokpal Bill, which had ignored each and every recommendation that he and his colleagues, who included a retired Supreme Court judge and two eminent lawyers, had made, he decided to go on a fast unto death.

This was not the first time he had done so. Five years earlier, he had forced the Maharashtra government to pass a Right to Information Act in a similar way. But it was the response of the people, and even more so of the youth among the middle classes that took everyone by surprise. For four days, as he fasted in early April 2011, tens of thousands of them came to share his vigil in New Delhi. Protest fasts and demonstrations erupted in 400 other cities across the length and breadth of the country. With the media giving the protests round-the-clock coverage, the government gave in and agreed to set up a ten-member drafting committee consisting of five members each from the government and civil society, which would frame a new bill that would give the Lokpal investigative as opposed to advisory power, and enable it to initiate prosecution in courts of law. In sixty years of freedom, this was civil society's most resounding victory over the Indian state.

But all was not smooth sailing thereafter. Two months later, the drafting committee had reached a deadlock. While the representatives of the India Against Corruption movement insisted that the Lokpal should have the power to investigate charges of corruption against not only members of parliament and civil servants, but the prime minister and higher judiciary, which included judges of the High Courts and the Supreme Court, the government dug in its heels and insisted that this was completely unacceptable. On June 17, the two groups decided to submit separate draft bills to the cabinet for its consideration. Knowing what the outcome was likely to be, Anna Hazare played his last card and announced that if the civil society draft was not accepted he would go on a fast unto death on August 16.

Unlike his first fast in April, this second fast divided his followers. One of his colleagues in the drafting committee, a former Supreme Court judge, announced that he would not attend any more of its meetings if Hazare did not withdraw his threat. Sri Sri Ravishankar, a widely respected religious guru with a nationwide following, advised him to be flexible and consolidate the very substantial gains he had made.

Others who resented the attempt to impose reforms under duress also joined the chorus against Hazare. Reflecting a growing suspicion that Hazare's fast was being promoted by its political opponents, especially the BJP, Sheila Dixit, the three times elected chief minister of Delhi expostulated: 'I am not against the Lokpal, but I want to know...what is civil society? What is its purpose? The Prime Minister represents the party which has received the mandate of the people. It is for the party to decide whether the Prime Minister should be removed or not.'

Many others who had openly supported Hazare were also wondering whether it was wise to risk half a loaf in the attempt to seize the full one. Salman Khurshid, a lawyer and pro-reform cabinet minister who was one of the government's negotiators in the committee put this succinctly to the *Indian Express*: 'If you look at the Bill that we had drafted, and look at this Bill, this is a far better, superior Bill... Let us give credit [to civil society] that this draft has come out of a collaborative effort between them and us'.

These eminently sensible remarks did not dissuade Hazare and the diehards of the India Against Corruption movement because the chasm of distrust between them and the state had become too wide to bridge. By 2011, ten previous attempts to pass an even less stringent Lokpal bill had failed for lack of a quorum because MPs had simply not turned up to vote when they were tabled. The IAC's representatives were, therefore, convinced that if they ceded an inch now the government would take an ell, and the battle against corruption would again be lost. But even this unprecedented uprising of civil society, fuelled by idealism and moral outrage, eventually ran aground on the reefs of political inertia and institutional resistance. In the end, the Lokpal that emerged was a pale shadow of what had been demanded—and the status quo, bruised but intact, endured.

This was a turning point, not only for the movement but for

the nation. For many, it marked the end of faith in incremental reform and the beginning of a search for stronger, more decisive leadership—regardless of the cost. This was the moment when the longing for accountability was quietly overtaken by the need for control. But to try and understand how a movement born out of the desire to deepen democracy ended up preparing the ground for its hollowing out, let us first ask: where did India take the wrong road?

CHAPTER FOUR

# Where Did India Take the Wrong Road?

The answer to the question the title of this chapter asks is: At its very birth.

Nehru's historic speech, 'A Tryst With Destiny' on August 14, 1947, gives a clue to what was about to go wrong: in that entire speech he did not once utter the word 'democracy'. This was not because he was not a democrat but because his faith in it was unquestioning. Nehru took it for granted that India would adhere to the Westminster pattern of democracy that had already been introduced in a limited way by the British through the Government of India Act of 1935. The members of the Constituent Assembly, who laboured through 1948 and 1949, obviously shared his belief that India already had a democracy that needed only a widening of the electorate to *universal* franchise—from the then much restricted one—to meet its future needs. This is the only explanation for the two crucial omissions in the Constitution that have now brought India to the brink of destruction.

The first was the absence of any provision for financing the functioning of the nation's *political system*, as distinct from its *administration*. The second was the failure to create any legal means by which the people could hold the administration, as distinct from their political leaders, accountable for its omissions and mistakes. This happened almost without thought, through the inclusion of clauses of the Government of India Act of 1935 that were intended to indemnify officers of the colonial government from legal action against them by civilian petitioners.

Financing administration through taxation is normal: rulers have been doing this to meet the costs of running an administration in war and peace since the birth of the nation-state. All states have elaborate systems to ensure that the money in their coffers is spent responsibly. But to the members of the Constituent Assembly the idea that the *political system* also needed a similar clean, transparent and audited system for financing perhaps appeared superfluous. The Congress, during the freedom movement, had been able to rely on mass enrolment in it, signalled by the four-anna membership fee, and on funding by Indian industrialists, to meet its then limited financial needs. What the Constituent Assembly did not realize was that this unity of purpose had ended with the achievement of independence. As a result, the very idea that accountability of resources would be needed not only to run the government but also the political system was utterly alien to all but a few members of the Constituent Assembly.

An illustrious member of the Assembly, Lokanath Misra of Orissa (now Odisha), who went on to become the governor of Assam, Nagaland and Arunachal Pradesh in the 1990s, moved an amendment to the Draft Constitution proposing that the *state* should meet the cost of elections for the candidate. But since he linked this to a proposal that the electorate should be limited to the panchayat members chosen by the villagers in each village, it was summarily rejected.[1] There was general agreement that money was a corrupter of democracy, so its use had to be discouraged: 'to come to the Assembly is not a profession or a profiteering business', as Misra said. But the only discussions the Assembly held on election finance centred on the need to *limit* spending by candidates.[2] The tenor of the debates was that, through universal suffrage, the people had been conferred a right that they would be anxious to exercise, and they would select their candidates spontaneously. Almost from the first elections in 1951, therefore, the lack of a proper system for financing politics led to parties and candidates raising money from clandestine sources.

The only palpable reason for their omitting a proper system on electoral funding was their unthinking emulation of British practice. Britain's unwritten constitution had no provisions for electoral funding. So, the Constituent Assembly believed that the Indian constitution didn't need them either. What its members did not take into account was the huge difference in the size of the constituencies. The average British constituency is 375 square kilometres in size and has around 60,000 voters. A candidate for parliament can therefore get into his car every morning, visit several towns and villages and return home every night.

In India, by contrast, the average parliamentary constituency is 6,000 square kilometres in size, contains more than a thousand villages—a hundred and fifty just in an assembly constituency—and even in 1951 had an average of 350,000 voters. Today, the number of voters exceeds a million, and is scattered over more than a thousand villages in each parliamentary constituency. The failure of the Constituent Assembly to understand how the huge difference in size between the British and the Indian parliamentary constituency made it impossible to copy the British model in India is therefore surprising, to say the least.

This oversight was almost certainly rooted in the Constituent Assembly's use of the Government of India Act of 1935 as the frame for the Indian constitution. Somehow, it overlooked the fact that the 1935 Act limited the right to vote to the owners of property above a certain size. In 1935, these made up no more than six to seven per cent of the population. That was a small enough electorate for a candidate to be able to reach out to without the need for financial assistance. But the Constituent Assembly was determined to introduce universal adult suffrage.

Had it looked beyond Britain in its search for an appropriate model, its members would have found that other democracies too had faced the same problem, and solved it in different ways. Western European democracies, for example, had resolved it by adopting proportional representation. Under this system, each party created a list of candidates, and asked the electorate to vote for the party first, and then its preferred candidates within the party's list.

The Continental system may have been ruled out because it required a prior acknowledgement of the political party as an *intermediary* between the people and their representatives in parliament, while the unwritten British constitution postulated a direct relationship between the voter and his or her candidate. But the USA, which had also adopted the first-past-the-post system of voting, had recognized the problem as far back as in 1865. By 1948, it had passed eight amendments to its electoral laws to ease and legitimize electoral financing.

To man the 1,000 to 1,200 polling booths in an Indian parliamentary constituency on polling day, political parties have to employ at least three times that number of persons. The cost of hiring, training and rehearsing with them is enormous, but it is the least part of the expense, for it does not take into account the cost of printing tens of thousands of posters, meeting the expenses of scores of election agents, and hiring dozens of vehicles for a month or more.

The Constituent Assembly's oversight could have been remedied with a constitutional amendment at a later date, but instead, in 1967, Mrs Indira Gandhi took the country in the opposite direction and choked off the only legitimate source of funds that had sprung up in the intervening years. This was the donations from corporations that all parties except the communists had begun to depend upon.

Mrs Gandhi took this decision weeks after the Congress party came close to defeat for the very first time in the general elections of 1967. Not only did its tally in the Lok Sabha fall from 353 to 282—only ten more than what it needed for a majority—but for the first time it lost the assembly elections in six major states. Her government first repealed the tax concessions on donations to political parties and followed it up three years later with a complete ban on company donations to political parties. But while choking off the political system's main source of funds, *she deliberately did not create an alternative.*

The purpose of the ban on company donations was not, therefore, as the Congress party claimed, to reduce the influence of big business on politics, which by then was all pervasive, especially for the twenty big industrialists who had cornered the bulk of the industrial licences. It was to cripple a rising threat to its complete dominance of Indian politics and economics from economic liberals, by depriving the Swatantra Party and the Bharatiya Jana Sangh, the precursor of the BJP, of funds.

In 1967, the pro-market Swatantra Party, formed by C. Rajagopalachari in 1961, and the Jana Sangh had fought the elections together and become a serious threat to the Congress in three states. These were Madhya Pradesh, where the BJS won seventy-eight out of the 296 seats, Gujarat where the Swatantra Party won sixty-six out of 168 seats, and Rajasthan where, by together winning seventy-two seats, they succeeded in preventing the Congress from passing the halfway mark in the assembly.

More than the rise in their share of the seats, the Congress feared the rise in their share of the vote, for this threatened to turn them into a magnet for the then numerous smaller parties and independents that dotted the political scene. A two-party, or at least two-coalition, political system therefore seemed on the point of being born. This was a threat that proved too unsettling for the Congress to stomach. Mrs Indira Gandhi, who had succeeded Lal Bahadur Shastri as India's third prime minister in 1966, therefore knowingly passed a law, and a constitutional amendment, that were designed to starve the opposition of funds. These were the ban on company donations to political parties, and the abolition of the privy purses that had been granted in perpetuity to the Indian princes who had acceded to India. Many of these had already gravitated towards the Jana Sangh, but this became a rush after the abolition of the privy purses threatened them with destitution.

In theory, the ban on company donations applied to all political parties, but the Congress knew that, with all the reins of political and economic power in its hands, it could flout the ban and force the corporate sector to keep financing it with impunity.

The Constituent Assembly's second oversight was its failure to realize that the only way to transform a bureaucracy from being the ruler of the people into its servant was to include provisions in the constitution that would allow the people to hold it accountable for its actions before a court of law. Considering the long struggle the Congress had had to wage for independence, and the years that many of its members had spent in jail, it is surprising that the Constituent Assembly did not see the need for this. The only explanation for this lapse of judgement is that in the first flush of freedom its members thought that accountability to an elected Indian parliament, in place of a British Viceroy and his Executive Council, would suffice. So, with no discussion whatever, they retained a provision in the Government of India Act, 1935 that gave civil servants virtual immunity from prosecution in a court of law without the express permission of the state. It became Article 311 of the Indian Constitution,[3] which reads:

> No person who is a member of a civil service of the Union or an all India service or a civil service of a State or holds a civil post under the Union or a State shall be dismissed or removed by an authority subordinate to that by which he was appointed.

This injunction applies not only to civil, but to criminal cases as well. The wording sounds innocuous, but for the all-India and central services the empowered 'authority' is the President of India; for the state civil services it is the Governor. In practice, therefore, this has meant that no prosecution can by initiated without the permission of the central or state government. As the dismal experience of the Central Vigilance Commission has shown, in civil cases this permission is rarely given.

In the Jain Diaries case, a famous 'Hawala' (illegal money laundering) scandal of 1996, which involved several senior politicians and no fewer than thirty-seven civil servants, the sanction did not come for months and in several cases was never given. This forced the Supreme Court to issue a directive that the limit of three months to grant sanction, which was prescribed in the Prevention of Corruption Act, 1988, had to be observed. But the civil service remained unfazed. Not only did it pay scant attention to the directive but it tried to extend the scope of Section 19 of the penal code to cover retired public servants as well. Luckily, the amendment was not ratified by the Rajya Sabha.[4]

Thus, till today, there is no law that allows a member of the public to prosecute a civil servant for not doing his or her duty to the public. Until the Right to Information Act was enacted in 2005, there was no law that even required a civil servant to reply to an inquiry from a member of the public within a specified period of time. Since people's plans, businesses, often their very lives, depend upon the timely issue of official government permits and licenses, this lacuna has disempowered citizens, and given bureaucrats virtually unlimited power to extort money from them through blackmail.

This disempowerment has been felt most keenly in their relations with the police. The police enjoy virtually unlimited power under the Indian Code of Criminal Procedure, 1973. This code, familiarly referred to as the CrPC, not only retained the draconian powers of apprehension given to the police in British days, but expanded them through subsequent changes of procedure and interpretation to an extent that few could have imagined even in the most oppressive periods of British rule. These permit a police officer, defined as the senior person in charge of a police station at the moment of action, to arrest anyone without a warrant immediately upon receipt of a written complaint (called the first information report or FIR), sweat a confession out of him or her, using 'third degree' methods including physical torture, before sending him or her into judicial custody.

This requires no preliminary investigation of the charge, no inquiry into the antecedents or motives of the accuser. All that the police officer is required to do is maintain a written record of his action and the grounds for taking it. As a succession of Law Commissions of India reports have pointed out, this requirement is honoured mainly in the breach.

But this is the lesser cause of the fear that the police now inspire in the poor. The greater part arises out of its systematic abuse of the Code of Criminal Procedure to harass, arrest, and extort money from its chosen targets. For the Code allows police officers to arrest anyone without a warrant, merely on the suspicion that they may be planning, or *intending*, to commit an unlawful act. It hedges this power with the requirement that the suspicion be 'reasonable' and 'credible', but this determination rests with the arresting officer alone. Such awesome discretionary power was bound to be abused, and was abused liberally in the pre-Independence days. But the abuse to which subjects of British India were subjected has paled into insignificance before that heaped upon the people of 'free' India by their Indian successors.

Today, all the safeguards provided in the Constitution for people's civil rights and liberties apply, fitfully at best, to the urban middle classes and the upper strata of landowners who live in the villages. For the poor, and the rural poor in particular, the police are not only the apprehenders of criminals but their executioners as well.

The following passage, from a detailed report on the state of the Indian police, brings out the utter inhumanity and injustice of the policing system in India, at least as it was in 2009, when the report was published:

> 'This week, I was told to do an "encounter",' a police officer we will call Officer Singh told Human Rights Watch in January 2009. He was referring to the practice of taking into custody and extrajudicially executing an individual, then claiming that the victim died after initiating a shoot-out with police. 'I am looking for my target,' he said. 'I will eliminate him.'
>
> Working in Uttar Pradesh, Officer Singh is the kind of police officer who should be in prison for misusing his authority. Instead he is protected by his superiors. It is in this way that impunity continues to thrive in India—and the reputation of the police continues to slide.
>
> But as we spoke to Officer Singh, we heard about other

> aspects of the reality of policing in India. Officer Singh said he had hardly a day off since he began working as a sub-inspector, or investigating officer, for the Uttar Pradesh police ten years ago. 'I've slept ten hours in the last three days. How is a person who hasn't slept in three days supposed to behave properly?' he asked. 'The pressure cooker will burst.'
>
> Officer Singh described hours crammed with too many duties: patrolling events, escorting VIPs, investigating crime, and, he added without hesitation, fabricating police records. He said he was working on a murder case but had at best a few hours at night to devote to solving it. 'I sent evidence to the forensic lab five months ago, but the case is still pending,' he said. Nonetheless, he said he was under tremendous pressure from superiors to solve the case, or face suspension. He admitted that in the past, in similar straits, he had beaten suspects to elicit confessions—that's what his superiors expected of him. 'It is presumed that I'm doing it,' he told Human Rights Watch. 'It's done before them. Sometimes they are doing it.'
>
> Despite his willingness to beat people he determines are criminals—and he made it clear that he had beaten many—Officer Singh said he did not initially intend to be a dishonest and abusive crime fighter. 'No one is born corrupt. It's a tailor-made system: if you're not corrupt, you won't survive.'[5]

The most egregious of all our failures with respect to the criminal justice system has been the steady erosion of the limitation of twenty-four hours placed by the writ of *habeas corpus* upon detention by the police without a warrant, till under the Modi government, it has now virtually ceased to exist. Over the past seven decades, the right to hold a person in jail without conviction increased from twenty-four hours to three days, then to a week, and then to a maximum period of fifteen days in police custody, followed by up to sixty days of judicial custody. Under amendments to various laws such as the Unlawful Activities Prevention Act and the Prevention of Money Laundering Act, this period of custody became virtually limitless. What is more, instead of requiring the police to present its *prima facie* case within the fortnight given them, magistrates allowed the accused to be taken back from judicial into police custody repeatedly, provided the total period of interrogation did not exceed fifteen days. In all but a handful of cases, magistrates routinely allow the police to remand the suspect to judicial custody for long periods on the grounds that he or she is a powerful/influential/rich person who is capable of leaving the country, or threatening potential witnesses and must not therefore be given bail till it has completed preparing its case. But more and more frequently, even these draconian rules are honoured in the breach. For hundreds of thousands of prisoners in jails all over India, judicial custody extends for years because the police are reluctant to admit that the case has gone cold, or because prisoners are too poor to afford bail, let alone a lawyer to represent them. (I'll come back, though briefly, to the topic of judicial custody in the new criminal codes of 2023, in Chapter 15.)

The same delays in the administration of justice have enabled the rich, and the criminally powerful, to evade the law for decades, to siphon billions of dollars abroad with the help of complicit bank employees, and acquire citizenship in countries that offer it in exchange for 'investment', with no questions asked.

Such glaring disparities in outcomes leave little doubt that something has gone fatally wrong. The foundational oversights that I single out—born not of malice but of misplaced assumptions, borrowed models and an excess of trust in inherited institutions—set India on a perilous path. What began as structural flaws in a young republic hardened over time into instruments of exploitation and control. The cost of these errors, deferred for decades, has now begun to reveal itself in full measure. To grasp the enormity of this descent, we must turn to the consequences that have unfolded in the life of the Indian republic.

CHAPTER FIVE

# How Did India Criminalize Its Democracy?

In the fifty years that have elapsed since the ban on company donations came into force, our 'mistakes' have come close to blighting India's future as a viable, democratic state. The absence of a legal system for funding elections has sent all aspiring politicians, and political parties, on a never-ending chase of money. In the 1950s, finding money to meet election expenses had already become a headache for most political parties, but it was a manageable headache. However, funding requirements ballooned in the 1960s because of the inflation unleashed by two severe droughts and two wars within five years, and a precipitous devaluation of the rupee in 1967. This intensified political competition. And the separation of central from state elections by Mrs Gandhi in 1971, to take advantage of India's victory over Pakistan in the Bangladesh War, *doubled electoral expenses overnight*.

With election and day-to-day expenses shooting upwards, political parties turned a blind eye to the sources of their funds and political support. Since elections are a gamble even for the candidates of the incumbent party, only gamblers were prepared to provide the funds. These fell into two categories—those with large amounts of 'black' money who wished to invest some of it in the acquisition of political power, and criminals who were prepared to terrorize candidates into withdrawing from the fray and voters into casting their vote for the party of their choice, in exchange for protection from the police.

The resulting 'deals' criminalized politics almost instantly. But this was only the beginning of the rot that set in. Since politicians needed complaisant bureaucrats and police officers to carry out the wishes of their new patrons, there was a rapid erosion of the integrity and, by degrees, the political neutrality of the bureaucracy.

As the cost of politics continued to soar, the reliance of the political system on black money and 'muscle power' continued to grow. When Mrs Indira Gandhi banned company donations altogether, the distinction between 'good' and 'bad' money, and between 'influence' and 'coercion' disappeared. From 1970 onwards, the sole purpose of every party machine and all of its candidates became to find the money they would need for the next election. The ban on company donations therefore completed the conversion of the developmental state that Pandit Jawaharlal Nehru had sought to craft in the fifties into a predatory, clientelist democracy that thrived on shortages and black markets, and preyed upon rich and poor alike.

## The End of the Two-party Democracy Dream

The change, which has had four decades to work through the Indian political system, has had a profound impact on the functioning of democracy. Its immediate effect was to destroy the moderate, centrist opposition in Indian politics and strengthen its ideological extremes. The first victim was the Swatantra Party, which had been set up by C. Rajagopalachari, India's first Governor-General, in 1961 as a liberal counterpoise to the by then heavily socialist and autarchic Congress party. It was born out of the strong feeling, shared by Rajagopalachari, that the Congress had used the first generation of India's industrialists to finance them during their long struggle and then betrayed them.

The pioneering role this generation had played in giving India an early start in industrialization has now been forgotten, but it was this small handful of industrial houses—the Tatas, the Birlas, the Mafatlals, the Bajajs, the Ruparels, the Goenkas, the Godrejs, the Singhanias, the Kirloskars, Larsen and Toubro and a dozen others whose names have now faded into history—that fought every obstacle the British government could put in the way of their development to create what was then the second most powerful industrial country in Asia. From the 1880s, when the first modern textile mills challenged the dominance of Lancashire in the Indian market, till the early 1940s, when a machine tools industry sprang up in India to cater to the British need for armaments to halt the Japanese advance from Burma into Manipur and Nagaland during the Second World War, they had set up their enterprises not only without protection from competition through tariffs on imports, as Germany, France and the USA had done, but in the teeth of the Doctrine of Imperial Preference (1932) that guaranteed duty-free entry to India for British manufactures while shutting out European goods. Indian industry had therefore attained very high levels of efficiency. In 1947, its cotton textiles industry was the most competitive in the world, and a few years later, in 1951, the Tatas' iron and steel plant in Jamshedpur was adjudged by the World Bank to be the lowest cost steel producer in the world. By the time India became independent, these and other smaller companies had established a significant hold on the Indian market in no fewer than seventeen sectors of production.[1]

The only favour that these industrial houses had asked of the Congress throughout the three decades in which they were its principal financiers was that they would end the enforced free trade and impose protective duties upon all manufactured imports, and the Congress had readily agreed to its request. Indeed, the Congress government kept its promise: in fact, barely a decade after Independence, it banned all 'non-essential' imports entirely. But with one twist to its 'concession': it simultaneously all but banned the growth of private industry!

It did so through its second Industrial Policy Resolution, unveiled in 1956, which was designed to implement a party resolution passed two years earlier. Declaring that its goal was the creation of a 'socialist pattern of society', it first stopped the further growth of the textiles industry, by imposing a ceiling on the number of looms that existing mills could operate and banning the establishment of new ones. It then banned private players from entering seventeen modern industries, which it reserved for development by the public sector. These included aluminium, copper, zinc, heavy engineering, petrochemicals and pharmaceuticals. The list also included steel, in which, although the Tatas and two smaller existing manufacturers were not nationalized, they were banned from increasing their capacity.

The Swatantra Party had been born out of industry's protest against this monumental betrayal by a movement that it had nurtured through three decades of growth to its final triumph. It also attracted most of the princes who had acceded to India in 1947 and were alarmed by the increasing populist demands within the Congress to withdraw the privy purses assigned to the rulers at the time of accession. In 1971, Mrs Indira Gandhi scotched this threat by amending the Constitution to withdraw their privy purses, thereby rendering most of them indigent. Not surprisingly, therefore, the Swatantra Party was the first to cave in. In 1974, two years after the passing of C. Rajagopalachari, it threw in the towel, dissolved itself and encouraged its state units to merge with the Jana Sangh. Not surprisingly also, the impact of the *de facto* merger was felt most acutely in the states where both industry and the princes abounded—Maharashtra, Gujarat, Rajasthan and Madhya Pradesh. These have remained the stronghold of the Jana Sangh, later BJP, from 1967 till today.

At the opposite end of the political spectrum, the two socialist parties, the Praja ('Citizens") Socialist Party (PSP) and the Samyukta ('United') Socialist Party (SSP), had also made significant inroads into the Congress party's vote banks in northern India. After the ban on company donations, these were the next to go. The first of these had been formed in the early 1950s, when Jayaprakash Narayan's Socialist Party merged with the Kisan Mazdoor Praja

Party of J.B. Kripalani; the SSP had resulted from a 1964 split in the PSP. When the ban on company donations came into effect, both fell back on caste loyalties to survive and fragmented further.

Only the two most ideological, and cadre-based, parties survived relatively unscathed. These were the RSS-backed Jana Sangh and the Communist Party of India (Marxist) (CPI (M)). The former had been able to create a stable vote base in Gujarat and Maharashtra. The merger of the Swatantra Party with it extended that base to Rajasthan and Madhya Pradesh. The CPI (M), by 1970, had begun to dominate Bengal and Kerala.

The Indian intelligentsia had once fondly hoped that the simple majority voting system, which consistently magnifies the seat share of larger parties at the expense of smaller ones, would force a merger of smaller parties with their nearest political neighbours, both in the states and at the centre, to eventually create a two-party system similar to that of Britain or the USA. By the late seventies, however, this dream seemed to have died a natural death.

## The Death of Intra-party Democracy and Political Accountability

A second, more serious, effect of the ban was to stifle democracy within the political parties. Mrs Gandhi had deliberately not created an alternative, transparent system of election financing because she believed, or was persuaded, that as the dominant party which held the reins of power at the centre, the Congress could squeeze the donations it received from large industry out of it in cash. In the very first election after the ban came into effect, which was held in 1971, it found out that this was far harder to do than it had imagined. It was therefore compelled to replace its relatively small but stable cadre of large donors with thousands of widely dispersed, and more often than not shady, donors who had both the capacity and the willingness to contribute money to political parties in cash.

Over time, the sheer difficulty of doing this every few years made them extremely reluctant to disturb a financing network once it had been established. The system hardened for both the Lok Sabha and Vidhan Sabha in the 1970s, and was described in detail by Stanley Kochanek in his book, *The Congress Party of India: The Dynamics of a One-Party Democracy*. It pointed out that financing by anonymous moneybags spread all over the country and gave them an increasing say in the making of not only local but national policy by the ruling party. India thus turned with surprising suddenness from a popular into a 'clientelist' democracy.[2] These anonymous donors insisted upon special favours such as licences and land grants to open petrol pumps by highways, cooking gas agencies, and permissions to encroach upon government lands, particularly forest lands, to clear them of their timber. These were only the most blatant examples of their use of their newfound power in politics. As the networks hardened, they also chose the future candidates for their constituencies, preferably from the family of the parents. The choices of Jyotiraditya Scindia and Sachin Pilot after the deaths of their fathers in a helicopter and car crash, respectively, were the most salient examples of a universally followed practice.

In the eighty per cent of the constituencies that are rural, or centred round small towns, these networks were inevitably local. All the deals that had to be made to establish them centred on gaining the favour of not only the party in power but, more specifically, the candidate who represented it in the legislature. The actual deals were, and continue to be, struck by self-appointed lieutenants, who give the candidates the elbow room necessary to modify, or get out of, conflicting commitments. Once a network was established, and especially once it had succeeded in getting its candidate elected, the lieutenants had a major stake in making sure that it was not threatened by a rival. The longer a party stayed in power the more embedded did the financial network become.

The arteries of the Congress' non-ideological rivals did not harden to the same extent because their grip on power was less sure, but in states where a two-party or two-coalition system has stabilized, they too have established similar clientelist networks based upon the exchange of money and local influence for privileged access to the state. Thus, the more Indian democracy has matured, the more has it succeeded in shutting new people out of politics unless they too are prepared to become a part of the existing clientelist networks.

A corollary to this has been the rise of the so-called 'princelings'—a second generation of political leaders in Indian politics who have inherited and not earned their places in Indian politics. In Western democracies, when a long-term member of the parliament, national assembly or congress dies, the party chooses his or her successor usually on the basis of latter's standing in the constituency. In India, the death of a senior politician triggers a rush by party members from the constituency to Delhi or the state capital to make sure that there is no contest within the party for the vacant seat, and that the dead leader's son or daughter is nominated to take the parent's place. They do this because, sentiment apart, this is the best way of making sure that the network of financial and other relations, upon which their personal fortunes rest, is not disturbed. While some of the 'princelings' like Omar Abdullah or Rahul Gandhi, regularly capture the headlines, they make up only a small visible fringe of the phenomenon. A study by historian Patrick French of the composition of the 2009 Lok Sabha, for example, showed that 28.6 per cent of all MPs (156) and 37.5 per cent of the Congress MPs (78 out of 208) were selected as candidates because of their family connections.[3]

These figures were disturbing in themselves but became more so when correlated to the age of the MPs. In his analysis posted on the website of the University of Pennsylvania's Centre for the Advanced Study of India, French pointed out that 'nearly half of all Members of Parliament aged fifty or under are hereditary, selected to contest a seat primarily because they are the children of politicians. The situation is most serious in the Indian National Congress, where *every MP under the age of thirty-five is hereditary.*

If you extend the survey across the whole Lok Sabha, thirty-three of the youngest thirty-eight MPs entered parliament because of their birth' (emphasis added).

'If you do not come from an established ruling family,' French concludes, 'you have almost no chance of progressing in national politics, unless you join an ideological party such as the Bharatiya Janata Party or the Communist Party of India (Marxist), where lineage is not important.'[4]

### The Dissipation of Central Power

A wholly unforeseen consequence of the absence of legal provisions for raising funds has been the weakening of the national leaderships of the non-ideological, and therefore non cadre-based, parties. Here, the Congress, which initiated it, has been the main sufferer. When donations were legal, the money used to come directly to the president or treasurer of the political party.[5] This ensured that the reins of financial power remained in the hands of its leaders whom the public recognized and could hold accountable for the way it was collected and spent. But once money began to be raised clandestinely, financial power slipped into the hands of anonymous, unaccountable and, more often than not, unsavoury characters. As mentioned above, local financial networks grew stronger, with control over the new money collectors passing more and more out of the hands of the central party leaders and into those of the leaders in the states.

Over time, the price that the fund raisers demanded kept growing and, with it, the power of the elected leaders to choose candidates or determine policy declined. One of the first victims of the change was Mrs Indira Gandhi herself. Scholars have severely criticized the way in which she concentrated power within the Congress in her own hands during the Emergency, but in reality this was a defensive action to stem a weakening of her control over the party that only she fully sensed. For by the mid-seventies she had all but lost control of several charismatic Congress chief ministers, such as H.N. Bahuguna in UP and V.P. Naik in

Maharashtra. Both were able administrators, and Bahuguna, in particular, had restored efficient government to UP after a lapse of several years since the 1969 elections—a period that followed a year of President's rule and saw the chief ministership change hands three times before Bahuguna assumed office. The main reason why Mrs Gandhi felt obliged to withdraw her trust from them was that they were no longer obeying the Congress High Command's directives. In all, Mrs Gandhi changed the chief ministers in the Congress-ruled states no fewer than fifteen times between 1975 and 1977. That she did this during the twenty-one months of the Emergency showed how much she felt weakened by the changes that she had herself triggered within the party. But she never acknowledged her mistake and turned down repeated suggestions that she create a state financing system for elections. And her troubles continued.

To some extent, the increased assertiveness of state leaders may have reflected a consolidation of ethnic identity in the major states after the linguistic reorganization of the states in 1957. But this was not the main cause of Mrs Gandhi's problems, for she shuffled chief ministers as frequently in the northern and western states as she did in the south, despite the fact that ethnic consolidation was much more pronounced in the latter. The more important cause was that state leaders were becoming less and less dependent upon the central leadership to raise funds, thanks to the new law having forced fund-raising to localize, making even the constituency-level leadership more powerful at the centre's expense. (I obtained this insight from a discussion with H.N. Bahuguna at the *Indian Express* guest house in Chennai in the summer of 1980. Its full significance dawned upon me only after the outbreak of the Khalistani insurrection in Punjab, in 1983.) In state assembly elections in Haryana, held a little over a year after her return to power in 1980, her attempt to choose the candidates to be nominated by the party met with stiff resistance from the state party bosses. When she insisted on having her way, many of them encouraged their candidates to stand as 'rebel'

Congressmen. In the election, a larger number of the rebels won, while the Congress lost its majority. Mrs Gandhi was forced to allow the Haryana leaders to bring the rebel Congressmen back into the party in order to form a government. This was the first unequivocal sign that even in the Congress, power within the party had shifted from the central, known and deeply respected leaders to largely unknown state leaders and their supporting client networks who were willing to contribute money in exchange for future favours.

The weakening of the central High Command and the strengthening of Congress' state units reduced the capacity of the national leaders to take decisions in the national interest that imposed short term costs upon its state units. In 1967, Mrs Indira Gandhi was able to overcome the resistance of a powerful regional chief minister in Assam, B.P. Chaliha, and separate Meghalaya from Assam. Sixteen years later, her inability to carry her state unit in Punjab, which was bent upon fracturing the Akali party by helping surreptitiously to create an extremist challenge to it from the far right, spearheaded by the maverick preacher Jarnail Singh Bhindranwale, precipitated the Khalistani insurgency in the state.

Not only was the Punjab Congress responsible for the rise of Bhindranwale, whom it actively fostered in an attempt to break the Akali Dal, it repeatedly sabotaged agreements that Mrs Gandhi arrived at with the Akalis in 1983 over certain long-standing demands that, if conceded, would have ended the rise of separatism in Punjab. This was because she was unable to persuade the state Congress leaders in Punjab (and Haryana) to endorse anything that would give the Akalis an edge over them in the next election. The country paid the price for her failure with ten years of insurgency and 61,000 civilian lives. Two thirds of the victims were Sikhs.

## MPLADS: The Re-feudalization of Democracy

The final chapter in the political disempowerment of the people was also written by a Congress government—in 1994, on the recommendation of former Maharashtra Chief Minister A.R. Antulay. As the only Muslim ever to rise to such eminence in Maharashtra politics, Antulay had remained, throughout, somewhat outside the crony-criminal network that the perpetual need for money had spawned. Therefore, when he became the chief minister, he hit upon a novel way of raising the funds that he needed to finance his succeeding elections. This was to create a trust of which he was the sole executor, to which any Mumbai builder who wanted an allocation of cement, at the then fixed price of Rs 12 a bag of 50 kilograms, would have to 'contribute' Rs 40 per bag. (The black market price of cement at that time was around Rs 60.) Because this was a registered trust the scam soon came to light and Antulay was forced to resign. When, some years later, the Congress resuscitated him, it was as a one-man committee to propose reforms of electoral finance! Antulay paid no attention to the rising cost of fighting elections, the doubling of political parties' expenses after the separation of the central from state elections in 1971, and the feverish growth of competition. Instead, he suggested that each sitting member of parliament and state legislatures should be allocated a discretionary quota of Five Year Plan funds—initially, one crore rupees (Rs 10 million) for an MP—to disburse on developmental projects within his or her own constituency. This became the MPLADS (Members of Parliament Local Area Development Scheme) and MLALADS (Members of Legislative Assembly Local Area Development Scheme).

On paper, this power was hedged with elaborate safeguards to prevent misuse. The most important of these was that the MP could only propose projects to the district magistrate (collector) in which his constituency lay. But in practice, these requests were rarely if ever refused, except on the grounds of feasibility. Besides, there was as little monitoring of how the money was spent as there was of any of the other central or centrally-sponsored scheme for which Plan funds were routinely allocated. This opened the way to the consolidation of political power through the use of public funds. The state assemblies lost no time in following the lead given by the centre, and as prices (and greed) rose, the allocations were steadily raised. In March 2011, although civil society was convulsed by the 2G scam, the Congress-led government of Dr Manmohan Singh raised the MPs' discretionary development funds from Rs 2 to Rs 5 crores. The state assemblies promptly followed suit and raised MLAs' quota from Rs 1 to Rs 2 crores. In all, this bestowed over Rs 7,000 crores a year on the MLAs and Rs 4,500 crores on the MPs. In a Five Year Plan period, this diverted Rs 57,500 crores from public agencies to wholly unaccountable private individuals. Since then, the Modi government and several state governments have raised the sums allocated to MPs and MLAs even further, which has given the finishing touches to the clientelist, essentially predatory, democracy that India has become.

## The Criminalization of Politics

But by far the worst consequence of the ban on company donations was the entry of criminals into politics. Since the Congress was in power at the centre and in a majority of the states at the time when the ban on company donations was enacted, it was the first to pioneer clandestine ways of funding politics. When other national parties came to power in a state, and later at the centre, they had only to continue the systems already in place. But new political parties back then, with no access to funds, were compelled to find other ways of mobilizing their potential vote. They did so by enrolling local musclemen to capture polling booths, intimidate rival voters and win seats. In UP, Bihar and Madhya Pradesh in particular, this led to a virtual takeover of the new, mainly caste-based, parties by dacoit gangs.

Their enrolment forced other parties to follow suit. Within a decade of the ban on company donations, the exchange of muscle power for protection from the law had become an integral part of state politics. For instance, by 1980, UP had more than a score of dreaded dacoit gangs which would descend with utter impunity upon the villages they chose to target and carry away everything of value from grain to jewellery, to cattle to, sometimes, young women. Madhya Pradesh and Bihar were not far behind. Since each of these gangs was allied to a political party that could come to power at any time, the police chose to stand impotently by.

But the criminals soon found out that the promise of protection was too tenuous to guarantee their safety. When V.P. Singh was appointed chief minister of UP in 1980, he vowed that he would rid the state of its dacoit gangs within two years, and gave the police a free hand to deal with them. In the next two years, the UP police killed, captured or forced into surrender an estimated 2,000 dacoits including all but one or two of the gang leaders. But paradoxically, this only made matters worse. For the criminal associates of the political parties learned the bitter lesson that protection from the law was not enough to ensure their safety. They had to *become* the lawmakers.

Since nothing was done to legalize the funding of politics even after V.P. Singh's valiant effort in UP, political parties were in no position to resist their demands. V.P. Singh's attempt to break the nexus between politics and crime therefore proved to be the last. Fifteen years later, when Kalyan Singh, the leader of the BJP in UP, induced defections from the Bahujan Samaj Party and the Congress to unseat the BSP leader, Mayawati, and form a BJP-led government, nineteen of the thirty-one defectors whom he accommodated in a mammoth ninety-eight-member council of ministers were facing charges that included murder, armed robbery, kidnapping, rape and the illegal possession of arms. One of these, former Congressman Hari Shankar Tiwari, whom Kalyan Singh made his minister for science, was facing seven indictments for murder at the time of his elevation.

Tiwari was not the first openly indicted criminal to have become a minister to an Indian government. In 1996, Prime Minister H.D. Deve Gowda appointed Taslimuddin, a known local mafia leader who dominated Kishanganj in north Bihar through sheer terror, the minister of state for home affairs in the national government in Delhi. He did this in spite of there being a report by the Bihar Legislative Council that had found *prima facie* evidence that Taslimuddin was involved in cases of rape, kidnapping, dacoity and several counts of murder. Gowda could be forgiven because he was from Karnataka and did not know Taslimuddin's antecedents. But the same could not be said of Lalu Yadav, chief minister of Bihar for fifteen years, who gave Taslimuddin the ticket to fight the Lok Sabha elections. To him, Taslimuddin's antecedents did not matter. All that mattered was the Robin Hood relationship he had built with the large Muslim community in Kishanganj.

Gowda dispensed with Taslimuddin when the Bihar Police confirmed the substance of the Legislative Council's report. But for a few weeks, India had had one of its more notorious criminals in charge of the department that was tasked to hunt him down.

Today, India's criminal class is firmly ensconced in its parliament and state assemblies. A hundred and fifty-five out of the 543 members elected to the 2009–14 Lok Sabha were facing serious criminal indictments in their home states and cities. The ratio of members with criminal records was much higher in the state assemblies: 44.6 per cent of those elected to the Bihar assembly in 2011 were facing similar criminal charges at the time of their election. In the May 2011 state elections, seventy-five MLAs of West Bengal, thirty-six MLAs of Tamil Nadu, eight of Assam and two of Puducherry declared serious criminal cases pending against them, including charges of murder, kidnapping and extortion.[6] An analysis by the Association for Democratic Rights revealed that 46 per cent of the 543 Lok Sabha members in 2024 had criminal cases registered against them, and that the percentage had steadily grown over the years. This was true even for MPs with serious criminal cases against them, for which the figure stood at 31, 29 and 21 per cent for the 2024, 2019, and 2014 elections, respectively.[7]

The figures for other states are all in the same ballpark as the ones cited above. This criminal element has not confined itself to exploiting parliamentary immunity and hamstringing the police and the bureaucracy. It too has built clientelist networks, mainly by acting as an intermediary between the people and the organs of the state. But unlike the networks that have given birth to the princeling phenomenon, these are criminal networks, which mobilize criminal funds and protect criminal enterprises like smuggling, bootlegging, timber theft and poaching.

Over time, the two types of clientelist networks have merged, through education and inter-generational mobility. This is most clearly visible in the Shiv Sena in Mumbai, a party that raised funds through a series of mafia-type protection rackets, and whose leader, Bal Thackeray, openly admitted that many of Mumbai's most notorious dons, like Arun Gawli, began life as members of the party but then, as he put it, 'went the wrong way'. (He reportedly said, 'If they have Dawood [Ibrahim], we have Gawli.' By 'they', he meant the Congress.)

## The Rise of the Predatory State

The transformation of what began as a developmental state into a predatory one has taken place in four stages. As mentioned earlier, in the immediate aftermath of the ban on company donations, the Congress party's fund managers themselves were at a loss as to where to raise the money to fight elections from. In the 1971 Lok Sabha and 1972 state assembly elections they therefore went back to the same companies and trade organizations from whom they used to accept tax-deductible cheques in the past, and demanded cash. Although most of them complied, they did so unwillingly. Raising money to meet electoral and administrative expenses therefore became more difficult than it had been before. But the gap was filled by owner-managers of small and medium sized enterprises and trade associations, which had earlier played a minor in funding politics. One result of this was a diffusion of the sources of party funds, and a relative shift in the balance of financial power within the Congress party, from the national towards the state units of the party. This came back to haunt Mrs Indira Gandhi till her untimely death in 1984.

The defeat of the Congress in the 'post-Emergency' 1977

elections triggered the *second* phase of the development of the predatory state. This was the first time that it had lost control of the centre, but its state units were far less affected by the debacle. The party as a whole therefore became significantly more dependent upon the state units that remained in power to meet its expenses. This tilted the scales within the Congress sharply in favour of the state units of the party. To restore its pre-eminence, the central party organization concentrated on restoring the financial pre-eminence of the centre. It did this by institutionalizing a system of kickbacks and commissions on foreign and domestic government contracts, most frequently in defence and energy. State Congress leaders and the opposition parties followed suit.

The effect this had on the economy was insidious and, cumulatively, disastrous. In no market economy, whether dominated by private or, as in China, by communist party 'cadre' investors, has it been possible to eliminate kickbacks and commissions altogether. The challenge these have posed to the state is to build a regulatory structure that maintains the accountability of the contractors for the quality of their products and the timeliness of supply, *in spite* of these kickbacks. Countries like the US and Singapore have succeeded by enacting stringent laws that impose harsh punishments on those who break them, and creating an effective system of adjudication to mete these out. India, however, has gone the other way. By making itself a party to skimming money off projects, the state has developed a powerful motive for crippling even the legal and regulatory framework that it had inherited from the British.

Over five decades, the cost borne by the people, in terms of opportunities foregone, has been astronomical. Two early examples, highlighted by the media at the time when they occurred, show how it has been paid. In the late seventies, the Janata Party government obtained World Bank financing for the first of a new generation of fertilizer plants for utilizing the natural gas from Bombay High to be set up at Thal-Vaishet, south of Mumbai. Based upon international bidding, the consultants employed by the World Bank had recommended that the contract should be given to an American firm, CF Braun. But when the Congress returned to power in 1980, it began to negotiate independently with several firms, including Toyo Engineering of Japan and Haldor Topsoe of Denmark, a subsidiary of the state-owned Italian engineering giant, Snam Progetti. When the World Bank refused to reopen the bid, and pulled out of the project, the government began beating the nationalist drum against foreign dictation, hinted that the World Bank's subservience to the US government was its reason for choosing CF Braun, and proclaimed that India would finance the plant from its own (then perennially straitened) foreign exchange resources.

Eventually, it awarded the contract not only for the Thal-Vaishet plant but for four others to Haldor Topsoe. At the time, there was widespread suspicion that the government had given the contract to Haldor Topsoe in exchange for a handsome kickback. Only later did the public come to know how much the country had to pay for that deal.

CF Braun had been chosen because it had by far the most energy efficient technology and lowest overall manufacturing cost of all the bidders. Had the original project been implemented with all the safeguards recommended by the World Bank, it would have set the benchmark for the entire future generation of gas-based plants. But it would, unfortunately, have made kickbacks on future projects much harder to obtain.

The award of a single contract for five plants without any international bidding led to an inflation of the capital costs of all the plants. To make matters worse, Haldor Topsoe's ammonia making technology used 15 per cent more energy per tonne of output. These two disadvantages ensured that these plants would never be able to produce urea at internationally competitive prices. The Thal-Vaishet project therefore created a much higher benchmark for capital costs in later plants. These and its higher energy costs had to be offset by subsidies. And since subsidies were designed to ensure a minimum return on capital invested, this gave a ready excuse to private investors to 'gold-plate' the cost of future plants. Indian taxpayers have been subsidizing inefficient fertilizer plants ever since.

Even while the Thal-Vaishet project was being renegotiated, the ministry of defence had begun a similar re-negotiation of major defence contracts entered into by the Janata government. Two that were eventually reinstated at immensely higher prices (and with much higher kickbacks) were for the purchase of Jaguar ground-hugging long-range fighter-bombers for the Air Force and the Harrier vertical/short take-off aircraft for the Navy, from Britain.

But we had to wait another five years to gain the first unequivocal proof of the cost that the by then ubiquitous system of kickbacks was imposing upon the country. We got this from an exposé in the Swedish newspaper *Dagens Nyheter* in March 1987 of what came to be known as 'the Bofors Deal'—a contract for howitzers for our military with Swedish weapons manufacturer AB Bofors. The investigations that followed the Swedish exposé revealed no fewer than three layers of kickbacks, totalling a mammoth 17 per cent of the $1.3 billion contract. So great was the public indignation aroused by the Swedish exposé that the revelation of yet another massive kickback, of 6 per cent on the purchase of submarines from the German firm Howaldtswerke-Deutsche Werft (HDW), went virtually unnoticed.

Public indignation led to the partial shelving of the Bofors deal, and a reduction of the number of submarines ordered from HDW. But the inflation of costs due to the kickbacks and the delays in striking deals is the least part of the harm that the institutionalization of kickbacks has done to the country. A much greater loss is that of time. This has left the country dangerously undefended for long periods while the deals are being struck. For instance, both Pakistan and India decided to equip their armies with 155 mm howitzers at more or less the same time in the late seventies. The Pakistan army got its guns by the early eighties. The Bofors deal was only finalized in 1985.

By the time the Bofors deal was shelved, a substantial number of the guns had already been obtained and deployed in the Nathu La region where their capacity to fire at high elevations had enabled the Indian army to push Chinese troops out of the sensitive Chumbi valley that separated Sikkim from Bhutan in 1986. But thirteen years later, when the Kargil War with Pakistan caught India unawares, the government had to pay up to 10,000 times the price of certain key spares and replacements that the armed forces had been unable to get for years through the defence procurement process, to enable them to wage war. The payment of these colossal prices was revealed by a report of the CAG. The defence minister at the time, George Fernandes, was unable to say a word in defence of his actions and acquired an enduring and undeserved reputation for corruption.

So tenacious, however, had the system of kickbacks become that the Kargil War changed nothing. At a closed door meeting in 2014, a former army chief openly lamented that it was still taking the army an average of three years to get their requisitions met.

The Thal-Vaishet fertilizer plant was only the trailblazer for what has followed. For the institutionalization of kickbacks has also ensured that contracts do not go to the most qualified bidders because these have the least need to pay kickbacks in order to secure contracts. Four decades later, this practice has become so pervasive that it no longer evokes dismay or outrage in civil society.

In the five decades since kickbacks became the main avenue for financing politics and slaking politicians' greed, the practice has spread to every corner of the country and permeated every level of its government. Today, there is hardly a contract, from the purchase of a new generation of the main battle tank to the construction of a rural road, that is not being preyed upon to extract money. Over the years, bureaucrats at every level, from the secretariats in New Delhi to the block development officers in each sub-division, have learned that they can do with even greater impunity for themselves what their political bosses want them to do for their parties.

The omission of time schedules, the obfuscation of penalty clauses and, once a 'deal' has been struck, the shaping of the tender specifications to ensure that only the chosen firm will qualify—abuses have crept into each stage of the tendering system.

Another notable feature of government contracts, even those awarded for giant contracts requiring state-of-the-art technology, is the absence of international consultants. This too can be traced back to the fact that the presence of independent consultants makes deal-making more difficult, a lesson that was learned from the World Bank's anger at the cancellation of the contract it had awarded to CF Braun in favour of Haldor Topsoe in 1978.

State governments shunned not only international expertise, but took advantage of this deliberate insularity to develop a stratagem for extracting money from projects that only Indian ingenuity could have dreamed up: they chopped up large projects into numerous smaller parts in the name of preserving competition and invited separate tenders for each part. This allowed ministers and bureaucrats to award contracts to small companies without the capital base, equipment or track record required to qualify for large projects, but willing to offer almost anything in return for getting a piece of the cake. Highway and urban development are the most flagrant examples of such parsing for profit. The cost, in terms of delays, inflation and shoddy work can be judged from the fact that the 'Golden Quadrilateral' highway project, to link Mumbai, Delhi, Calcutta and Chennai, started by Prime minister Atal Bihari Vajpayee in 1999 with the express purpose of providing a fiscal stimulus to the Indian economy after two years of recession, and intended to be completed by 2006, was not even half completed five years after the scheduled time of completion, and was declared operational only in 2012. It had remained incomplete because there were unfinished portions (and there still were till several years later) in every section of the four highways that made up the quadrilateral. This situation had arisen because, instead of dividing the project into segments of several hundred kilometres each and inviting world-wide bidding, the National Highways Authority chopped each highway into 20- to 30-kilometre segments. This enabled scores of fly-by-night companies to bid for each segment. Many turned out to have little or no capital or highway building experience but had secured the contracts nonetheless because of political connections and promises of massive kickbacks. Inevitably, in each segment, one or more contractors were unable to meet their deadlines. The ensuing court cases have gone on for years, and as of the date of writing, many are still unresolved. It was only after Narendra Modi came to power, and Nitin Gadkari took over the transport portfolio in the cabinet, that this practice of fragmenting contracts into smaller packages was given up and the construction of modern highways dramatically modernized.

The cost imposed on the nation by the state's abdication of its role as the guardian of the public interest, and its joining the ranks of the predators, cannot even remotely be computed. On November 23, 2009, i.e. well before the Commonwealth Games, 2G and other such scams were unearthed, *Outlook* had estimated that in eighteen years after economic liberalization, thirty-three major 'scams' had cost the nation an estimated 73,00,000 crores ($1.7 trillion at the 2009 exchange rate) or about $100 billion a year.[8] This turned out to be a hugely inflated estimate, but at the time when it was released it summed up the cost of corruption to society as nothing had before.

There is no way of computing the kickbacks being extracted from the hundreds of thousands of smaller contracts that central and state governments, the *zilla parishads* (District Development Councils) and the Rural Development Agencies (set up to implement rural infrastructure projects) sign every year. But even that figure, were it available, would not capture the cost that the absence of accountability caused by the kickback system has imposed upon the nation.

How huge the loss is can be judged by comparing the 'Golden Quadrilateral' project with construction projects executed by China. We have seen above the inordinate delays in the completion of the project. What is more, most of the roads do not meet the quality standards of roads in Europe or Southeast Asia. By contrast, in 2010, Chinese companies had built 1,000 kilometres of four-lane highways of European specifications and another 500 kilometres of high-grade two-lane roads in Kenya in just three years.

In their own country, their performance is even more impressive. China placed its first order with two Japanese companies, Kawasaki and Shinkansen, for twenty complete bullet trains to ply on a single high-speed line in 2004. Eleven years later, by the end of 2015, China had 19,000 kilometres of special track on which 2,300 trains were linking more than a hundred destinations.

*

Economic liberalization—by stealth after 1975 and openly after 1991—led to the *third* stage of development of the predatory state. When the corporate sector ceased to be an embarrassment to the state and became the spearhead of its attempt to join the global manufacturing network, politicians ceased to be chary of flaunting their links with industrialists. To circumvent the still numerous hurdles to investment, such as the acquisition of land and the provision of electricity, water and transport and communication facilities, industrialists began to 'take care of the expenses' of individual MPs and ministers. A practice that was still rare in the eighties soon became commonplace and then evolved into another of the tacitly accepted norms of Indian democracy. Thus was born the crony-capitalist state that Indians had derided in Indonesia, the Philippines and elsewhere till only a decade earlier.

The *final* act in the development of the predatory state opened with the end of Congress dominance in the 1996 elections, and the creation of a United Front government, a coalition of central and regional parties that spanned the gap between the BJP and the Congress. When, to everyone's surprise, the Congress was unable to decide upon a leader within the deadline given by the

President, and the UF was asked to form the government, it did not have a leader of the coalition to put forward. None of the latter had had any serious ambition to rule the nation. The UF eventually persuaded H.D. Deve Gowda, a former Congress leader in Karnataka who was then the chief minister of the state, to leave the state and come to Delhi to head the new government. Gowda agreed, but with the proviso that he would stay as prime minister only for a year. This, he said, would give the UF sufficient time to decide upon his successor. Deve Gowda stuck to this and resigned on April 21, 1997. By then the UF had chosen Inder Gujral to be the next prime minster, so the transition was smooth, but the former's firm resolve highlighted the extent to which, for the state governments, the central government had become a milch cow waiting to be milked. Power-sharing at the centre therefore became their favoured response to the perennial problem of raising funds in their home states.

One has only to examine the composition of the five coalition governments that have held power in Delhi since 1996 to perceive that while the major partner has retained the prime ministership, and the home, defence, external affairs and finance portfolios, most of the other lucrative 'economic' portfolios—industry, commerce, energy, the railways, telecommunications and civil aviation have gone to the coalition partners.

The lure needed to bring them into the coalition has been, and remains, the opportunity to make money—and reward their financiers and supporters in the states. To recoup their expenses on fighting elections, political parties and their chosen leaders have relied upon kickbacks on the award of government contracts and, since the one cannot be separated from the other, to enrich themselves and their more influential supporters.

## Preying Upon the Poor

Since the national media are overwhelmingly urban, they have paid only sporadic attention to the corruption and extortion that exists at the state and local levels of government. But this has done infinitely more harm, for it has inflicted death by a thousand cuts upon the legitimacy of the Indian state.

The need for money and muscle power to fight elections has led to a replication of the predatory political system at every level of local government. If parties in power at the centre have filled their coffers by demanding kickbacks on infrastructure projects, and commissions on large defence and other purchases made abroad, parties in power in the states have done exactly the same thing same thing on projects that fall within their purview. Thus, those bidding for contracts to build state highways, school buildings, bridges, small hydro-electric and thermal power projects, and any kind of urban development or improvement project, become automatic targets for the concerned ministers. In earlier days, when the Congress was the dominant party in the central and state legislatures, the normal mode of extraction was to ask the bidder to put down a percentage of the estimated cost of the project as a token of their seriousness at the time of bidding. This money was not always refunded.[9] More recently, the extraction of bribes has become more predatory. Under the Modi government, bribery was refined further by the issue of anonymous electoral bonds that contributors could buy and give to any party of their choice. (This is discussed in greater detail later in this book.)

Since land is needed for virtually any enterprise a person may want to start, it is the most highly prized bargaining chip in the hands of local politicians. It is not surprising therefore that most of the corruption and lawlessness that characterizes the clientelist state that India has become centres around its acquisition. Local mafias regularly battle for its control and anyone who dares to report on their activities does so at the risk of his life.

As a general rule, the smaller the size of the constituency the greater is the importance of muscle power. Thus, it should come as no surprise that muscle power has been deployed most frequently in the panchayat and zilla parishad elections. This has created a circle of predatory exploitation that has ensured that very little of the funds intended for rural development, health and education have filtered down to the intended beneficiaries. In 1985, a study of poverty alleviation programmes in Bihar which he had commissioned from a highly respected civil servant, Ajit Mazumdar, made Prime Minister Rajiv Gandhi expostulate at the Congress' centennial celebrations in Mumbai that only 15 per cent of the funds intended for the poorer sections of society ever got to them.

But Rajiv Gandhi's expostulation at the centennial celebration slipped off the hardened carapace of the Congress party as easily as water off a duck's back. Throughout the nineties and 2000s, as evidence accumulated that rural poverty was not declining anywhere nearly as fast as the sums being spent on its alleviation merited, the central government began to bypass the state administrations and inject funds directly into 'centrally sponsored' schemes for rural development, education, nutrition and health, and into special schemes like the National Rural Employment Guarantee Scheme, which transferred the responsibility for implementation directly to the gram panchayats.

The seriousness of the effort can be judged from the fact that annual outlays for rural development rose by fifteen times in nominal, and almost six times in real terms between 1990 and 2011. But if the UN's Human Development Index is a reliable indicator of performance, very little of the money has reached the beneficiaries, for India's position on the ladder stayed virtually unchanged at between 123rd and 127th.

Instead, as the sums devolved by the centre to the states and districts rose, so did the stakes in controlling the disbursement of these funds. The competition this unleashed between rival, and equally predatory, political parties resulted in growing violence in state assembly elections. To control the violence and especially to put an end to the practice of capturing polling booths and stuffing the ballot boxes, the Election Commission began to hold these elections in phases, accompanied by a growing deployment of paramilitary forces during each phase.

## The Co-optation of the Executive

Needless to say, none of the above stratagems for capturing and retaining political power would have worked without the willing or unwilling cooperation of the bureaucracy and the police. Politicians have needed their connivance to facilitate the receipt of kickbacks, cite regulations and precedents where necessary, and put the gloss of public interest upon the most private of transactions. And they have needed the connivance of the police to protect the suppliers of muscle power for local and state level elections. Article 311 of the Constitution has not only removed the single main threat to their connivance with their political masters, but has also made it fatally easy for them to go into the business of extortion on their own.

Till the digitization of transactions with the government, which began in earnest around 2010, there was hardly a transaction between the public and the state—whether it was the collection of one's pension or income tax refund, one's ration or Below Poverty Level (BPL) card, the passage of an architect's plan, the receipt of a 'completion' certificate for construction, the registration of a property sale, the payment of the stamp duty, or the renewal of a license no matter what it was for—that did not require the payment of a bribe—more strictly, an extortion 'price'—to a petty civil servant.

Posts in the bureaucracy that involved contact with the public were informally classified according to the amount they could yield by way of these bribes. Inevitably, therefore, within each ministry entire systems developed for 'auctioning' these posts to aspirants within the department, in exchange for a private 'fee'. Often the fee was so high that the aspirant had to take a loan to pay it. And there was no dearth of people willing to provide the money, on the understanding that it would be repaid in kind when the aspirant secured the post.[10]

Since then, the rapid growth of online transactions with the government has reduced face-to-face contact of the public with government officials, and greatly reduced the scope for corruption. This is the single greatest contribution that the digital age has conferred upon India and, one suspects, other developing countries as well.

But the bulk of the beneficiaries have been urban dwellers. In the rural areas, politicians have continued to need the help of the police even more than the bureaucracy. They have obtained this through a combination of inducement and blackmail. As pointed out in the 2009 report *Broken System* by the US-based Human Rights Watch:

> Since the late 1970s, senior police officers have remained at the mercy of state and local politicians who, acting on ambiguously worded supervisory authority in the Police Act of 1861, intervene in everyday police operations: officers are frequently told to drop investigations against people with political connections and sometimes told to harass or file false charges against political opponents. Refusal means transfer to remote areas, and with it the loss of prestige and the hardship of removing children from good city schools.
>
> Senior police officers have also lost the ability to discipline their ranks as politicians patronize junior-ranking police, intervening in recruitment, appointment and promotions. Former Inspector General of Police S.R. Darapuri said: 'There is a flaw in the recruitment process itself. Selection is very much biased and based on recommendations or corruption. Deserving candidates rarely get into the service. And therefore insubordination is a big problem in the force. Seniors are not able to control their juniors because these people have political connections.'
>
> A superintendent of police in Uttar Pradesh explained the pervasiveness of the system of political patronage: 'It has become obvious that the police cannot be neutral. Either you comply with every order from the political masters, or you have some strong backing of a leader who protects you. That is how policing is done here.'[11]

When you do your boss' dirty work, the boss does yours. It does not come as a surprise, therefore, that according to the National

Crime Records Bureau's (NCRB) annual report *Crime in India 2007*, which the 2009 HRW report relied on, only a little over a quarter (28 per cent) of the 282,384 complaints filed against the police between 2003 and 2007 for the violation of peoples' human rights led to departmental, magisterial or judicial inquiries. There were only 1,070 trials and 264 convictions.[12] Fifteen years later, there was little improvement in the situation. The NCRB data from 2021 revealed that around 49,000 complaints were filed against police officers, yet fewer than 28 per cent resulted in any disciplinary action.[13] In small towns and villages, the police are so greatly feared that it must have taken great courage on the part of the victims to report even these infractions. One can therefore assume that the remainder of the indicted policemen went back and extracted revenge from those who had dared to complain against them.

The National Crime Records Bureau recorded 853 custodial deaths between 2010 and 2018—seventy of them in 2018 alone. But the National Human Rights Commission (NHRC) put the death toll much higher at 1,636 deaths for this period. According to a 2020 report, only three policemen had been convicted by then for these deaths.[14] But even NHRC figures can be lower than the actual number. The registered number of deaths with the NHRC from January to December 2020, for example, was ninety. However, a report published by a consortium of NGO's against torture documented deaths of 111 persons in police custody across the country that year, out of which fifty-one were alleged to have died during torture and thirty-five allegedly committed suicide.[15]

What is more, Indian prisons are now crowded to bursting. In 2021, the NCRB reported that there were 488,511 prisoners in Indian jails at the end of 2020. Of these, 371,848 prisoners, i.e. 76 per cent were awaiting trial. The high number of pre-trial detainees had caused severe overcrowding in the prisons.

*

A tragic example of the toxic mix of crime, bureaucratic corruption and politics is furnished by the burning of Shahjahanpur-based Hindi journalist Jagendra Singh, on June 1, 2015, which led to his death. The report of his tragic death after a week's struggle in hospital, written by *The Hindu*'s correspondent Mohammad Ali, is reproduced below:

> In a dying declaration on video, shot before he breathed his last because of burns, he said, 'Why did they have to burn me? If the Minister and his people had something against me, they could have hit me and beaten me, instead of pouring kerosene over me and burning me.'
>
> In the video, [a copy of which Ali lodged with his newspaper], the journalist blamed Ram Murti Verma, Minister for Dairy Development, for his death.
>
> Singh was set on fire allegedly by a group of policemen and goons allied with Mr Verma on June 1. He battled for life for a week at a hospital in Lucknow before he died.
>
> The Shahjahanpur journalist who wrote extensively against alleged cases of corruption and illegal mining by the Minister had received repeated threats to his life.
>
> 'Prakash Rai [police inspector] was there and along with him were present four–five police personnel. The police team, led by Prakash Rai, barged into the house and started assaulting me. They could have as well arrested me,' said Singh, while crying in pain.
>
> Singh used to singlehandedly run *Shahjahanpur Samachar*, a page on Facebook which had a wide following in local circles. Most of the time, his reports were followed up by mainstream and local publications and TV channels, something which had allegedly angered the Minister.[16]

An FIR was registered by the victim's son Raghvendra, after his father died during treatment at the hospital. In it, he accused the minister Ram Murti Verma and Inspector Prakash Rai, and four others named Gufran, Akash Gupta, Amit Pratap Singh and Bhure for killing Jagendra, at Puwayan police station of Shahjahanpur.[17]

But nothing came of it. The dying declaration of Singh, his two sons Rahul and Raghvendra claimed, only proved the involvement of Mr Verma, who as per indications coming from a meeting of the top brass of the Samajwadi Party was expected to be dismissed. This did not happen.

### The Full-blown Predator State

When the 2G scam was exposed and the government was forced to take action, two charge sheets were filed by the CBI in April 2011 against Swan Telecom, one of the bidders which had secured a 2G broadband allocation. This brought to light, for the first time, the vast reach of the crony network that had been built over the previous four decades to sustain the predatory state, a network that stretches from Dubai and Lichtenstein, to Singapore, from Chennai to Delhi, from the metropolis to villages and tehsils, and from cabinet ministers to criminal dons currently residing in Dubai and Pakistan.

The story pieced together reads like the script of a Bollywood gangster movie, but its actors have been drawn from the entire power elite of the Indian state. The story begins with the rise of two dynamic young MDs aged thirty-seven and thirty-eight, who head (in one case headed) the fastest growing real estate companies in Mumbai and Chennai, and owed their meteoric rise to the powerful political patronage they enjoyed. The first of these companies is DB Realty, in Mumbai; the second is Green House Promoters, in Chennai.

The celebrated examples discussed below demonstrate the crime and politics nexus that has made a mockery of democracy, overwhelmed the Indian state and significantly eroded the public's trust in its institutions.

#### *Mumbai, Maharashtra*

DB Realty was created in 2006 by two families in Mumbai, those of a small hotelier, Usman Ebrahim Balwa, and a real estate dealer, Krishna Murari Goenka. In the next four years, DB Realty grew at a pace never before witnessed even in Mumbai's rambunctious real estate sector. By early 2011, it had put 21 million square feet of new residential and office space on the market and had another 40 million square feet under construction. Its thirty-seven-year-old managing director, Shahid Balwa, the younger son of Usman Balwa, had assets worth 1.06 billion dollars and was listed by Forbes as the sixty-sixth richest man in India.

How did a newcomer in the real estate business become one of the largest builders in Mumbai in as little as five years? In the Maharashtra secretariat, it was an open secret that DB Realty owed its dizzy growth to the complete backing it was receiving from a top politician in the state. Files concerning DB Realty, the *Times of India* reported, were processed, and permissions granted, within days.

Who was DB Realty's mysterious backer? Niira Radia, the lobbyist employed by Tatas, Unitech and a score of other companies, revealed in an interrogation by the CBI that 'As per the general perceptions in Mumbai and outside, DB Realty is controlled, directly or indirectly by Sharad Pawar and his family'. This created a sensation in the media, but most people still did not know that DB Realty may also have been a conduit for investments by its most notorious gangland don, Dawood Ibrahim.

According to Zameeruddin Ansari, an associate of Dawood's brother Anees Ibrahim, whom the Mumbai crime branch arrested in September 2004, Krishna Murari's son Pramod Goenka's real estate company was a conduit for the 'D' Company's investments in Mumbai's skyrocketing real estate market. This disclosure had come after a far more damning accusation made six months earlier, in October 2003, by a rival Mumbai builder Rajesh Patange, who accused Krishna Murari of having placed a 'supari' (contract) on his life in a dying declaration after he had been shot by four hitmen in a typical Mumbai contract killing. But neither in 2003 nor in 2004 did the Mumbai police even interrogate, let alone charge him for either offence.

The Maharashtra police also had evidence, gleaned from

arrested gangsters, that Shahid Balwa's father Usman Ebrahim Balwa was closely associated with another notorious underworld don, Chhota Shakeel. In all, the police and central security agencies, sent seven reports to the state government between 2003 and 2008 against the Goenka and Balwa families, but no one paid them the least attention. 'We invest so much resources [in the collection of this information] because there are serious issues of national security,' a Delhi-based official, probably belonging to the Research and Analysis Wing, our foreign intelligence agency, lamented to the *Times of India*, 'But governments just ignore them.'

In 2011, it remained to be seen how much of the above information would be included in the CBI's charge sheets against Shahid Balwa and Vinod Goenka, Krishna Murari's other son and Balwa's partner in DB Realty. But the media and the public had no difficulty in joining the dots, and connecting not only the Balwas and the Goenkas with Sharad Pawar and Dawood Ibrahim, but Pawar to Ibrahim.

***Chennai, Tamil Nadu***

A similar set of connections was exposed by the investigation of a case against A. Raja, the DMK minster in the central government who issued 2G licenses in 2007 at prices fixed on the recommendation of the Telecommunications Regulatory Authority (TRAI) in 2003, on a first come, first served basis. The government of Dr Manmohan Singh had agreed to TRAI's fixed price recommendation because the first round of thirty-four licenses which had been awarded through competitive bidding had pushed mobile telephony charges so high that few people bought mobiles and fewer of them used these for more than the minimum period of time. As a result, the operators had expressed their inability to meet their commitment to pay and asked for a shift to revenue sharing in order to meet their commitments. After studying their complaints and counter proposals, TRAI had conceded the validity of the former and viability of the latter in

2003, and recommended shifting to a Unified Access Services Licensing system for all future contracts in which there would be a fixed access price-*plus*-revenue sharing with the government by the telecom operators.

This change of pricing policy brought the cost of mobile calls crashing down till it was among the lowest in the world. The poor of the country, and India's more than 100 million migrant workers in particular, were the greatest beneficiaries. But in the meantime, the pricing policy change had been vetted by the Comptroller and Auditor-General's office which produced a damning report that accused the government of having foregone Rs 42,000 crores of actual revenues by way of auction fees foregone because of the change of policy, and presumptively another Rs 176,000 crores by way of future fees and mobile charges. These colossal estimates unleashed a storm of accusations of corruption against both the Manmohan Singh government and A. Raja in particular. These were eventually dismissed by the Delhi High Court in a scathing judgement in 2010.[18]

But the intense investigative reporting that the accusations hurled against Raja the CAG report had unleashed had the unintended effect of casting a flood of light on how he had built his political career. It revealed how the constant hunt for money with which to fight elections had thinned the dividing line between politics and crime even for serious, well respected politicians.

Early in his career as a local lawyer in Perambalur, Tamil Nadu, A. Raja had once defended a young man who had a small real estate business in the rural Karur district, buying plots of land with margin payments and completing the payment when he sold the land to someone else. His name was Sadiq Batcha. Batcha had sought legal help from Raja when some of his deals went sour. This became the foundation of an enduring and lucrative partnership. When Raja later entered politics, he apparently began to feed Batcha with information about where the government intended to buy land for new projects in any given area. To Batcha, such information was worth its weight in gold because whenever the government announced a project in a particular neighbourhood, and especially in Perambalur, Raja's constituency, it had to buy it from Batcha, inevitably at much higher than the original price.

In 2004, when Raja first became a union minister in the NDA government, Batcha set up a real estate firm named Green House Promoters. His joint managing director in the company was A. Raja's elder brother, A. Kalaiperumal. In the next few years, the company expanded at a dizzy pace, always buying land cheap and selling it dear to the government, or to major real estate companies. Within a few years Green House Promoters, which had been started with an equity capital of just one lakh of rupees, reported a revenue of Rs 600 crores—sixty thousand times its equity base, and had opened offices in Bangalore and Singapore. Raja's wife, nephew and various other relatives were employees and directors of the company.

After one intense interrogation by the CBI in February, when faced with a second summons from the CBI, Batcha, *apparently*, took his own life on March 16, 2011. The CBI was trying to track down where the presumed payments made to Raja had been salted away, and had come across evidence that suggested that they may have been put into accounts in six countries.

At the time of Batcha's death, Green House was describing itself as a company engaged in exports. According to some newspaper reports, the CBI had wanted to interrogate Batcha to learn the identities of four persons from the D Company, the gang of criminals being run by Dawood Ibrahim, whom it suspected of having set up the Singapore account. Batcha's suicide could not therefore have come at a more convenient time for all concerned, but especially for Dawood Ibrahim.

Much of what has appeared since in the media is, nonetheless, still conjecture. Apart from the fact that they knew each other well and may have had business relations with each other, everything described above about Raja's connections with Batcha is conjecture. By the same token, when Anil Ambani may or may not have acquired 10.71 per cent equity in Balwa's Swan Telecom,[19] to use it as a front for buying more than the permitted bandwidth, he may not have known about DB Realty's murky origins. But in the court of public opinion, not only these companies and their owners and managers, but the entire Indian state stood condemned. For the sustained reporting on the 2G scam, and its attendant disclosures, had exposed a web of shady transactions and a systemic abuse of state power that stretched all the way from a powerful minister in the central government, through some of India's most respected industrialists, managers, lobbyists and journalists, to a political party in Tamil Nadu with an otherwise enviable record for good governance, to hitmen in Mumbai's underworld employed by two of its most detested dons, one of whom—Dawood Ibrahim—was a self-proclaimed enemy of the Indian state who had actively aided terrorist attacks in Mumbai in 1993 that had claimed scores of lives.

What is particularly troubling is the way these disclosures reinforced the long-held suspicion, that Bal Thackeray's off-the-cuff allegation that the Maharashtra Congress, headed by Sharad Pawar, had been the political patron and protector of Dawood Ibrahim in the eighties and early nineties was true. For if DB Realty was only formed in 2006, who was the powerful patron, hinted at by the Mumbai Police and central intelligence agencies, who shielded Krishna Murari Goenka from a charge of murder in 2003 and his son from interrogation for having business dealings with Dawood Ibrahim, his brother Anees Ibrahim, and a Karachi-based real estate dealer known to be associated with them in 2005? And if Pawar, who had been the chief minister of several Congress governments in Maharashtra, and was a powerful minister in Dr Manmohan Singh's cabinet, had felt no qualms in dealing with, and protecting, Dawood Ibrahim, a gangster alleged to have organized the 1993 serial bomb blasts in Mumbai on behalf of Pakistan's ISI, then is there anything left sacred in the Indian state?

The public also knows that the 2G scam is one of not hundreds but thousands that take place every year. It cannot therefore be blamed for concluding that the Indian state today bears not even a passing resemblance to the nation that Mahatma Gandhi and Pandit Nehru had tried to found, for in it every principle has been abandoned, except the relentless accumulation of money for personal and political gain. Coming on top of Bal Thackeray's remark, mentioned above, Niira Radia's casual reference to Pawar's personal interest in DB Realty came close to destroying people's faith in Indian democracy.

## Democracy at its Breaking Point

The stories related above are by no means the worst. But they suffice to show how completely the working of Indian democracy had become divorced from the moral values and lofty ideals that had been enshrined in the Constitution.

When the second great explosion of public discontent took place in 2010, the Congress-led United Progressive Alliance (UPA) had been in power for six years and had four more to go. It had won a comfortable victory in 2009, securing 322 seats, forty more than needed to secure a majority. In Dr Manmohan Singh, it had a prime minister of unimpeachable integrity, whose government had overseen more than six years of the fastest growth in industry and GDP that the country had ever known. In these years, the number of non-agricultural jobs created every year had exceeded the number of new job-seekers for the first time in the country's history and done it so comprehensively that industry had begun to draw as many as four million youth out of rural areas annually into urban jobs.

The Congress was therefore uniquely placed to initiate the structural reforms of the political system that the country was craving for. Briefly, these were

(i) to end the all-pervasive corruption and criminalization of the democratic system by creating a state financing system for meeting recognized political parties' electoral expenses;

(ii) to create a system of administrative law, similar to France's *droit administrative* overseen by administrative tribunals similar to the French *Cours de Cassation*, in which citizens can hold the bureaucracy and the police accountable for dereliction of duty and give them the power to prosecute politicians, officials and policemen who accept bribes from the rich and powerful to look the other way while they break the law; and

(iii) a judicial system that citizens can rely upon to give them speedy and affordable justice.

The nationwide response to Anna Hazare's first fast had convinced Sonia Gandhi, the president of the Congress, of the urgent need for reform. She therefore convened a meeting of the All-India Congress Committee, the party's highest representative body, to discuss what needed to be done. After two days of discussions, she set up four committees to frame concrete proposals for reform. But nothing came of this initiative. This did not come as a surprise because the Congress was both the architect and the main beneficiary of the clientelist system of government against which the people were rebelling. So, the party machine had no difficulty in snuffing it out the moment public attention shifted to other issues.

Fifteen years later, it has become apparent that this was the Congress' last chance to rehabilitate itself in the eyes of the people by reforming Indian democracy. When the party made light of the wishes of its own president and made no attempt to do so, it lost the vestigial faith people had reposed in it till then. Even so, had it managed to sustain the high growth rate that had begun in 2003–04 through the rest of its three years in office, it might have been returned to power in 2014. Indian democracy would then have continued on its creaky road for some time longer. But industrial growth collapsed in 2011, falling from close to 10 per cent a year in the previous eight years to barely 3 per cent. Employment growth fell equally dramatically, from an average growth of seven million a year to about a third of that figure. And, as a 2019 paper by the Modi government's former chief economic adviser, Arvind Subramaniam, has shown, GDP growth too fell dramatically.[20]

For the youth, this was the last straw: after eight years, when almost no one who looked for a job had failed to find one, all of a sudden there were no jobs for most of them. Shorn of hope, large numbers of them turned to the BJP. Forty-four per cent of young voters gave their vote to Narendra Modi's BJP. As a result, the Congress' share of the vote plummeted from 28 per cent in 2009 to 18 per cent in 2014, while the BJP's vote rose from 18 per cent to 31 per cent. For the first time since it was formed, the BJP came to power entirely on its own, winning 282 out of 543 seats.

The completeness of their victory has put the survival of democracy in jeopardy. For the BJP that came to power in 2014 was not the BJP that had first come to power in 1998 under Atal Bihari Vajpayee. While Vajpayee was a staunch democrat who considered India's ethnic diversity and religious pluralism to be the sources of its strength and resilience, the Sangh Parivar (lit., 'family') of today is the sworn enemy of every 'Gandhian' value that informs the Indian Constitution—its acceptance of ethnic diversity, its secularism, its respect for all religions, and its marked preference for non-violent accommodation over coercion, cultural assimilation and violence as ways of settling differences within and between countries.

The BJP's second, even more convincing victory in 2019, brought India face to face with the grim realization that its victory in 2014 was not caused by a chance conjunction of events, but the outcome of a profound change in the nature of Indian society that caused almost two-fifths of the country to reject the unique federal democracy that had drawn unstinting praise from President Clinton in 1994, and support its replacement by a fascist, Fuehrer-led state. What is this profound change and how has it come about? To understand this we need to stop thinking of Fascism as a term of abuse and understand the forces that give birth to it.

CHAPTER SIX

# What Is Fascism?

## *A Necessary Digression*

*Fascist* is perhaps the most widely used term of abuse in the language of politics today. The term comes from the Latin word *fascio*, which means a bundle of sticks. In Roman times, it referred to a bundle of sticks with an axe-head. Since the Second World War, the term has been used so routinely by liberals to describe authoritarian governments they disapprove of that its original meaning has been all but lost. But it is an appropriate description for the authoritarian impulse that the RSS has been seeking to harness to its goal of creating a *Hindu Rashtra*. For the forces that are driving this impulse in India are the same ones that gave birth to Fascism in Europe after the First World War, and are doing so today in a growing number of developing countries, ranging from Iran and Turkey to Venezuela and Brazil.

What are these forces, and how have they manifested themselves in the realm of politics so far? In her maiden speech in the Lok Sabha—the lower house of the Indian parliament—in June 2019, Mahua Moitra, a London-based investment banker who returned to India to serve her country and joined the Trinamool Congress in Bengal, described the Narendra Modi government as a fascist government because it exhibited seven of the twelve features of Fascism that are listed on the wall of the Holocaust Museum in Washington, DC. These are: (i) a powerful nationalism that is superficial, dogmatic and narrow; (ii) a mobilization of support using hate and exclusion as its driving force; (iii) an intermingling of religion and myth and their incorporation into government; (iv) an obsession with national security, that constantly fans an irrational fear of the unknown and creates new enemies in order to justify the suppression of dissent and enforcement of conformity within the country; (v) a relentless extension of control over the mass media through the abuse of law; (vi) an utter disdain for intellectuals, the Arts, and for all knowledge that conflicts with dogma; and (vii) rampant sexism.

As the following chapters will show, all of these were visible in the thirteen years of Modi's chief ministership of Gujarat from 2001 till 2014, and have been prominent characteristics of the Modi-led central government since 2014. But, one may ask, haven't these characteristics been present to a greater or lesser extent in all authoritarian states since the end of monarchy. If so, how then is a fascist state different from a tribal, military or communist dictatorship?

This question preoccupied an entire generation of scholars and political scientists after the Second World War. The question to which they sought an answer was: 'Why, after a century of "enlightenment", that had advertised progress and emancipation from prejudice as its dominant pursuits, did basically similar movements—avowedly hostile to the present and fearful of the future—arise throughout Europe at almost the same historical moment?'[1] Two decades of intense study of the rise of fascism during the inter-war years (1918 to 1939), from the mid-forties of the last century till the late sixties, did not yield a consensus because almost any salient characteristic of Fascism in one country was often found to be absent in another.

For instance, fascism developed in Italy and Germany as a reaction to the threat from communism. But fascist movements also sprang up in several industrially backward and largely agrarian countries of Eastern Europe, such as Hungary, Romania, Croatia and Slovenia, that had no serious communist movement.

Second, mature fascism created, and then glorified an absolute leader—Hitler in Germany and Mussolini in Italy. But fascism arose in Eastern Europe without producing, and then glorifying, a single supreme leader.

Third, fascist regimes in Germany and Italy drew their strength from the urban petty bourgeoisie—small traders and manufacturers—but in Spain and Eastern Europe, fascism attracted peasant farmers, artisans, the lower rungs of the land-owning aristocracy, and elements of the military that had been disbanded after a war they had lost.

Most of this ambiguity has arisen because in sharp contrast to democracy, where the concept long preceded its revival in the industrial age, fascism had to be defined *after* movements with similar characteristics had already sprung up in a number of countries at almost the same time. What were these common features? *First*, fascism was born out of what may be termed economic 'intermediacy': in its full-blown form, as found in Italy and Germany, it was a movement of the *middle* and *lower middle* classes that developed in the *early and middle stages* of the transformation to capitalism. If any social class enjoyed a privileged position in fascism, it was the '*small man*'—the businessman or farmer—the 'healthy' German *Mittelstand* (middle class) or the Italian '*productive bourgeoisie*'.[2] This middle stratum was supported by a large fringe of artisans, shopkeepers, petty civil servants and skilled workers who considered themselves a part of the 'bourgeoisie' and were, as a result, the most zealous defenders of their status.[3]

Fascism was also 'intermediate' in a *second* sense. This was that it was most readily accepted in countries that were in the middle stages of the transition from traditional to modern societies. It fared best in countries that were late starters in industrialization; were relatively young nations where the fires of nationalism burnt especially bright[4] and had only recently begun to experiment with parliamentary democracy. This description fitted Italy and the fascist regimes of Eastern Europe best but was not a bad fit for post-First World War Germany and France either.

Germany had a mature industrial economy, with a high level of urbanization and a very large and well-established working class. But the Weimar Republic was not even a decade old when it was forced to contend with the first repeated buffets of fascism. These were delivered in rapid succession by the humiliation of defeat in the war; the draconian reparations forced upon Germany at the Treaty of Versailles in 1919; the resulting hyper-inflation of 1923; and the onset of the Great Depression in 1930 only three years after the German economy had begun to recover from the last of these blows.

France, on the other hand, had a well-established democracy, and a mature industrial structure, but much of this was in the hands of a large and insecure small business and peasant proprietor class, which felt continually threatened by the growth of modern industry. In both countries, as also in Italy, it was this class of owner-proprietors that formed the backbone of the fascist movement and provided the collaborators who did the Germans' dirty work of rounding up the Jews in Vichy France. Marshall Philippe Petain's tame surrender to the Germans after the fall of Paris allowed this insecure petty bourgeois class to survive till well after the end of the Second World War. It did so in the form of *Poujadisme*—a tax protest movement of the 1950s named after the French populist politician, Pierre Poujade—and survives to this day as Marie LePen's Front Nationale.

*Third*, the catalyst for the rise of fascism in all the countries of Europe was a sudden and deep attack of insecurity. In one or other form, all the post-Second World War analyses agree that the middle and lower middle classes forsook democracy out of fear. The fear was triggered by the savagery of the Great Depression, which drastically weakened their economic viability even while it triggered a sharp rise in working-class militancy.[5] This was greatly aggravated by the rise of communist regimes in Russia and Hungary, the nearly successful communist putsch in Germany, and the fear of social *anomie*—of being reduced to irrelevance—inspired in this middle bourgeoisie by the rise of giant corporations on one side, and a mass social and economic culture, heavily influenced by communism, on the other, which found its political expression in its support of the Social Democratic Party.[6]

To sum up, therefore, the fascism of the inter-war years was the *defensive* reaction of an insecure middle strata of society that regarded themselves as victims of forces over which they had no control, and were afraid of becoming the losers from industrialization and the development of the market economy. This numerous, but economically weak, stratum had been able to seize power almost simultaneously in several European countries because of the powerful external shock of defeat in war, followed by hyperinflation and the sudden onset of the Great Depression of the 1930s. This destroyed the authority and credibility of pre-war state structures and of the then nascent democracy in the more mature of these nations, to wit, Italy, Germany and France.

## The Economic Roots of Fascism

In the years after the Second World War, the study of fascism became intertwined with the study of anti-Semitism, and German Nazism. But one political scientist, A.F.K. Organski, continued to trace it to the stage of *economic* development of the countries in which it emerged. Fascism, he wrote, is a product of the tensions that are generated in a society during the middle stages of its modernization.[7] In this intermediate period, economic development, political modernization and social adjustment proceed at different paces. It creates severe stresses in society when the three get far out of line with each other. Fascism can result from society's attempt to bring the three back in line by either hastening the pace of one of these, or slowing down the pace of another.

The stresses are likely to be most severe at two different points in the continuum of industrialization. At the earlier point the conflict is likely to be between the modern (commercial-industrial) and traditional (peasant-artisanal) sectors of society. At a later stage, it can be between the emerging elite in a modern, industrialized society—what the Left in India called 'Big Business'—and an intermediate stratum of small and middle-sized, usually family-owned, businesses that finds itself being pushed out by the superior organizational and productive power of the former. At both points of the continuum, the conflict is between the winners and losers from the advance of capitalism.

Implicit in Organski's analysis was the perception that economic change usually races ahead of change in political institutions, and even further ahead of change in social attitudes. The attempt to reconcile the three in order to minimize conflict is invariably a reaction to changes that are already in motion. It is thus reactionary in the limited sense of trying to hold back, if only temporarily, the process of economic modernization. Organski therefore provided a single, coherent explanation for why fascism bloomed in the 1920s not only in the industrialized countries of Europe—Germany, Italy, France and, more weakly, in Britain, but also the largely agrarian societies of Spain, Portugal, Hungary, Romania, and the Balkans. In the former, it was a 'revolt' of a middle and lower petty bourgeoisie against the threats posed by economic recession, hyperinflation and militant socialism from below, and the concentration of capital in the hands of giant, professionally managed, enterprises from above.[8] In the latter, it occurred because of the same external shocks, but these were borne by peasant proprietors, artisanal industry and small traders who were already struggling to cope with the early stages of the onset of capitalism.

Most of the differences in fascist ideology displayed by the nations of continental Europe in the inter-war years can be traced to the stage of capitalism through which they were passing at the time of its birth. In countries which were at an early stage of industrialization, fascism tended to look backwards and romanticize a real or mythical past. In countries where industrialization was already far advanced, as in Germany, it was more radical, attacked the Church, pitted itself against the landed gentry and big bourgeoisie, and called itself 'socialist'. Thus, the German fascists labelled themselves the National Socialist German Workers' Party (NSDAP). The label of socialist was missing in the names of the fascist parties of Eastern Europe and the Balkans.

This ideological progression reflected the changing goals, and power, of those who were opposing the advance of capitalism. The exaltation of the past during the early stages of modernization reflected the fascists' desire to arrest the process that was marginalizing the new middle class. It also reflected their awareness of the weakness of their economic support base and therefore the need to enlist the traditionalists, the monarchists and the Church. Such fascist impulses could go both ways: they could die a speedy death either by getting absorbed by the true traditionalists, as happened in Spain, or by getting absorbed by the traditional conservatives on whose support they had come to depend, as happened to the National Front in Britain. When either happens, fascism, defined as an impulse of the *middle* propertied stratum to oppose the elites of the past and the future, dies a natural death.

The alternative is to take control of the state and use its *political* power to slow down the rise of a modern industrial class. Fascist movements have a much better chance of doing this during the middle stages of industrial transformation when the burgeoning petty bourgeoisie is numerous and economically strong. That is what happened in Italy, and Germany. In Germany, as noted above, it was aided by the weakening of the large industrial houses by defeat in the First World War and a cruelly high burden of reparations imposed upon Germany; hyperinflation in the mid-twenties; and the Depression of the 1930s. It was only after 1930 that the fascist impulse flowered in Germany, as a revolt of an underprivileged, insecure and politically powerless Mittelstand against a weak and discredited democratic state. Its goal then was not so much to reject an industrial future as to control its arrival, in order to minimize the threat of impoverishment. It was in this middle stage of industrialization that fascism developed its ideology of 'corporativism'—a trusteeship between employers and employed based upon respect for hierarchy and loyalty to a Supreme Leader—to its fullest extent.

To eliminate class conflict, Corporativism stressed the organic unity of the state, and legitimized curbing the growth of power at the extremes of the social spectrum. These were the organized trade unions and the large industrial houses. The cost was a slowing down of growth and an increased toleration of inefficiency. But to small business, the propertied middle strata of society, the economic security it provided far outweighed its cost.

## The Inherent Instability of Fascism

Fascism was therefore inherently unstable. It curbed the rise of the big bourgeoisie through an elaborate network of controls, but these caused delays in investment and created shortages in the market. Since these shortages attracted imports, high tariffs soon followed. The resulting economic autarchy, was justified by appeals to nationalism. Heightened nationalism therefore became an inherent feature of the fascist impulse.

The long-term effect of trying to limit the development of the market economy is the emergence of a regime of permanent shortages—a permanent seller's market that permits the small, independent manufacturers and traders to co-exist with the large. The cost of this stability, however, is an aversion to technological change, because this keeps creating new winners and new losers all the time. The result is the slowdown of economic growth. This is what ultimately destabilizes a fascist regime.

To avoid this, Hitler's government in Germany harped constantly on German nationalism, and the need for *lebensraum*—room for the German race to expand. This allowed him to create a massive new war machine. To do this he established a *concordat* with German industry that gave his government the industrial muscle-power to take on Europe, Russia and America single-handedly and keep them at bay for five long years before crashing in flames.

## The Fascist Impulse in Today's Developing Countries

Nearly all the studies of fascism during the first two decades after the Second World War contained one unspoken premise—that it had been a European phenomenon, and was therefore not relevant to the recently decolonized, newly industrializing countries of Asia, Africa and South America. This has proved a crucial error[9] because in the three quarters of a century that has elapsed since the end of the war, the fascist impulse has re-surfaced, and authoritarian governments have arisen in country after country across Asia, Latin America and Africa.

This book describes the slow strangulation of democracy and development of an authoritarian state in India, but even in the 1980s and '90s, India was far from being the only country where a fascist impulse had begun to develop in the middle stages of industrialization. Another large and important developing country where this happened was Iran, which is indeed the more striking example. In Western writing, Iran is routinely described as a theocratic state, but it became one only after the revolution that ousted Mohammad Reza Pahlavi, the Shah, and brought Ayatollah Khomeini to power. In the days of the Shah, it was a rapidly developing country and was, in fact, a nation of traders and small manufacturers known locally as the *Bazaaris*, an Iranian Mittelstand, that felt seriously imperilled by the Shah's haste to modernize the economy, and sought legitimacy for its opposition to it through an alliance with the Shia clergy. The rise of Ayatollah Khomeini was not the cause, but the outcome, of this economic radicalization.

## The Roots of the Iranian Revolution

Till as late as December 1978, the US embassy in Tehran still believed that the Shah was not seriously threatened by the populist '*Bazaari*' movement that had sprung up in the country.[10] Nor did anyone seriously believe that the downfall of the Shah would lead to the establishment of an Islamic theocratic state.[11] The outcome confounded the US government, and Western observers, because none of the established political groups that had long opposed the Shah came to power. What did come to power was a group of clergy backed by a class of people to whom no one at the time assigned any social identity or capacity for mobilization—the merchants, shopkeepers and artisans of Iran, who made up 17 per cent of its urban population.

In the aftermath of the coup, no fewer than five theories were put forward by analysts of the Iranian revolution: four by scholars and the fifth by the Shah himself. These ranged from seeing it (i) as a revolt against authoritarian rule, brought on by the fact that the rapid pace of Iran's modernization under the Shah was not matched by its political democratization; (ii) as a revolt against modernization which was deemed to be against all Islamic values and tenets; to interpreting it (iii) as a *product* of modernization which had pulled hordes of people out of their villages into the cities, broken down social cohesion and uprooted traditional institutions; and (iv) as a reaction in the new urban classes to economic distress and social anomie. Finally, there was the Shah's belief that (v) the revolution had been plotted by foreign powers, although he never could pinpoint which ones, or why they should have turned against him.[12]

All of these theories, with the exception of the last, give important insights into the causes of the revolution, but none is able to explain its most puzzling feature: why did revolution occur in a country where the per capita income had grown *thirty* times in thirty-two years between 1946 and 1978, and reached the then relatively high level of $2,150 in the latter year; where the non-oil gross domestic product was growing at 15.2 per cent and doubling every 4.5 years when the revolution took place; where unemployment was as low as 1 per cent and the country had had to import one million foreign workers, who made up 10 per cent of the labour force?[13]

The belief that it was a popular uprising against an assault on Islam by the Shah has gained its credibility from the fact that this is what Ayatollah Khomeini, and the regime he set up, repeated tirelessly both before and after the revolution. But it loses most of its plausibility when one considers that although the hold of religion, and of the clergy, is far greater in the villages than the towns, *the villages did not join the revolt until its last stages when the fall of the regime was virtually certain.*

The revolution began in the cities and towns, and was led by the Bazaaris, the traditional merchant class and their workers. Their numbers and wealth had swollen greatly as Iran's national income soared on the back of the OPEC's (Organization of the Petroleum Exporting Countries) oil price hikes in the 1970s. The Bazaaris were religious in much the same way as the *kirana* traders of India are religious. But religion alone cannot explain why they spearheaded the revolt while the far more conservative rural peasantry did not.[14]

Nor can the breaking of traditional cultural ties and social anomie resulting from hectic, unplanned urbanization explain a revolt against a regime that had accomplished so much in so little time. It can, at most, explain why so many people were discontented and tacitly or overtly approved of the revolt once it had begun. The hypothesis that it was a revolt against a tyrannical monarch and the SAVAK, his savage secret service, also loses credibility because the very people who threw the Shah out submitted tamely to a far worse reign of terror for the next eleven years. The autocratic, highly personalized rule of the Shah only explains the sudden and complete success of the revolt, for it had made him lose touch with the social changes that were being brought about by sudden wealth and urbanization, but throws little light on what caused it.

The explanation that most closely fits the facts is that the Shah was dethroned by a revolt against capitalist industrialization, spearheaded by a large and powerful 'old' petty bourgeoisie, consisting of merchants, shopkeepers, artisans and small manufacturers, that felt directly threatened by modern industry and the rapid growth of non-bazaar, modern commerce. The pivotal role of the Bazaaris in the Iranian revolution has been extensively written about, but it has been most clearly identified as a *reaction* to a threat from the state to their economic interests by Misagh Parsa.[15] Parsa has treated the Iranian revolt as an illustration of a more general theory of revolt in Third World countries. According to him, revolts are inevitably, perhaps even tautologically, fathered by those who perceive themselves to be losers within a given politico-economic dispensation. The reason why this discontent crystallizes into an attack on the state, instead of discharging itself less harmfully as class conflict, is the role that the state plays in creating the environment that fosters the change.

When the state cuts out the private sector and makes itself the sole investor we get communism. But when the state relies on private investors for industrialization one all too often gets crony capitalism. This politicizes the discontent that inevitably arises among those whom modern industry disempowers. These are the traditional artisanal and cottage scale manufacturers. The close relationship between modern capital and the state therefore leads inevitably to the politicization of discontent.

Parsa's analysis shows that the Bazaaris clearly perceived that the threat came from economic modernization—the growth of modern industry and commerce 'outside the bazaar'. They responded by turning against the regime because they perceived it to be actively and energetically favouring the industrialists and traders in the modern sector of the economy.

Precisely because Iran's economic growth was so hectic, it provides an even more clear-cut example of a successful revolt against capitalist development than did Germany in the thirties. The much, much higher rate of economic transformation and consequent social restructuring compressed the time period in which everything happened and threw the causes of the revolt into high relief. In every sense of the term, the time was ripe for such a revolt in 1977–78. Even after keeping the oil sector out of the picture, the share of agriculture in the rest of the economy had fallen to 14 per cent and that of industry risen to 29 per cent, in 1978, the year when the Shah was deposed. The change had been dramatic, for the share of agriculture had been 32 per cent in 1963–64 and that of industry just 21 per cent.[16]

In 1976, Iran's workforce was also almost exactly divided between agriculture and industry, with 34 per cent employed in agriculture and 34.2 per cent in industry.[17] (Iran therefore met one of Organski's key preconditions for the rise of a fascist-type movement. This was that the proportion of the workforce employed in industry should not be far short of the proportion that remained in agriculture.[18]) Property relations in industry and trade were also at the precise stage of evolution at which small property owners were not only numerous but also lacked the social security that their counterparts in Europe had secured. Of the total workforce, 17.5 per cent—717,690 persons—were engaged either in commerce or were self-employed manufacturers. They were thus in the same position as the German Mittelstand had been at the beginning of the 1930s Depression.[19]

At the same time, the ownership of property was extremely inegalitarian. The top tier of beneficiaries in the modern sector of the economy consisted of 150 families that owned two-thirds of all industries and financial institutions (measured by the value of output). Within this uppermost stratum, forty-seven families owned 85 per cent of all enterprises with a turnover of more than ten million rials. At the very top were the royal family and ten others close to it which owned 496 out of the 527 largest corporations and financial institutions in the country.

The second stratum consisted of around 8,500 employers in factories, i.e. modern industry. The third stratum consisted of 40,000 smaller enterprises in the traditional sectors, mostly food products and textiles. The fourth and most insecure was a large artisanal sector, in which carpet manufactories alone numbered 135,000. In all, no less than 98 per cent of industrial establishments belonged to the Iranian counterpart of India's small and medium sized enterprises, concentrated in traditional industries like textiles, food, carpets, shoe-making, copper and silverware. These employed over two-thirds of the workforce. Finally, there were over 540,000 traders and shopkeepers, a few of whom were rich, but the vast majority of whom were small specialist vendors of a few products.[20]

The pattern of property ownership in agriculture was equally skewed. One per cent of the landowners owned more than 20 per cent of the arable land. Unlike India, Iran had had no land reforms. In the most fertile agricultural areas, therefore, the concentration of land in the hands of the aristocracy was even greater. In Mazanderan vilayet, for instance, 19 per cent of the land was owned by 0.26 per cent of the owners, nearly all of whom were members, or close associates, of the royal family. At the other end of the scale, 31 per cent of the farm families owned less than one hectare of land and 65 per cent owned less than five hectares. According to official data, the minimum viable agricultural holding in Iran then was estimated to be seven hectares.[21]

There is a textbook quality to the way the hectic economic modernization and development of the sixties and seventies marginalized large sections of the population of Iran. The marginalization began long before 1973, when OPEC raised oil prices by a common decision for the first time.[22] Iran's petrodollar boom, and the attempt to step up an already very rapid growth rate still further, exacerbated the fear and insecurity already present in the losers from this hectic modernization, to the point of revolt.

In agriculture, the marginalization of the small farmers and sharecroppers began, paradoxically, with land reforms that were intended to have exactly the opposite effect. The impact of these reforms was similar to that of land reforms enacted in India in the late 1940s. The principal feature of the Iranian reforms, which began in 1961 and were completed by 1973, was the redistribution of a part of the land of absentee landowners to the sharecroppers who did the actual cultivation. But only sharecroppers who had had formal agreements with the landlords were allowed to benefit. This led to the eviction of large numbers of sharecroppers who had only oral leases. These became, almost overnight, a new agricultural proletariat.[23]

That was only the beginning of the process of marginalization. Throughout the sixties and seventies, government policies continued to favour the industrial sector and the very rich among the agriculturists. Low interest loans, for instance, were available only to the mechanized farms. The entire sector was starved of investment: capital formation in agriculture rose in price adjusted terms by only 20 per cent between 1963 and 1971, a compound rate of just over 1 per cent a year. Then, in 1975, it declined suddenly, in absolute terms, by 22 per cent. Agricultural modernization, which was being discouraged anyway, suddenly took a nosedive. In 1975, the entire sector had only 41,000 tractors and 2,633 combine harvesters. This in a country that had already begun to benefit hugely from a tripling of oil prices after the cartelization of OPEC in the beginning of the 1970s. Not surprisingly, therefore, the production of cereals grew by no more than 3 per cent a year, which was simply not fast enough to meet the needs of a 3 per cent a year rise in population and 7 to 8 per cent rate of growth of the towns.[24]

Indeed, the oil boom played havoc with agriculture, for the flood of petrodollars pushed up prices, drew workers off the land, and pushed up real wages in agriculture, while the sudden, huge surplus in the balance of payments effectively prevented any devaluation of its currency to offset the high rate of inflation it unleashed in the domestic economy. Faced with rising costs, an absolute dearth of labour, and declining real incomes in terms of what their money could buy in terms of manufactures, the farmers reacted in the only way that was left open to them—they abandoned their lands and went into the towns in search of work. In the rice-growing province of Dezful, the area under paddy fell from 130,000 hectares in the sixties to a mere 6,000 hectares in 1978.[25] Needless to say, therefore, the sector was given no protection against imports.

This drastic loss of status and, quite possibly, income, did not, however, trigger any kind of revolt, because of the frenetic pace of industrialization. The Enclosure movement in Britain—a process of privatizing previously communal lands—four hundred years earlier had forced English peasants off their farms in the sixteenth and seventeenth centuries in a manner very similar to what was happening in Iran. But the displaced English peasantry were protected from destitution by the Elizabethan Poor Law which required every parish in the country to ensure that none of its poor starved or lacked an opportunity to work.

Iran had no such legal buffer against destitution but the rapid rate of economic growth performed a similar function for the Iranian peasantry. Between 1956 and 1976, at least 1.9 million agriculturists—almost two-fifths of the workforce that the land would have had to support in the absence of industrialization—migrated to the towns to take up employment in factories and shops. As Parsa puts it, 'The separation of producers from their means of production in Iran was non-violent *and was carried out through a combination of market forces and government inaction...* but was replete with suffering nonetheless'[26] (emphasis added).

The marginalization of traders and small manufacturers was equally rapid. But here, in contrast to agriculture, the losers had nowhere else to go. The seeds of the Iranian revolt were sown by the increasing helplessness of this class. In Iran, the bazaar had a long tradition of collective action in response to state policies that adversely affected its interests. Bazaaris played a role in the revolution of 1905–11, and were an important pro-Mosaddeq element in 1951.[27] Neither of these movements can be traced to the effects of economic development, but stem from the unique features of the bazaar—its strong guild organization and its physical compactness and interconnectedness. Both are caused by and, in turn, help to perpetuate its unique configuration. The bazaar consists of artisans and traders who work side by side along single lanes or alleys as specialist producers and sellers. The bazaar is thus the Iranian counterpart of the *souq* of the Arab countries. Geographic proximity and specialization leads to intense competition among producers and sellers of the same wares. This makes them nervous, unusually sensitive to any threat to their survival, but also more than normally predisposed to acting together to ward off a common threat. The power of the merchants' guild derives from the latter feature.[28]

The Bazaaris had first revolted against the state as a reaction to the Shah's so-called 'White' revolution in 1963.[29] The underlying cause was the same as the one that caused them to revolt again in 1978. One of the Shah's first acts after being restored to the throne in 1953 had been to liberalize imports. Between 1954 and 1959, imports grew by six times. Along with debt servicing, this far outstripped even the rise in oil revenues and brought on a foreign exchange crisis. That forced the government to ask for a loan from the International Monetary Fund in 1959 and accept a stabilization programme monitored by it. The latter entailed a ban on the import of luxury goods, imposition of high import duties on non-essentials, and a sharp reduction in domestic money supply to bring down prices. As a part of these deflationary moves, the government sharply reduced credit to the Bazaaris. Since the economy had also gone into recession, the combined effect was to trigger a large number of bankruptcies among them. Thus, when Ayatollah Khomeini gave a call for a revolt against the Shah's social and economic reforms in 1963—which included the extension of voting rights to women, profit sharing in industry, and the establishment of a literacy corps for adult education in the villages—sensing a threat to their economic security in these reforms, sections of the Bazaaris joined him and became the backbone of his revolt.[30]

The revolt fizzled out after three days. The traders and manufacturers' guilds were outlawed and only permitted to re-establish themselves in an emasculated form in the late sixties. But the 1963 uprising against the White Revolution established the precedent for co-operation between Mosque and Bazaar that brought down the Shah fifteen years later.

In retrospect, these fifteen years were a golden period for Iran, for the long period of prosperity that followed the 1963 uprising did more to de-politicize the bazaar than the repression that had followed the suppression of the 1963 revolt. In 1975, the Bazaaris did not respond to Khomeini's call to commemorate the twelfth anniversary of the suppression of the 1963 uprising. The reason, as it was soon to become clear, was that in the general prosperity of OPEC's heyday, and especially the period that began in 1972, the Bazaaris had no reason to be discontented. This was a period of boundless foreign exchange, and rapidly rising imports, and the bazaar handled the sale of 30 per cent of those imports.

Its estrangement from the Shah's regime began only after the economy overheated. It was in the period of high inflation and rising public distress, which led to the 1963 uprising, that the connection between religion and the Bazaaris was forged. The Shah exiled Khomeini in 1964, initially to Bursa in Turkey where he stayed for over a year as the guest of a high-ranking officer in the Turkish Military Intelligence. In 1965, Khomeini was allowed to leave Turkey and stay for the next fourteen years in Karbala and Najf in Iraq. During these years, Khomeini exalted the notion of martyrdom, and preached revolt against injustice and tyranny, describing these as intrinsic to Shi'ism. He also urged Muslims to reject both liberal capitalism and communism, on the grounds that these were ideas imported from the West. In their place, Khomeini developed the ideology of *velayat-e faqih* (guardianship of the jurist) as the appropriate form of governance for Muslims.

Khomeini's ideas gained little traction in the sixties, and even less after the flood of petrodollars began in 1973. This brought a surge of prosperity, and caused a sharp increase in the already high rate of inflation after the oil boom began.[31] The main beneficiaries were the Bazaaris and small manufacturers, but their gains were largely at the expense of the substantial working class in the cities, 73 per cent of whom, according to an official assessment, were earning less than the statutory minimum wage.[32]

To alleviate the plight of the working class, the government belatedly imposed price controls on no less than 2,600 items in August 1975, and announced a host of other anti-profiteering measures which it implemented with the utmost of vigour. The

Bazaaris became the special target of its anti-hoarding and black marketeering drive. In the first few days after the price controls were imposed, the police arrested 7,750 merchants for violating the order.[33] By October 1977, 109,800 out of Tehran's 200,000 merchants had been investigated, and by the end of that year 20,000 had been jailed. Countrywide, by the autumn of 1978, 220,000 shopkeepers had been found violating the controls and fined, jailed or exiled to other parts of the country. But price control measures were nearly all implemented at the retail level without any serious attempt to hold down manufacturing costs and profits. As a result, the Bazaaris, especially the sellers of foodstuffs and essential consumer goods, where the controls were most vigilantly supervised, found themselves sandwiched between rising procurement costs and fixed sales prices. Many tried to get out of the business and put their money into some other investment, but the government also forbade them to close their shops. Five hundred Tehran food retailers applied for licenses to sell other goods but were also refused, so the proprietors of 130 bakeries simply downed shutters and disappeared.[34]

The assault on the middle stratum was not confined to price controls, nor to the shopkeepers alone. Rising prices and labour costs, without a compensating devaluation of the rial, made Iranian carpets, a very largely export oriented industry, more and more uncompetitive. Thus, the largest single class of independent artisans and small businessmen faced the threat of extinction. To make matters worse, machine-made carpets began to be imported. Between April and December 1977, thirty-six out of eighty carpet shops in Ahvaz, an important city in western Iran, closed down.[35] Not till September 1978 did the government impose controls on the import of machine-made carpets. But by then it was too late to stem the revolt.

An official policy of confrontation and repression, combined with the perception that manufacturers were getting off lightly at the expense of traders and artisans; that dealers in essentials were bearing the brunt of the price controls while those who dealt in luxuries for the elite were exempted; and that the richest merchants and those with connections were getting off with light fines while the rest had their shops closed down or went to prison undoubtedly paved the way for revolt by the Bazaaris.

But why did the workers join them? For the latent hostility between traders, who are regarded as the price makers, and workers, who are the 'price-takers', that every developing country has experienced, must have been present in Iran too.

In most traditional countries, traders are regarded as parasites. Therefore, measures aimed at curbing their power are invariably popular with the masses. Why, then, did the Shah's anti-inflationary measures backfire? No analysis of the causes of the Iranian revolution would be complete if it does not explain this. Several additional features played a key role in converting the Bazaari revolt into a general one.

The first was inflation, which hit the urban working class the hardest; the students, whose cost of education skyrocketed, were in any case opposed to the autocratic rule of the Shah. The second was the continuing marginalization of the peasantry, which has been described above. Although this did not lead to a peasant revolt, the displaced marginal landowners who flocked to the cities in search of jobs brought their hangover of resentment with them. Therefore, when inflation pushed down their real wages while quadrupling their house rents,[36] their earlier passive resistance flared into active rebellion against the King.

These were the economic forces that created the alliance between the Bazaaris and the mosque. This alliance may have been cemented by the fact that the mosque was the only place that was relatively secure from the agents of SAVAK, the Shah's secret police. But that does not explain why more than 20.4 million of the country's 22.8 million eligible voters voted for Khomeini's Islamic republic, in an election in which the monarchy was given as the only alternative.[37] The conclusion is inescapable: this was a revolution to end the monarchy and not a revolution to create a theocratic state.

A better understanding of the driving forces behind it can be had by considering that it had not one but two foci. The clergy, headed by Khomeini, were capable of offering an alternative state structure—the theocratic state—but incapable of mobilizing support for it on the basis of appeals to religion alone. The Bazaaris were capable of creating a powerful anti-government movement against the existing monarchical state, based upon economic insecurity and a pervasive sense of injustice, but had no alternative state structure to offer. It took the fusion of the two, therefore, to create the revolution.

Can the Iran that emerged from the revolution be called 'Fascist', after the term is shorn of its exclusively European connotations? In terms of Organski's model, the answer has to be 'yes', for it had all the requirements that had created the fascist movements of Europe: economic intermediacy, an insecure new middle stratum of property owners in search of support against economic adversity, an ancient artisanal class being wiped out by mechanization, a new urban proletariat consisting of peasants displaced from their land in desperate search of a new identity, and an established church and clergy ready and willing to give them that identity and security.

The Iranian revolution provides a vindication of the hypothesis that forms the core of this book. This is that the near-simultaneous rise of fascism in several European countries between the two world wars was not a historical accident but an organized expression of resistance to the rise of industrial capitalism that brought together all those who stood to lose from it. This resistance is not a new phenomenon. Karl Marx had seen the struggle erupt in his lifetime in Germany and France. He summed it up in the *Communist Manifesto* in 1848 as follows:

> The lower middle class, the small manufacturer, the shopkeeper, the artisan, the peasant, all these fight against the bourgeoisie, *to save from extinction their existence as fractions of the middle class*. They are therefore not revolutionary, but conservative. *Nay more, they are reactionary, for they try to roll back the wheel of history.* (Emphasis added)

CHAPTER SEVEN

# India's Journey from Hindu Nationalism to Fascism

The threat fascism poses is greatest during the early to middle stages of the economic transformation under capitalism. It is one to which several other newly industrializing countries, notably in South America, have also succumbed. It is not surprising, therefore, that this reactionary, authoritarian impulse has emerged in India too, and has now become the single greatest threat that the Indian nation faces. The source of the threat is the rise of Hindutva which is little more than fascism clothed in saffron. The following chapters show how the Hindu nationalist impulse that gave birth to the RSS in 1925 became transformed by stages into the fascist impulse that brought Narendra Modi to power in 2014.

## The Nationalism of Tilak

The belief that in order to fight British colonialism the Indian freedom movement had to harness religious nationalism to patriotism was first articulated in the 1880s by the great Congress leader Lokmanya Bal Gangadhar Tilak. In recent years, it has become fashionable to ascribe the rise of Hindu chauvinism, and specifically of the RSS, to his writings. Even authors who have not gone so far have conceded that his overt appeal to a collective Hindu consciousness to create a popular base for the nationalist movement disturbed and alienated the Muslims and contributed to the eventual partition of India. This is a particularly egregious example of re-interpreting the past through lenses acquired in the future.

Bal Gangadhar Tilak was a nationalist. He believed that freedom would not be gifted to India by the British but would have to be wrested from them. This would require a large mass base similar to that which was created in 1857. His goal in his writings was to create the moral and psychological base for such a mass movement. The road to this, he firmly believed, lay through the revival of pride in India's heritage. He fostered this assiduously by reminding his readers of the greatness of Hindu philosophy and culture and of the need to purge the poorly concealed contempt for pre-Islamic India that authors like Vincent Smith, a prominent historian and member of the Indian Civil Service during the British Raj, and his followers had ingrained into the teaching of Indian history.

The common theme of these 'imperialist' writings was that there was some intrinsic weakness in the Hindu character that made Hindu kingdoms incapable of sustaining unity and order. India had therefore always needed foreign invaders to create cohesive empires in the sub-continent. So complete was their success in brainwashing the emerging Indian middle class that till as recently as the 1960s, two decades after India gained its freedom, history textbooks still paid scant attention to ancient India, and almost none to the Hindu kingdoms of the south. Therefore, two generations of students who had learned about the invincibility of Alexander's army and the details of how he defeated Porus on the banks of the Indus, did not learn of the might of the Nanda Empire, and the way the sheer size of the forces it had assembled on the banks of the Chenab compelled Alexander to turn back and return to Greece.

Nor did they learn about the splendour and might of the Vijayanagar Empire, which prevented the southward spread of Mughal rule and confined the Deccan sultanates to the Krishna-Cauvery belt for two centuries till the Muslim expansionist impulse faded away. The title of the first book in English on the Vijayanagar

Empire, which appeared only in 1900, is revealing. Robert Sewell, its author, called it '*A Forgotten Empire (Vijayanagar): A Contribution to the History of India*'.

Tilak's unswerving goal throughout his life was to revive the country's pride in ancient (and therefore by default, Hindu) India. Based at Ferguson College in Pune, and writing in both English and Marathi, it was natural that he would extol the rise of the Maratha Empire, and festivals like *Ganapati Puja* and *Shivaji Jayanti*, to encourage the development of a collective consciousness. He spread his ideas through two powerful newspapers that he founded, *Kesari*, in Marathi, and *Mahratta*, in English. But these reflected only the lesser part of his thinking. The greater part was in his re-interpretations of the *Ramayana* and *Mahabharata*, and particularly of the *Bhagavad Gita*, all of which he tried to purge of the emphasis on renunciation, highlighting instead their exhortation to selfless action, to do one's duty without considering the cost. This was the doctrine of *Anasakti Yoga*, which became the guiding light for Mahatma Gandhi till the last moments of his life on January 30, 1948.

The influence of Tilak's writings upon the emerging, modern, Hindu elite of the time, and indeed upon the Congress party itself, cannot be denied. It probably played an important part in the wholehearted support the Congress gave to the British proposal, made in 1885, to conduct the competitive services examinations in English, a move that historians like Anil Seal have concluded drove the first wedge between the Hindu and Muslim elites of the time.[1]

Tilak's goal, in his writings, however, had not been to create a platform for future Hindu hegemony over India. It had been to free the Hindu mind from the shackles of British thought, and that could only be done by a deep and thorough understanding of British history and the development of British democracy. He did not feel any need to exhort the Muslims to do this because in the 1880s they had still not reconciled themselves to the loss of their political and cultural hegemony over the sub-continent, and were viewed with wariness and suspicion by the British. However, another consideration that may have weighed with him was the problem that India faces even today—if Indians had to be inducted into the ICS, in which language should the examinations be held? Hindi would have left more than half of the country out of the competition, and a multi-lingual exam, as the UPSC now attempts with very little success to hold every year, would then have been impossible. For Tilak, the hurdle to *Swarajya* was the acceptance of British, and more generally Western, intellectual hegemony by the Indian intelligentsia and the Congress in particular. It could only be discredited by those with a thorough understanding of its strengths and shortcomings.

His political horizons widened dramatically after his passionate opposition to the partition of Bengal in 1905 drew him into backing the use of terrorism in the freedom struggle in Bengal. His lawyer, when he was tried for sedition, was none other than Muhammed Ali Jinnah, the future founder of Pakistan. When he came back from jail and exile in Mandalay in 1914, he re-joined the Congress and became a signatory to the Gandhi–Jinnah Lucknow Pact of 1916. Among the pact's main clauses was the creation of a separate electorate for Muslims.

Tilak's lament for Swami Vivekananda on the latter's death sums up his view of Hinduism:

> No Hindu, who has the interests of Hinduism at his heart, could help feeling grieved over Vivekananda's samadhi. Vivekananda...had taken the work of keeping the banner of Advaita philosophy forever flying among all the nations of the world and made them realize the true greatness of Hindu religion and of the Hindu people... At the fag of the 19th century, the second Shankaracharya is Vivekananda. His work has yet to be completed. We have lost our glory, our independence, everything.[2]

Tilak was eulogizing the same Vivekananda who told the World Conference of Religions in Chicago in 1893 that Hinduism did not *tolerate* but *accepted* all religions as being equal, because like paths up a mountain, or rivers running into the sea, they were all seeking the same end.

The only connections between Tilak and the Rashtriya Swayamsevak Sangh were indirect and of little significance. Keshav Baliram Hedgewar, the ideological founder of the RSS, had been influenced by Tilak early on. Before 1925, he had been a member of the Hindu Mahasabha and a protégé of one of its leaders, Balkrishna Shivram Moonje. Moonje had belonged to the Congress but had broken away because he did not believe that *Swarajya* (independence) could be won through non-violent means. Hedgewar, who was in prison when the RSS was formed, broke away from the Hindu Mahasabha upon his release a year later, and joined the RSS.

V.D. Savarkar, whose writings would have tremendous influence on the RSS later on, was as a student deeply influenced by Tilak. He would go on to become the president of the Hindu Mahasabha in the 1930s. Savarkar had taken note of the speed and ease with which the Indian Muslim community had come together to oppose the abolition of the Ottoman Caliphate. But he was not driven by Islamophobia. The *Khilafat* movement (1919–22) made him conclude that India's capacity to fight for its freedom had been significantly weakened by the absence of a similar capacity to rally around the banner of religion and history.

**Savarkar: The Origins of Hindutva**

The RSS' commitment to creating a Hindu Rashtra had different roots from Tilak's bid to harness pride in one's Hindu identity to the freedom movement. Its ideology was shaped by Vinayak Damodar Savarkar, an ardent nationalist who studied in England from 1906 till 1910, was deeply offended by the Viceroy Lord Curzon's attempt to partition Bengal, and became an ardent advocate of the 'revolutionary terrorism' that swept through Bengal province at that time. In England, Savarkar joined a group of Indian students who wished to return and join the movement.

Around this time, he wrote a pivotal book, *The Indian War of Independence, 1857*, in which he took the now accepted view that the Sepoy Mutiny of 1857 was the first expression of an Indian mass rebellion against British colonial rule.

In London, he instructed a group of students in terrorism and sabotage, was arrested in 1910 and sent back to India to stand trial. While being tried on the first count he was indicted on a second charge of involvement in the assassination of a British magistrate, sentenced to life imprisonment, and sent to the Cellular Jail in the Andamans, where he was assigned a cell directly above the execution chamber, where he could hear the trapdoors clang open every time there was an execution. After ten years in the Andamans, Savarkar was brought back to India, incarcerated in a normal jail for a further three years and released in 1924. It was while he was in jail that he wrote *Hindutva: Who is a Hindu*, which became the bible of the RSS, an organization that had been formed a year before his release.

Central to defining Indian nationhood according to Hindutva were a common nation (*rashtra*), a common race (*jati*), and a common culture or civilization (*sanskriti*). The impress of Europe on his thinking is reflected by the similarity of this slogan with the slogan that the NSDAP, i.e. Germany's Nazi party, had coined: *ein volk* (one people), *ein reich* (one nation), *ein Fuhrer* (one leader). And just as the Nazis decided that Jews could not be a part of this 'volk', Savarkar believed that Muslims and Christians could not belong to the Hindu jati, because their sanskriti and their prophets originated outside the Hindu civilization.

Savarkar did not exclude non-Hindus from the Hindutva fold. But to belong they had first to accept that they belonged to the Hindu sanskriti. This has remained the core requirement of Hindutva to the present day. Its corollary was the exclusion of those who did not wish to belong. Those who wished to belong had to *profess* their 'Hinduness' and allegiance to Hindu Rashtra. Savarkar thus placed pre-conditions for being included in the Hindu fold that were strikingly similar to the baptism and *bar mitzvah* rites that bring Christians and Jews formally into the fold of their respective religions. As in Catholicism and Islam, the reward for accepting the true faith was the promise of absolution for sins committed in the name of God and Hinduism. Savarkar may not have realized this at the time he wrote his book, but unwittingly he had made Hindutva a pale copy of the three messianic religions—Christianity, Judaism and Islam. This was, and remains to this day, the very antithesis of true Hinduism.

In the 1920s, Savarkar's advocacy of Hindutva could be condoned because it was a counsel of despair. The Congress was still a middle-class debating society; Mahatma Gandhi's doctrine of Satyagraha was still largely untried; and the British had taken to shooting, or summarily hanging, freedom fighters after labelling them terrorists. But the last shred of justification for it ended when India gained its freedom. For the creation of Pakistan fulfilled the main goal that Savarkar and Hedgewar had set for the RSS—it had 'cleansed' India of all the Muslims who did not accept that they were part of the Hindu sanskriti!

Two-thirds of the Muslims of British India ceased to be Indians because they became Pakistanis. The one-third that remained were Muslims who had chosen consciously to stay in India. They had therefore demonstrated their allegiance to 'Hindu sanskriti' by not voting with their feet. What is more, after Partition, the Muslims numbered only forty-five million—about 12 per cent of the country's population. So, what fuelled the frantic rage against Partition that the RSS vented in its immediate aftermath? What made it condone and later glorify the assassination of Mahatma Gandhi, and want to deify his assassin Nathuram Godse? And what has made them demonize the Muslims who chose to remain Indian?

The answer is that from its inception the RSS' goal was not simply the 'negative' freedom India would get from the departure of the British, but the 'positive' freedom of creating a 'Hindu' nation purged of the 'impurities' of thought and practice introduced by Muslim and Christian invaders over a thousand years. Nothing less would satisfy them.

Today, the Sangh Parivar is trying to pass off Savarkar and Keshav Baliram Hedgewar as freedom fighters. But as the biographer of Hedgewar, and some of the remarks of his successor Golwalkar show, from the Dandi Salt March in 1929 till Gandhi's Quit India call in 1940, the RSS stoutly opposed every attempt to secure freedom through Satyagraha and even offered its cohorts to the government to act as civil guards to quell the popular unrest that Gandhi's call would generate. To the RSS, even in the heady days of 1947, freedom was less important than power. It needed more time to create the Hindutva legions with which it hoped to storm to power.[3]

Caught by surprise by the advancement of Independence from June 1948 to August 15, 1947, it made contingency plans, nonetheless, to seize power if the opportunity arose, in the wake of the turmoil that Partition would unleash. In one of his fortnightly letters to the chief ministers of the provinces, Pandit Nehru explained the need to ban the RSS and imprison its leaders by referring to a plot they had hatched to do so.[4] This was cut short when, after finding RSS *shakhas* ('branches') celebrating Gandhi's assassination, Sardar Patel, who was both the home minister and the deputy prime minister, banned the organization. He lifted the ban more than a year later, only after the RSS agreed to frame and publish a written constitution, accept the Tricolour with the Ashoka Chakra as the national flag, pledge its loyalty to the soon-to-be-promulgated Constitution of India, and publish the procedure for the choice of the *sarsanghchalak* (supreme leader) of the organization. Golwalkar eventually gave in, having stiffly opposed these initially, but he never fulfilled his commitment to publicize the method of selection of the sarsanghchalak, or the names of the pre-adolescents it recruited into its shakhas.

## Democratization of Hindutva: The Creation of the Bharatiya Jana Sangh

The ban on the RSS after Mahatma Gandhi's death gave the leaders of the RSS time to rethink their strategy. They arrived at two conclusions: first, that the Gandhian concept of India was antithetical to a Hindu Rashtra, and to root it out would require a long period of 're-education' of the people. Second, since the route to power lay through democracy, the Sangh would need to create a political party that could ceaselessly represent its alternate vision to the people, and provide a political alternative to the Congress when the time was ripe. This resulted in the transformation of the Hindu Mahasabha into the *Bharatiya Jana Sangh* in 1950 under senior RSS leaders Deendayal Upadhyaya and Balraj Madhok. Joining the organization soon after its formation was a young Atal Bihari Vajpayee.

One of the first actions of the new party was to remove all the 'traditionalists' of the Hindu Mahasabha from their positions in the organization. Their positions, from the district to the central level, were taken over by cadres of the RSS. One of Deendayal Upadhyaya's first actions was to explicitly shun forming coalitions with other parties, which Syama Prasad Mukherjee, the president of the Hindu Mahasabha, had advocated in 1948. He did so on the grounds that coalitions were bound to 'degenerate into a struggle for power by opportunist elements coming together in the interest of expediency'.[5] His goal was to build the party at the grassroots patiently till it was able to offer the people an ideological alternative to the Congress. This was the first explicit declaration of an ideological, and undemocratic, goal for the Jana Sangh.

And yet the India that this first generation of political leaders envisaged was very far removed from the one that Narendra Modi's government is bent upon creating today. For their avowed goal was not '*Hindutva*' but '*Bharatiyata*'.[6] In December 1949, shortly before the Jana Sangh was set up, K.R. Malkani, who became one of the party's most eloquent spokespersons in the 1950s and 1960s, wrote the following: 'The [RSS] must take part in politics not only to protect itself against the greedy design of politicians, but to stop the *un-Bharatiya* and *anti-Bharatiya* policies of the Government.'[7] For the Sangh, then, Bharatiyata was shorthand for a composite but indigenous culture. The name 'Bharat' was juxtaposed primarily against 'India', and not against 'Hindustan', the Urdu name for the country. It was understood that this culture was predominantly non-Muslim, i.e. Hindu in origin. But there was no hint of religious bigotry in it. In fact, the Jana Sangh went out of its way to recruit eminent Muslims into the party and gave them important functions within it.

What is more, Upadhyaya's admonition notwithstanding, the Jana Sangh began to enter into anti-Congress coalitions, first tacitly with the Swatantra Party in the 1962 elections, and then explicitly from 1967 onwards. With the RSS' blessings, it entered into a Grand Alliance (which included the Swatantra as well as the Socialist parties) ahead of the 1971 elections, supported the JP movement that triggered the Emergency in 1975, and actually merged itself with the Janata Party in 1977 after Mrs Indira Gandhi lifted the Emergency, to make sure that the Congress did not return to power. Although the merger proved short-lived, it turned out to be a spectacularly successful tactical move for gaining acceptability within the disillusioned middle class and the nascent Indian civil society that had borne the brunt of the repression during the Emergency.

### From Bharatiyata to Hindutva: Harnessing the Fascist Impulse

The RSS had watched the development of coalition politics with some unease. But it had learnt important lessons from it. The first was that coalition politics paid high dividends. Cooperation with the Swatantra Party, which began in the 1962 elections, and led to the virtual merger of the two parties after the ban on company donations, had further diluted the communal bias within the parliamentary party, and greatly increased its acceptability in the intelligentsia of the country.

It also became clear that most of the Jana Sangh's following was concentrated in urban areas. This was revealed by the voting pattern in the 1967 elections—the first held after Jawaharlal Nehru's death—and by the student-led JP movement of 1974–75. The concerns of the youth were mostly economic, not ideological. Their growing anxiety about their future stemmed from rapid inflation, caused by the droughts of 1965 and 1966 and the devaluation of the rupee in 1966; food rationing, endemic shortages, and above all the very slow growth of employment in the modern sector of the economy that had resulted from the successive Five Year Plans' heavy bias in favour of capital-intensive development. This had resulted in growing joblessness among the educated youth and a disquiet that flared into student demonstrations and violence in 1966.

The Sangh Parivar learned its third lesson from the Emergency, which had brought the Jana Sangh and the centrist opposition together for the first time on an issue that had nothing to do with the RSS' communal agenda. This was a fight to save democracy. For more than eighteen months, leaders of the main opposition parties had lived together in jails all over the country. Their shared discussions and experiences had created a mutual respect and camaraderie that resulted in the merger of the two Socialist parties, the Congress (Organisation)—the faction of regional party elites after the INC split in 1969—and the Jana Sangh to form the Janata Party, after Mrs Indira Gandhi lifted the Emergency in January 1977.

But the RSS was not a part of this experience. Mrs Gandhi had banned the organization during the Emergency (its second ban), but tacitly accepted its claim to be a social and cultural organization, without political ambitions, as had been asserted by its chief Balasaheb Deoras in multiple letters to the Prime Minister. Its leaders did not therefore go to jail. Thus, it watched the formation of the Janata Party with considerable trepidation and was more than relieved when the merger proved short lived.

As it had done after the murder of Mahatma Gandhi in 1948, the RSS used the ban to rethink its strategy for creating Hindu Rashtra. The main change was a decision to shed its reservations about participating in politics. These had already been diluted by M.S. Golwalkar, who had succeeded Hedgewar as its sarsanghchalak and remained in that position till his death in 1973. Golwalkar had already restructured the RSS to mirror the constituency-wise division of the Jana Sangh in the country, and allowed its members to campaign for the party during elections. The RSS shed all of its remaining reservations after Mrs Gandhi stormed back to power in 1980.

In 1982 and 1983, it decided to give the party added muscle through two additional organizations that reported directly to it, whose purpose was to speed up the dissemination of what was no longer called *Bharatiyata* but *Hindutva*, among the masses. The first was Vishwa Hindu Parishad ('World Hindu Organization', or 'Association'), which Golwalkar had created two decades earlier to give Hinduism a congregational character similar to Christianity, Islam and Sikhism, and which was now revived. The second was the Bajrang Dal, named after Hanuman, the monkey king who was Sri Ramachandra's principal ally in his fight against Ravana in the *Ramayana*. As its name implied, the Bajrang Dal were intended to be the storm troopers of the Hindutva movement, to be deployed when muscle power was needed to achieve its goals. With their formation, the RSS acquired all the instruments it needed to create a violent mass movement that could one day seize power in the country. But like the VHP when it was first set up, and like many of the RSS' organizations even today, these might have remained dormant organizations had Indian democracy not, almost simultaneously, taken a turn towards fascism within months of their formation.

## How the Congress Opened the Doors for the Fascist Impulse to Bloom

Four nearly simultaneous developments in the mid to late eighties were responsible for the change of direction—three initiated by the Congress and the fourth by the Janata Dal government of V.P. Singh. The first was the Congress party's adoption of a new strategy in sustaining its political dominance. This was the polarization of the Hindu community between its upper and lower castes. This polarization, immediately nicknamed the KHAM (Kshatriya, Harijan, Adivasi and Muslim) alliance, first occurred in the state of Gujarat, in 1984–85, but spread to other parts of northern India as the Congress began to feel its grasp on the upper-caste Hindu vote begin to slip.

The second was the overruling by the Congress government of Rajiv Gandhi of a Supreme Court judgement that gave Muslim women the right to appeal to the judiciary against dowry settlements made to them by Muslim Waqf boards under Islamic law.

The third was the re-ignition of a dispute over a dilapidated mosque, called the Babri Masjid, at the supposed site of a once grand Rama temple in the ancient city of Ayodhya, which was renamed Faizabad in 1722 by the Nawabs of Awadh. The dispute arose from the belief that the Babri Masjid had been built by a general of the first Mughal Emperor Babar, at the birthplace of Sri Ramachandra, the God-King of the *Ramayana*, after pulling down the grand Hindu temple that had stood there.

The first of these alienated upper-caste Hindus from the Congress; the second was seen, and rightly so, as a betrayal by the Congress of the secular principles that it had itself enshrined in the Constitution. It was the third that legitimized the rise of violent Hindu nationalism and began the transformation of the RSS into a fascist movement.

(A fourth development, one that took place in the economic sphere, and the least understood at the time, was a sharp relaxation of the controls that Mrs Indira Gandhi had imposed upon private investment in modern industry between 1970 and 1973. We will come back to it in the discussion on the economic roots of fascism in India.)

### *KHAM: How Democracy Polarized Hindus by Caste*

In 1985, the western state of Gujarat was racked for nine long months by a caste-cum-communal conflict that brought its thriving economy to the verge of collapse. The conflict actually began a year or more earlier, over the sensitive question of reservation of jobs and seats in educational institutions for boys and girls from the Scheduled Castes and Tribes—the former untouchables and tribal aborigines of India—the most socially disadvantaged sections of society. This policy, instead of being phased out gradually over the years had been progressively extended under one pretext or another, by a succession of governments intent on cornering the sizable (more than 25 per cent) SC/ST vote. What sparked off a students' revolt was the government's decision to carry over vacancies in this category to future years. This meant that there was no certainty left about how many seats would be available for those seeking to secure admission to engineering and medical colleges, and other centres of higher learning, on the basis of merit in any particular year. This uncertainty proved too much for the students to swallow, so they took to the streets.

However, it was the Congress party's reaction to their agitation that did the real damage. Through the early eighties, the leaders of the party in the state tried to build a coalition of Backward Classes, Scheduled Castes and Tribes, and Muslims, labelled KHAM, to take on the upper-caste Hindus—mainly landowners and traders—who had begun to transfer their vote to the BJP, successor to the Jana Sangh, formed in April 1980. While attempts to woo various castes were normal in Indian politics, this was the first time that an attempt had been made to bring not only the Backward Classes and the Scheduled Castes and Tribes together on the same platform, but also to include the Muslims. What was thus being attempted for the first time was to divide society on the basis of class and not caste. The attempt created a new kind of insecurity—one with which the Gujarati Hindu middle class in particular was completely unfamiliar. They were familiar with the rhetoric of the Communists and had seen, over a series of elections, that it had only a limited appeal for the poor in India. But a polarization along class lines that used the powerful mobilizing tools of caste and religion was another matter altogether.

In 1985, this unease was vague, as yet ill-defined and touched only the periphery of the middle class' perceptions, especially outside Gujarat, but it prepared the ground for what was to happen when the National Front, a coalition of five parties that came to power under former Congress finance minister V.P. Singh in 1989, tried to revive such a grand coalition of the lower castes to fortify its own stability while simultaneously stemming the rise of the BJP.

### *The Shah Bano Case: The First Betrayal of Secular Ideals*

The second shock was administered by the Congress government in New Delhi. In 1985, an elderly Muslim lady called Shah Bano Begum petitioned the Supreme Court of India to award her a larger divorce settlement than had been fixed under Islamic law at the time of her marriage, some forty years earlier. She pleaded that the settlement was fixed a long time ago, and that since then inflation had reduced the amount to a pittance. Since her husband was a man of comfortable means, he could afford to pay her more. The Supreme Court ruled in her favour but in the process established a new precedent: this was to subordinate Muslim personal law to the civil courts and therefore the civil and, by definition, secular law of the land. The decision touched off an uproar among orthodox Muslims in the country. By undermining a provision of the Shariat (Islamic law) the Supreme Court, they claimed, had imposed a uniform civil code on the country by the back door. Since the Shariat was ordained by God, the Supreme Court had put itself above Allah! This was an intolerable insult to the Muslims of the nation, one that the community's conservative leadership had been resisting since the dawn of freedom.

A member of parliament belonging to the All-India Muslim League, G.M. Banatwala, introduced a private member's bill in parliament proposing an amendment to the law that would overturn the Supreme Court's ruling and put Muslim personal law above challenge in any court of law in the future. The Rajiv Gandhi government initially decided to oppose the bill, but suddenly and without warning, decided to adopt the bill instead. Since the Congress had 415 members in the 543-member parliament, its passage was now a certainty. The shock this decision gave to Hindus throughout the country is difficult to overestimate. Nor was it confined to Hindus. Arif Mohammed Khan, energy minister in Rajiv Gandhi's cabinet, resigned from the government because he had been asked to spearhead the Congress party's initial opposition to the Banatwala bill in parliament and then been left high and dry by his party's sudden *volte-face*.

The bill was also assailed by progressive Muslim women all over the country who joined hands with women's civil rights groups to take to the streets. But all that was of no avail. The Congress had decided for reasons of its own that it had to appease the Muslims, and that meant the Sunni Muslim clergy, who commanded the greatest support in the community.

*

The two developments described above took place at almost the same time. The government took over the Banatwala bill at the tail end of 1985, just as the Gujarat agitation reached the peak of its bitterness. Together, they set large numbers of upper-caste Hindus wondering for the first time whether the democratic system was not inimical, if not as yet an outright threat, to their aspirations. Hindu society had always been stable because the upper castes had set the goals and aspirations for the lower ones. Upward social mobility was slow, but as described by M.N. Srinivas, one of India's greatest sociologists, it took a form that he termed 'Sanskritization': caste groups that succeeded in improving their political, economic or military status would lay claim to belonging to higher caste, the most common being reclassification as Kshatriyas. Over two or three generations they would get accepted, and the seal of acceptance would be placed by a Brahmin priest carrying out a holy ritual in their homes or under their acknowledged patronage. Sanskritization, which would inevitably accelerate as India became richer, more mechanized, and more militarized, would have loosened caste bonds and eliminated ritualistic taboos against the lower castes without creating a cleavage within the Hindu fold. The KHAM coalition did precisely that. In the late eighties, no political leader, other than India's almost forgotten prime minister, Vishwanath Pratap Singh, realized that by empowering the peasant castes the Green Revolution of the 1960s had made such a challenge from a horizontally composed middle stratum of castes unavoidable.

### *Babri Masjid: The Second Betrayal of Secular Ideals*

The third shock to the political system was a direct consequence of the second. On December 6, 1992, Hindu zealots belonging to an organization known as the Vishwa Hindu Parishad broke through steel and barbed wire fencing and barricades to demolish a 460-year-old mosque supposedly built by Mir Baqi, a general of Babar, the first emperor of the Mughal dynasty in India (1526–30). In the week that followed, 1,179 persons were killed either in communal rioting, or by the police, which opened fire to control rampaging mobs. A large number of temples were damaged by irate Muslims, but a number of mosques too suffered the same fate, especially in the twin cities of Ayodhya and Faizabad. The demolition of the mosque at Ayodhya had its repercussions in Pakistan and Bangladesh, where scores of Hindu temples were damaged or destroyed and a few Hindus killed or injured by mobs of enraged Muslims. Nor was this the end of it. A month later, riots again erupted in Bombay and Ahmedabad, two important commercial centres on the west coast of India, with large resident Muslim populations. This time they were less spontaneous, and were targeted at choice pieces of real estate, but no less brutal. Another 200 to 300 persons were killed, and middle-class Muslim families began to flee from the city of Bombay. It was apparent that organized gangs of hoodlums were behind the riots, and that their aim was to drive Hindus or Muslims away from specific areas so that the land, houses or shops that they vacated could be picked up for a song.[8]

From the beginning of the eighteenth century, the belief had grown among the Hindus not only that Ayodhya, the small pilgrimage town in eastern UP, was *the* Ayodhya of the *Ramayana*, but that the Babri Masjid had been built in the sixteenth century on the exact spot where Lord Rama had been born.[9] Hindus believed that there had been a grand temple to Lord Rama there, which had been destroyed to build the mosque. The presence of a number of pillars used as supports for the dome of the mosque which were clearly of Hindu or Buddhist origin reinforced this belief.

As Muslim power waned, the Hindu sects in Ayodhya became more and more assertive. From the middle of the nineteenth century, the site was fought over frequently. On two occasions, *sadhus* (holy men or ascetics) of different Hindu orders occupied the mosque, driving out the *imams*. On the second occasion, they actually broke one of the lesser domes of the mosque. The conflict was especially bad between 1853 and 1855, when a sect called the Bairagis occupied the mosque. This provoked a Muslim cleric to declare a *jihad* (holy war) against them. A pitched battle was fought between his followers and the troops of the Nawab of Oudh, under whom Ayodhya fell. Eventually, after another fracas in which seventy people were killed, the mosque was recovered by the state and returned to the Muslims.[10]

After 1855, Muslims continued to pray at the mosque, while the Hindus prayed at a raised platform a little to one side of the mosque, called the *Ram Chabutra* (Lord Rama's platform). However, Hindu sects never gave up their claims to the mosque, and trouble sputtered on.

The present conflict began on the night of December 22, 1949. Some fifty or hundred local Hindus entered the mosque, placed a statue of the infant Rama on the floor right below the imam's pulpit and claimed, the next day, that there had been a miracle. The idol, they said, had come out of the earth at that precise spot. This, they claimed, was proof that the mosque was indeed built over the birthplace of Rama, and that He wanted a temple to be rebuilt on that spot.

Muslim organizations immediately went to the courts demanding the removal of the idol. Over the years, case piled upon case but their number and nature, and quite possibly their political sensitivity, made the Allahabad bench of the UP High Court extremely reluctant to pass a judgement. The government of the day in Uttar Pradesh closed the mosque and the Ram Chabutra for prayer, and there the dispute rested for the next thirty-seven years. Year after year, Hindu organizations made representations and moved the courts to open the mosque at least to the extent of letting a priest enter and look after the idol which lay there neglected. The petitions were regularly turned down.

This went on till February 1, 1986, when a sub-judge of a lower court conceded this demand after receiving a 'nod and a wink' from the Congress state government,[11] and prayers began regularly to be said at what was once a mosque. That brought the dispute to life once again, but in a wholly different form.

Whereas in 1949 the original dispute over what was called the Ram Janmasthan (Rama's birthplace), was entirely a local one, in 1986, all the protagonists were strangers to Ayodhya and hailed from the far corners of India. While before 1949, people were fighting for possession of a particular piece of land, in 1986, the site, and the mosque standing upon it, became symbols of a far larger, more abstract conflict.

To the Muslims of the twin cities of Ayodhya and Faizabad, the mosque had lost its importance and therefore most of its significance. Willy-nilly, the Babri Masjid, as the mosque was known, had ceased to be a mosque from December 22, 1949. Indeed, the official gazette recorded that it had fallen into disuse as far back as 1935 or '36. What cannot be doubted was that by 1986 it was in a highly dilapidated state.

A large proportion of the Muslim families of the twin cities had migrated to Pakistan after Partition. The remaining mosques in town were more than sufficient to meet the needs of the remainder. The Muslim community would therefore have lost nothing in concrete terms if its leaders had yielded to the wishes of Hindu organizations asking for the site.

But the Muslim religious organizations that had taken up the fight to save the Babri Masjid under the rubric of the Babri Masjid Action Committee decided that this was not possible. A reference by them to the Islamic Council of India elicited the opinion that under Muslim religious law, no mosque could ever be moved. This was endorsed by the academy of Muslim jurists at Jeddah. The academy concluded, after studying the relevant texts, that Islam did not permit the relocation of a mosque in any part of the world.[12] It did this even while both the Saudi and the Pakistani government next door thought nothing of pulling down, or shifting, mosques that got in the way of other projects. But in India, the BMAC had the edict that it wanted: for it, the defence of the now derelict mosque, even though there were Hindu idols in it, became a defence of Islam itself.

Lest this reasoning prove a little too esoteric for some of their flock, the BMAC put forward a second justification for its obduracy. If the Muslims gave in on the Babri Masjid, the floodgates would be opened for the re-location of all mosques that had been built on the sites of Hindu temples. The VHP had listed no less than 3,000 such sites, so the defence of the Babri Masjid became a last-ditch defence of all their mosques and holy places. As has been mentioned already, neither of these explanations related to the piece of land on which the mosque had been built. Instead, the Babri Masjid became a surrogate for the grand principles of Islam and its defence became a defence of Islam itself.

Precisely the same change had taken place over the previous thirty-seven years in the Hindu position on Rama's birthplace. To the VHP, too, the Babri Masjid was only a symbol. Although its immediate demand was for restoring Rama's birthplace to Rama, its leaders made no secret of the fact that their goal was to wipe the stain of Islam off the face of Hindu India—a stain that was reflected by the destroyed temples, desecrated shrines, and defaced sculptures of its gods and goddesses. Its immediate targets after Ayodhya were a mosque built supposedly by Aurangzeb, the last of the Greater Mughal emperors, at the site of Krishna's birthplace in Mathura, 140 kilometres from Delhi, and another built by the same emperor at Kashi (modern Varanasi) after partially destroying the great Vishwanath Temple, the holiest shrine in the city.

This was not an esoteric Hindu fundamentalism but the hyper-nationalism made familiar to our generation by the fascist nation-states of inter-war Europe. It had all the ingredients to which the late Sir Isaiah Berlin drew attention in his celebrated essay on nationalism—humiliation over past defeats, anger at the attack on one's culture by the conquerors, the desire to re-establish the cultural link with the past and to avenge one's defeats, not historically, since that was not possible, but symbolically.[13]

## Betrayal Compounded: The Extension of Job Reservation to the Backward Classes

The final push was given, albeit unintentionally, by the National Front government of V.P. Singh. On August 7, 1990, it announced that it was reserving 27 per cent of the jobs in the central government and the central government-owned public sector undertakings for members of the 'Backward Classes'—a congeries of no less than 3,600 castes that fall between the 15 per cent elite castes of the country and its 23 per cent Scheduled Castes and Tribes. Since 23 per cent of government jobs and places in educational institutions had already been reserved for the latter in the Constitution, this new dose of affirmative action would have put fully half of the available jobs, and seats in government schools and colleges, out of reach of candidates from the upper castes, and religious minorities, i.e. Christians, Parsees (Zoroastrians), Muslims and Sikhs.

The demand for an extension of reservation to the Other Backward Classes (OBCs) was a longstanding one. A commission led by a former chief minister of Bihar, B.P. Mandal, had recommended it to the Janata Party in 1979. When the Congress came back to power in 1980, it accepted the report but did not implement it. When V.P. Singh came to power in December

1989, he was acutely aware that his was a minority government dependent upon both the Communists and the BJP to stay in power and that the BJP's support was conditional upon his finding a compromise solution to the Babri Masjid dispute. In July 1990, when all his efforts to find a compromise solution to the Babri Masjid dispute had come to naught, and he found out that the RSS had secretly instructed the Vishwa Hindu Parishad to resume its preparations for the march to Ayodhya in October, Singh decided to stymie the VHP's plan by implementing the Mandal Commission's recommendations.

V.P. Singh's purpose was to frustrate the VHP's march. He was convinced that although the BJP had given a string of assurances that its purpose was only to perform a floral *shilanyas* (laying of a foundation stone) at a spot ninety metres from the mosque, once lakhs of RSS and VHP volunteers congregated there, nothing would stop them from bringing down the mosque. He chose to prevent this by forging an alliance of backward castes, a *Mandal Rath*, that would crush the *Ram Rath* under its wheels, as one Backward Class leader, Sharad Yadav, put it. The extension of job reservations to the OBCs was his way of sealing the alliance. Unfortunately, it came at a time when, despite an acceleration of industrial growth following Rajiv Gandhi's liberalization of the economy, there were still around fourteen million educated unemployed in the country, three million of whom had college degrees. The move, which was announced with absolutely no attempt to prepare the public and soften the blow, sent college students into a frenzy of despair. Between the 14th of September and the 10th of October, 267 students committed suicide, either through self-immolation or other means, or fell to police bullets. Overnight, V.P. Singh became the *bete noire* of the urban middle class.

The job reservation scheme broke the last tenuous restraint that moderates in the BJP, like its parliamentary leader, Atal Bihari Vajpayee, were able to exercise on the party's policies, and allowed the RSS to take over. On September 6, 1990, the BJP formally reneged on its promise to keep out of the Ayodhya dispute, and warned the government that if it tried to prevent the VHP from starting the construction of the temple that was designed to replace the existing Babri mosque, it would withdraw its support from the government. Five days later, the president of the BJP, L.K. Advani, announced that he would personally undertake a *rath yatra* (chariot pilgrimage) across India to drum up support for the construction of the temple.[14] By September 1990, therefore, the VHP was in full command. The BJP's role was reduced to being the political front organization for the VHP and the RSS and, because of its more secular immediate past, of legitimizing the fascist upsurge in the eyes of the Indian intelligentsia and professional middle class.

CHAPTER EIGHT

# The Economic Roots of Fascism in India

Coming on top of each other, the four seismic developments of the second half of the eighties completed the alienation of the upper-caste Hindus from the Congress and the Janata Dal. But what gave staying power to this shift was a simultaneous, and sudden, rise of insecurity in the intermediate bourgeoisie that industrialization within a closed, autarchic economy had created in the previous half century. This had begun almost surreptitiously with the removal of several restrictions on imports in 1978 and a relaxation of India's industrial licensing laws in 1980 and 1981. But the pace of economic liberalization had accelerated dramatically in 1985 after Rajiv Gandhi became the prime minister. In his first budget, presented in February 1985, the government abolished industrial licensing for about half of all industrial production. In the next few months, it also took a large number of controls on industrial modernization off the rule book, reduced duties drastically on the import of capital goods, and eased the import of new technology.

This rapid shift away from the crippling controls of the previous three decades, and the consequent return of modern industry into the consumer goods sector, fulfilled the essential economic requirement for the development of the fascist impulse that I discussed in Chapter 6, for it turned the seemingly solid ground that near-total import control, and a chronically shortage-ridden market, had created for the small and medium sized, owner-managed enterprises into quicksand. The shock this gave to it was almost as great as the shock that the onset of the 1930s' Great Depression had given to the Mittelstand in Germany.

## The Rise to Political Ascendance of the Intermediate Class

At first sight, India's industrial landscape in the 1980s and '90s did not look very different from that of other industrialized countries during the middle stages of their transformation into modern market economies. There was the same sprinkling of large, professionally managed, multi-product firms at the top of the hierarchy, followed by a body of medium and small enterprises that grew wider as their size became smaller.

But the similarity in the size distribution of industry was deceptive. For while in countries where the growth of capitalism had been unhindered, or actively encouraged by the state (as in the 'tiger' economies of East and Southeast Asia), the relationship between small and large industry had evolved naturally from competition to symbiosis. As technology progressed and the minimum scale of efficient production expanded, small industry turned increasingly from producing final goods sold directly to the consumers to providing components, ancillaries and specialized services for supply to the large industrial companies that produced and marketed the finished goods. In sharp contrast, the vast majority of small scale producers in India continued to produce final goods for the market in direct competition with the now liberated large scale enterprises till the very end of the twentieth century.

The reason for this 'arrested development' of capitalism was a singular, and in retrospect tragic, convergence of economic and political compulsions. Before 1957, the Indian government had followed a relatively open trade policy because it had accumulated large sterling balances during the Second World War, and therefore did not foresee the need to husband the use of foreign exchange. Its first Five Year Plan (1952–57) therefore emphasized infrastructure, community development and agriculture, and left industrial development to the private sector.

Economic autarchy was ushered in by the Second Five Year Plan, which emphasized self-reliance, and gave priority to the establishment of heavy industry. This would have required tighter controls on non-essential imports anyway, but what really brought about a sudden and complete ban on all non-essential imports was a severe foreign exchange crisis in 1957 when the government belatedly realized that it had exhausted its sterling balances and was not exporting enough to carry on with its earlier liberal import policies.

Since this crisis occurred before the World Bank had shifted its focus from European reconstruction to economic development in the Third World, and before the era of liberal US economic aid ushered in by President John F. Kennedy, the government had no option but to pull down the shutters and ban virtually all but the most essential imports. The near-complete ban on the import of consumer goods that followed created the market space for the rapid rise of an intermediate industrial class in the country.

At that time, India produced very little for export except textiles, jute, tea and a few other simple manufactures. Everything from lead pencils to liquor was imported. Importers had seen the foreign exchange crunch coming at least a year before the government, and had spared no effort to corner as many import licenses as possible. When the government lowered the boom, these licenses began to change hands at fantastic premia. Premia of 1,000 and 1,200 per cent were not unknown.[1] Those with import licenses received a windfall profit of staggering dimensions overnight. Denied future imports, many of them asked their suppliers to help them set up manufacturing units for what they had previously been importing. Most manufacturers obliged, and sent equipment, often second-hand machinery that was to have been phased out, and took equity shares in the enterprise in return. In this way, commercial capital was converted into industrial capital overnight, and a new class of small and medium sized enterprises was created. For the next ten years, hectic import substitution enabled industrial production to grow at an average of 9 per cent a year. By the time the foreign exchange crisis petered out, this new owner-manager class was firmly established and ready to make a bid for power. Its opportunity arose when Prime Minister Indira Gandhi abolished the privy purses of the princes and, in 1969, enacted the ban on company donations to political parties, described earlier, without creating an alternative mode of financing elections and electoral politics. Since political parties, including the Congress, still had to meet their expenses they still needed large amounts of money, but now in cash. The intermediate class stepped into the breach and began to provide it.[2]

The change in the financial patrons of the Congress party did not take long to get reflected in economic policy. Professionally managed businesses found it far more difficult to give unaccounted donations. When they said so they were told openly by party treasurers and fund raisers to find ways of doing so 'or else…'. The relationship between government and big business therefore changed overnight from one of cosy co-operation to one of barely concealed hostility.

The businessmen who found no difficulty in giving cash were the owner-managers of small enterprises, and traders. This class led an insecure existence at the best of times. Its control over the market was virtually non-existent; its access to bank finance at reasonable rates of interest was limited; its dependence upon the government for infrastructure—power, water, communications and transport—was total. Consequently, its 'transaction costs' (the bribes it had to pay) were higher. It lived in mortal dread of any policy change that would enable modern enterprise to enter the fields it had chalked out for itself. Mrs Gandhi's ban on company donations to political parties, and its consequent need for clandestine donations, gave it the opportunity to convert its growing economic power into political power. Within a decade, the Congress had transformed itself from being an ally of modern, large scale industry into an ally of this new, intermediate bourgeoisie.

Between 1970 and 1973, the Indira Gandhi government passed a spate of laws that cut all remaining links with big business, and turned India into an inward looking siege economy. A Monopolies and Restrictive Trade Practices Act defined monopoly companies as those with total assets of more than $7 million and those that controlled more than one-third of the market for a product. An Industrial Licensing Policy amendment act barred 'big business' from investing in any but the core sector, i.e. basic metals, heavy engineering and chemicals industries. It permitted even this only when they could further prove that the proposed investment would not make them a monopolist.

By an amendment to the Foreign Exchange Regulation Act, the government also banned foreign investment *except in 100 per cent export oriented ventures.* Its most draconian enactment was a 'conversion clause' that permitted investment banks to convert 40 per cent of their loans to any company into equity shares, at their discretion. Since the promoters seldom owned more than a third of the equity capital of the company, and since all the three institutional investors in the country—the Industrial Development Bank of India, the Industrial Finance Corporation and the Life Insurance Corporation—were almost wholly owned by the state, the conversion clause became a way to nationalize private concerns by the back door. This sowed an enormous fear of growth itself in large industrial enterprises, which was heightened when these institutional investors began to convert the loans they had given to the most successful enterprises into equity instead of those given to struggling companies to keep them afloat. Not surprisingly, the conversion clause put an end to new large scale investment by private companies for more than a decade.

As if all this did not give sufficient protection to small scale industry, the government also explicitly reserved more and more products for manufacture exclusively by it. The number of such products rose from an already high 177 in 1972 to 837 in 1983. So comprehensive was this list that it virtually blocked any large company from entering the consumer goods sector. From garments to electrical goods, to transistor radios and household appliances, virtually every Fast Moving Consumer Good (FMCG) was reserved for the small scale sector. Thus, in the mid-eighties this 'intermediate' manufacturing sector had 853,000 industrial units, produced 5,000 consumer products, employed 9.6 million workers and, including the output of the public sector, accounted for over 40 per cent of total industrial output.[3]

By 1984, therefore, the structure of Indian industry bore a remarkable resemblance to that of Germany at the end of the 1920s when the Great Depression began, and of Iran in the 1960s and '70s. In the 1980s, India had entered the middle stages of transformation into an industrialized economy. It had the same overt hostility towards big business; the same handful of favoured cronies among such businessmen; the same elaborate regime of controls to curb the growth of big professionally managed concerns; the same xenophobia towards foreign businesses; the same autarchic determination to be self-reliant at any cost; the same benevolent attitude towards small enterprise; and the same elaborate structure of party middlemen to 'fix things' with the government, that Germany had had in the 1930s and Iran in the 1970s.[4]

While this 'intermediate class' was protected from competition by the Congress, and could rely on it to pass and maintain laws that would curb the growth of the large industrial houses and keep foreign investors out, it had no need to look for another patron. Thus, Hindu nationalism remained without the third essential ingredient that had been responsible for the rise of fascism in Europe. Paradoxically, that ingredient was provided by the success of Rajiv Gandhi's partial liberalization in 1985. This led to a burst of investment in industry that pushed manufacturing growth up from 4.9 per cent between 1980 and 1984 to 10.4 per cent between 1985 and 1990.[5] The rapid growth of income, and consumer demand, that resulted from this jump in production softened the impact of the initial economic liberalization upon the intermediate stratum of manufacturers. But this proved a temporary reprieve.

Rajiv had lifted controls only upon the domestic market and left India's highly overvalued exchange rate untouched. This kept Indian manufactures out of the world market and ensured that little of the jump in production went into exports. The vast bulk—nine tenths or more—went into satisfying the pent-up demand of a growing middle class within the country and pre-empted the further expansion of the small scale enterprises. Almost overnight, therefore, the intermediate class lost a large part of the comforting, secure 'economy of permanent shortages' that Mrs Indira Gandhi had created for it between 1970 and 1973.

But that was only the first blow. The jump in manufacturing led to a jump in imports. Since that was not matched by an increase in exports because of India's overvalued rupee, the government met the balance of payments gap through commercial borrowing from the international money market. In five short years, this turned India from one of the least to one of the most indebted countries in the world. It then required only the spike in international oil prices to trigger the worst foreign exchange crisis the country had ever faced. This finally convinced the government that economic reforms could not be done piecemeal and needed to be synchronized in all sectors of the economy if they were to succeed. As a result, after the briefest of returns to a closed economy to cope with the foreign exchange crisis in 1990, India's intermediate stratum of manufacturers found itself facing the full blast of competition from both domestic and international, professionally managed, industry.

Denied the time to shift from being manufacturers of final consumer goods to manufacturers of intermediate products and ancillaries, the Indian mittelstand found itself facing ruin with a suddenness not unlike what the German Mittelstand had faced during the Depression of the 1930s. Its members therefore began to look for new patrons, and found them in the RSS, one of whose organizations, the Swadeshi Jagran Manch, had continued to campaign vigorously against opening the economy up to imports.

Domestic industry got a second reprieve in 1993 when there

was a huge jump in the growth of GDP and industry that lasted till 1997. The impact of the shift from a closed to an open economy was further softened by the gradualness with which Dr Manmohan Singh, the finance minister in the Congress government headed by Prime Minister Narasimha Rao, introduced the second round of reforms. While the government devalued the rupee, ended import controls and lowered import duties in stages, it—and its two successor governments, the United Front (1996–98), and the BJP under Prime Minister Atal Bihari Vajpayee (1998–2004)—kept more than 500 consumer goods reserved for the small scale sector till the beginning of the twenty-first century. So slow was the withdrawal of protection that thirty-five products were still reserved for production by the small and medium scale industries in 2008, four years after the Congress returned to power.

The small and medium enterprises sector got a third reprieve when, after a relatively mild recession from 1997–98 till 2002–03, the growth of GDP almost doubled from 4.5 per cent in this period to 8.4 per cent from 2004–05 to 2010–11.[6] Even in 2009–10 and 2010–11, despite the onset of the global recession in 2009, a sharp cut in interest rates allowed industrial production in India to continue growing at more than 10 per cent a year. But a high interest rate policy adopted by the Reserve Bank of India to control inflation and minimize a further devaluation of the rupee caused a sharp slackening of industrial growth. That plunged the small and medium sized industries and the construction sector into yet another crisis. A study by the Associated Chambers of Commerce (ASSOCHAM) in 2012 showed that while this sector still accounted for 45 per cent of total industrial production and employed nearly eighty million people, 25 per cent of the enterprises in northern and central India had either pulled down their shutters or were on the verge of doing so. Nine-tenths of the enterprises ASSOCHAM surveyed reported causes that were beyond their control. While two out of five were facing insufficient demand, three out of four cited inadequate, delayed and very expensive credit, and an erratic supply of power.[7]

The sheer helplessness that the Indian small and middle business class had begun to feel once more as recession and a simultaneous sharp increase in competition began to take away their markets goes a long way towards explaining its yearning for a decisive leader who promised swift action to ease their plight if he came to power. The BJP's Narendra Modi, who had presided over a decade of rapid growth in Gujarat as its chief minister, seemed to fit the bill. So, with the backing of the RSS, he was nominated as the BJP's prime ministerial candidate for the 2014 election to the Lok Sabha, the Indian parliament.

## Enter the Storm Troopers

By the beginning of the new millennium, all but one of the pre-conditions for the transformation of Hindutva into a fascist movement were in place. The exception was a cadre of 'storm troopers' with the necessary lack of a stake in the prevailing social system, and therefore the anger and ruthlessness, to smash it at their command. This got created by the very same social changes that industrialization, urbanization and globalization were bringing about in society. While there were several contributory causes, one can be singled out for the seismic effect it had on India's future. This was the introduction of colour television, and the creation of Doordarshan, a nationwide state-owned television network, in time for the Asian Games, held in Delhi in 1982.

Television broke the wall that had divided traditional, rural India from the modern India that was developing in the cities. Till then the villagers encountered urban India in the subdivisional and district towns where they went to conduct business with the government, or buy what they did not grow or weave. Their main connection with urban India, and in particular with national affairs, took place through All India Radio. There they heard different voices, different kinds of music and discussions of a different order of concerns—one that spanned the entire nation. When migrant workers returned from the cities their relatives *heard* of a different kind of life, but they could not see, much less experience it. Their only visual interaction with urban India was through the cinema, but the fact that what they were watching was fiction perhaps lent a touch of unreality to the world they were seeing.

Television changed all that in a single stroke. It brought not only the Asian Games, but middle-class sitcoms set in affluent urban middle-class homes, fashion parades and glamourized versions of the Hindu epics, the *Ramayana* and the *Mahabharata*, into people's homes. Finally, with the advent of satellite TV in the early nineties, it also brought sex and violence into their homes.

Taken together, these created an immense desire for urbanization. The number of migrant workers multiplied, the number of crimes involving sex and violence also increased exponentially. But TV also created the awareness that this new lifestyle was unattainable without education. One consequence, that initially surprised demographers like Leela Visaria, was a sharp drop in the fertility rate among rural women. This was not confined to the states with higher per capita incomes, and higher levels of education, but was noticeable in the poorer, less educated ones as well. One of the more important reasons, she noted, was 'changing perceptions of the costs of children's care and education'.[8] In sum, the social changes brought about by economic development, and highlighted by television from the late eighties onwards, made even poor, uneducated women decide that they would prefer to have fewer children but give them an education.

The result was an explosion of secondary and university education that caught both the centre and the state governments by surprise. Between 2006 and 2016, enrolment of children in secondary schools jumped from 58 per cent to 90 per cent. The enrolment of college students also rose from 11 per cent to 26 per cent of those who had completed secondary school.

Since the government schooling system was more or less defunct, especially in northern India, private schools advertising 'English Medium' sprang up in the countryside like mushrooms in spring. Even farm labourers began to set aside Rs 150 a month or more—a substantial sum in the nineties—to pay for the education they wanted their children to have. Initially, the state governments considered this an encroachment on their hitherto exclusive prerogative to keep the poor uneducated, so the RSS leapt in to meet the demand. The first Sangh school designed to spread the Hindutva ideology had been set up in 1946 at Kurukshetra, in Haryana (then undivided Punjab) with the personal blessing of the RSS chief M.S. Golwalkar. In the following years, the RSS set up other schools modelled on it, mostly in northern and western India. In 1978, it brought these under an apex body, the Vidya Bharati. By the early 1990s there were 5,000 such schools across India.

Then their number skyrocketed. By 2003, there were 14,000 Vidya Bharati schools with an enrolment of 1.7 million students. This was followed by a decade of consolidation and relentless expansion. In 2016, there were 12,000 Vidya Bharati schools, but with three million students. Seven years later, in 2023, the Vidya Bharati website listed 12,828 schools with an enrolment of 3.4 million students.[9] Assuming that the average student spends eight years at a Vidya Bharati school, this means that the RSS has been sending around 400,000 partially or fully indoctrinated young people to join the electorate every year, and has been doing this for the best part of twenty years.

Hundreds, if not thousands, of these students have gone on to become the storm troopers of the Sangh Parivar. On December 15, 2019, at the school day function of a VB school, the Sri Rama Vidya Kendra High School in Kalladka, Karnataka,[10] in a singular act of calculated contempt the students were made to enact the demolition of the Babri Masjid barely a month after the Supreme Court of India ruled that it had been a 'violation of law'.

Of special note are the RSS' military schools. One such is the Bhonsale Military School (BMS) in Nagpur, which has been linked to several terrorist attacks by Hindu terrorists against Muslims in the recent past. During its investigation of a bomb blast at a mosque in Malegaon, Maharashtra, in 2008, and another at

Nanded, also in Maharashtra, in 2006, the Maharashtra Anti-Terror Squad (ATS) found that several of the accused had attended military training camps organized at the BMS and a similar school at Pune, both in Maharashtra, where the RSS was born a century ago. It also found that meetings had been held in the BMS between the accused, senior RSS leaders and their affiliates to plan the bombings.[11]

In addition to the syllabus prescribed by the NCERT, the National Council for Education, Research and Training, the Vidya Bharati schools teach five additional courses: *moral education*, which includes stories of heroes, songs, honesty, and personal hygiene; *physical education*, which includes yoga and martial arts; *music*; *Sanskrit*; and *Vedic mathematics*. In religiously plural schools, this would have been unexceptionable. But these schools are the opposite of pluralist, for in them there is no corresponding celebration of Muslim, Sikh or Christian festival days, and an almost complete absence of non-Hindu enrolment.

Their choice of heroes is also skewed deliberately to serve the RSS' anti-Muslim agenda. For there are no Muslim rulers in its pantheon of heroes. There is no reference to the way in which the Delhi Sultanate's most powerful ruler, Ghiyasuddin Balban, and Alauddin Khilji, repelled every Mongol invasion of India for six decades from the 1240s till 1305 and inflicted such mass slaughter upon them that they never came back again. It was only this foresight of a Muslim Sultan that confined the creation of the Mongol empire to Central Asia and Europe.

Nor is there any reference in its teaching to Tipu Sultan, who kept the British at bay in Karnataka till one of his own generals betrayed him for money and opened the rear gate of Srirangapatnam Fort, where Tipu made his last stand alongside his soldiers and died.

The RSS has also added some of its own books to the prescribed texts. These blame the 'internal disunity' of Hindus for the invasions of Turks, Mongols and Mughals. They describe Christian pastors as instruments of colonialism, completely ignoring the fact that the British conquered India with upper-caste Hindu sepoys, using *hundis* (letters of credit) issued by powerful financiers like the House of Jagat Seth, to purchase supplies along the way for their wars against the Marathas, Tipu Sultan, the Sikhs and others in northern and central India.

In these books, RSS founders Hedgewar and Golwalkar are listed alongside Hindu divinities and historical heroes, in a subliminal attempt to put them on the same pedestal. There is also more explicit political conditioning through prayers recited and songs sung at morning assembly that are steeped in religious devotion and the spirit of patriotism.

The Vidya Bharati schools preach religious exclusivism, and therefore prepare the ground for an easy injection of animosity towards the Muslim community. But the opportunity to do this was created for the RSS by the skewed definition of secularism that was adopted by the Constitution, and ratified by the first Congress governments of the country. Relying upon a definition of secularism borrowed mindlessly from Europe, it enshrined a definition of secularism that banned all religious education *except in so-called minority, i.e. non-Hindu schools.* In a country of nearly half a billion people practising all the seven major religions of the world, there was no attempt to balance this by including a course in comparative religion that would have taught children what Emperor Akbar realized four hundred years earlier: the fundamental truth that all the great religions of the world, regardless of their claimed origins, preached the same moral code and way of life.

This cultural vacuum was deepened by not making the teaching of at least one classical language, ideally Sanskrit or Persian, compulsory, which would have put students in secondary schools in direct touch with their historical past. As a result, over six decades, the public education system created a cultural and philosophical vacuum that Vidya Bharati filled, albeit to meet the RSS' own skewed, and often perverted, ends.

## Collapse of Economic Autarchy: The Final Ingredient

As has happened in most other developing countries, the schools and universities have prepared their students for jobs in industry and non-traditional services. So, those who have devoted a decade or more of their lives to studies look for regular, secure jobs in these sectors first, and consider returning to the occupations of their parents an admission of failure. When they do not find the jobs they want, a significant proportion decide to wait till these come their way. When these still do not come their way, they turn in despair or anger to drugs, crime, and politics. The best index of the increasing mismatch between the jobs the youth want and the jobs available is to be found in the labour force participation rate (LFPR), which measures the proportion of the population between the ages of sixteen and sixty that is employed, or is actively looking for work, and by the same token, therefore, what proportion of the labour force has stopped looking for work.

Data published by the government's Ministry of Statistics and Programme Implementation, show that the LFPR reached an all-time high of 63.7 per cent in 2004–05 but then began a continuous fall that had not ended even by the end of 2022. It fell gradually at first to 57.1 per cent in 2011–12, then more precipitately to 49.8 per cent in 2018–19 and still more rapidly to 46.9 per cent in 2022. Till 2011–12, the fall was almost certainly voluntary, because housewives were withdrawing from the work force and rural youth were staying at school longer and going to colleges. But after 2011–12, the withdrawal was involuntary, and was taking place because jobs had dried up.

The sheer magnitude of this catastrophe is better revealed by absolute numbers. India's labour force numbered 446.1 million in 2005, 457.5 million in 2011, 482.7 million in 2019, and 501 million in 2021. Thus, while eighteen million people between sixteen and sixty left the work force during the boom years, almost certainly voluntarily, another twenty-one million did so in the eight years that followed, almost certainly involuntarily.

All or more of the loss of hope that followed occurred in just six years after 2011, for between 2003–04 and 2011–12 the economy had grown by an average of 8.3 per cent and created *more jobs than aspirants* for perhaps the first time in India's history. Precise figures quoted by labour economist Santosh Mehrotra show that until 2012 nearly 7.5 million non-agricultural jobs were being created per year. There was a slight economic slowdown thereafter, but still the average GDP growth over the decade 2004 till 2014 remained at 8 per cent per annum.

However, employment growth virtually dried up after that because of two droughts and a high interest rate policy inflicted upon the economy by the government. This brought non-agricultural employment growth down to 2.9 million per year. Nearly all of this demand was met by urban youth, and so, close to five million rural youth who were coming into the cities in search of jobs were forced to stay back in their villages. Nearly all of them were educated at least till the class 10 level, and were therefore reluctant or unable to go back to farming. The steep fall in the labour force participation rate was the result.[12]

This was revealed by the Periodic Labour Force Studies of the National Sample Survey, which showed that between 2004–05 and 2011–12, urban unemployment among those with a secondary or higher education had fallen for both males and females till 2011–12, but had then risen at a dizzying pace in the next six years:

Table 8.1. Urban educated unemployment rates, 2004–05 to 2017–18:

| *Year* | *2004–05* | *2011–12* | *2017–18* |
|---|---|---|---|
| Female | 15.6 | 10.3 | 19.3 |
| Male | 5.1 | 4.0 | 9.2 |

Table 8.2. Youth unemployment rates, 2004–05 to 2017–18:

| *Year* | *2004–05* | *2011–12* | *2017–18* |
|---|---|---|---|
| Rural Male | 3.9 | 5.0 | 17.4 |
| Urban Male | 7.5 | 8.8 | 18.7 |
| Rural female | 13.1 | 14.9 | 27.2 |

The close tally between the two sets of figures tells the same story outlined above: of an unemployment crisis that first the Congress-led UPA government unintentionally unleashed upon the country, but which the Modi government did not have a clue on how to reverse. In absolute terms, between 2004–05 and 2011–12, more jobs were created than entrants into the work force. But then there was a loss of jobs so severe that thirty million or more of the educated youth did not enter the job market at all.

It was from the anger and disillusionment of these thirty million, and of the forty or fifty million more who had even stopped trying to look for work, that the fascist movement within the Sangh Parivar began recruiting its storm troopers. As Christophe Jaffrelot, one of the most widely read and respected students of the Sangh Parivar, pointed out in an interview in December 2018,

> This feeling of victimization partly explains the anger of young Hindus who, sometimes, have no job, little money, and nothing to do, and consider that they have become second-rate citizens in their own country. They take revenge against the *other*, par excellence... For them, Modi is not only a saviour who has promised jobs, but also a hero who has never said 'sorry' for the Gujarat riots...and a victim, like them, of an English-speaking, secular, liberal establishment which has accused him on television and in the courtroom, for years, for what had happened in Gujarat.[13]

CHAPTER NINE

# Gujarat—the Laboratory Where Indian Fascism was Created

The event in Gujarat that Jaffrelot referred to began with a fire that broke out in carriage number S-6 of the Sabarmati Express, at 7.38 am on February 27 at Godhra, a wayside station in Gujarat, about 160 kilometres from Ahmedabad. The train had originated at Varanasi in Uttar Pradesh and had passed through Ayodhya. At Ayodhya, it had been boarded by more than a thousand *kar sevaks* (devotees offering worship through manual labour), who had come to the town ostensibly to build the Rama temple but in reality were there to keep the Babri Masjid dispute alive. When the train reached Godhra, carriage number S-6 was carrying 150 to 200 passengers against its designated capacity of seventy-two. As is described in the next chapter, the fire that killed fifty-eight persons was most probably an accident. But since the train was packed with kar sevaks, and had been stationary at a railway signal, called Signal Falia, beside a village populated almost entirely by Muslims of the Ghanchi community when the fire broke out, it was immediately assumed that S-6 had been set alight by locals and some other Muslims who were seeking revenge for the misbehaviour of kar sevaks with Muslim women on the station platform.

### Not a Riot but a Pogrom

Like the attack of gonorrhoea that the Mughal Emperor Shah Jahan suffered 350 years earlier, this almost certainly accidental fire changed the course of Indian history.[1] It became apparent within hours of the tragedy that Narendra Modi, Gujarat's new chief minister, and cohorts of the VHP, had been waiting for something like this to happen. For the killing and rapine that it unleashed was not only unprecedented but planned to a degree that had almost never been seen before. More than two decades later, the Indian media still shy away from using terms like pogrom and massacre to describe what happened next, and prefer to call it a 'riot'. This is comforting to their consciences because it brings what happened at Ahmedabad and scores of cities and villages in the next two weeks on a par with communal clashes of all sorts that have occurred since the Partition. But several features of the massacre that followed suggest that the violent and murderous reaction to the fire, if not the fire itself, had been pre-planned. For the killing that followed began instantly and was wholly one-sided. It was not a riot, therefore, but a pogrom.

The official tally, provided reluctantly by the Gujarat government in answer to a starred question in the Indian parliament in 2005, was that it left 1,044 dead, 223 missing, and 2,500 injured. Of the dead, 790 were Muslim and 254 Hindu. But this was a large, and deliberate underestimate, for it was given by the state government after a delay of more than three years, and then under pressure from the parliament in Delhi. By then a detailed and much more accurate estimate had already been prepared and submitted by an eight-member Concerned Citizens' Tribunal set up by the Peoples' Union of Civil Liberties. The Tribunal was headed by Justice V.R. Krishna Iyer, the legendary former chief justice of India, who had had the courage to declare Prime Minister Indira Gandhi guilty of election malpractice in 1975, and three other retired judges of the Supreme Court and the Maharashtra High Court, along with four other highly respected social activists. The CCT had collected the names of 1,926 persons who had been killed.[2] Subsequent estimates put the figure even higher, at more than 2,000.[3] The CCT's estimate is the most credible because it is indirectly supported by the estimate of the intelligence department of the Gujarat Police.

Nine out of ten of the victims were Muslims. Therefore, to call what happened in Gujarat between February 28 and March 10, 2002 a riot is to deliberately describe a tiger as a tabby cat.

On March 9, ten days after the Godhra fire, the government of Gujarat set up a one-man commission presided over by Gujarat High Court judge K.G. Shah to look into the incident. But following outrage among families of victims and in the media over Shah's alleged closeness to Modi, it added retired Supreme Court judge G.T. Nanavati to the Commission and made him its chairman. After six years of going over the details, the Commission submitted a preliminary report which concluded that the fire was an act of arson, committed by a mob of one to two thousand locals. It described one Maulvi Husain Haji Ibrahim Umarji, a cleric in Godhra, and a dismissed Central Reserve Police Force officer named Nanumiyan, as the 'masterminds' behind the arson. The Nanavati–Shah Commission took twenty-four extensions to prepare its final report, which it presented on November 18, 2014, after Modi had become the prime minister, and its findings had lost their relevance. The Commission's report was immediately discredited by a video recording released by *Tehelka* magazine and Aaj Tak TV channel, in which Arvind Pandya, the Gujarat government's special counsel before the Nanavati–Shah Commission was seen claiming confidently that the Commission would exonerate Modi and the BJP because Shah was 'our man' and Nanavati could be 'persuaded'.[4]

Based upon the Commission's findings, in February 2011, a trial court in Gujarat had convicted thirty-one people of conspiring to commit murder and acquitted sixty-three others. Of those convicted, eleven were sentenced to death and the other twenty to life in prison. Along with sixty-two others, the court acquitted Maulvi Umarji, who had been presented by the Nanavati–Shah commission as the prime conspirator, for 'lack of evidence'. The possibility cannot be ruled out that Umarji chose to endorse the government's version of events to buy his freedom, but by then there was so much definitive evidence that the fire had not been set by Ghanchi Muslims at Signal Falia, a kilometre outside Godhra station, as claimed by the government and the Gujarati press, that the proceedings at the Nanavati–Shah Commission had been reduced to pantomime.

As we will see later, the fire almost certainly started inside the carriage S-6 of the Sabarmati Express, at Godhra. It cannot altogether be ruled out, as several commentators have suggested, that it was a small fire, started by *agents provocateurs* to create the excuse for starting a riot, that went out of control. But it is more likely that it was started by a kerosene stove being used by a high-caste Hindu to make an early morning cup of tea, or heat some food, that was knocked over by someone's foot in the hugely overcrowded compartment. It is a common practice among high-caste Hindus to cook their separate meals.

It is therefore unlikely that either the VHP or the Bajrang Dal, whose members were later to be indicted, had anything to do with the way it started. But the way in which Modi—then a greenhorn chief minister who confessed in a rare moment of candour that he did not even know how to read a file when he assumed office—seized the opportunity the fire provided to consolidate his, and the BJP's, hold on Gujarat, and then ruthlessly eliminated any threat to his continued hold on power, showed that Indian fascism had finally found the leader it had been waiting for.

## How Did Gujarat Become the Laboratory of the 'Hindu Rashtra'?

Narendra Modi began his political life on Diwali, 1958, at the age of eight when, with his father's blessings he joined the RSS as a *bal swayamsevak* (child volunteer) in his home town of Vadnagar in Gujarat. From that early age, it was apparent that he had a restless energy that made him different from other boys of his age. 'Narendra always wanted to do something different. Something more than what we did in our daily routine at home and in school. And the RSS *shakha* provided him just that,' Sombhai Modi, Narendra's oldest brother, told Vinod K. Jose, who wrote an insightful and the most deeply researched profile that has appeared so far of Modi in the monthly magazine, *The Caravan*, in 2012.[5] At school, Modi's Sanskrit teacher told Jose that he remembered Modi as 'only an average student. But he showed keen interest in debates and theatre. I set up the debating club at the school, and I remember Narendra was among the regular students in the club'.

In 1969, after he had finished high school, to get away from an unconsummated marriage that had been arranged for him when he was three years old, Modi, then eighteen, left his home and visited a variety of religious shrines in the Himalayas. For two years his family did not know where he was, till he returned to Vadnagar and announced that his *sanyas* was over, and he would move to Ahmedabad and work in his uncle's canteen. After a short stint at his uncle's canteen, Modi opened his own teacart on a cycle near Geeta Mandir. According to a senior RSS *pracharak* (propagandist), who was then in Ahmedabad—and who insisted that he not be named for fear of angering the chief minister—it was at this point that Modi decided to return to the RSS.

'Some pracharaks used to have tea at his cart after they returned from their morning *shakha*,' he told Jose. 'Modi made an impression on them, given also his background in the *shakha* in Vadnagar.' He soon wound up his teacart and moved to Hedgewar Bhawan, the RSS headquarters in Gujarat, as an assistant.

The Ahmedabad that he came to in 1971 was a city transformed. In September 1969, shortly after Modi went away to the Himalayas, it had been racked by the first ever communal holocaust in Gujarat, which claimed more than 1,100 lives. Of the 685 incidents of communal violence recorded in urban Gujarat in the decade 1961–71, 578 occurred in 1969. Starting with Ahmedabad, the worst affected city, the communal violence had spread to several other places including Vadodara. The description of one incident during a riot in Ahmedabad on September 20, 1969, given to the Concerned Citizens' Tribunal by a human rights activist who was an eyewitness, captured the animosity that had developed between Hindus and Muslims in the state:

> A young Muslim, enraged by the destruction of his property said he would take revenge. Upon this the crowd seized him, showered blows on him, and tried to force him to shout *Jai Jagannath*. Staying firm, the youth refused even if that meant death. To this, someone in the crowd responded that he might indeed be done away with. Wood from broken shops was collected, a pyre prepared in the middle of the road, petrol sprinkled on the pyre as well as on the youth, and he was set alight with ruthless efficiency. What is remarkable is that there was no resistance from any Hindu. The wails of the Muslim inhabitants of the area were drowned in the celebration of the incident by the Hindus.[6]

What entrenched this malevolent hatred in the years that followed was the presence of cash rich, armed gangs of smugglers and illicit liquor vendors in *both* the Hindu and the Muslim communities. These had been created by decades of prohibition, on the one hand, and the smuggling of gold and contraband from Dubai and elsewhere in the Persian Gulf, on the other. Prohibition had created similar gangs in other states as well, notably adjoining Maharashtra, and in Hyderabad city in the then undivided state of Andhra Pradesh. By the end of the twentieth century, economic liberalization, and the end of prohibition, had weakened the economic base of these gangs in Maharashtra and elsewhere in the country. But in Gujarat, prohibition had remained intact and the smuggling of gold and other contraband, including huge consignments of wines and liquors by boat from the Persian Gulf, had remained a thriving business. So, turf battles between Hindu and Muslim smugglers and illicit liquor vendors that often morphed into communal riots had continued.

It would have been surprising indeed if Modi had not been shaped by these events. In Hedgewar Bhawan, he impressed his seniors with his organizing ability, his single-mindedness in his work, and his impeccable honesty in issues involving money from the beginning. As a result, he was selected to attend the one-month, level one, officer training course at the RSS headquarters in Nagpur, central Maharashtra. When he returned, at the very young age of twenty-one or twenty-two, Modi was made the RSS pracharak in-charge of the student wing of the RSS, the Akhil Bharatiya Vidyarthi Parishad (ABVP) in Gujarat, a position he held throughout Prime Minister Indira Gandhi's Emergency (1975–77). These were formative years for the BJP, and for Modi's career. The ABVP was at the centre of the students' movement against corruption and high prices triggered by a drought in 1972, which led to the formation of the Navnirman Yuvak Samiti in 1974 in Gujarat, heading the protest movement for *navnirman* ('constructive reform'), and set off the train of events that led to the Emergency in 1975.

But it was also while he held this position, of in effect being the secret liaison between the RSS and the ABVP, that Modi first showed his penchant for becoming a loose cannon. As summed up by Jose, 'The Sangh *pracharak* in-charge of a frontal organization like the ABVP is supposed to function like an underground guide—to be like a vein hidden under the skin, exercising authority away from the public eye—but Modi's personal style, which chafed at such restrictions, was already making itself evident.'

'Modi had firm opinions on even smaller things, and the senior leaders thought that he was attention-seeking,' a second senior RSS pracharak, who was a member of the Gujarat ABVP in the 1970s, told Jose. 'The Sangh leaders did not like it.'

The pracharak related to Jose an incident that occurred during the Emergency:

> We in the ABVP were told to organize agitations against the government, from neighbourhood to neighbourhood, and one day we were holding a meeting at the Bhulabhai Char Rasta (crossroad) in Ahmedabad. We were supposed to speak against the government, but in a sober tone, because that was the Sangh style, and also the police and the intelligence agencies were watching over us. But while the meeting was on, Narendrabhai passed by on a cycle. He was furious at the composed serenity in our protest. He jumped onto the stage, grabbed the mike and

> began giving a rabble-rousing speech, spitting abusive words, and not hiding his anger against the (Congress) government.
>
> The audience loved it. But that night, at Hedgewar Bhavan, the senior Sangh leaders scolded Modi for his detrimental and unwarranted act—for a nearly-underground Sangh *pracharak* to come out in the open. 'Forget about speaking,' they lectured him, 'you shouldn't have even gone there. Even if the meeting failed, it would be okay, but discipline and obedience to one's role is superior to all.'[7]

Modi listened, but remained unchastened. His desire to step out of the shadows into the limelight grew stronger as he grew older. It led, over the years, to increasingly frequent conflicts with senior BJP leaders like Shankersinh Vaghela and Keshubhai Patel, both of whom had served as BJP chief ministers in Gujarat. Vaghela recalled that even as a very young man Modi chafed at minor strictures of the Sangh. 'He always used to do things differently from others in the group—if all of us wore long-sleeved kurtas, he used to wear short sleeves, and when all of us wore khaki shorts, he wore white shorts.' One day, Vaghela remembered, when the sarsanghchalak of the RSS, M.S. Golwalkar was visiting Gujarat, he 'question[ed] Modi in public about his [penchant for] keeping a trimmed beard.' Golwalkar, who also had a beard but did not trim it, died in 1973 when Modi was only twenty-three. So, his gentle reprimand must have come very shortly after Modi had begun to frequent Hedgewar Bhawan in Ahmedabad.

Writing in January–February 2012, Jose could not foresee that these seemingly unimportant assertions of individuality were early signs of the flamboyancy in speech and dress that was to become the hallmark of Modi's style of leadership after 2014.

To the RSS, however, his value as a peerless organizer, and his unbounded energy, outweighed his penchant for self-promotion. After two more training courses at Nagpur in 1981, the RSS made Modi its liaison in Gujarat with all its frontal organizations in the state. The lone exception was the BJP, the apex of the Sangh Parivar's political pyramid. But Modi crossed that barrier six years later when the RSS made him its organizational secretary for Gujarat, and therefore its conduit for coordination with the BJP. However, by then, Vaghela told Jose, Modi was no longer satisfied with simply advising the BJP and other frontal organizations of the Sangh Parivar. 'Modi interfered in the day-to-day operations of running the BJP, when that job was mine, as the president of the party… According to the party constitution, the organization secretary shall give only directions to the party, but not execute things on his own.'

To increase his power, Modi worked ceaselessly to set Vaghela and Keshubhai Patel, the BJP's other major leader in Gujarat, against each other. His machinations against Vaghela eventually caused the latter to revolt and threaten to split the party. A part of the compromise he accepted, when the BJP high command in Delhi made him the chief minister, was the exile of Modi from Gujarat. In 1995, therefore, Modi was shunted out of Gujarat to Delhi as the BJP's national secretary for India's northern region, comprising Punjab, Haryana, Chandigarh, Himachal Pradesh, and Jammu and Kashmir.

But, with his restless energy and skill in intrigue, Modi turned this 'exile' into a stepping stone to power. By the time he came to Delhi, a clear pattern had been established. Senior BJP leaders did not like or trust him, but his organizational skills continued to pay him dividends in the RSS. When Shankersinh Vaghela defected from the BJP in Gujarat, and formed a short-lived government with the Congress, Modi was vindicated. In 1998, a few days after Atal Bihari Vajpayee took office as prime minister, the RSS made Modi the organizational secretary of the BJP for the whole of India, and therefore the bridge between the parliamentary party and the RSS for all of India.

Modi had had only three predecessors in this position and all had followed the organization's dictate to avoid publicity and work behind the scenes. Modi broke this tradition and increasingly began to grab the spotlight. He did this by making political speeches that reeked of animosity towards Muslims and towards Pakistan in particular. 'During the 1999 Kargil War and the subsequent failed peace talks between Vajpayee and General Pervez Musharraf,' Jose observes, 'Modi held frequent press conferences and often appeared on television, demonstrating the jingoistic fervour that would become his signature. Asked during one TV debate about how to respond to provocations from Pakistan, his answer was: "*Chicken biryani nahi, bullet ka jawab bomb se diya jayega*—we won't give them chicken biryani, we will respond to their bullets with bombs."' (Fifteen years later, in October 2014, when he was the prime minister of India, he fulfilled this promise by ordering the Indian army to respond to random firing across the Line of Control in Kashmir from Pakistan with a 'ten-for-one' retaliation using mortar and other heavy weapons. Muslim baiting within India and a relentless demonization of Pakistan, as we shall see, became the leitmotifs of Modi's first term as prime minister of India.)

Never entirely trusted by the local BJP leaders in Gujarat, Modi had gravitated towards the Vishwa Hindu Parishad, the RSS' muscular agitational wing. Having with his usual efficiency organized several vast meetings for it, he developed close relations with leaders within it like Pravin Togadia, an oncologist turned agitator, even riding pillion behind him on his motorcycle from 1983 onwards on some of his recruitment drives for the VHP. While Modi was in Delhi climbing the RSS-BJP ladder, the VHP was building its cadres in Gujarat. The endemic communal violence in Gujarat made it the most fertile ground for making its first bid for power. Modi joined the recruitment campaign that followed with enthusiasm. And so, in the 1990s, Modi spent more of his time at the offices of the VHP than the BJP.

By the late nineties, the RSS' campaign for a Hindu Rashtra had borne its first fruit. After a brief taste of government in 1995, the BJP had come to power in Gujarat for the first time in 1998. Pravin Togadia had begun to refer to Gujarat as the laboratory where the Hindu Rashtra of the future would be forged within the next two years.[8] Modi's chance to become the chief minister came in October 2001 when, after a string of three defeats at the hands of the Congress in bye-elections to the state legislature, the RSS felt the need to replace the incumbent chief minister, Keshubhai Patel, with someone more capable of converting the growing animosity of Hindus towards Muslims in Gujarat into support for the BJP. They chose Narendra Modi.

One of Modi's first acts was to appoint Gordhan Zadafia, Togadia's right-hand man in the Gujarat unit of the VHP, as his state minister for home affairs and give him charge of the police. The two fell out later. Zadafia, who had been in the VHP for fifteen years before joining the BJP, left the party in 2007. He was implicated in the pogroms of February 27, 2002, but not convicted. Still, it is Modi's personal link with the VHP that explains much of what followed in Gujarat after he assumed office.

CHAPTER TEN

# Fire in the Sabarmati Express

## *Accident or Conspiracy?*

Had carriage S-6 of the Sabarmati Express not burnt down outside Godhra station in the early morning of February 27, 2002, Modi's chief ministership could easily have ended as early as April 2003, when another state assembly election was due to take place, for the BJP had lost the gram panchayat (local government) elections in 2001 and some Vidhan Sabha bye-elections in October of the same year. But the fire on the Sabarmati Express created an opportunity for him to galvanize Hindu chauvinism and use it to shore up his hold on power.

The presence of kar sevaks, their past misbehaviour with Muslim vendors at the Godhra platform both en route to Ayodhya and on their way back, the heated altercation between them and local Muslim vendors just minutes before the incident, and the fact that the burning train stopped directly in front of a shanty colony of feisty Ghanchi Muslims, who had acquired a bad reputation in earlier communal riots, all reinforced the conclusion that the latter were responsible for torching the carriage. By the afternoon of the 27th, local Gujarati newspapers had accepted that explanation: someone had pulled the emergency chain shortly after the train left the station and brought it to a halt opposite the Ghanchi colony where the crowd, forewarned, had already assembled; they poured kerosene into the carriage and threw burning oil-soaked rags into it through its windows to set it on fire.[1]

All of this information was made available to the Gujarati media within hours of the fire by nine self-proclaimed eyewitnesses who came forward to describe what they had seen. All of them confirmed that the carriage had been set on fire from the outside by the Muslims assembled beforehand at a railway signal called Signal Falia. All claimed that they had been at the station to greet and felicitate a VHP leader who was travelling back from Ayodhya on that train. None of them was able to explain how they knew that the Sabarmati Express would arrive at 7.00 am, when its scheduled time of arrival was hours earlier—2.55 am.

The precise cause, or causes, of the fire and the subsequent holocaust have been hotly debated over the past two decades, and the debate will continue because of its importance for understanding the sea-change in Indian politics that has followed. What follows below is the most accurate account of the way the tragedy developed that this writer has been able to find:[2]

> **February 27, 2002—07.42 am:** Sabarmati Express, Train No. 9166 UP, carrying kar sevaks on their way back from Ayodhya arrives on platform number 1 at Godhra railway station. The train is nearly five hours behind scheduled arrival time 0255.
>
> As kar sevaks come down, they shout slogans and there are several reports of provocations:
>
> a) They clash with Muslim tea vendors on the platform.
> b) There is a rumour that a Muslim girl, Sophiya Shaikh, has been abducted by the kar sevaks.
> c) The Muslims on the platform start pelting stones at the train.
>
> **07.47 am:** The train driver, Rajendrarao Raghunath Rao, gets a green signal at 0745, but as soon as he starts moving, the chain is pulled and the train stopped. Some kar sevaks were yet to board the train.
>
> **07.55 am:** The Sabarmati Express train starts again.
>
> **08.00 am:** After moving a short distance, once again the train comes to a halt because of the automatic brake system, on account of dropping of vacuum near Cabin-A, about a kilometre from the station.

A mob has chased the train from the station, and heavy stone pelting continues. All windows are shut, and blinds are pulled down. (S-6 was a non-air-conditioned, 3-tier sleeper coach with metal-grilled sliding blinds.)

**08.20 am:** Smoke is first seen rising from coach S-6.

**08.20 am:** Fire brigade operator receives the call about the fire.

**08.26 am:** District Collector Jayanti Ravi receives a telephone message from Deputy Superintendent of Police Raju Bhargava that the Sabarmati Express train is under attack.

**08.30 am:** DSP Raju Bhargava reaches the scene, disperses the mob.

**08.35 am:** The only working fire brigade engine in Godhra arrives at the scene (the other two had been lying broken).

**08.50 am:** By the time the District Collector Ms Jayanti Ravi reaches the scene, the fire has been put out.

**09.00 am:** The Home Secretary of Gujarat informs Chief Minister Narendra Modi and the Home Minister of Gujarat.

**09.39 am:** Narendra Modi talks to VHP leader Jaideep Patel—later to be a principal accused in the riots facing two separate charges.

**12.40 pm:** Sabarmati Express is sent on its onward journey, with 3,000 passengers.

**04.30 pm:** Modi arrives at the scene, and immediately calls the attack a pre-planned conspiracy.[3]

The Gujarati newspapers swallowed the official statements wholesale. By early afternoon, the entire state was flooded with the news that the fire was an act of revenge for misbehaviour by the kar sevaks with Muslim tea sellers at the station, in particular with the granddaughter of one of the tea stall owners. These reports, backed by the endless repetition of video clips showing charred bodies being brought out of a still smoking carriage, tipped the simmering Hindu animosity towards Muslims over the brink into a towering rage.

At 8.38 pm on the day of the tragedy, Dilip Trivedi, the general secretary of VHP, Gujarat general secretary Jaideep Patel and joint secretary Kaushik Mehta, declared in a joint statement that 'innocent *Ram Bhakts* had been attacked and hence they had declared a Gujarat Bandh. They also stated that the attack was pre-planned by the Muslims. Innocent ladies were molested, compartments were set on fire and *Ram sevaks* were burnt alive.'[4]

The substantial number of Hindu deaths—254 of the 1,044 of the official tally—has enabled the BJP, and other apologists for the Modi regime, to foster the impression that what started in Ahmedabad and spread to the rest of Gujarat in three days was only a communal riot that had gone out of control.

But there is little or no evidence of any organized resistance, let alone a counter-attack, by the Muslims, for only a handful of the Hindus were killed by Muslims trying to defend themselves. For instance, of the ninety-seven persons killed in the Naroda Patiya massacre, one of the three worst atrocities committed on February 28, only one was a Hindu. In the attack on the Gulberg Society, which is described below, only three out of the sixty-nine persons killed were Hindus.

Apart from deliberate misrepresentation, there are two possible explanations for the official estimate: the first is that the majority of the non-Muslim casualties could have occurred among Dalits or migrant workers living cheek by jowl with Muslims in villages and shanty towns, who were killed when the riots spread from Ahmedabad to the rural areas. The second is that this figure is a concoction of the Gujarat government, forced out of it in 2005 by the Congress-led UPA government, by means of a starred question in parliament.

The fortuitousness of the fire in the train, and the horrified reaction of the Indian and international media to the slaughter that followed, served to inflame Gujarati nationalism and fuse it with the easily reawakened Hindu communalism in the state. Modi's relentless use of both sentiments after he came to power, both in Gujarat and in New Delhi, has led many observers to speculate that the fire in carriage S-6 may have been a 'false flag' operation similar to the burning of Germany's parliament building, the Reichstag, in 1933 to provide Hitler with a pretext for imprisoning every known communist in the country.[5] But in 2005, a high-level committee set up by the Railway Ministry, consisting of a retired judge of the Calcutta High Court, U.C. Banerjee, came to the conclusion that the fire was an accident, probably caused by a short circuit, or by someone who kicked over a stove on which somebody was cooking a meal. (The Concerned Citizens' Tribunal had interviewed railway officials who, notably, said that flour and other raw foodstuffs had been found in the debris left by the fire.) A five-man team of experts appointed by a Delhi-based NGO, Hazards Centre, came to the same conclusion. The investigating team comprised professionals from engineering disciplines relevant to the issue: A.K. Roy of the Hazards Centre was a chemical engineer with expertise in hazards and safety; Dinesh Mohan, professor of biomedical engineering at the Indian Institute of Technology, Delhi, had expertise in human tolerance to injuries; Sunil Kale, professor of mechanical engineering, also at the IIT, Delhi, was an expert in thermodynamics and fluidization; and, S.N. Chakravarty, a Mumbai-based consultant had been a mechanical engineer in the Indian Railways for ten years, with an expertise in the manufacture of railway coaches.

The team came to this conclusion after examining six carriages burnt in other fires, which had been preserved by the railways for forensic reference. Its crucial discovery was the extraordinary similarity of the smoke and burn patterns in Sabarmati Express' coach S-6 with a burnt-out coach (No. 16526 GSCN) which the Railways had kept at their yards at the town of Jagadhri. In the latter, the fire had started somewhere in the centre of the carriage, and spread outwards and upwards, eventually enveloping the entire carriage. This coach had caught fire while under maintenance in the washing line at Delhi Junction on November 21, 2003.[6]

The Banerjee Commission's finding was fiercely disputed, even ridiculed, by the Sangh Parivar. Its spokesman then, Arun

Jaitley, who went on to become the finance and defence minister in Narendra Modi's first cabinet in 2014, raised the procedural objection that the railway ministry, even when belonging to the central government, had no right to conduct such an inquiry. 'If it was an accident, what prevented passengers from jumping out?' he further asked, rhetorically.

When one of the Hindus who claimed he had been injured in the fracas on the Godhra platform in 2002 challenged Justice Banerjee's report in the Gujarat High Court, the judge lost no time in declaring the formation of the Banerjee Commission 'unconstitutional, illegal and null and void', and also declared it a 'colourable [*sic*] exercise of power with *mala fide intentions*' and quashed *all* of its findings. As if that was not enough, following Jaitley's lead, he went on to berate the central railway ministry for daring to set up the Commission when the state government had already appointed the Shah Commission, later joined by retired justice G.T. Nanavati on March 8, 2002. This learned judge also entirely dismissed the right of the central railways ministry to set up a high-level committee to ascertain how a fire had started on its own property, even when its purpose was to make sure that such a tragedy did not happen again.[7] As is described below, this was the first of a string of questionable judicial pronouncements by the courts in Gujarat that made the Supreme Court of India decide that cases pertaining to the 2002 riots could no longer be tried in a court located in Gujarat.

The fire in the Sabarmati Express immeasurably strengthened the fascist impulse within the Hindu community in northern and western India. Modi not only refused to believe that it may have been an accident, but went out of his way to conceal any doubts he may have had, and went instead on a campaign to hold Muslims, as a whole, responsible for the conflagration in the Sabarmati Express. The fire was an accident, but having jumped to, and enormously profited from, the conclusion that it was set by Muslims to kill kar sevaks, this was something that Modi simply could not later admit. That is the only plausible explanation for the release of a second report on the cause of the fire, prepared in early May, *two months* after the tragedy.

A first report had already been put out after an on-the-spot examination of the coach by the Gujarat Police, which had confirmed the commonly accepted explanation described above. It had found windows on the right side of the train, the side on which the crowd from the Ghanchi Muslim slum had collected, broken by extensive stone pelting, and concluded that the kerosene had been introduced into the carriage from outside. Based on its report, a trial court in Ahmedabad promptly convicted thirty-one of the ninety-four Muslims accused of the crime, and awarded ten of them a death sentence which was only commuted to life imprisonment on appeal fourteen years later in 2017.

The second, more detailed forensic examination, was carried out by another team of experts from the Forensic Science Laboratory (FSL) in Ahmedabad, headed by Dr M.S. Dahiya, its assistant director-general, on May 1, 2002. It explicitly rejected the first report observing:

> It was found that the height of the window of the coach was around 7 ft. from the ground at the place. Under this circumstance, it was not possible to throw any inflammable fluid inside from out side the coach from any bucket or carboy, because by doing this, most of the fluid was getting thrown out side. At the place of the incidents there was one heap of grit of three feet height at a distance of around 14-ft. in the southern side of the coach. Water was thrown on the windows of the coach with the help of bucket standing on the top of the said heap, in that case only about 10 to 15% of the water went inside and the rest of the quantity was spilled outside itself. Thus if the inflammable fluid is thrown from outside then major part of it would fall around the track outside and catch fire and cause damage to the outer part of bottom side of the coach. But after examination of the coach and the track, no effect was found of the fire on bottom side below the windows of the coach. By taking into consideration this fact and also the burning pattern

> of the outer side of the coach, a conclusion can be drawn that no inflammable fluid had been thrown inside from outside of the coach.
>
> There also appears to be no possibility that any inflammable liquid was thrown through the door of the bogie.[8]

But, having demolished the first explanation, Dahiya and this second team put forward an even more bizarre explanation of how it was the Muslims of the shanty town, nonetheless, who had set fire to the carriage. The explanation was that they had boarded the train when it stopped opposite the Ghanchi village by cutting through the flexible interconnecting passage between the two carriages and poured sixty litres of an 'inflammable liquid', which could be kerosene or gasoline, from one end and set a match to it.

To confirm their finding they first threw buckets of water at the train from the top of the large rubbish heap on the bund beside which the train had come to a halt and found that 85 per cent of it fell on the outside of the carriage or the ground beneath it, and only 15 per cent entered the compartment through the broken windows.[9] Then they took buckets of water into the carriage and poured more and more of it onto its floor from one end until the water had travelled almost all the way till where the fire had reached, close to the other end, and measured the amount they had had to pour. Based on this they concluded that '60 litres of inflammable liquid was poured…by using a wide-mouthed container'.

This explanation seemed plausible at first glance, but, as several commentators pointed out within hours, had more holes in it than a cheese. First, since very few buckets in everyday use are large enough to carry more than twenty to twenty-five litres of liquid, sixty litres would have needed at least three standard buckets. The report did not even hazard a guess as to how local Muslims, whose features and dress would have singled them out immediately, could have carried such a large quantity of gasoline or kerosene, both of which have a strong smell, onto a train jam-packed with hostile kar sevaks who had already been in a fracas with Muslim vendors a few minutes earlier and were spoiling for a fight. If, as some commentators hazarded, the Muslims had somehow got the buckets onto the train at the Godhra station itself, how were they not stopped immediately by the kar sevaks and other passengers standing in the packed vestibule of the carriage the moment they began to pour it out?[10]

These objections were raised by many analysts, including the Concerned Citizens' Tribunal, but the biggest 'mistake' in the report went completely unnoticed, and has remained so till the present day. This is that the FSL experts had based their finding upon a test carried out with water, not kerosene, poured when the carriage was empty, not *jam-packed with people whose shoes and luggage would have blocked, and largely absorbed, the kerosene or gasoline, before it could travel far down the vestibule*. For the tally of the dead and injured, given name by name in the CCT report, shows that there were at least 103 persons in the carriage when the fire broke out, not counting those who escaped from the opposite end, and possibly through a broken window, before the rush of panic-stricken passengers to the doorways began.

Why did the Modi government ask for a second forensic examination in the first place, and why only two months after the tragedy had occurred? The only plausible explanation is that it had learned through the state intelligence department, which had been shadowing the members of the CCT ever since they entered Ahmedabad, that the latter had decided to visit Godhra in the beginning of May. The Ghanchi Muslim revenge plot explanation for the fire was therefore about to come apart, so the government had to find another, at least halfway plausible explanation, before the CCT blew up the first explanation and exposed the BJP, VHP and Bajrang Dal for the murderers they were. So, whatever else the FSL found, it had to arrive at a conclusion that would justify the VHP's call for a bandh (paralysing of the state machinery) on the evening of February 27, and the 'collective punishment' on Muslims that it intended to inflict, the next day.

The Concerned Citizens' Tribunal had fixed its visit for May 7. The FSL team therefore visited the site and the burnt-out carriage on May 1, and submitted its report on May 3. By demolishing the government's earlier finding and presenting a second, more detailed, and more sensational, explanation, it stole the CCT's thunder and kept the moral justification for killing nearly 2,000 Muslim men, women and children alive and healthy. This was Modi at his devious, ruthless best. What did the absurdity of two reports coming to diametrically opposite conclusions on how the fire broke out but blaming the same culprits matter, so long as it kept the coals of self-righteousness smouldering warmly in the Hindu belly?

There was also eyewitness testimony that disputed the official account. Hariprasad Joshi, an employee of the Income Tax Department based in Ahmedabad travelling in coach S-6 with his wife, said he saw smoke but no fire. He even testified before the police that he saw no inflammable liquid being poured into the coach. He survived by crawling out of the compartment, though his wife, seated near the window, was unable to escape in time and succumbed to asphyxiation. Joshi himself suffered no burn injuries—significantly, despite having crawled along the floor. Had petrol indeed been spread and ignited on the floor, as was later alleged, it is unlikely he would have emerged unscathed. Most of those who died in the compartment appear, in fact, to have died not of burns but of suffocation.

The Deputy Superintendent of the Railway Police, in his testimony, also cast doubt on the conclusions drawn by the FSL. He stated that he did not observe petrol—or any other flammable liquid—being carried into the compartment by anyone. The injuries sustained by the survivors, moreover, were largely superficial and confined to the upper parts of their bodies. Had petrol been poured onto the floor and set alight, the pattern of injuries would have been markedly different: one would have expected burns primarily on the lower limbs.[11]

## Very Few of the Victims Were Kar Sevaks

An analysis of the persons who were in the ill-fated carriage at the time when it caught fire also strongly suggests that very few, if any, of those who actually died were kar sevaks. The railway booking chart for the carriage at Lucknow shows that forty-three of the seventy-two berths in carriage S-6 had confirmed bookings from there. Of these, nineteen were for adult males, nineteen were for adult females, and five were for minors. More than half of the booked passengers were therefore families travelling together and unlikely to have been kar sevaks.[12] Another twenty-three booked passengers had boarded the train at intermediate stations.[13] So, the kar sevaks boarded the S-6 coach of the train at Faizabad when it was already more or less fully booked. Therefore, all but a few of them would have had standing room only and many would have been in the vestibule or the two ends of the carriage, from where escape would have been easy. This surmise is strengthened by the fact that forty-three passengers managed to escape, and all had only minor burns and injuries. That meant that there were only four empty berths that the kar sevaks could have occupied.

Forensic examination of the dead, carried out at Ahmedabad three days later, confirmed this for it showed that while twenty of the dead were men, twenty-six were women, and twelve were children! In all, therefore, *thirty-eight of the fifty-eight dead were of the wrong sex and age to have been kar sevaks*. Among the male victims, a large number, probably the majority, would have been those who refused, or were reluctant, to leave their families and succumbed therefore to the smoke. Taking all this into account, it is unlikely that more than a handful, if any, of those killed were kar sevaks. The number may have been even smaller for, as the Concerned Citizens' Tribunal headed by Justice V.R. Krishna Iyer hinted, all but a fraction of them would have been physically fit young men who, having muscled their way onto the train, would have easily been able to force their way out.[14] That most of them did manage to do so is suggested by the fact that only five of the forty-three persons who escaped from the carriage needed to be hospitalized.

## Modi's Reaction

Confronted by a tragedy of such magnitude, any responsible government would have immediately appealed for calm, and announced a thorough probe into its cause before leaping to a conclusion. But showing a heartlessness with which the whole of India would become familiar in the coming decades, Modi did the exact opposite. On February 27, even before leaving for Godhra, Modi first addressed the Gujarat legislative assembly which was in session then, and announced without a moment's hesitation that the arson had been 'a pre-planned terrorist act and was a result of a conspiracy'.[15]

In Godhra, instead of urging people to stay calm, not take rumours and reports at face value, wait for the authorities to identify the victims and inform their next of kin, Modi set about extracting every ounce of political capital from the tragedy. This may have been his intention all along because, along with sundry ministers and advisers, he also took with him Jaideep Patel, the general secretary of the Gujarat unit of the Vishwa Hindu Parishad. Patel became the key instigator of the carnage that followed the next day.[16]

The first indication of what Modi had in mind came at around 2.00 pm when, over the strenuous objections of the Deputy Commissioner (Collector) of Godhra, Jayanti Ravi, he gave the order to stop the post mortems that were being carried out in the station. He also ordered that the charred corpses of the dead be shipped to the Sola Civil Hospital on the outskirts of Ahmedabad, where they would be received by Jaideep Patel, whom he had sent back forthwith after seeing the carriage and corpses, grasping what a political bonanza this could be.

Ms Ravi had kept Godhra calm throughout the day, at the expense of severely angering zealots in the local media who were already bent upon revenge,[17] by assuring the people hour after hour over the radio that the fire had been accidental, or had been set by miscreants who had yet to be identified. Although, in the two decades since, she has not spoken in public about precisely what passed between her and the Chief Minister, that the subsequent instruction had to have come from him was confirmed by M.L. Nalvaya, the executive magistrate of Godhra and immediate deputy to Ravi. He told the Special Investigation Team set up by the Supreme Court in 2008 that the order to send the bodies of the victims to the Sola Civil Hospital, without completing the post mortem that had already begun, and hand them over to Jaideep Patel there had come from his 'senior officer', i.e. Ravi. When he raised objections, he was told that the orders had come from 'higher up'.

Everything that followed had the feel of a choreographed ballet. The report of the Concerned Citizens' Tribunal summed it up as follows:

> It was the chief minister who declared that the Godhra incident was pre-planned when the investigating agencies had not reached such a conclusion. Shri Modi's cabinet, notably the minister for home, Shri Gordhan Zadaphiya, reiterated strongly that Pakistani hands were behind the Godhra act. These statements were irresponsible, given the sensitivity of the situation and the anger that they generated. Once they generated a climate ripe for apportioning blame, the entire Ghanchi Muslim community of Godhra was branded as criminals for the purported acts of a few among them. This allowed the Modi government in Gujarat to justify, even if it did not instigate, the systematic massacre, plunder, loot and cultural decimation of the entire Muslim community in Gujarat thereafter.

The CCT therefore rightly concluded:

> [I]t was the chief minister who decided that the charred, unidentifiable dead bodies be taken from Godhra to Ahmedabad in a motor cavalcade. As the cavalcade headed for Ahmedabad, senior members of his party and organizations affiliated to it shouted slogans and incited mobs to retaliate. The CM's role in condoning this behaviour, and in using official machinery to propagate the unsubstantiated view that the Godhra tragedy

> was a sinister conspiracy, is condemnable. *Thus, it was the chief minister who was primarily responsible for the spread of violence, post-Godhra, in the rest of Gujarat.*
>
> The VHP gave a call for a Gujarat *Bandh* on February 28 and for a *Bharat Bandh* on March 1. The Gujarat BJP president, Shri Rajendrasinh Rana, was quick to announce the state BJP's support for both the *bandh* calls, giving a clear signal to the administration that it need not take a hard line against those who enforced the *bandh*. The state government's reluctance to take adequate steps in the wake of the proposed *bandhs* amounted to an abdication of all its responsibilities and an open invitation to anarchy.[18] (Emphasis added)

In the evening of February 27, the Vishwa Hindu Parishad issued a call for a state-wide bandh in sympathy with the kar sevaks who had allegedly died in the fire. With a BJP government in power, this effectively prevented the Gujarat Police from taking the normal preventative action that police in India have been taking since times immemorial to prevent the outbreak of communal riots, which is to round up all known troublemakers—called 'history sheeters'—and put them in preventive detention for a few days till tempers cool down. As a result, while the police in Maharashtra, Andhra Pradesh and Rajasthan, the three adjoining states, detained between 7,000 and 16,000 'history sheeters' on February 27, according to its own website, while the Gujarat Police deployed a large number of policemen in defensive positions to prevent riots, they detained only two persons that night, and both were Muslims.[19]

### The Massacre That Followed

In Ahmedabad, Jaideep Patel readied cohorts of the VHP to receive the bodies when they arrived at the Sola Civil Hospital and carry them in processions around the city. The bodies arrived at around 4.00 am. In the next few hours, they were visited by virtually every BJP dignitary in the city including Pravin Togadia, Maya Kodnani (a gynaecologist and BJP legislator whom Modi later elevated to his cabinet as minister for women and child development), and Modi's home minister, Gordhan Zadafia. Then the bodies were hoisted onto the shoulders of the processionists, and the death marches around the city began.

What followed was so awful that most readers of the newspaper reports emanating from Ahmedabad (including this writer) either expressed disbelief or just blocked it from their minds. The events of just one single day in the single blackest week of India's existence as a free nation suffices to capture the horror of what followed. This is an excerpt from the Concerned Citizens' Tribunal's report on the violence that took place in Gulberg Society, Ahmedabad on February 28, which describes the killing, among others, of Ehsan Jafri, a respected Congress leader and former member of parliament from the city:

> At about 10.30 am, police commissioner Pandey, with Ambalal Nadia, the Congress *mahamantri*, Ward No. 19, and Kannulal Solanki from Ward No. 20, visited Jafri and gave him a personal assurance that they would send reinforcements and that he would be fully protected. Within five minutes of the CP's [Commissioner of Police's] departure, at 10.35 am, the Zahir Bakery and an autorickshaw just outside Gulberg society were burnt. The stoning of Gulberg society began around 11.15–11.30 am. Forty-five minutes later, at about 12.15–12.30 pm, stones, acid bulbs, bottles and petrol bombs were thrown at Gulberg Society from the rear side of the complex of buildings and bungalows. From the terrace of an adjacent bungalow belonging to a non-Muslim, between 12.30 and 12.45 pm, there was heavy stone throwing, including big boulders. This caused the biggest damage, because, without this frontal attack using premises from within the residential colony itself, the residents might have been able to protect themselves. The volley of huge stones, along with acid bulbs and burning cloth balls, continued until 1–1.15 pm. Around 1 pm, one Yusuf, a resident of the society, was caught, cut up and torched. Fear amongst the residents had mounted. By this time there were nearly 80 persons in Jafri's house. Amid shouts of '*Ghusijao*' ('Get in!'), between 2.30–2.45 pm, suddenly

the gate at the rear end of the Society, near the railway tracks, was broken down. Between 2.30–2.45 pm, Ahsan Jafri, who was clearly a specific target, allowed himself to be dragged out of his own house. There, just outside the home that he had so painfully created, for 45 minutes, he was brutally dismembered and then finally decapitated. He was stripped, paraded naked, and asked to say, '*Vande Mataram!*' and '*Jai Shri Ram!*' He refused. His fingers were chopped off and he was paraded around in the locality, badly injured. Next, his hands and feet were chopped off. He was then dragged, a fork-like instrument clutching his neck, down the road, before being thrown into the fire. A man who had devoted his life to public service, had met a brutal end. In this attack, Jafri was killed along with his three brothers and two nephews.

At this time, 2.45 pm, Anwar, another resident, was also killed. The main accused…brought in logs from the nearby Sansar Bakery and began, ominously, to prepare four funeral pyres. Anwar was killed and then cut up into pieces and burnt. There was a relentless barrage of stoning, throwing of fireballs and frontal attacks on Jafri's house in particular. This was confirmed by many eyewitnesses to the tragic carnage, all of whom deposed before the Tribunal.

After this, Shafi Mohammed Munawar Sheikh was also cut into three pieces, and burnt alive. It was between 3.30–4.30 pm that 10–12 women were first raped, then cut into pieces with *guptis*, and then thrown into the fire. The police finally arrived between 4.30–5.00 pm. At 5.20 pm, the police party that was trying to rescue the people, was stoned. Finally, at around 7 pm, the survivors were taken out of the area under police escort.

One of the eyewitnesses who was with Jafri until the end, a Parsi woman whose 12-year-old son has been missing since that day, gave the CCT an elaborate testimony. She had contacted an influential relative, a legal luminary, for help and the latter had rushed to meet the police commissioner in person. The CP then telephoned the witness and asked her, 'How many from your family are trapped there?' 'Three, Sir,' she replied, implying that there were only three Parsis trapped there—she, her daughter and son—since her husband was at the Meghani Nagar police station. She then saw the other victims around her, quickly recovered herself and said, 'No there are 40 persons here.' He then took the address but the help, when it came, was too late.

This witness had been in her verandah, in the same building as Jafri, when about 6–7 persons came to the neighbourhood to close down everything because of the *bandh*. A boy who was standing opposite had closed his shop, but they ran to beat him up. He was shouting for help, and there were 6–7 policemen also standing there, who were watching, but did not help. When his brother came to help him, they started beating him up as well. Then the first boy ran inside, to be followed by a boy with a knife. She could see them because they were in the society, but she could not see what happened to the other boy.

This witness testified that she had seen Jafri go out to meet CP Pandey at 10.30 am. Jafri returned after a few minutes, apparently reassured that forces would be sent soon. He told others that he had told the PC that if they could not send forces they should escort the Gulberg Society residents out. Children from the different homes in Gulberg Society were taking their morning tuition classes when, in panic, parents had to summon them back home.

The attackers first torched all the vehicles outside. The mobs were shouting '*Jai Sri Ram!*' and '*Kill! Slaughter! This is what they did to us in Godhra. We will do the same to them here!*' Eyewitnesses who deposed before the Tribunal deposed that the attackers had used gas cylinders from the abandoned homes as ammunition for their attacks. Chemicals were sprayed into the room, then gas cylinders thrown in after removing the seals. With fireballs providing the spark, the gas cylinders exploded like bombs. The blasts were so powerful that they made the plaster peel off walls, so much so that the structural steel rods were exposed. The attackers were pulling out the girls and killing anyone who came out of Jafri's home, either with swords or by pouring kerosene over them and torching them.

By 11 am, women had collected in Jafri's flat, bringing their valuables, fearing the worst. Witnesses also saw the mob throwing something that would fall near their houses and then burst into flames.

Despite the Police Commissioner's visit to Gulberg Society, the police did not come. Jafri kept looking outside with apprehension while he made calls to all the influential people listed in his diary. He made numerous calls including calls to Congressman Amarsingh Chaudhry, the commissioner, and the local police station.

By then, the mob had started breaking windows. They threw burning tyres inside and the women inside would catch them and throw them out. In fact the witness' hands were singed. There was no water in the house because it had all been consumed and the water from the tanks below had been leaked out by the mob. Inside, the people did all they could to save themselves in those terrible two hours. They ripped off carpets so that they did not catch fire.

At about 2–2.30 pm, the phone was disconnected. By then Jafri had begun pleading with the mob for forgiveness—he was speaking in Gujarati—and telling them to let them go. He said that all the residents of Gulberg would leave without any belongings, only their lives. But the leaders of the mob said, 'You burnt our parents, our sisters, so we will not spare you.' The Parsi lady even said, 'I am a Parsi—we are neither Hindus nor Muslims,' to which they replied, 'We know no Parsis or anything else.' They were in such a murderous mood at the time. They had been burning the kitchens in all the houses first. At about 3 pm, they even poured petrol over this witness and her 11-year-old daughter. They had brought petrol in plastic bags and they threw the bags at them so they were soaked with petrol. By this time only one room of Jafri's home was not on fire but the rest were full of smoke. Many persons collapsed due to asphyxiation. There were bodies of women and children everywhere. Many died choking from the smoke. Only the strong and the lucky could survive. The police arrived at about 4.30 pm. When the victim-survivors were escorted out by the police, the mob stoned the van. That is when PI Pathan gave orders to shoot into the crowd rather than in the air. If he had not fired, and dispersed the crowd somewhat, even the rest would have died. Even when they got into the van, the victim-survivors had only the driver with them; there were no other policemen.

There are 21 eyewitnesses to the entire case who have been consistent in their depositions before other human rights and fact-finding teams. Each of these have lost from 1–7 family members in the brutal violence. The Tribunal benefited from the detailed records of this incident, the FIRs, etc., published in *Communalism Combat*'s 'Genocide—Gujarat 2002' issue. The accused, who have been identified by eyewitnesses to have launched the first attack, are: Girish Prabhudas Sharma, Bharat Rajput, Kapil Kumar Munna…

Several eyewitnesses saw the CP arriving and talking to Jafri. 'He said to Jafri, "We are making all arrangements for you and sending additional police force—you don't worry." Jafri *sa'ab* told Pandey *sa'ab*, "If you cannot make arrangements for us and if you don't have enough men, then arrange for us to go away from here—just let us know."'

Within minutes of the commissioner's car leaving from one side, a mob appeared from the other and started throwing stones. From the Asarwa side, the ex-corporator and BJP worker, Chunilal Prajapati, was leading the mob, swearing at Muslims and shouting, 'Kill! Slaughter! See what they did in Godhra. They killed our Hindus so now kill them all, destroy their society.' From the Om Nagar side, ex-Congress municipal councillor, Meghsingh Dubsingh was leading the mob, which also started throwing stones. Jafri had opposed Dubsingh's receiving a ticket in the last elections. Muslims from the surrounding *chawls* also came into the society for protection. There is a railway line behind Gulberg Society, and from that side, where there are servants' quarters, a mob of about 5–6,000 came. They were led by Jagrup Singh Rajput, who was deputy mayor of Ahmedabad when the BJP held a majority in the municipality. Stone throwing started from the back as well. Thus, from all four sides of Gulberg Society, stone throwing was going on.

In his desperation, Jafri made over 200 calls that day. He called PC [*sic*] Pandey, Amarsingh Chaudhry in Gandhinagar, Naresh Rawal, and even the chief minister and the home minister. According to a witness, 'At about 2.30 pm, Jafri *sa'ab*, who was standing at his door with folded hands, was pulled out by four men. The four who pulled him out were: Narayan Kabra, a cable operator in Chamanpura, Ramesh Choti, a "Bhaiyaji", Manish Jain, son of the owner of Rajasthan grocery store, and Krishna, son of Champaben. (Eyewitnesses have also recorded these names in the statements made during police investigations.) As they were pulling him out, they were slashing him with a sword and they cut him up into three pieces. After burning Jafri *sa'ab*, the people who had come in started burning tyres, etc. They broke all the doors of Jafri *sa'ab*'s house and torched it from all sides. There were 35 children and everyone was begging with folded hands but they could not go out. By about 3.15 pm, Jafri's house had filled with smoke and all persons trapped inside for their safety were finding it difficult to breathe.'

Some women from inside were lured out on the pretext that they would be kept safe. Eyewitnesses who testified before the Tribunal saw Dinesh Prabhudas Sharma, who was carrying a sword, killing Yusuf [a resident of the society]. It was Lathia [*sic*] who tore the clothes off the niece of one eyewitness, raped her and then killed her. Lala Mohansingh Darbar, who was also involved in the incidents of torching earlier, killed another woman.

At around 4.45 pm, an eyewitness who had hidden himself in a cabin at the back of the small garden, heard shouts of 'Run, run!' and guessed that the police had come. This eyewitness asked ACP Tandon to rescue some of the persons suffering from asphyxiation who were trapped inside Jafri's home, but Tandon was reluctant to do anything. The attack had been planned so meticulously that the water in the tanks in Jafri's house and garden as well as those in neighbouring houses had been emptied so that the fires could not be put out.[20]

## New Delhi's Reaction

When news of the slaughter commencing in Ahmedabad on the morning of February 28 reached the Prime Minister's Office in Delhi, Vajpayee was appalled. For throughout the afternoon of February 27, and till the early hours of February 28, 2002, the one thing that Modi had not done was to call either for reinforcements, or for the army to come to the aid of civilian authority. Throughout the morning of February 28, Prime Minister Vajpayee phoned Modi repeatedly, but the phone was picked up by a lady officer, a joint secretary in his office, who kept repeating that Mr Modi was not available. In desperation, at around noon, the Prime Minister decided to send his defence minister, George Fernandes, to Ahmedabad to see Modi, and personally call in the army in defence of civil authority. Fernandes arrived in Ahmedabad in the afternoon, was appalled at the total absence of preventative measures and the inaction of the police and immediately called in the army.[21]

Unfortunately, at the time, India was engaged in Operation Parakram, the massive activation of the Indo-Pakistan front that had been ordered after Pakistani Mujahideen had almost succeeded in occupying the parliament building while a session was in progress in December 2001. So, the two brigades assigned to aid the Gujarat government were a considerable distance away.

The first brigade arrived in Ahmedabad at the midnight of the 28th, but the Gujarat government had assigned no civil authority to guide them and set them their duties, so they remained helpless all night long. The second brigade arrived in the morning, and was similarly denied civilian support, till about four hours later. Thus, it was only in the mid-morning of March 1 that the army was able to begin flag marches in the worst hit parts of the city with a magistrate accompanying each brigade to guide it and give it the order to resort to firing, if the situation warranted it. By then the huge wave of violence that had swept through Ahmedabad on February 28 had subsided (but not ended), and had spread to other cities.

In the days that followed, every action Modi took and every statement he made showed that he had already made up his mind to foster the belief that this was the result of a Muslim plot against the kar sevaks, and to extract every ounce of political capital he could squeeze out of it. On February 28, his government's initial stand was that the 'riots' were 'a spontaneous reaction' to the Godhra train carnage and that the state government and ruling party had nothing to do with it. But two days later, Modi changed his stance and aligned his government, morally, with the rioting mobs by declaring that the slaughter had resulted from the 'natural and *justified* anger of people'. He went on to add the next day that 'the five crore people of Gujarat have shown *remarkable restraint* under grave provocation'. Ten days later, after all of India had erupted in horrified protest against what he had allowed to happen in Ahmedabad, in an interview to *The Tribune* of Chandigarh, he introduced what was to become his clarion call to the people of Gujarat to rise in defence of their state and country. He blamed Pakistan for instigating the riots and said that the people of Gujarat would not tolerate attempts at giving such a 'distorted image' of the state.[22] This was the first instance of what became a common practice for him a decade later—diversion of blame for the failings of his government onto Pakistan or, during his second term as prime minister, onto the opposition.

In Delhi, Prime Minister Atal Bihari Vajpayee was horrified by Modi's deliberate dereliction of his duty during these crucial days. It is widely believed that he had intended to ask Modi to step down from the chief ministership of Gujarat at the meeting of the BJP's National Executive held in Goa on April 10, 2002, but was pre-empted by the hero's welcome that Modi received when he came to the meeting. That welcome resulted from the near-universal belief that Modi had succeeded in creating, and which persists to the present day, that all those who were burnt to death at Godhra had been kar sevaks, and that the fire in carriage S-6 was the result of a deliberate Muslim plot, and that the Muslims deserved what they got.

In April, the Concerned Citizens' Tribunal had not yet visited Gujarat, let alone written its report. So, the BJP National Executive's adulation of Modi, and the absence of unimpeachable evidence that Modi had turned a deliberate blind eye to the slaughter of Muslims tied Vajpayee's hands. He therefore chose to back down, and although he harped, in his speech, upon the secular nature of Hinduism and its acceptance of all religions as equally valid routes to salvation, he placed the blame for what had happened in Gujarat upon Muslim zealots.

'What happened in Gujarat?' he asked his audience rhetorically. 'If the conspiracy to burn alive the innocent, helpless and blameless travellers on the Sabarmati Express had not been hatched, the Gujarat tragedy could have been averted. But this did not happen. People were burnt alive. Who were those people [the culprits]? The government is inquiring into it. The intelligence agencies are gathering all the information. But we must not forget how the Gujarat tragedy began. The later incidents are condemnable, but who started the fire? How did the fire spread?'[23]

### Modi's Triumph

This was the victory over Vajpayee that turned Modi into the leader that the till-then nascent fascist movement within the BJP was looking for. It was what made the BJP, and the RSS, jettison not just Vajpayee but also his closest associates in government, L.K. Advani and Murli Manohar Joshi, after Vajpayee's electoral defeat in the 2004 parliamentary election. It also explains the RSS' choice of Narendra Modi as the BJP's prime ministerial candidate in 2014, a full eight months before the 2014 elections—another significant departure from its earlier reliance upon collective identity, ideology and service to the nation to fight elections. For, in Gujarat in 2002, and in the eleven years that followed, Narendra Modi demonstrated that he had all the traits needed for becoming the Supreme Leader of an authoritarian party that held democracy in contempt: the decisiveness needed for taking difficult decisions, the determination needed to see them through, and the demagogic power needed to make the masses believe anything he wanted them to.

CHAPTER ELEVEN

# Gujarat, 2002 to 2014

## *The Birth of an Authoritarian State*

Narendra Modi had what it would take to bring the Sangh to power. He had the capacity to sway vast numbers of people by stoking fear, grievance and righteous anger in them; to turn this anger against a minority community in order to unify the majority; to silence dissent and ensure that only one version of the truth prevails; and to build slavish loyalty by disproportionately rewarding submission and compliance with his dictates.

### Harnessing Gujarati Ethno-nationalism

Modi faced universal condemnation for failing to prevent the pogrom in Gujarat. He was condemned in the Indian media, ostracized abroad and banned from entering the USA for life—a decision that was reversed only when he became the prime minister of India. But Modi's response was to take the criticism head-on; blame 'the Muslims' incessantly for having brought it upon themselves by attacking and killing kar sevaks returning from Ayodhya; and strongly hint that they had been instigated by Pakistan. What is more, the criticism that came his way was depicted as an attack on Gujarati 'nationhood' by the rest of India and the world.

Within days of the pogrom, he approached the Election Commission and demanded that the state assembly elections, which were scheduled for April 2003, be advanced to July 2002. When the Chief Election Commissioner demurred, citing the need to first redraw the electoral boundaries of the constituencies and insisting that this could only be done after peace had returned to the state, he stopped the supply of essentials to the refugee camps, closed them down and sent a report to the Commission in July that everything had returned to normal when in fact the traumatized survivors of the carnage were still refusing to return to their burnt homes and neighbourhoods, subsisting on food and other essentials sent by the truckload by humanitarian organizations from all over the country.

Receiving no contrary inputs from the central government, the Election Commission reluctantly agreed, but advanced the elections to December 2002. That advancing of the state assembly elections served Modi's purpose: it not only denied Hindus the time for reflection and regret, but kept alive Gujarati indignation over the way in which their community had been demonized when it was *their* kar sevaks who had been the first victims. He never once said sorry, nor admitted to having second thoughts, on any future occasion. His relentless aggression kept his opponents on the defensive and steadily enlarged his larger-than-life image in Gujarat. These tactics worked, for the BJP swept back to power with 127 seats in a house of 182, ten seats more than they had won in 1998, and the Congress' share of seats went down from fifty-three to fifty-one. The BJP has not lost a single assembly election in Gujrat since then.

### Taming Big Business

But Modi did not stop there. Having aroused Gujarati hyper-nationalism to win the elections, he used it again, within months, to tame the captains of Indian industry. The detailed account in the monthly journal *The Caravan*, written thirteen years later, described the ruthlessness with which he did this:

> In February 2003, the Confederation of Indian Industry (CII)—the country's biggest and most important business trade

> association—held a special session at its auditorium in New Delhi: 'Meeting with Narendra Modi, the New Chief Minister of Gujarat'. The meeting was organized after a special request from Modi: he had just won a resounding victory in state elections in the wake of the riots, but he was still facing public condemnation from national business leaders and dealing with an economy reeling from the impact of the violence…
>
> In the months after the riots, some of corporate India's biggest names had publicly voiced their anger and concern… compared the violence against Muslims in Gujarat to 'a genocide'… Two of Bangalore's biggest IT chieftains, Narayana Murthy of Infosys and Azim Premji of Wipro, issued strong public condemnations. At a CII national meeting in April 2002, the chairwoman of the energy major Thermax, Anu Aga, received a standing ovation after delivering an impassioned speech about the suffering of Muslims in Gujarat.
>
> Modi knew he was under pressure But he also knew that… Gujarat, riots or no riots, was of critical importance to the chieftains of Indian business. He came to Delhi to mend his image with the captains of industry, but…on his own terms.

After being severely criticized by both his co-speakers, Rahul Bajaj, chairman of Bajaj Motors, the world's largest producer of two-wheelers, and Jamshed Godrej, scion of one of the oldest engineering companies in India, he responded:

> 'You and your pseudo-secular friends,' Modi roared at the leaders of Indian industry, 'can come to Gujarat if you want an answer. Talk to my people. Gujarat is the most peaceful state in the country.' … [T]urning to Godrej and Bajaj Modi continued: 'Others have vested interest in maligning Gujarat. What is your interest?'

Returning to Gandhinagar, he showed his mettle:

> Within a few days, a group of Gujarati businessmen close to Modi—including Gautam Adani of Adani Group, Indravadan Modi of Cadila Pharmaceuticals, Karsan Patel of Nirma

> Group, and Anil Bakeri of Bakeri Engineers, established a rival organization, which they called the Resurgent Group of Gujarat (RGG), whose members threatened to withdraw from the CII on the grounds that it had humiliated and insulted Modi *and all Gujaratis* and demanded that the Gujarat chapter of the CII resign for 'failing to protect the interests of the state'.
>
> Faced with an open revolt from a crucial state and its powerful business community, Tarun Das had good reason to worry: more than 100 companies from Gujarat were threatening to leave the CII, which would cripple the organization's presence in Western India.[1]

After several consultations in Delhi, from which he learned that Modi would accept nothing less than a written apology from CII, its chief Tarun Das wrote the following letter: 'We, in the CII, are very sorry for the hurt and pain you have felt, and I regret very much the misunderstanding that has developed since the 6th of February, the day of our meeting in New Delhi.'[2]

Three months later, in a further gesture of reconciliation, the CII helped Modi organize his first international meeting with investors in Zurich, under the aegis of the World Economic Forum. Modi's victory was complete.

But that victory did not make Modi complacent. Having created the myth that Godhra had been a Muslim plot to take revenge upon devout Hindus, he tirelessly reinforced this version of 'the facts' by constantly accusing 'Muslims' of seeking Pakistan's aid in order to take revenge for the massacres of February and March. With a born actor's instinct for drama, Modi made himself the target of most of the plots, allegedly hatched in Pakistan, that the police later claimed to have foiled.

## Merging Hyper-nationalism with Paranoia: Attack on the Akshardham Temple

The opportunity to bring Pakistan into the picture arose when two terrorists, Murtaza Hafiz Yasin and Ashraf Ali Mohammed Farooq, alias Shakeel and Abdullah, who belonged to the Pakistan-based Lashkar-e-Tayyiba and the Jaish-e-Mohammed, forced their way into the Akshardham Temple in Gandhinagar, the capital of Gujarat, on September 24, 2002, and opened fire with machine guns and grenades indiscriminately upon whosoever came within their sights. The two were killed after a fourteen-hour gun battle, but not before they had killed thirty men, women and children including two police officers and two commandos, and injured another eighty, including twenty-three policemen.

The investigation by the Gujarat Police that followed confirmed the identity of the terrorists, and established that they had had local help. But on August 29, 2003, three days after the Commissioner of Police informed the media that it had arrested five Gujarati Muslims for having aided the assassins, and that the plot had been hatched in Riyadh, Saudi Arabia, the Jammu and Kashmir Police announced that it had arrested a key Indian link in the plot, a man named Chand Khan who hailed from Bareilly, in Uttar Pradesh, and claimed that he had brought the two terrorists down from Kashmir to Ahmedabad. Chand Khan maintained that the plot had not been hatched in Riyadh but by the LeT chief in Anantnag, a hotbed of militancy in south Kashmir.

The timing of his arrest, and the alacrity with which he gave an interview to the *Times of India* while in custody, giving precise details of how he had brought the terrorists down to Ahmedabad, were suspicious because they seemed designed to sow reasonable doubt into the Gujarat Police's case against the five whom it had arrested.[3] His claim that he had done it for the Rs 30,000 the LeT chief in Anantnag gave him was also unconvincing, because it seemed too small a sum, even in 2002, to risk one's life for. But in a significant disclosure, he also claimed that the LeT's original plan had been to assassinate Modi when he launched his first *Gaurav Yatra* to reinforce Gujarati pride, on September 8.

Chand Khan's confession forced the Gujarat Police to widen its inquiry in order to find a way of including him in its indictment. This proved difficult because, by September 2003, most of the conspirators he named had taken shelter in Pakistan, and Saudi

Arabia, with which India did not have an extradition treaty. The police, however, eventually got its convictions for the trial court convicted all six defendants, and sentenced three of them, including Chand Khan, to death in 2006.[4]

The struggle the police had had to wage to get the Akshardham trial concluded must have left a sour taste in the mouths of its departmental heads and hardened their resolve to short circuit the process of obtaining 'justice' and discourage future attacks within Gujarat. This is probably why, in the four years that followed, a police force that had once been considered among the most disciplined in the country went on a killing spree. Between 2003 and 2006, there were no fewer than twenty-one 'encounter killings' in Gujarat, and in nearly all of these the victims were labelled as assassins sent, or recruited, by Pakistan to kill Narendra Modi.

To Mr Modi, however, the attack on Akshardham, and Chand Khan's well publicized statement that Modi had been its original target, provided another opportunity to burnish his image as a fearless leader of the Hindu race and consolidate his hold on power. If he did not ask the police to pass off its 'encounters' as successful bids to foil attacks on his life, he certainly did nothing to dissuade the police from doing so.

### Taming the Administration

The immediate challenge Modi faced after returning to power was to ensure that the bureaucracy and police toed his line. This was not an easy task because the independence of the bureaucracy was guarded not only by the Constitution but by layer upon layer of subsequent legislation designed to prevent the filing of cases against specific officials in courts of law. But there was one yawning gap in this hedge of protection: all of it was designed to protect the civil service against assaults from outside the government, e.g. by civil society, through the judiciary. None of these were designed to protect it from attacks by its political bosses. Modi took full advantage of this vulnerability to make the bureaucracy and police into the principal instrument of his transformative policies. He did so by punishing those who opposed him and rewarding those who served him faithfully, with a cavalier disregard for civil service rules, norms and ethics.

The most serious accusation that Modi faced after the 2002 riots was that he had not only turned a blind eye to the orgy of killing that began on February 28th but had instructed his police chiefs at a late evening meeting after he returned from Godhra on February 27, not to 'control the Hindu backlash' that the arrival of the corpses in Ahmedabad the next morning was bound to provoke. If this could have been established it would have ended his political career. The fact that he went on to become the prime minister of India makes it evident that none of these attempts, right till the final one before the Supreme Court of India in 2022, succeeded. On the contrary, in 2012, a Special Investigation Team (SIT) appointed by the Supreme Court to investigate several especially brutal killings in Ahmedabad, indicted a large number of VHP, Bajrang Dal and BJP members but absolved Modi of all charges of incitement and collusion. The Supreme Court ignored the report of its own *amicus curiae* on the SIT's functioning and conclusions, and accepted the report of the latter. The cloud under which Modi had lived for ten years finally lifted.

But guilt or innocence in a court of law depends upon how high the judges decide to raise the bar of proof. And in Modi's case, as in some others discussed below, there is a widespread consensus that not only various commissions of inquiry, but the Gujarat High Court and even the Supreme Court have raised the bar of proof too high.

### *How Modi Turned a Blind Eye to the Slaughter of Innocents*

If Modi did not *instruct*, as distinct from *suggest* or *indicate* what he wanted done, there is abundant evidence that his officials, with only a few exceptions, took the cue from his inaction and his calculated silences, and acted according to his wishes. The CCT's account of the assault on the Gulberg Society presented in the previous chapter provides ample proof of this: 'The attack on

Gulberg society…was launched with military precision from 7.30 am to 4.30 pm on Thursday, February 28. A 20–25,000-strong mob surrounded the Chamanpura area in the heart of Ahmedabad city. The FIR lodged by K.G. Erda[5] of the Meghani Nagar police station itself gives a detailed account of the utter failure of the police to put off the assailants or protect the trapped residents. The FIR admits that the arson and destruction began from that morning itself.'

The behaviour of the Gujarat Police, all throughout that fateful day, and in the months that followed, suggests that it had to have been acting under some kind of severe constraint imposed upon it from above. P.P. Pandey, the commissioner of police, visited Ehsan Jafri at 10.30 in the morning after receiving agonized calls from him, and promised to send police to protect the society, but none came till 4.30 in the evening, by when Jafri, his three brothers and sixty-five other people had been killed, raped, hacked to pieces, and burned.

All over the town the police received reports of the premeditated and organized slaughter that was taking place but did very little. When it did use extreme force, it was mostly against Muslims. For in May 2002, the Gujarat Police admitted that of the 184 persons it had killed in the aftermath of Godhra, 104 had been *Muslims*, although nearly all the violence the state had experienced had been initiated by enraged *Hindu* mobs.[6]

As that dreadful day wore on, a pattern of behaviour by the police gradually emerged. Two reports obtained by the Associated Press from the Ahmedabad police records, show just how helpless conscientious local police personnel must have felt throughout the day:

> Kirit Erda, senior inspector-in-charge of the Meghaninagar police station reported that nine people, including local Bharatiya Janata Party leader Deepak Patel, headed the mob that burned to death 42 people, including former Parliament member Ehsan Jaffrey, in the Muslim neighbourhood known as Gulberg Society in Meghaninagar. 'These persons, armed

> with weapons, led a mob of 20,000 to 22,000, which attacked Gulberg Society and set it ablaze. They first burned to death 18 residents and later burned 24 more persons in the same place,' Erda wrote in Gujarati.
>
> A separate report dealing with the Naroda Patia killings squarely blamed members of the [Vishwa Hindu Parishad]. 'The carnage at Naroda Patia was the handiwork of a mob of 6,000, which was led by Babu Bajrangi, Kishan Kosani, T.J. Rajput, Harish Rohit and Raju Goyal,' wrote N.T. Bala, an assistant police sub-inspector stationed at the local police station. 'These people, possessing deadly weapons, led the mob of about 6,000, all belonging to the Hindu community,' Bala's report detailed how the mob set fire to 24 homes, killing the 65 Muslims inside.[7]

In the deluge of requests for instructions and reinforcements that the police control room must have received, there had to have been several that specifically requested reinforcements, and permission to open fire on the mobs if the need arose. That permission was almost never given. A report by Human Rights Watch detailed why:

> Panicked phone calls made to the police, fire brigades, and even ambulance services generally proved futile. Many witnesses testified that their calls either went unanswered or that they were met with responses such as: 'We don't have any orders to save you'; 'We cannot help you, we have orders from above'; 'If you wish to live in Hindustan, learn to protect yourself'; 'How come you are alive? You should have died too'; 'Whose house is on fire? Hindus' or Muslims'?' In some cases phone lines were eventually cut to make it impossible to call for help.[8]

At the Gulberg Society, not only did the police not come to the rescue of the besieged Muslim families till 4.30 pm, *nine hours* after the attack had begun, but Sub-Inspector Pathan, as the CCT report mentions, only gave the order to open fire on the Hindu mob when it began to stone the police van in which he was evacuating the survivors. In short, the police opened fire on the mob *only in self-defence, when it came under attack*. This suggests that the station house officers and police inspectors were not in the loop. If there was an order given, or even an understanding, that the police should go easy on rioters extracting 'revenge' from Muslims for Godhra, it had been communicated only to the senior police officers. Lack of instructions and support from above did the rest.

That would explain why no sooner had a senior police officer, Praveen Gondia, registered FIRs charging Jaideep Patel and Maya Kodnani with participating in the massacres than he was transferred, and the FIRs mysteriously vanished.[9] It would also explain why Erda's reports from Meghani Nagar received no response; why P.P. Pandey's visit to Jafri was followed by *six hours of inaction* till the killing at the Gulberg Society had all but ended; and why the call data records sent to his seniors by Rahul Sharma (more on him later), superintendent of police of Bhavnagar district, later disappeared, like Gondia's FIR.

Finally, it would explain why Modi posted two cabinet ministers unconnected with police matters, I.K. Jadeja and Ashok Bhatt, at the Gujarat and Ahmedabad Police Control Rooms, respectively, throughout the day. Neither had any connection with the police, so could not therefore have been there to give them instructions. Their purpose could only have been to act as monitors to ensure that *instructions that had already been given were being carried out*.

This was the conclusion to which the Supreme Court arrived in September 2003 while hearing the National Human Rights Commission's petition challenging a series of acquittals by the Gujarat High Court of persons accused in the Best Bakery case—which involved the burning down on March 1, 2002, of a bakery in Vadodara where a Muslim family had taken refuge, resulting in the deaths of fourteen people. Chief Justice V.N. Khare of the Supreme Court told the Gujarat government's lawyers: '*I have no faith left in the prosecution and the Gujarat government. If you fail to act then we will have to step in. We are not sitting here as mere spectators.*' When that still did not have the desired effect, the Supreme Court transferred the case out of Gujarat. While doing so, Justice Arijit Pasayat[10] of the SC declared in April 2004:

> The modern day 'Neros' were looking elsewhere when the Best Bakery and innocent children and helpless women were burning and were probably deliberating on how the perpetrators of the crime can be saved or protected…
>
> When the investigating agency helps the accused, the witnesses are threatened to [make them] depose falsely, [the] prosecutor acts in a manner as if he was defending the accused, and the Court is acting merely as an onlooker, there is no fair trial at all, [and] justice becomes the victim.[11]

Modi maintained steadfastly that he had no knowledge of the events at Gulberg Society until he was briefed by police officers later in the evening of February 28. But Sanjiv Bhatt, who was then the state deputy commissioner (Intelligence), but later became one of the principal targets of Modi's wrath, told Vinod Jose, writing for the *Caravan*, that Modi was lying. Bhatt insisted that Modi, who was also the home minister then, was in regular contact with the senior police and intelligence officers throughout the day, and was well informed about what was happening on the ground. He himself had spoken with Modi over the phone several times before 2 pm, and reported that a mob had circled Gulberg Society. He said that he met Modi at his office in the afternoon to report that the situation demanded immediate intervention.[12] Bhatt goes on:

> 'His response was very strange. He listened and then said, "Sanjiv, try to find out if in the past Jafri has been in the habit of opening fire."
>
> 'Outside the chief minister's office, in the corridor, I bumped into the former chief minister Amarsinh Choudhary and former home minister Naresh Rawal,' Bhatt continued, referring to two Congress leaders. 'Naresh Rawal was my minister earlier, so we talked. They told me "Gulberg Ehsanbhai has been giving [us] frantic calls", and they had come to meet Modi. I said I had briefed the CM, "but you also go and tell him".'

What followed, according to Bhatt, was stranger still:

> 'I then got a call on my cell phone from my informer on the site at Gulberg, telling me that Jafri had opened fire. I was surprised. But when I reached my office, a short report was lying on the table saying Jafri opened fire in self-defence. That was when I realized that this man [Modi] knows things even before I come to know of them.'[13]

This could only have happened if Modi had been directly in touch with at least some key members in the murdering mobs.

Bhatt also confirmed that others had tried desperately to intercede with Modi on Jafri's behalf, but were met with no response. If Bhatt was telling the truth to Jose, Modi's question was not an idle one. He had already heard that Ehsan Jafri had opened fire on the mob attacking the Gulberg Society and was looking for a reason to put the blame for the slaughter that followed upon Jafri himself. It became the explanation his government later gave for the massacre in every inquiry that followed.

Modi was therefore already looking for ways to protect his political future. In this he succeeded beyond what would then have been his wildest dreams. For in its report exonerating him, the SIT appointed by the Supreme Court of India reported that 'In his interview the CM has clearly referred to Jafri's firing as "action" and the massacre as "reaction". *It may be clarified here that in case the late Ehsaan Jafri had fired at the mob, this could be an immediate provocation to the mob, which had assembled there to take revenge of Godhra incidents from Muslims.*' (Emphasis added)

The SIT did not ask itself why Jafri would have taken the most provocative action anyone could have taken—to open fire on an agitated crowd that had not yet turned violent, when as a seasoned politician, he could not but have known how it would react. This was one of several conclusions it reached that show that its setting up was no more than a charade designed to exonerate Modi of any blame for the slaughter that had taken place. It managed to retain its credibility while doing this by pointing the finger of guilt at thirty-four others. These included Maya Kodnani, a minister in Modi's government, Jaideep Patel, the deputy chief of the VHP who had accompanied him to Godhra and arranged the reception and parading of the corpses in Ahmedabad the following day, and Babu Bajrangi, the head of the Bajrang Dal in Ahmedabad at that time. It was only when it came to Modi's culpability, for the inaction of the police, that the SIT raised the bar of proof so high that it virtually ruled out the possibility of a court entertaining a case against Modi in the future.

### *The Persecution of Rahul Sharma*

Not all the bureaucracy cooperated with Modi on February 28th. This brought out the vindictive worst in his personality. Among the first to be 'punished' for doing his duty was Rahul Sharma, the superintendent of police of Bhavnagar district. A young man in his mid-thirties who had joined the All-India Police Service in 1992, Sharma ordered the police to fire on a mob of several hundred rioters that was attacking a *madrassa* that housed 300 school children, and saved their lives, but at the cost of the lives of some of the attackers. For this, he was transferred immediately to a desk job in the police control room in Ahmedabad. If this was intended to tame him it failed miserably for, at the suggestion of a senior colleague, A.K. Sirolia, he obtained the call data records of mobile phones used in the Ahmedabad area on February 28 from two private companies, saved them on his home computer, and copied them onto two CDs which he sent to his senior officers. One of the recipients was the Commissioner of Police, P.P. Pandey, the same officer who had visited Jafri on February 28, but not fulfilled his promise to send the police to protect, or evacuate, him and his family. To Sharma's surprise, the records simply disappeared, and he heard nothing more about them until he was asked to testify before an inquiry commission under a former Supreme Court judge, G.T. Nanavati, on the events of February 28 in Ahmedabad. This gave him an opportunity to enter the call data records into the evidence on the riots.

Sharma also gave the records to two other commissions of inquiry, the Justice U.C. Banerjee Commission set up by the Congress-led government of Dr Manmohan Singh in 2005, and to the Special Investigation Team set up by the Supreme Court in 2008. He also gave them to the Jana Sangharsh Morcha, a legal-aid NGO helping the Naroda Patiya victims. The JSM's analysis of the call data for February 28 showed that Jaideep Patel and Maya Kodnani had been in touch with the Chief Minister's office, and with the minister of state for home affairs, Gordhan Zadafia, throughout the day, and that their calls had originated from the Naroda Patiya and Naroda Gam areas, where some of the worst pogroms, involving the killing of women and children, had taken place. This became a principal document in the trial of Kodnani and Jaideep Patel that followed several years later.

The call data records that Sharma had obtained also showed that throughout the day the police control room had received innumerable phone calls from officers in the field asking for directives on what they should do, but they had been issued none. On the contrary, Inspector K.K. Mysorewala, the senior police officer at the Naroda Patiya police station, was found to have been in constant touch with Bipin Panchal, one of the main accused in the Naroda Patiya massacre, and with Jaideep Patel.

The persecution of Rahul Sharma did not end with his transfer in 2002. In August 2011, alarmed by the evidence provided by him and its potential impact on the state's politicians, including Chief Minister Modi, the Gujarat government issued a charge sheet against him accusing him of gross misconduct and violation of his service rules. Sharma resigned from the police and is now practising law in Ahmedabad.

### *The Punishment of Himanshu Bhatt*

Another police officer who was punished for doing his duty was Himanshu Bhatt, the superintendent of police at Banaskantha, a district headquarter close to the Pakistan border, 200 kilometres from Ahmedabad. He was among the handful of courageous police officers who resisted the government's pressure to minimize action against the rioters. He immediately suspended a police sub-inspector whom he caught brandishing a sword after joining the rioters. Bhatt was actually reprimanded by the government for doing so and transferred to a junior post in the intelligence branch. Bhatt took study leave to pursue a course at Harvard University. When he returned, he was denied any posting in his parent cadre, and was forced to resign from the police. In an act of singular vindictiveness, the government reinstated the sub-inspector whom Bhatt had suspended, and put him in charge of the same police station from where he had joined the rioters and terrorized the Muslims.[14]

In another similar vindictive act, the government removed M.D. Antani from the post of superintendent of police of Bharuch (formerly Broach) district, at the mouth of the Narmada river, and parked him in a desk job at Ahmedabad. His crime too was that he stopped a mob of rioters intent upon murder in the city.[15]

### *Jayanti Ravi and Raju Bhargava: Modi's Animus Against Muslims on Full Display*

Modi's determination to crush the independence of the bureaucracy and police remained undiminished. In July 2002, he transferred Jayanti Ravi, the collector of Godhra, and Raju Bhargava, superintendent of police of the Panchmahal district (in which Godhra falls) to other, relatively minor, posts. Ravi had vehemently questioned Modi's decision to send the bodies of the Godhra victims to Ahmedabad. In July, she got shifted to the post of commissioner for the mid-day meal scheme. Ravi has spent the rest of her career in the Indian Administrative Service in a succession of low-profile posts, many outside the state. At the time of writing, she was the chairperson of the Auroville Trust at Puducherry.

Raju Bhargava was also transferred in July, on the very next day. He had incurred the wrath of local BJP leaders by preventing them from indulging in the orgy of killing that followed the burning of the train. Local newspapers exposed the punitive nature of these transfers by reporting that they were designed to appease the district unit of the BJP, which had protested vehemently against the widespread arrest of party leaders in the district after the February–March violence. The BJP MP from Godhra, Bhupendrasinh Solanki, had been adamant in his demand because these two officers had arrested nearly 250 BJP leaders in the district. The transfers came only days after Ravi and Bhargava had been highly commended by the National Human Rights Commission for containing violence in the district where the anti-Muslim pogrom had begun. The Commission had observed that while the Gujarat courts had given bail to nearly 90 per cent of the persons arrested for substantive offences, they had been unable to do so in Panchmahal because of the thorough job done by the police. As a result, the majority of those arrested were still behind bars.

Modi's reaction to this was not to commend Ravi and Bhargava, but to punish them. More than his other controversial and widely discussed actions, it is this targeting of two junior officers, who were performing their duty quietly and unassumingly with immense courage two hundred kilometres from Ahmedabad, that reveals the depth of his animus against Muslims, his contempt for the law and his determination to trample on anyone or anything that stood in his way. Bhargava's fellow police officer, Sanjiv Bhatt, who was to become the principal target of Modi's vengefulness a few years later, noted, 'If anyone likes to speak out the truth the government ensures that there is a strong message to other officers that we [*sic*] will not tolerate truth coming out.'

### *Geetha Johri and Rajnish Rai*

Yet another police officer who also bore the full weight of Modi's wrath was Rajnish Rai. Rai fell foul of the Modi government and blighted his career when he arrested three senior police officers, D.G. Vanzara and R.K. Pandian of the Gujarat Police, and N.K. Amin of the Rajasthan Police, for the murder of Sohrabuddin

Sheikh. The latter, a small time gangster, was killed in a faked encounter on November 26, 2004, on the grounds that he had become an accomplice of the Pakistani terrorist organization, the Lashkar-e-Tayyiba, in its planned assassination of a 'prominent local leader', i.e. Modi, in revenge for the 2002 pogrom.

When Sohrabuddin's brother Rubabuddin filed a petition in the Supreme Court asking for a full investigation of his killing, the Court asked the Gujarat government to investigate the circumstances of the killing and submit a report to it. The state government delegated the task to the Indian Police Service's first ever female police officer from Gujarat, Geetha Johri. Johri concluded that this had been a faked encounter, planned and executed by the above three officers who had, for good measure, also murdered Sohrabuddin's wife, who was with him when he was arrested. Among the many pieces of evidence that led her to that conclusion was the fact that the motorcycle Sohrabuddin was allegedly riding while trying to escape belonged to the cousin of a policeman.

Johri had also listed several reasons for suspecting that the killings had been done at the behest of Modi's minister of state for home affairs and principal confidant in Gujarat, Amit Shah. This had brought her into direct conflict with her superiors in the police, who took the investigation away from her and gave it to another, very senior, police officer. That happened to be Deputy Inspector General Rajnish Rai.

Rai proved an even harder nut to crack than Johri for, without further ado, he arrested the three officers she had indicted for the murder of Sohrabuddin Sheikh and his wife, Kausar Bi. This set the cat among the pigeons because the three were part of a select group of officers that had been involved in virtually all of the encounter killings of alleged Pakistani terrorists that had built Modi's larger than life image in Gujarat. Taking advantage of a protest that Rubabuddin had lodged with the Supreme Court earlier, the government handed the case back to Johri. Johri reportedly had a major confrontation with her superiors, but the version of the report that finally went to the Supreme Court had amendments that evidently dissatisfied the judges. So, they came to the conclusion that the Gujarat administration could no longer be trusted and directed the Central Bureau of Investigation (CBI) to take over the case.

Geetha Johri's report could not, however, be suppressed indefinitely. On May 5, 2007, *The Hindu* published a report that blew the lid off the case and fully vindicated Johri and Rai. Disclosing that it had been given a photocopy of the twenty-four-page report by 'a privileged source within the Bharatiya Janata Party', *The Hindu*'s report stated the following:

> In Part B of the report, she [Johri] records these 'important facts' relating to repeated attempts by the accused and Mr Shah to sabotage the enquiry. The IGP and Mr Solanki [member of Johri's investigative team] faced 'no hurdle' in their enquiry up to a point. 'However, as soon as the statements of witnesses pertaining to confinement of Sohrabuddin and Kausarbi in the Farm House of Shri Girish Patel at Ahmedabad came to be recorded, it came to the knowledge of Shri Vanzara and Shri Rajkumar Pandian [two of the accused officers]. It is further learnt that these officers brought the above facts to the notice of Respondent No. 2, Shri Amit Shah, Minister of State for Home, Government of Gujarat.'
>
> The report states that Mr Shah 'brought to bear pressure' on the enquiry process, with the result that Ms Johri was directed to suspend the enquiry and the enquiry papers were taken away from her 'under the guise of scrutiny'. The report also links [Sheikh's associate Tulsiram] Prajapati's 'escape' from jail and subsequent fake encounter death to the 'stalled enquiry'.
>
> Mr Shah even 'directed Shri G.C. Raigar, Additional Director General of Police, CID (Crime & Railways) to provide him with the list of witnesses, both police and private, who are yet to be contacted by CID (Crime) for recording their statement in the said enquiry. Such direction of Minister of State for Home goes beyond the scope of his office, was patently illegal and apparently designed to provide the same list to accused police

> officers…so as to enable them to take measures in their defence.' Mr Shah's influence also led to Ms Johri being instructed 'orally' not to register a First Information Report.
>
> But this was not all. Mr Shah called a meeting of senior police officers, including the DGP, at Circuit House, Gandhinagar on January 30, 2006. 'In that meeting,' the report says, 'he attempted to influence the Investigating Agency into believing that Smt Kausarbi was not a lawfully married wife of Sohrabuddin and that she might have run away somewhere. It is reliably learnt that the Minister in [the] course of [the] conversation with the senior officers had admitted in a cavalier manner that Smt Kausarbi had been killed as well.'[16]

This did not help Rai, however. He faced a continued barrage of harassment, with frequent transfers to punishment postings in remote places. He first took refuge in a three-year study leave at the Indian Institute of Management in Ahmedabad, then a request for a transfer to the central government, and finally resigned from the Indian Police Service. However, before he handed back the investigation to Johri, he had managed to retain a copy of the call data records of the three policemen which showed extensive discussions with the Home Minister. He handed these over to 'his senior officers', one presumes in the CBI.[17]

### *The Fate of Sanjiv Bhatt*

Severe and unjust as it was, the victimization of these officers paled into insignificance before that of Sanjiv Bhatt. In the aftermath of the Gujrat pogrom, no one was treated more harshly by the Modi government than its first whistleblower, Sanjiv Bhatt. Bhatt was a superintendent of police in the intelligence branch of the Gujarat Police in 2002. As has been described earlier, he had spoken to Modi several times during the early afternoon of February 27th to inform him of the pogrom that was developing and the urgent need to direct the police to intervene. He said nothing in public about his role, however, preferring to swallow his discomfort and carry on with his duties. But when the Supreme Court-appointed

SIT summoned him to depose before it in 2008, this same sense of duty, and the oath he had to swear, made him tell it everything he knew, and what he revealed was dynamite.

In an affidavit he submitted to the SIT, he said that he had attended the meeting at the Chief Minister's residence on February 27 in the place of his chief, D.C. Raigar, who was on leave when the crisis began. Bhatt stated that he had driven there with the director general of police, Chakravarthi, and been followed there by his car driven by his driver K.D. Panth. He produced an affidavit from Panth attesting that he had indeed driven behind Bhatt to the Chief Minister's residence.[18]

Bhatt stated in his affidavit that

> Mr Narendra Modi said that the bandh call had already been given, and the party had decided to support the same, as incidents like the burning of kar sevaks at Godhra could not be tolerated. He further impressed upon the gathering that for too long, the Gujarat police had been following the principle of balancing its actions against the Hindus and Muslims while dealing with communal riots. This time, the situation warranted that the Muslims be taught a lesson to ensure that such incidents do not recur ever again. The Chief Minister, Mr Modi, expressed the view that emotions were running very high amongst the Hindus, and it was imperative that they be allowed to vent out their anger.

The officials present, he went on, tried to warn Mr Modi that his decision to bring the bodies of the kar sevaks burnt in the Godhra train carnage to Ahmedabad could cause widespread communal riots across the state, and that the police neither had the manpower nor resources to deal with such a situation. Mr Modi, however, was unrelenting and told the police officers that an incident like the burning of the kar sevaks could not be tolerated. The Muslims had to 'be taught a lesson'.[19]

Unfortunately for Bhatt, he got no confirmation of his statement from any of the others who had been present at the meeting. In their depositions before the SIT, all of the officers denied that Sanjiv Bhatt had even been present at the meeting. Nor was even one of them prepared to confirm that Modi had given any such specific instruction.

When Bhatt's driver, Panth, also announced his intention to withdraw his earlier affidavit, Bhatt asked the SIT for permission to be present when it questioned him. But far from conceding his request, which was understandable because of the driver's sudden 'U' turn, the SIT accused him of deliberately trying to intimidate a witness, thereby tampering with evidence, and accused him of acting on behalf of 'rival political interests', i.e. the Congress. But *Bhatt had not lied*, for as Harsh Mander, a former Indian Administrative Service officer turned civil rights activist later revealed, a BBC correspondent had also accompanied the driver in Bhatt's car to the Chief Minister's residence.

No one in the Gujarat government contacted BBC to find out if this was indeed true, but DGP Chakravarthi's driver, Tarachand Yadav, told the *Indian Express* on April 23, 2011, after Bhatt's affidavit to the Supreme Court had become public, that he had indeed driven Bhatt with Chakravarthi to the meeting, with the former's car following them. He also told *The Hindu* that the SIT had been extremely hostile to him, had grilled him six times, demanding that he prove he was speaking the truth by giving the license plate number and make of the car he was driving. When he said that after nine years had passed, he had driven countless cars in between, and that he could no longer remember the number and make of Bhatt's car, the SIT threatened to send him to jail if he did not tell the truth. For the SIT, 'impartial investigation' obviously meant turning over every stone in an attempt to find reason hidden beneath one of them.

This bias in the SIT's report was fully exposed by Raju Ramachandran, the *amicus curiae* who was appointed by the Supreme Court, in a parallel case filed by Zakia Jafri, the widow of Ehsan Jafri. In a searing analysis of this report, Ramachandran, who had been given all of the records of the proceedings of the

SIT, concluded that Gujarat Chief Minister Narendra Modi could be proceeded against for various offences during the 2002 riots, including 'promoting enmity among different groups'.

He strongly disagreed with a key conclusion of the former CBI director R.K. Raghavan-led SIT: that IPS officer Sanjiv Bhatt was not present at a late-night meeting at the Chief Minister's residence on February 27, 2002. He said there was no clinching material available in the pre-trial stage to disbelieve Mr Bhatt, and that, given its seriousness, the veracity of his claim could be tested only in court. 'Hence, it cannot be said, at this stage, that Shri Bhatt should be disbelieved and no further proceedings should be taken against Shri Modi,' he concluded.

Highlighting the glaring divergence between the SIT's findings in its preliminary report, and its final conclusions, the *amicus curiae* also disagreed vehemently with the SIT's reasoning that 'even if Mr Modi had told the police during the riots to allow the Hindus to vent their anger over the massacre of 56 kar sevaks in the Godhra train burning incident, the mere statement of those in the confines of a room does not constitute an offence… Further, even if such allegations are believed for the sake of argument, mere statement of alleged words in the four walls of a room does not constitute any offence'. In other words, an instruction could not be considered to have been given if it was not in writing.

The reasoning behind the SIT's conclusion defies understanding. The VHP had announced its bandh just after 8.00 pm in the evening. The meeting at the Chief Minister's residence therefore had to have taken place at the latest between 9.00 and 10.00 pm. The purpose of the meeting should not, indeed could not, have been just to mull over what might or might not happen, but to chart a course of action that would minimize violence the next day. So, if Mr Modi did not instruct them to 'allow the Hindus to vent their anger over the massacre of 56 kar sevaks in the Godhra train burning incident', what *did* he discuss? Did he discuss how to contain the anticipated Hindu reaction? Did he discuss police deployments? Did he ask the Home Secretary to deploy the state's armed constabulary? Did he ask his officers which areas of the state were likely to be the most violence prone? Did he instruct them to call out the BSF, the CRPF, or the two brigades of the army designated to assist civilian authority in the maintenance of public order that are assigned to every state government? The fact that no one present mentioned that any of these issues had been discussed shows that *the prevention of the violence they anticipated the next day was not on their agenda.*

It is the *absence* of these questions from the SIT's report that exposes the dishonesty of its members. All of them seem to have known from the beginning that their task was to identify for punishment not the *planners* of the anticipated violence but only its *perpetrators*. Only on this basis could it have concluded that a mere statement by the chief minister within the four walls of a room of what was likely to happen the next day did not constitute an offence.

'In my opinion', *amicus curiae* Ramachandran wrote, 'the offences which can be made out against Shri Modi, at this prima facie stage, are offences, *inter alia*, under Sections 153 A (1) (a) & (b) (statements promoting enmity between communities), 153B (1) (c) (imputations and assertions prejudicial to national interest), 166 (public servant disobeying a direction of the law with intent to cause injury) and 505 (2) (statements conducing to public mischief) of the IPC.'

On the SIT's dismissal of Bhatt as an unreliable witness Ramachandran said: 'The stage for believing or disbelieving a witness arises after trial, i.e. once the entire evidence is placed before the court for its consideration… [T]he question whether Shri Bhatt was present at the meeting…and whether Mr Modi had indeed made such a statement, can only be decided by a court of law.'[20]

Ramachandran conceded that Mr Bhatt had not behaved like 'a detached police officer' and had actively strategized with others, but did not agree that this alone was sufficient to disregard the weight of his testimony at the preliminary stage of a police investigation. 'It does not appear very likely', he concluded, 'that a serving police officer would make such a serious allegation against Mr Modi, the Chief Minister of the State, without some basis.' Significantly, he added that 'There is *no documentary material of any nature whatsoever which can establish that Shri Bhatt was not present in the meeting on 27.02.2002*' (emphasis added).

It was not till *Tehelka* journalist Rana Ayyub published *The Gujarat Files*, a book based upon an eight-month-long sting operation in which, posing as a Hindu NRI filmmaker from the USA, she interviewed and secretly recorded dozens of officials and politicians who had been in the government in 2002, that an explanation for Sanjiv Bhatt's simultaneous presence and absence in the February 27 meeting finally surfaced.

Speaking informally to a person he believed to be a Hindu NRI filmmaker from the USA, former Director General of Police K. Chakravarthi, who had categorically denied Bhatt's presence when he deposed before the SIT, said: '...he was an SP [Superintendent of Police] level officer in the intelligence, and Mr Raigar was the additional DIG... [The latter] was absent that crucial day. So [Bhatt] must have thought he should go and represent [his chief]. But since it was a meeting of heads of departments...he was [present but] not a participant.'[21] Chakravarthi may not have known then that Ayyub had already met Raigar and he had told her that Bhatt used to accompany him to similar coordination meetings in the past. It is also possible that on this occasion Raigar may have instructed Bhatt to go because *in the weeks before the Godhra tragedy, the intelligence branch had sent at least twenty warnings to the Home Minister that the VHP and Bajrang Dal were cooking up something unusual for this kar seva trip to Ayodhya.*

With a vindictiveness that has become the hallmark of his regime, within months of Modi becoming prime minister in 2014, the Gujarat government dismissed Bhatt dishonourably from the IPS, in 2015.[22] This is the highest administrative punishment that an officer can face, and is reserved for only the most serious transgressions. But Bhatt was dismissed for taking a few days of unauthorized leave.

Modi's vengefulness did not end there. For he knew that Bhatt dismissed was a free man, and as a free man he would be more dangerous than as a serving police officer. Modi had already been made uncomfortably aware of the threat that a disgruntled police officer could pose by the letter of resignation to the Gujarat Police that D.G Vanzara, Amit Shah's 'encounter specialist', had sent in 2013. In that letter, he had asserted repeatedly that he had carried out every task assigned to him by Home Minister Amit Shah, and accused him of having abandoned Vanzara and others in their hour of need. Modi and Shah had immediately realized that after he left the police his lips would no longer be sealed. So, they rejected his resignation, and freed him with the offer of a BJP seat in the next assembly election.

But both knew that Sanjiv Bhatt could neither be coerced, nor bought. So, perhaps not coincidentally, in September 2018, Bhatt was arrested on the charge of having falsely arrested a man after placing one kilogram of drugs on him in 1996, and was held in jail without bail. While he was still in jail, the government worked feverishly to find something to pin on him to keep him there. Ten months later, he was sentenced to life imprisonment for the custodial death of a member of a 133-strong Hindu mob during a communal riot in Jamnagar in 1990.

The verdict marked a new low point in the Gujarat's already besmirched record for dispensing justice. The death had occurred twenty-nine years earlier. The man, Prabhudas Vaishnani, had been in custody for nine days. When he fell ill, he was granted bail and sent to a hospital. He died not in jail but in the hospital, so he was in custody only in a purely technical sense. According to the local newspapers, the hospital's medical records had given the cause of death as 'renal failure'. Renal failure is the failure of *both* kidneys at the same time. The possibility of massive beating causing a simultaneous failure of both kidneys is so remote that the page on kidney failure of the Mayo Clinic's website, for example, does not even mention it.[23]

On the other hand, the webpage of the American Urology Care Foundation devotes an entire section to Blunt Force Trauma and describes how well guarded the kidneys are by the ribs, pelvis and spine. It would be possible for a brutal beating to damage one kidney beyond repair, but two, both completely and at the same time, would have been so rare that no hospital would have dismissed it with the diagnosis of 'renal failure', which is a term routinely used to describe kidney failure caused by disease or diabetes.

The sentence passed on Sanjiv Bhatt raises another equally knotty question that the state's prosecutors did not even bother to ask: When the police arrested 133 persons, why was Prabhudas Vaishnani singled out for such massive and sustained beating? Why was no one else even hospitalized? It is just barely possible to imagine a scenario during a riot in which one person becomes the target of the police's savagery. But how Prabhudas became that person needed to be asked and answered. None of the reports of Bhatt's trial suggested that this had been done. It is difficult not to conclude, therefore, that Modi and Shah have railroaded him into prison for life for the same reason they had earlier railroaded him out of the police. *He knew too much!*

### *The Victimization of R.B. Sreekumar*

The seniormost officer in the Gujarat Police to be punished in this way was R.B. Sreekumar, the additional director general of police (Intelligence) during the 2002 riots. Sreekumar was the only senior officer who had uncompromisingly deposed before the Nanavati–Shah Commission that the government had ordered the police to be partisan during the riots. In retaliation, the government denied him promotion to the rank of director general of police, to which he qualified on the basis of his seniority in the police service. Sreekumar took his case to the Central Administrative Tribunal which ruled in his favour and directed his reinstatement even after his retirement. The Modi government appealed against the CAT's decision, but the Gujarat High Court upheld the CAT's ruling.[24]

The state to which Modi has reduced a once exemplary police force was described by R.B. Sreekumar at a 2011 press conference that was held in Mumbai to protest against the arrest of Bhatt on the charge of 'Giving or fabricating false evidence with intent to procure conviction of capital offence', Section 194 of the Indian Penal Code. (This arrest and suspension in September 2011, in which he was granted bail the following month, had been based on a complaint filed by his junior, K.D. Panth.[25]) At the conference, he said that the police and administration of Gujarat were in the grip of a 'Modi phobia' in which no one dared any longer to oppose his will on any issue. Sanjiv Bhatt's arrest was intended to scare all those who dared to oppose him.

Sreekumar told the assembled gathering that he had sent as many as twenty intelligence reports to the Home Ministry before the burning of the Sabarmati Express, that the VHP and Bajrang Dal were preparing for a major operation. But, he added, 'When I was the ADG intelligence, any information related to the role of Sangh Parivar was suppressed.'

Arresting whistleblowers was essential for maintaining this level of compliance, Sreekumar claimed. He also described the former Gujarat home minister, Haren Pandya, who was murdered in mysterious circumstances in March 2003, as the 'first whistleblower about Modi's role in the Gujarat riots'. The implication was obvious.[26]

## A Spate of 'Encounters': The Building Blocks of Modi's Rise

The immense publicity the media gave to the Akshardham attack, and the admiration it generated for the Chief Minister and the Gujarat Police, created a template that the government used without restraint to keep support for it at fever pitch in the years that followed. Sensational reports would flash on the front pages of newspapers and on television screens about men and women gunned down in encounters with the state police. In nearly all the cases, the police claimed that these were dreaded terrorists who intended to assassinate Chief Minister Narendra Modi or another senior leader of the BJP in revenge for the Gujarat pogrom. But in each case, the authorities had been able to gather advance information of their plans and apprehend the terrorists, almost miraculously, just in time. The sheer number of encounters, the disturbing similarities between them, and the constant refrain from Gujarat that these had all been 'terrorists' sent by Pakistan to kill Chief Minister Modi, provoked deep disquiet in civil society.

The first of these 'encounters' took place on January 13, 2003, less than four months after the Akshardham attack, and ended in the death of one Sadiq Jamal Mehtar. Although the Supreme Court's Justice Bedi, who presented a report to the Supreme Court on the alleged fake encounters in Gujarat between 2003 and 2006, did not peg this as a custodial killing, a considerable volume of evidence, collected later by *Tehelka* journalist Rana Ayyub suggests that it might well have been.[27] According to the police's FIR, Sadiq Jamal was a resident of Bhavnagar in Gujarat, but had been living in Dubai where he had developed close connections with members of the Mumbai gangland boss Dawood Ibrahim's inner circle. When Jamal saw what the police euphemistically described as '*incidents* of communal violence in Gujarat that had erupted after the Godhra *carnage*', 'he had made up his mind to kill Narendra Modi'.

A very different version was disclosed, however, by a shady Mumbai journalist, Ketan Tirodkar, who, in the process of covering crime in the city, had developed a close friendship with the Maharashtra's 'encounter specialist' policeman, Daya Nayak. Daya Nayak is a folk hero in Maharashtra. Six movies have been made on him, and events in his life as an 'encounter specialist'. Nayak is credited with having killed more than eighty members of Mumbai's underworld in the 1990s when the Maharashtra government launched a no-holds-barred campaign to break the stranglehold that rival underworld gangs had established on the city. Tirodkar stated, in a sworn affidavit, that he had known Jamal from Dubai, that Jamal had been a servant in the home of one of Dawood's associates, had managed to get back to India against his employer's will, and had asked for Tirodkar's help in getting two minor cases expunged from his record. He further stated that on January 9, 2003, at Nayak's request, he had lured Jamal to the Sanjay Gandhi National Park north of the city, and handed him over to two policemen from Gujarat, one of whom he later claimed, after seeing him on television in 2008, was Gujarat's 'encounter specialist' D.G. Vanzara. According to Tirodkar, he and Nayak had been asked by the Gujarat Police to supply it with a young Muslim who had some kind of criminal record. Jamal had fit the bill.[28] Four days later, Jamal was dead.

Other encounters followed. In reply to a question asked in the Gujarat legislature, the police replied that twenty-one persons had been killed in encounters with the police between 2003 and 2006. The descriptions the police gave of the circumstances in which many of these deaths occurred were for the most part clumsy and unconvincing. Six of the people killed were actually in police custody when they died. No one tried to explain how they managed to secure firearms while in police custody and, thereby, force the latter to kill them in 'self-defence'. Nor did they explain how none of the policemen involved was injured. The police described all of the twenty-one as dreaded terrorists who had come from, or been recruited by, Pakistan to assassinate Modi or other senior BJP leaders, or to launch other terror strikes against civilians as they had done at Akshardham. But there was rarely any convincing evidence to back these allegations.

In 2007, B.G. Verghese, one of India's most respected journalists, a former editor of the *Hindustan Times*, and a former adviser to Prime Minister Indira Gandhi, filed a petition in the Supreme Court asking for an inquiry into the twenty-one encounter killings by the Gujarat Police between 2003 and 2006. He was joined in this by lyricist Javed Akhtar and social activist Shabnam Hashmi. In all, twenty-two cases were brought to the attention of the court, twenty-one by Verghese, and the twenty-second, the case of one Sameer Khan, by Akhtar and Hashmi.

Verghese pointed out that the encounter killings 'spanned a

range of persons that included workmen who have come in from outside the state, to suspected terrorists. The ages of those killed are in the range between 22 and 37. It is not clear if the families of those killed are even aware of the fate of these young persons'. There were other disturbing similarities which were not confined to these encounters alone, but fed the plaintiffs' suspicions about these: nearly all the 'encounters took place in the early hours of the morning; in a field or other open space. In all of them the accused had snatched, or tried to snatch the weapons of the police and opened fire upon them, forcing them to fire back in self-defence; in all of them all of the accused had died, but not a single policeman had been injured'.

'There is a need to investigate this pattern,' Verghese had concluded, 'and there must be a system [put] in place to ensure that armed personnel do not easily do away with lives of citizens.'

Highlighting the killing of one Sameer Khan Pathan in his written submission before the bench, Javed Akhtar pointed out that in all these cases the police version was invariably that the 'victims' were terrorists from the Jaish-e-Mohammed or Lashkar-e-Tayyiba on a mission to assassinate Modi.[29] Both the petitioners sought independent investigations by the CBI or a Special Investigation Team appointed by the Court, to investigate what they claimed were murders carried out in cold blood.[30]

The Supreme Court ordered an inquiry and set up a monitoring committee under former Supreme Court judge M.B. Shah. But the wheels of justice grind slowly in India, especially when the police, on whom the courts depend for hearing the prosecution's case, are themselves the defendants. So, it took eleven years and a change of judge to get a final report in December 2018. This report confirmed that three of the seventeen encounter killings that the monitoring committee had studied, including that of Sameer Khan,[31] had undoubtedly been faked encounters, i.e. extra-judicial killings—and recommended harsh punishment of the policemen involved. By then, Verghese had been dead for four years, Modi and Shah had moved to Delhi and controlled all of the central government's investigative agencies. So, to no one's surprise, no action followed.

As far as Modi was concerned, the twenty-two encounters, whether genuine or faked by the police, had served their purpose. At an election rally days before the December 2007 elections, while forty-two Gujarat Police officers and men were languishing in jail waiting to be tried for the faked encounters described above, the Chief Minister invited his audience to celebrate the murder of Sohrabuddin Sheikh. 'Modi called out his name, with each slowly enunciated syllable—"Sohrrraa-budeeeeen"—leaving no doubt as to his religion,' writes Vinod Jose. He got what he deserved, Modi said, and asked the crowd: 'What should have been done to a man from whom a large number of AK-47 rifles were recovered, who was on the search list of police from four states, who attacked the police, who had relations with Pakistan and was eyeing to enter Gujarat?' To which he got the reply, '*Mari nakho, mari nakho*' (kill him, kill him).

'Does my government need to take permission of Soniaben [Congress leader Sonia Gandhi] for this?' he then asked, and declared, '[Merchants of death] will be dealt in the same fashion on the land of Gujarat.'[32]

CHAPTER TWELVE

# Faked Encounters

## *A Foretaste of India's Lawless Future*

Justice H.S. Bedi, who had taken over from Justice M.B. Shah in 2011, did not take up three of the twenty-one cases because these were already before other courts, had resulted in several convictions, and were being appealed against. These were the cases of Ishrat Jahan, a nineteen-year-old girl from Maharashtra, her employer/friend, and two alleged Pakistani terrorists killed on June 15, 2004; of Sohrabuddin Sheikh and his wife Kausar Bi, killed on November 26, 2005; and of one of Sheikh's partners in crime, Tulsiram Prajapati, killed on December 28, 2006. The deceased were described as *fidayeen* (suicide attackers), recruited by terrorist organizations in Pakistan, supported by its Inter-Services Intelligence, who had also been tasked with the assassination of Chief Minister Modi.

Ishrat Jahan Raza was a college student from Mumbra, a small town turned distant suburb of Mumbai in Maharashtra. The three men killed with her were Javed Ghulam Sheikh, whom she called 'Uncle Javed', Amjad Ali Rana and Zeeshan Johar. The police claimed that all four were operatives of the Lashkar-e-Tayyiba (LeT), and that Rana and Johar had been sent from Pakistan to assassinate Narendra Modi.

According to the police's version of the plot and the encounter in which they met their deaths, Javed Ghulam Sheikh was born

Pranesh Pillai, the son of Gopinath Pillai, a native of Kerala. He converted to Islam and changed his name in 1991 in order to marry a Muslim woman named Sajida whom he had met three years earlier. They were married in 1994 and had three children. After his marriage he had migrated to Mumbra and had drifted into the fringes of the Mumbai underworld which was rife with inter-gang rivalry at the time. Within a few years he had been arrested by the Mumbai Police in four assault cases in Mumbai and Pune, and been charged with being involved in a fake currency racket. At the time of his death, he had two passports, one in his Hindu and the other in his Muslim name. Javed Sheikh had travelled to Dubai in 2003 and to Oman in 2004. His wife Sajida said that he had been radicalized by the stories he heard there about the slaughter of Muslims in Gujarat, and had come back a changed man.

Ishrat Jahan met Javed Sheikh in Mumbra sometime early in 2004, and introduced him to her family on May 1, when he asked for their permission to employ her as a salesgirl in his shop. In her deposition, Ishrat Jahan's mother, Shamima Kausar, explained that while the family lived in an apartment block and had middle-class pretensions they were severely pressed for money to feed their two sons and five daughters. Ishrat was in her second year studying for a bachelor's degree in science. According to Shamima, she eked out the family income by giving tuitions to between twenty and twenty-five school children. And so, she accepted when Sheikh offered her a position as a salesgirl in his shop at a salary of Rs 3,000/- per month.

The Intelligence Bureau later claimed that Sheikh had no such shop, so the 'job' was a cover for Ishrat's frequent meetings and travels with Sheikh, because by then he had recruited her into the LeT. A third possibility, that the job offer could have been a cover for an amorous relationship was not suggested, nor seriously pursued.

Amjad Ali and Zeeshan Johar, on the other hand, may well have been Pakistani fidayeen belonging to the LeT. Johar, according to the Gujrat Police, belonged to Gujranwala district of Pakistani Punjab, and Amjad Ali Rana (alias Salim) to Sargodha.

In August 2004, more than six weeks after Ishrat Jahan and Javed Sheikh's death, Shamima Kausar filed a writ petition in the Gujarat High Court alleging that her daughter had been killed in cold blood, in a faked encounter, and asked the court to order an investigation by the Central Bureau of Investigation into the circumstances in which her daughter met her death. She had probably been provoked into going to the court by the widespread publicity that the Indian media had given to a report published on July 14 by the Lahore-based *Ghazwa* ('Holy War') *Times*, a mouthpiece of the LeT, that had hailed Ishrat Jahan as yet another martyr for their cause. She made this stipulation to ensure an impartial inquiry, because the CBI came under the central home ministry, over which the Modi government had no control.

Shamima Kausar's belief in the innocence of her daughter and her lack of trust in the Gujarat Police was vindicated by the three inquiries that followed her daughter's sensational death. On August 7, the Gujarat High Court asked the state government to investigate the allegation, but the police procrastinated, claiming that it had already asked its *Mahila* ('Women's') Cell to investigate her death and was waiting for the report. The Mahila Cell gave its report only twenty-two months later, on June 8, 2006, and stoutly confirmed that the June 15 shootout had been a genuine encounter. Sadly for the Mahila Cell, in Lahore, on the very day that it submitted its report to the Gujarat Police, the Jamat-ud-Dawa, the parent organization of the Lashkar-e-Tayyiba, published an apology to Shamima Kausar *for having wrongly described her daughter as a member of the LeT*. It also confessed that it had drawn this conclusion hurriedly and uncritically from the extensive reporting of the encounter in the Indian media and the unanimous view that Ishrat Jahan had, at the very least, been lured into becoming an accomplice by an employer she respected, and whom she may have been drawn to.

Since some officers of the IB, the central government's

Intelligence Bureau, had also been involved in the shootout, the Gujarat High Court had also asked the central government for an explanation. Again, inexplicably, despite it being a Congress-led regime at the centre, the IB dragged its feet over giving one for *three* whole years and submitted its reply only on August 6, 2009. In its reply, it too reiterated that Ishrat Jahan had been a member of the LeT and dismissed its 2006 disowning of Ishrat Jahan as having been intended to throw dust in the Indian public's eyes. The only explanation of this tortuous vindication of Gujarat Police's encounter killing was that the IB had been a part of the plot to trap Sheikh, Rana and Johar, and was now trying to limit the damage to its reputation and its involved personnel, by claiming that Ishrat Jahan had not been the innocent victim that her relatives and the media were claiming her to be.

What blew this elaborate construction of blame apart was a second, independent report, commissioned by the Gujarat High Court, from S.P. Tamang, the chief metropolitan magistrate of Court No. 1 in the Ahmedabad High Court. The High Court had commissioned this because it was not satisfied by the Gujarat Police Women's Cell's 2006 report, and the Home Ministry's 2009 rejection of Shamima Kausar's accusation. Tamang's report landed like a bombshell on the judges' table. It proved conclusively that this had not only not been a faked encounter of the common or garden kind—in which the police, driven to desperation by the endless procrastination of the courts, and its inability to prevent the assassination of key witnesses by the gangsters released on bail, takes to executing well-known criminals in elaborately staged escape attempts—this was also the cold-blooded murder of at least one completely innocent young girl, whose only fault was to have been at the wrong place at the wrong time.

A summary of the deposition before Tamang of Inspector J.G. Parmar, the only policeman involved in the alleged fatal shootout who gave one, boils down to the following:[1]

Around June 1, 2004, K.R. Kaushik, police commissioner, Ahmedabad city, received an intelligence input from the central government's Intelligence Bureau through its ACP (Intelligence), G.L. Singhal, that two Pakistani fidayeen belonging to the Lashkar-e-Tayyiba had departed from Kashmir separately, to reach Ahmedabad to meet a resident of Pune, Maharashtra named Javed who was also a terrorist recruited by the Lashkar-e-Tayyiba to establish a local network for the two fidayeen. Their aim was to mount a suicide attack to kill Narendra Modi. For this purpose they were conducting reconnaissance at Ahmedabad, and in Gandhinagar of the Chief Minister's residence, his office, the places he visited and the roads he travelled on.

Kaushik, P.P. Pandey, the joint commissioner of police (Crime), D.G. Vanzara, additional commissioner of police (Crime) for Ahmedabad, and Singhal put together a force of policemen and directed them to maintain a 'discreet vigilance' till Singhal could give them more precise information.

On June 14, at about 11.00 pm, Pandey received 'concrete intelligence from his secret sources' that Javed Sheikh had left Mumbai for Ahmedabad in a blue Indica car bearing the number plate MH-02-JA-4786 with both the Pakistani fidayeen terrorists carrying with them weapons and ammunitions, and that the car was likely to enter Ahmedabad early the next morning. Vanzara immediately summoned both the Additional Commissioners of Police and police inspectors of the Crime Branch under him and briefed them. Under his guidance, a foolproof plan for blockading every junction and choke point in Ahmedabad was prepared. Teams of police were deployed at six key points and they took their positions at about 1.30 am. At 4.00 am, the blue Indica entered a checkpoint called Narol Chokdi on the main road into the city from Mumbai and got onto the road to Naroda (the mainly Muslim area that had seen some of the worst killing in the 2002 riots). The police at the checkpoint informed the others and gave chase. The Indica (possibly having become aware it was being chased) abruptly turned onto the road to the airport in a bid to escape but, informed by wireless, police at other checkpoints were able to scramble into their vehicles, and intercept it, coming from the opposite direction at a sharp turn near the Kotarpur Water Works. They had been able to do so by crossing the road divider to the opposite side and setting a trap just in time to stop the Indica by firing upon its rear left tyre, forcing it to swing towards the central divider and come to a halt there. A gun battle ensued in which the police fired eighty-one or more shots and killed all the four occupants of the car, but not before one of them, Amjad Ali, had been able to get out of the car, take shelter behind the divider, and return fire using a Chinese AK-56 submachine gun.

### An Elaborate Fabrication

The story sounded entirely plausible, but Tamang did not believe it because he had already examined minutely the documents and reports that had been submitted to him for examination and not found a single shred of evidence to support the police's story. On the contrary, six key findings in the autopsy, forensic and ballistic reports on the four deceased convinced him that they had been shot elsewhere in cold blood and brought to the encounter site like props in a play.

First, the doctors who performed the *post mortem* found that *rigor mortis* was fully developed in all the bodies when they began. They had begun at 3.40 pm on June 15, ten hours and forty minutes after the alleged time of death but, as Tamang pointed out, rigor mortis sets in about two hours after death, takes about twelve hours to spread through the entire body, stays for another twelve hours, and takes a similar amount of time to dissipate. So, all four had to have been killed at least fourteen hours before 3.40 pm, i.e. not later than 1.40 am—more than three hours before the alleged encounter.

Second, the analysis of the contents of Amjad Ali's stomach reinforced this conclusion because it contained half-digested grains of rice. This confirmed that he could not have been killed more than three to four hours after he had had his last meal. Assuming that this would have been around 8.00 pm, Tamang concluded that Amjad Ali had been shot dead between 11.00 and 12.00 pm on the night of the 14th.

Third, ballistic evidence also strongly confirmed this finding. It showed that Amjad Ali had been killed with eight shots fired at close range into his neck and chest from different positions around him, but all at a steep downward trajectory. This suggested that he had been shot by one or more persons while he was sitting.

Fourth, both Sheikh and Johar had been killed with at least one shot from the same Chinese AK-56 that was found lying between Amjad Ali's legs on the road divider from behind which he was alleged to have made his last stand. *This meant that the AK-56 had been in the possession of the police and could not therefore have been brought to the encounter site by the two alleged Pakistani terrorists.*

Fifth, while Amjad Ali was described as having fired a large number of rounds at the police Gypsy (the Suzuki equivalent of a Jeep), there was not a single spent cartridge shell anywhere around him. Finally, sixth and most conclusive, there was no gunshot residue on either hand of any of the four alleged terrorists.

Piecing all this together, Tamang had concluded that Javed Sheikh had been killed first at around 8.00 to 8.30 on the evening of the 14th, and that Amjad Ali, Zeeshan Johar and Ishrat Jahan had been killed, probably at different places, at around 11.00 pm. The fact that Sheikh and Johar had been killed by bullets from the same AK-56 also destroyed the 'evidence' the police had relied upon to prove that the deceased were terrorists—the 17 kilograms of sulphur and urea (to build a crude bomb) and three full magazines of ammunition for the AK-56 it claimed to have recovered from the Indica after the encounter had to have been planted by the police. Tamang therefore not only concluded that the entire police version was fake but that in all probability the 'concrete intelligence' that P.P. Pandey had received at 11.00 pm, which set the police operation in motion, was the information that all the four were now dead. He therefore indicted the entire top hierarchy of the Gujarat Police, Commissioner K.R. Kaushik, Joint Commissioner P.P. Pandey, three additional commissioners of police, D.G. Vanzara, G.L. Singhal, and N.K. Amin, and sixteen inspectors and police constables, as conspirators.[2] He concluded that the purpose of the conspiracy was to eliminate the three men, that the police had not expected Ishrat Jahan to be with Sheikh, and that having killed Sheikh, they were left with no option but to kill her as well, which they did five hours later.

*

Tamang's finding dismissed the IB's frantic assertion that Amjad Ali and Zeeshan Johar had indeed been LeT operatives whom the IB had lured to Ahmedabad, and that Sheikh was their local contact. But he did not put forward an alternative explanation, or conjecture, about why the Gujarat Police had chosen these three, out of thousands of members of the Maharashtra–Gujarat underworld, to eliminate. So, the possibility that the IB was telling the truth, but could not provide proof as it would expose its methods and its agents, cannot be ruled out. The Ahmedabad riots of 2002 had sparked a thirst for 'revenge' that the LeT and Pakistan's Inter-Services Intelligence took full advantage of. The assault on Akshardham had been followed by two spectacular revenge attacks in Maharashtra: the planting of seven bombs in the first class compartments of a Mumbai suburban train with the express purpose of killing Gujarati businessmen on July 11, 2006, and the LeT's sea-borne attack on two hotels in Mumbai—the Taj and the Oberoi, on November 26, 2008. The first had killed 189 persons and wounded 800; the second had killed 174 and wounded more than 300. Both had had local support from a home grown terrorist organization, the Indian Mujahideen, which came into being in the aftermath of the Gujarat pogrom.

It was only in 2013, when the CBI began to investigate the Ishrat Jahan encounter, that a third possibility surfaced. This was that two Gujarati Muslims referred to as 'Asad' and 'Owais', whom the Gujarat Police had picked up and detained during its investigation of the murder of former Gujarat Home Minister Haren Pandya in March 2003, had agreed to become double agents, joined the

Lashkar-e-Tayyiba, gone to Pakistan, and lured Amjad Ali Rana and Zeeshan Johar to Ahmedabad. A third, referred to in the CBI charge sheet only as 'Javabhai', who had been Javed Sheikh's partner in running a company named Al Rahman Enterprises that supplied manpower to the Gulf countries, had placed the phone call that brought Sheikh to Mumbai. But his reasons for doing so never became known because he disappeared immediately after Sheikh, Ishrat Jahan, Rana and Johar were killed.[3]

Had it not been for Ishrat Jahan's youth, beauty and obvious lack of motive for becoming a terrorist, this obviously botched 'encounter' would have joined the long list of other extrajudicial killings by the police and faded from public view. What made Tamang's report a bombshell five years after her killing was that nearly all of the policemen he had indicted were already in prison facing trial for two other faked encounters in which alleged 'terrorists' were also planning to assassinate CM Modi. The core group of police officers and other ranks indicted for these encounters was virtually the same as the one involved in the Ishrat Jahan killing.

The most disturbing feature of the Tamang report, more even than its contents, was the lengths to which he went to keep his findings secret from the government and the entire city. Tamang did not employ a stenographer, or use a computer, but wrote his entire 243-page report in long-hand.[4] He then broke protocol and submitted the report directly to the Gujarat High Court, circumventing the office of the chief metropolitan magistrate who had assigned it to him. Tamang clearly did not trust even his personal staff and the inviolability of his chief's office. There can be no more eloquent testimony of the atmosphere of terror that the Gujarat Police had created to keep its misdeed secret.

To no one's surprise, the Gujarat government reacted with unbridled fury. It termed the report 'illegal and doubtful' because it 'didn't have the response of 20 policemen, including senior IPS officers, involved in the shooting' and demanded that the report be suppressed forthwith. But somewhat surprisingly, it also did not attempt to seek to rebut its conclusions. Instead, it gave an interview to a well-known journalist, Sheila Bhatt, in which it sought to justify the 'special measures' it had had to take to protect Prime Minister Modi in the wake of the Gujarat 'riots' of 2002.[5] This was a classic case of Modi–Shah tactics in action, which had been based from the day of the Godhra train burning on the maxim that attack is the best form of defence. Tamang's report made it clear that he would have given any of the police officers and men involved in the affair a chance to make a deposition. However, only one 'complainant' had responded. This was Inspector (Crime) J.G. Parmar, who gave an account of the encounter that did not deviate one jot from the original police version of 2004, to the extent that he too barely mentioned the presence of Ishrat Jahan in the encounter. Tamang had, in any case, been given all the medical and ballistic reports he needed to investigate the case. He based his findings entirely on those reports and only used Parmar's deposition as the foil against which to contrast his conclusions.

In a surprising, and possibly unprecedented, action the Gujarat High Court agreed to suppress the report, but asked the state government to set up a three-member Special Investigation Team and gave it access to the Tamang report.[6]

On November 21, 2011, the SIT confirmed Tamang's findings, so the High Court recommended the prosecution of the twenty-one officers and other ranks whom Tamang had named. The bench also recommended further investigations, observing that 'Somebody else may also be behind the encounter'. The judges wanted the SIT to continue with the investigation, for 'it is well-versed with the case'. And also considered handing it over to a central agency like the CBI or the then recently formed National Investigation Agency. By then the CBI had already indicted Modi's home minister, Amit Shah, in another case of a faked encounter. This was the killing of Sohrabuddin Sheikh and his wife Kausar Bi, in November 25–28, 2005.

## The Killing of Sohrabuddin Sheikh and Tulsiram Prajapati

Sohrabuddin Sheikh and his associate, Tulsiram Prajapati, were gangsters based in Rajasthan, who were enforcers and guns for hire for marble mine owners who were constantly fighting turf wars with each other over disputed seams of marble. In the 1990s, Sohrabuddin, who had been born Salim Anwaruddin Sheikh, had been a junior member of a gang whose chief, Abdul Latif, was a much feared illicit liquor 'don' in the 'dry' state of Gujarat. Latif had two lieutenants, Sharif Khan Pathan and Rasool Parti. Sohrabuddin was Sharif Khan's driver.

When Latif was killed in an encounter with the police in 1992, the liquor trade passed into the hands of the Hindu liquor mafia, and Latif's gang dispersed. Sharif Khan Pathan and Rasool Parti fled to Dubai. Others moved to Rajasthan where some of them continued in the illicit liquor business, while others, including Sohrabuddin, gravitated into the marble mining mafia. There he became an informer for the Gujarat Police. This was not happenstance. In 1995, a cache of twenty-six (by some accounts forty, or even forty-eight) AK-47s had been recovered from a well in Sohrabuddin's home in Ujjain, in Rajasthan. Sohrabuddin was able to avoid prison by getting bailed out. The *quid pro quo* was that he became a police informer. His 'handler' was a senior police officer named Abhay Chudasama, who was later one of the fourteen police personnel indicted for his killing.

No one would have heard of either him or Tulsiram Prajapati had the Anti-Terrorism Squad (ATS) of the Gujarat Police not gone into Maharashtra on November 23, 2004, pulled them, and Sohrabuddin's wife Kausar Bi, off an interstate bus bound from Hyderabad to Sangli, and taken them almost a thousand kilometres to a farmhouse outside Ahmedabad, where Sohrabuddin was shot. Kausar Bi went missing after this.

Sohrabuddin's brother, Rubabuddin, filed a petition in the Supreme Court claiming that the encounter was fake and wanting to know where his sister-in-law was. Inexplicably, despite his having witnessed the abduction, Prajapati was spared, and handed over to the Rajasthan Police to be jailed on some other charge. When quizzed about this by journalists, the police said that he was spared because he was an informer for D.G. Vanzara. This raised the possibility that it may have been Tulsiram who had informed the police of their travel plans in order to facilitate the abduction, a possibility that was confirmed by another associate of Sohrabuddin and Tulsiram thirteen years later. (See below.)

The Gujarat ATS claimed that Sohrabuddin was a terrorist who had links with the Lashkar-e-Tayyiba; that Sohrabuddin had come to Gujarat from Rajasthan to assassinate Chief Minister Narendra Modi; that the Rajasthan Police tipped off its Gujarat counterpart about him and even accompanied them to identify the man during the joint operation to capture him. When he tried to escape on a motorcycle, he was killed.

The allegation that Sohrabuddin had been an LeT terrorist was fiercely denied by his brother Rubabuddin Sheikh. The Supreme Court ordered the Gujarat government to investigate the killing and the disappearance of Kausar Bi, but nothing much happened for another year until drunken police officers boasted about it in front of a journalist, Prashant Dayal, who was a senior correspondent for the Gujarati language newspaper, *Divya Bhaskar*.

Dayal was no ordinary journalist. From an early age he had found the conventional curriculum in his secondary school so boring that he managed to fail all his subjects in his class eight examinations (which students take when they are fourteen). He then decided to stop wasting his parents' money, took a job in a garage and started going to night school. In college, he drove an autorickshaw at night to continue earning the money he needed to continue his studies. By then, he had found his vocation: he was determined to become a journalist.

After getting a degree in journalism, he managed to land a job but was refused salary on the grounds that he was an interne. This was common in Gujarati journalism: trainees and stringers were rarely paid but told to secure advertisements for the journal and live on the commission the paper paid them. Few internes managed to stay the course, but Dayal was so determined to earn a name as a reporter that he worked without a salary for more than a year, continuing to drive his autorickshaw at night.

By 2007, when he was interviewed by the online journal Rediff.com, Dayal had been a journalist for nineteen years and switched jobs fourteen times. 'I have never seen an increment or bonus in my career, because I could never settle down in a newspaper. Every day, I used to have a fight with the editors over stories.'

Over these years, however, he had earned a reputation as a reliable and well-informed crime reporter. He had done this by developing the habit of drinking alcohol with off-duty police officers, 'where I drink within limit, so that I can listen and grasp what the officers say when they open up after a few pegs'.

On one such evening, officers involved in the Sohrabuddin encounter case bragged before him how they had 'punished' and eliminated some anti-national elements. With this clue, the next morning Dayal cross-checked the details of the case. 'I got confirmation from the farmhouse in Ahmedabad that three persons were kept there. Then, from my sources in Vanzara's native village, I confirmed that Vanzara had been there with his team during the period. At the farmhouse, the servants confirmed that a lady in *burkha* was kept there. I suspected she must be Kausar Bi.'

All these facts matched with what he was told by the drunken police official, Dayal claimed. When he first filed the story, editors were hesitant to go with it, because they simply could not believe that 'there can't be documented evidence' of such crimes. But Dayal managed to convince them and the story came out on November 30, 2006.[7]

According to Dayal, and a subsequent Gujarat CID reconstruction of what had happened in November 2005, the three of them had been taken to a private farm outside Ahmedabad on November 25, with the consent of the owner. But the owner had given it for one night's stay only and asked them to leave the next morning. Upon Vanzara's request, another farm owner just outside Gandhinagar agreed to let them use his premises. From there Sheikh was taken to Ahmedabad and killed. The deposition before the CID inquiry by one of the policemen who helped stage the encounter was damning. Its report stated:

> Constable Ajay Parmar was asked to bring a Hero Honda motorcycle lying in the backyard of an ATS office here. Sohrabuddin was also brought here. A sub-inspector of Rajasthan police rode the bike for a short distance and jumped off it. As it fell, Sohrabuddin was pulled out of the car and thrown on the road. Four police inspectors fired eight rounds from their service pistols. Vanzara then asked Parmar to take Sohrabuddin to the civil hospital.[8]

Four weeks later, Prajapati was brought from Udaipur to Ahmedabad, produced in court on December 26, ostensibly to be questioned in another case, and taken away to jail. On his way out of the courtroom, he shouted in Hindi to the reporters, 'I know what is going to happen to me. They are going to kill me.' Two days later, he was killed in another staged encounter, involving alleged Pakistani terrorists in Chapri, a village close to the Pakistan border in Banaskantha district, 118 kilometres from Ahmedabad. It might not have been coincidental that, fifteen days earlier, D.G. Vanzara who was the DIG (Crime) in Ahmedabad at the time, had been transferred as DIG (Border Range) to Banaskantha.

Following hard on the heels of Dayal's exposé, the killing of Prajapati raised so many questions about his relationship to Sohrabuddin that the central government decided to club the two encounter deaths together, and widen its inquiry to cover the possibility of a wider conspiracy in which both the 'encountered' hitmen had been involved. The details of how Prajapati was killed were revealed during the CBI interrogation that followed, by Ashish Pandya, the police constable who allegedly pulled the trigger, and who was allegedly acting on the orders of his boss, the superintendent of police in Banaskantha, Vipul Agarwal.

Ashish Pandya not only exposed Agarwal's role in the

encounter but his nexus with the superintendent of police in the Gujarat Anti-Terrorism Squad, Rajkumar Pandian, and the very recently appointed DIG of the Border Range, D.G. Vanzara, in the planning and execution of the encounter. The CBI therefore concluded in its final report, submitted in 2010, that Vanzara, Pandian, Rajasthan DIG N.K. Amin, several other senior officers including Abhay Chudasama, and inspectors and constables from both states, had killed Sohrabuddin Sheikh in a faked encounter. They had then strangled his wife Kausar Bi after keeping her in the second farmhouse for two days, cremated her in the dead of night at or near Illol, Vanzara's home village, and killed Tulsiram Prajapati after Dayal's exposé because he could provide 'material evidence' of the murders of Sohrabuddin Sheikh and Kausar Bi.

## A System of Rewards

During his thirteen years as the chief minister of Gujarat, Modi established an enviable track record for backing his officers. This allowed them to take decisions without fear of a backlash from those adversely affected by their actions. But the reverse side of this was his demand for unquestioning obedience. Both played a part in the covering up of his instigation of the Ahmedabad riots.

Seven senior officers attended the fateful meeting at Modi's house on February 27. These were: Acting Chief Secretary Swarna Kanta Verma; Additional Chief Secretary (Home) Ashok Narayan; Director General of Police K. Chakravarthi; Ahmedabad Commissioner of Police P.P. Pandey; Secretary (Home) K. Nityanandam; Principal Secretary to Chief Minister P.K. Mishra; and Secretary to Chief Minister Anil Mukim.

When questioned by the SIT, two of the senior officers—Swarna Kanta Verma and Ashok Narayan—'pleaded loss of memory due to passage of time'. A third, Anil Mukim, claimed that he was not even present—a statement that turned out to be a blatant lie, spoken in order to allow him not to tell an even bigger lie. The remaining four firmly denied that Sanjiv Bhatt, the whistleblower, had been there.

Ashok Narayan not only got promoted to chief secretary, which would certainly not have happened had he not lost his memory, but kept being given post-retirement extensions as chief vigilance commissioner all the way till December 2008, four years after he reached the retirement age of sixty. P.P. Pandey and P.K. Mishra were two of the four who said they were not there. Pandey's subsequent reinstatement as the DGP, in April 2016—when he was still on bail in the faked police encounter killings of Tulsiram Prajapati and Ishrat Jahan—was so flagrantly a violation of the intent of the law, if not its letter, that it provoked Julio Ribeiro, a former chief of the Maharashtra Police,[9] to file a case in the Supreme Court against it. The Supreme Court dismissed the case on the grounds that since Pandey had not been dismissed from the police earlier, but had resigned, the government had the right to call him back. To say that his appointment as the DGP was unprecedented would be an understatement. As for Mishra, in 2019, he became principal secretary to Prime Minister Narendra Modi.

Police officers who stood by and watched the killing also got rewarded. M.K. Tandon, joint commissioner of police in a section of Ahmedabad where 200 were Muslims slaughtered, was promoted to inspector general of police in Surat, the richest, and third largest city in Gujarat. Three years later, in July 2005, he was promoted again to Additional DGP (Law and Order) for the entire state. This was in sharp contrast to what happened to Jayanti Ravi, the collector of Godhra, as we saw earlier.[10]

Modi continued his taming of the administration through a by now well-honed system of rewards and punishments after he became the prime minister of India. R.K. Raghavan, the disgraced CBI official who had been in charge of Prime Minister Rajiv Gandhi's security at Sri Perumbudur on May 21, 1991, when he got blown up by an LTTE suicide bomber, but who had been resuscitated by Home Minister L.K. Advani to head of the SIT that exonerated Modi of any dereliction of duty during the 2002 pogrom, was allowed to stay on in the same post, now nothing but a sinecure, for four years after he submitted his final report in 2012, and was then sent as India's Ambassador to Cyprus.

Similarly, in another move without precedent, Modi appointed Justice P. Sathasivam, who had headed the Supreme Court bench that uncritically accepted the SIT's initial and final reports exonerating Modi of culpability in the Gujarat riots, paying scant heed to the objections of Raju Ramachandran,[11] the Supreme Court's own *amicus curiae*, as the Governor of Kerala on August 31, 2014, only three months after Modi became prime minister and four months after Sathasivam retired as the chief justice of the Supreme Court of India. This was the first ever occasion on which a chief justice of India, one of whose tasks is to administer the oath of fealty to the prime minister of India, went on to swear a similar oath to the man whom he had elevated to that post.

## Modi Throws Vanzara to the Wolves

But there were limits to how far Modi could go towards suborning his bureaucracy to destroy its constitutionally mandated independence from politics. One of those whom Modi could not shelter was D.G. Vanzara, the head of Gujarat's ATS and widely known as the state's 'encounter specialist'. In the letter of resignation from the Indian Police Service that he wrote from jail on September 1, 2013, forfeiting all his post-retirement benefits, Vanzara wrote:[12]

> To the best of my knowledge, nowhere in any part of the country, [has] such a big number of police officers [been] arrested and continuously...kept in the jails for such a long period of time except in the state of Gujarat. The most notable part of the whole episode is that they are made to suffer in the jails, in spite of the fact that they had been, and are, loyal soldiers of this government who fought [an] incessant war against Pakistan inspired terrorism with complete honesty, integrity and sincerity without falling prey to any of the mundane temptations...
>
> With the passage of time, I realized that this government was not only not interested in protecting us but it also has been

> clandestinely making all efforts to keep me and my officers in the jail so as to save its own skin from [the] CBI on one hand and gain political benefits on the other...
>
> I, therefore, would like to categorically state in the most unequivocal words that the officers and men of Crime Branch, ATS and Border Range, during the period of years between 2002 [and] 2007, simply acted and performed their duties in compliance of the conscious policy of this government... [W]e have simply implemented the conscious policy of this government which was inspiring, guiding and monitoring our actions from very close quarters.

Vanzara's letter contains no tinge of remorse, but also none of communal rancour:

> A monstrous episode of Godhra train burning and equally horrible post-Godhra riots in Gujarat provided a pretext to Pakistan based terrorist outfits like Let, JeM and D gang under the direct supervision of ISI, to 'convert Gujarat into another Kashmir' by exploiting the sentiments of the Muslims all over the world.

Listing fourteen bomb blasts, five assassination attempts and two fidayeen attacks on the Rath Yatra and the Swaminarayan Temple at Akshardham, he concluded: 'I can say with pride that my officers and men not only successfully prevent[ed] Gujarat from becoming another Kashmir, but were also instrumental in providing a solid atmosphere of durable peace and security in the state.'

The bulk of the letter was a violent diatribe against the Modi government, and Amit Shah in particular, for having abandoned his police force when it most needed their support:

> This government suddenly became vibrant and displayed a spurt of sincere activities only when Shri Amitbhai Shah, former MOS, Home, was arrested by CBI. It [engaged] Shri Ram Jethmalani, the most learned, senior most and highest paid advocate of India...and got him released on regular bail within [the] record time of 3 months of his imprisonment.

> In contrast, when I, along with Rajkumar Pandian and Dinesh M.N., was arrested by the CID Crime, forget about providing the legal services, nobody from the government bothered even to provide a lip service to us or to our family members…
>
> [The] Gujarat police…used to be one of the finest…in the country till the coronation of this government in Gandhinagar. Today the same proud police…stands totally shattered and demoralized [by]…the continuous betrayal of jailed police officers [for the] last six years.

The chain of cause and effect described above is, admittedly, circumstantial. But it allows us to make sense of Modi's choice of Amit Shah for the key post of president of the BJP within weeks of his being sworn in as prime minister in 2014. Modi did this *while he was on bail facing three charges of murder*. In the confusion and unrest generated within the secular intelligentsia of the country by Modi and the BJP's victory, few of its members noticed the implications of the prime minister appointing a man facing three charges of murder as the president of the BJP. It meant that Modi already knew that Amit Shah would never be convicted on any of these charges before they had even been heard in court. What this appointment did was to provide the missing link that connected the string of extra-judicial murders that took place in Gujarat to the riots in 2002.

That link is motive. The three things that every judge looks for when deciding a murder case are motive, opportunity, and means. In situations where the murderer is not caught red-handed, motive is by far the most important of the three. Yet motive is the one question that neither the investigators nor the judges who set up the SIT chose to investigate.

If motive is essential to establish guilt, then absence of motive should suffice to establish at least sufficient doubt to set a man free. So, if these were faked encounters, and Narendra Modi and Amit Shah both did not order them, then what motive did thirty-two policemen, including officers, have for carrying these out? Had this question been asked, it could have evoked several possible answers: Gujarat's long coastline and its proximity to Dubai had made its coast a smugglers' haven for as long as anyone could remember. This had fostered powerful gangs with ample access to firearms. Gujarat is also an obstinately 'dry state' where prohibition has continued not because Gujaratis are puritans, but because powerful gangs have developed that deal in illicit liquor and therefore have a vested interest in its continuance. The police in Gujarat therefore have an especially dangerous job, so faked encounters have become one of the principal ways of keeping the power of these gangs in check.

But no one asked any searching questions, so no explanation was ever given. The immense popularity Modi and the police gained from foiling the terrorist attack on the Akshardham Temple gave the police a *carte blanche* to deal with undesirable elements in any way they chose, and Modi a readymade way of further inflating his already larger-than-life image as a defender of India and of Hindus against the evil Muslims of Pakistan.

The true answer was given, albeit indirectly, by D.G. Vanzara, in the letter of resignation quoted above. In it, Vanzara heaped all the blame on Shah, but whose orders was Shah following? It could only have been the Chief Minister who was also the home minister in the cabinet, and therefore Shah's direct superior in the home ministry. One indication that it was Modi himself was that there was a second person in constant contact with Rajkumar Pandian in December 2006. This was Parag Shah, an officer on special duty in the Chief Minister's office.

During the month of December 2006, Parag Shah spoke to Pandian ten times for a total of *10 hours and 48 minutes*. More than half of these calls took place in the two days when Prajapati had been brought to Ahmedabad from Rajasthan, to be interviewed by the CBI, before he was taken to Banaskantha, where he met his end. (See Appendix.)

In its final report, the Concerned Citizens' Tribunal observed:

Not only the criminal justice system, the entire Administration has failed. IAS and IPS officers who are supposed to be independent, have succumbed to the pressure of the Sangh Parivar. 'There is no civil service left in Gujarat', said the former Indian cabinet secretary Shri T.S.R. Subramanian. 'What has happened is something much more fundamental than Gujarat: The civil service is gone. There is no such thing left. Over the years, the civil service has turned from a steel frame to non-existent. And that is a shattering thought.

'When the government wants something done it has the ability, it has the *taakat* (strength). It can do it in village after village, town after town. That it has not done so in Gujarat is a telling indictment not only of the way of the present government, but also the collapse of the police and civil magistracy.'[13]

CHAPTER THIRTEEN

# The Mystery of Haren Pandya's Murder

Searching for a motive is also the only way to find an explanation for the most sensational political murder in the history of Gujarat—that of Haren Pandya, who had been the home minister of the state under Modi's predecessor, Keshubhai Patel, and therefore Modi's principal rival for the chief ministership after Keshubhai resigned in 2001. The moment one asks who stood to gain the most from Pandya's death, the 'needle of suspicion' stops at Narendra Modi.

There were three political leaders over whom he exercised no control. These were Sanjay Joshi, a general secretary in the national BJP, Modi's first deputy minister in the home ministry, Gordhan Zadafia, and Haren Pandya.

In the years that followed, two of the three were either discredited or intimidated. Sanjay Joshi was forced into political oblivion when a VCD showing him with naked women was anonymously circulated to top BJP leaders. The video was later found to be a fake.

Modi replaced Zadafia with Amit Shah, partly because Zadafia's primary loyalty was not to him but to the VHP chief Pravin Togadia. The fact that call data records and eyewitnesses had placed him in Naroda Patiya, where the worst killings had taken place on February 28, gave Modi a good reason to do so. But Zadafia took it badly. So, Modi kept him under surveillance. In February 2005, two years later, when Zadafia found a policeman from the state intelligence department following him around and learned from him that he was acting under the orders of Minister of State for Home Amit Shah, he decided to confront Modi at a meeting of BJP legislators held a few days later. He recounted the episode to Vinod Jose of *Caravan*:

> 'Narendrabhai, what kind of spy activities are you doing against your own party legislators?' I asked. 'Why is an intelligence man following me?' Then Vajubhai Vala, a senior minister, took the microphone and said, 'Okay Gordhanbhai, cool down. We will look into it, but this is not a question to be asked now.' Modi didn't speak at all, but I got a note from his secretary that said 'Please meet the CM'.
>
> I met him at his chamber after the meeting. Amit Shah was sitting there. Modi asked me, 'Why are you asking these kinds of questions in public?' I said, 'What shall I do? It is not a private matter.' Then he looked sternly into my eyes and said, '*Khatam ho jaoge*, Govardhanbhai… You're going to get finished.'
>
> I asked him, what kind of finishing? Physically or politically?
>
> He said, 'You complained against me to L.K. Advani and Om Mathur in Delhi.
>
> I said, 'Of course. There's no option for me other than to complain to the people in Delhi. But if you're saying you will finish me off, let me tell you, I'll die when my time comes. Don't try to threaten me again.'

'Modi understands only one alphabet, and that is the capital "I",' said Zadafia in conclusion. 'I was threatened with death by Modi himself… Haren was bold. He thought nothing would happen to him. That was a mistake.'

The difference between Joshi and Zadafia, and Haren Pandya was that while the first two could only complain to the party high command or try to discredit Modi through the media, Haren Pandya had the capacity to get him indicted on criminal charges that would force him out of office and possibly into prison. 'Pandya was a formidable political rival for Modi within the state BJP,' notes Jose. 'The two had clashed publicly for the first time in

2001, when Modi was in search of a safe assembly seat to contest after his appointment as CM. He wanted to run from Pandya's constituency, Ellisbridge in Ahmedabad—a very safe seat for the BJP. But Pandya refused to yield to Modi's wishes. As a state BJP functionary recalled, "Haren said, 'Ask me to vacate my seat for a young man in the BJP—I'll do it. But not for that fellow.'"[1]

Modi did not forget the snub. Shortly afterwards, he moved Pandya out of the home ministership to the relatively minor portfolio of revenue minister, keeping the home portfolio for himself and appointing Gordhan Zadafia as his deputy. Modi's thirst for revenge did not stop there. In the run-up to the December 2002 state election, he defied virtually the entire top leadership of the BJP and RSS and took the Ellisbridge constituency, which Pandya had represented for fifteen years, away from him.

The leadership of both the RSS and the BJP objected and asked Modi to relent, but he refused. Near the end of November, RSS leader Madan Das Devi went to meet Modi at his residence, carrying a message from the RSS supremo K.S. Sudarshan, his deputy Mohan Bhagwat, Advani and Vajpayee: Stop arguing, don't create division before the elections, and give Pandya his seat. Devi stayed late into the night, but Modi held his ground, the state party functionary whom Jose interviewed said: 'He knew he would start getting phone calls from [the RSS headquarters in] Nagpur and Delhi, since he did not listen to Devi. So that night, by 3 am, he got himself admitted into the Gandhinagar Civil Hospital for exhaustion and fatigue.'

Pandya, according to the same functionary, charged to the hospital to confront Modi. 'Haren told him, "Don't sleep like a coward. Have the guts to say no to me."' Modi refused to budge, and the RSS and BJP leaders finally gave in.

After the elections, Pandya started a campaign against Modi, warning every top leader in the BJP and RSS—in Delhi and in Nagpur—that Modi would destroy the party and the Sangh for his own personal gain. Since Pandya was considered a valuable asset to the party, senior BJP leaders decided to transfer him to the party headquarters in Delhi as a member of the national executive or a party spokesman.

Modi, who was only too aware that he owed his own rise to supremacy to his fortuitous expulsion from Gujarat to the party headquarters in Delhi, could hardly have failed to see the immense increase in threat to him that Pandya could become once he was established in Delhi. So, not surprisingly, Modi even tried to scuttle that, as Zadafia told Jose. Three months later, on March 24th or 25th, Pandya received a fax from the BJP president instructing him to shift to Delhi. *Perhaps coincidentally, he was murdered just one day later.*

**Haren Pandya**

Murders take a long time to organize, so it is unlikely that anyone connected Pandya's murder to his imminent departure for Delhi. But Pandya also presented a threat to Modi on an altogether different level. At a cabinet meeting Modi convened after receiving the news from Godhra, Pandya had reportedly objected to the bodies of the victims being brought to Ahmedabad, but had been shouted down by other ministers present at the meeting.[2] Unlike the police officers whom Modi met later that evening, Pandya was not a subordinate of Modi and could not therefore be controlled through threats and inducements. On May 23, 2002, Pandya deposed secretly before the Concerned Citizens' Tribunal that Modi had in fact issued the February 27th injunction to his officers to let the Hindus take their revenge. He was not present at the meeting, but claimed that he had been briefed by someone who had been present.

Pandya also spoke to *Outlook*, a weekly magazine published from Delhi. In its issue dated June 3, 2002 (which hit the newsstands a week earlier) the magazine published a detailed account of what Pandya had told them, but on Pandya' request, without naming him. The gist of his statement is reproduced below:

> [The minister told *Outlook* that in his deposition he] revealed that on the night of February 27, Modi summoned DGP

> K. Chakravarthy, commissioner of police, Ahmedabad, [P.P.] Pandey, chief secretary G. Subarao, home secretary Ashok Narayan, secretary to the home department K. Nityanand (a serving police officer of IG rank on deputation) and DGP (IB) [G.C.] Raigar. Also present were officers from the CM's office: P.K. Mishra, Anil Mukhim and A.K. Sharma. The minister also told *Outlook* that the meeting was held at the CM's bungalow.
>
> The minister told the tribunal that in the two-hour meeting, Modi made it clear there would be justice for Godhra the next day, during the VHP-called bandh. He ordered that the police should not come in the way of 'the Hindu backlash'. At one point in this briefing, according to the minister's statement to the tribunal, DGP Chakravarthy vehemently protested. But he was harshly told by Modi to shut up and obey. Commissioner Pandey, says the minister, would later show remorse in private but at that meeting didn't have the guts to object.
>
> According to his deposition, it was a typical Modi meeting: more orders than discussion. By the end of it, the CM ensured that his top officials—especially the police—would stay out of the way of Sangh Parivar men. The word was passed on to the mobs.
>
> (According to a top IB official, on the morning of February 28, VHP and Bajrang Dal activists first visited some parts of Ahmedabad and created minor trouble just to check if the police did in fact look the other way. Once Modi's word was confirmed, the carnage began.)

Before publishing what it had learned from Modi, *Outlook* contacted one of the members of the Concerned Citizens' Tribunal, Justice Hosbet Suresh, to confirm whether a senior minister of the government had indeed spoken to it. Justice Suresh gave *Outlook* a detailed account of what Pandya had told the Tribunal during his thirty-five–forty-minute meeting with its members.

> The minister told the tribunal that Modi was convinced that since he started the riots, he would be able to control the violence within a day or two. But the scale of the violence and the media backlash caught him by surprise. The more shocking

> aspect of the minister's testimony was what he told the CCT when it asked him how he would have handled the Godhra train conflagration if he had still been the Home Minister: 'Scores could have been settled in Godhra itself. Perhaps 100 people may have died there on the whole and that may have been the end of it. But Modi brought the riots to Ahmedabad. He took the riots to rest of the state.'

The riots were not born out of any ideology, according to the minister. They had a simple political background. The minister told *Outlook*,

> Modi was never a politician. He was a *pracharak*, a *pracharak* whose days were numbered because unlike others of his status, he was a man who liked the good life. He lived like a king. Not many liked him. Then one day, we were shocked by the BJP's defeat in the panchayat elections. And when the BJP lost the Sabarmati assembly seat and Sabarkanta parliamentary seat, we knew we would lose the general elections.

That's when Modi stepped in. According to the minister,

> Modi told the BJP high command that after all, he was more presentable than Keshubhai Patel and he swore that in the next elections he would bring the BJP back to power. The minister added that when, five and a half months into the job, Modi realized his charm wasn't working, he decided religious polarization was the only way to survive. As triggers go, Godhra was a strong one. But anything could have served as a trigger. *There was talk of making an issue of a cow slaughter video the party had got, but that plan was shelved.*

Modi could not have learned what Pandya told the Tribunal, but when the story appeared, he had a good idea of who the unnamed minister was. For the written records of Modi's office, accessed somehow by Vinod Jose while researching his story for *The Caravan*, showed that his principal secretary, P.K. Mishra, had instructed the director general of state intelligence to track

Pandya's movements, and in particular those related to the 'fact-finding panel'. The intelligence director took down the instructions in a register—the entry for June 7, 2002 read as follows:

> Dr PK Mishra added that Shri Harenbhai Pandya, minister for revenue is suspected to be the minister involved in the matter. Thereafter, he gave one mobile number 9824030629 and asked for getting call details.

Five days later, on June 12, 2002, there was another entry in the register:

> Informed Dr PK Mishra that the minister who is suspected to have met the private inquiry commission (Justice VR Krishna Iyer) is known to be Mr Haren Pandya. I also informed that the matter cannot be given in writing as this issue is quite sensitive and not connected with the charter of duties given to State intelligence Bureau vide Bombay Police Manual. It is learnt that the telephone number 9824030629 is the mobile phone of Shri Harenbhai Pandya.[3]

Pandya did not know at that time that he was already under surveillance. So, when he received a notice from the BJP president in Gujarat, Rajendrasinh Rana, asking him to 'show cause' as to why he should not be expelled from the party, Pandya took strong offence, wrote a sharply accusatory letter to Modi saying that he knew he was behind the show cause notice, and resigned from the government on August 6.

Seven months later, on March 26, 2003, he was shot dead in cold blood.

*

Two completely opposed accusations emerged within hours of Pandya's murder. Pandya's family have always maintained that Modi was behind it. His father, Vithalbhai Pandya, said as much when Modi came to the hospital where Pandya's body lay. But an alternative theory involving D.G. Vanzara, whom the government had put in charge of the investigation, also began to make the rounds within hours of Pandya's death. This was that he had been killed in a 'cut out' murder—in which 'A' had commissioned 'B', who had commissioned 'C' to do, or arrange, the actual killing.

According to this theory, 'Pandya had gone to Law Garden for a walk, as usual. As he parked, Asghar Ali [a known hitman from Hyderabad] had approached his car and shot him five times through a three-inch opening in the pane on the driver's side. Asghar's recruitment for the job was part of a plot hatched by Muslim elements—among them Mufti Sufian, a rabble-rousing cleric of Ahmedabad's Lal Masjid—that wanted to avenge the post-Godhra carnage.'[4]

The CBI team that took over the investigation two days after Pandya's murder was led by an IPS officer Y.C. Modi. Modi soon claimed that the team had uncovered an elaborate conspiracy that included links with Pakistan's ISI and gang lords of the Muslim underworld in Gujarat and Andhra Pradesh. The CBI wrapped up investigations in less than six months and filed its charge sheet on September 8, 2003.

Based on its finding, a special court convened under the Prevention of Terrorism Act (POTA) convicted twelve people, and awarded life imprisonment to nine of them on June 25, 2007. Asghar Ali was punished with imprisonment till the end of his natural life. Two others got seven-year jail sentences, and another person got a five-year jail sentence.[5]

This hurriedly concocted case had been eyewash from the start, for four years later, the Gujarat High Court reversed all the convictions with a scathing indictment of the CBI's inquiry. But it had served its purpose, for by then, the trail had run too cold for anyone to pick up again.

**Pandya Had Spoken to *Outlook* Again**

But it hadn't quite, for in August 2002, a week before he left the government, Pandya had given a second interview to *Outlook*, and this conversation was recorded. Four years later, *Outlook* released excerpts from the tapes. Then, in a searing revelation, in its issue dated November 12, 2007, the magazine published what he had said in his second conversation: Pandya confirmed what he had told *Outlook* earlier. 'The time, the place (of the February 27th meeting),' he said, 'was correct. Ask them to get the officers present to deny it. Let them say there was no meeting, no direct or indirect orders. Let them say it on paper with their signatures.' Needless to say, this never happened.

'Don't disclose my identity even verbally,' he had told *Outlook*, fearing the worst. '*My name should not be quoted in any story, not even as minister or BJP leader. If you write BJP leader, I will die. If you write minister, even then I will die.*' (Emphasis added)

He went on to say:

> I can't tell you how much I have been harassed [after the first *Outlook* story appeared]... See, whatever I told you, it was not as if some disgruntled man was saying it. I didn't say all those things because I was unhappy. There is nobody in my position who can fight him [Modi]. Outsiders can't do anything. So, it's important I remain an insider, in power, in position. That's why I want my identity protected.[6]

We now know that G. Subba Rao and G.C. Raigar were not present at the meeting, the latter having been on leave. Nor, obviously, was Pandya himself. But his description of what happened there tallies closely with that of Sanjiv Bhatt, Raigar's deputy, who made a deposition before the SIT in 2009, seven years later. Unless both Bhatt and Pandya were part of a conspiracy to defame, and oust, Narendra Modi that was hatched as early as May 2002, it is hard to doubt that Pandya had been briefed by someone who had served under him when he was the home minister till five months earlier. That person could have been Sanjiv Bhatt.

### A Political Cover-up

Pandya was killed at around 7.20 am on March 26, 2003, at or near his car in Law Garden in Ahmedabad, where he used to take a walk every morning. He was so eminent and respected that the entire force and skills of the Ahmedabad Police should have been concentrated on finding the killers. But everything about the police's subsequent behaviour reeked of a cover-up. First, the police did not get to know of his murder till a little past 10.00 am. This was not because no one saw his corpse inside his car, parked on an increasingly busy street, but because no one reported it to the police. Then, even after it got to know of the murder, the police took another hour to get to the car, although it was parked no more than ten minutes away from the Ellisbridge police station. The delay occurred because Ellisbridge, the closest police station, got a succession of conflicting orders on where to go.

On August 19, 2006, *Tehelka*, then one of India's most widely read and respected news magazines, whose correspondents had done more to expose the organized nature of the pogrom that had taken place in Ahmedabad in 2002 than any other publication in the country, published a detailed report from its executive editor, Sankarshan Thakur, that highlighted the many inconsistencies in the police's charge sheet.[7]

Thakur revealed that the post mortem on Pandya, carried out by the Forensic Science Laboratory in Ahmedabad, had shown that Pandya had been shot at least six, possibly seven, times but with two separate guns. Five of the bullet holes were of 8 mm diameter, while two were of 5 mm diameter. More puzzling still, one of the latter bullets had entered his scrotum and travelled upwards to pierce the abdominal wall. Not only would it have been impossible for anyone to shoot him from that angle when he was sitting in the car, but he would have bled profusely from a wound in that part of the body, where there is a convergence of arteries and veins. However, the FSL reported there was no blood in the car except for a small dab of it on the front passenger seat, and another on the key chain. There was no attempt then, and there has never been one since, to explain this anomaly. In the trial court, the CBI relied upon the statement of its lone eyewitness, and claimed that the trajectory of the shot that entered Pandya's scrotum could be explained by the fact that when Pandya sprawled to the side after being shot, his legs had gone up in the air. But as is explained further down, this was a manifest impossibility.

The only conclusion that could be drawn from the forensic evidence without denying the laws of physics was that Haren Pandya could not have been killed in the car. So, he had to have been kidnapped while he was taking his walk, taken to a place where he could be killed unobserved, shot dead with two small calibre bullets, allowed to bleed out till his heart stopped pumping, then brought back, seated in his car, and have five more bullets pumped into his dead body, which no longer bled, from a much larger calibre revolver or pistol.

Who could have committed this fiendish murder? And since it was not committed in the car, how could one man and a helper—be it Asghar Ali, Sohrabuddin or Tulsiram Prajapati—have carried the body back from wherever he was killed without at least a trolley to carry the corpse?

The cornerstone of the police's case was a statement obtained from a lone eyewitness, a Law Garden sandwich vendor named Anil Yadram Patel, who claimed to have been present at the time of Pandya's shooting and who, in the trial of the alleged plotters that followed, identified a known Hyderabad hitman, Asghar Ali, as Pandya's assailant.

But Yadram's testimony was so full of inconsistencies that it was beyond understanding how a judge at any level of the judiciary could not see the gaping holes in it. For not only was it refuted by the forensic evidence collected by the police, it was full of internal inconsistencies that the police did not even bother to explain and no judge till this day has probed.

First, he claimed to have recognized a man *whom he had never seen before* walk up to a car in which another man—whom, as his subsequent actions suggest, he certainly recognized as Haren Pandya—was sitting and shoot him dead with five shots of a handgun. Such eyewitness testimony is not always reliable, but in this case it would have been even less so, because Yadram would have had to be far enough from Pandya's car for the killer not to think it necessary to eliminate him as a potential witness.

Second, since Ellisbridge and Law Garden were in Pandya's constituency, he would have been well known there. It is inconceivable therefore that his body could have lain in a public place for almost three hours, without a crowd having gathered around him. So, why did no one report the murder to the police?

The inconsistencies between Yadram's testimony and the forensic evidence should have been sufficient to throw the case against Asghar Ali out of any court, but it is a third element, the inconsistency in Yadram's behaviour *after* the murder, that not only made his testimony truly suspect but pointed towards a completely different set of suspects for the murder. For instead of rushing straight to the nearest police station to report the murder, *Yadram stayed rooted to his spot for a whole hour and did absolutely nothing.*

Yadram claimed later that he had been too dazed by what he saw to be able to move. But an hour is much too long for such paralysis, and reeks of fear and indecision rather than shock. What is more, his natural reaction after he recovered from the shock should have been to go to the car and see who had been killed. So, what could have caused such intense fear that he neither ran to the car, nor to the police station minutes away?

An explanation for Yadram's strange behaviour can be found by looking at the behaviour of three other persons who got to know of Pandya's murder before the Ellisbridge police arrived at the scene. When he snapped out of his 'daze', Yadram went not to the police but to his *seth*, Snehal Adenwala. After hearing his account, Adenwala too did not report the murder to the police. Instead, he contacted one Prakash Shah, an associate of Haren Pandya. *Shah too did not call the police.* Instead, he called Pandya's secretary, Neelesh Bhatt, who was already at Pandya's house and had begun to worry about the absence of his employer. Bhatt too did not go to the police! Instead, he rushed directly to Law Garden to make sure for himself that it was indeed Pandya in the car.

The answer to why Yadram did not go to the police could have been a simple one: he might have feared that the police would try to pin the murder on him. But why did Adenwala, Shah and Bhatt, who were all men of influence and had nothing to fear from the police, also shun the police? The only disclosure Yadram could have made that would have made them all do so was that the people who brought Pandya's corpse back and placed it in his car were policemen.

Yadram's behaviour makes it difficult not to conclude that Haren Pandya's murder was also a faked encounter arranged by the Gujarat Police. Not only was his family convinced that he had not been murdered by a hired killer brought from Hyderabad by Muslim bigots who were bent upon killing a senior Guajarati politician in revenge for the Ahmedabad pogroms, as the police claimed, but both his wife and father remained convinced, the latter till his dying day, that this was a political killing. Both had tried and tried to make the police take it up but without success. Their view was widely shared in Ahmedabad at the time, because Pandya's security cover had been withdrawn without explanation just days before the killing. The Law Garden lane in which his body was found was also cleared of all carts and hawkers two days before he was found dead there. This was a strange action indeed for a government that went on to claim, in an on-the-record statement to the online journal Rediff.com only four months later, that the killing of Haren Pandya was one of the reasons why it had decided to create a structure designed to 'nip such threats in the bud'. Inevitably, therefore, public opinion in Ahmedabad, and more than one newspaper, concluded that this was 'a political murder'.

More than two decades after Pandya's murder, this allegation still remains to be proved, but it is the most plausible explanation for the anomalies that surround his death: the three-hour delay in the police getting to Law Garden; its insistence in the face of very strong forensic evidence that at least two guns had been used that there had been only one assassin, Asghar Ali; and its sole reliance for this claim on the word of Yadram, who would have been too terrified of the police to do anything but endorse its version of the murder. Strangely enough, the police was also unable to obtain phone records for Pandya's phone from Hutch for March when it was able to supply them for January and February.

Six years after the Gujarat Police and the CBI secured a conviction from a trial court in Ahmedabad in 2005, on August 29, 2011, the Gujarat High Court threw the conviction out with anger and contempt. 'What clearly stands out from the record of the present case', the Court said, 'is that the investigation in the case of murder of Shri Haren Pandya has all throughout been botched up and blinkered and has left a lot to be desired.' It faulted the CBI for relying heavily on a single eyewitness, Anil Yadram, whose testimony, it said, could not be believed owing to his behaviour, which it deemed 'unnatural'. It also detailed the inconsistency between his supposedly eyewitness account and the forensic evidence, highlighted by the absence of blood in the car. 'The investigating officers concerned', it concluded, 'ought to be held accountable for their ineptitude resulting in injustice, huge harassment of many persons concerned and enormous waste of public resources and public time of the Courts.'

The High Court's judgement immediately reopened the question that had lain dormant in Gujarat: if it was not a Muslim hitman hired by Muslim conspirators bent upon taking revenge for the Ahmedabad pogrom, then who had organized Haren Pandya's murder? To no one's surprise, the CBI and the Gujarat government immediately appealed against the acquittal to the Supreme Court.

Little was heard of the case after that for seven years till, for reasons that have never been made clear, the Supreme Court 'reserved' its verdict on January 31, 2019. It was only on July 5, 2019, three months after the Lok Sabha elections were over, that the two-judge bench led by Justice Arun Mishra gave its verdict. To the surprise and shock of the legal community, it took the virtually unprecedented step of totally reversing the High Court judgement and convicting all twelve of the conspirators all over again.

Reversals of the verdicts of lower courts by the Supreme Court are not uncommon. As a study by the National Law University, Delhi has shown, 55.3 per cent of the criminal cases it studied had resulted in a reversal of the verdict.[8] But as recently as December 22, 2021, the Supreme Court has laid down that reversal of an *acquittal* by a trial court is permissible only if the acquittal is 'not only erroneous but also unreliable and perverse'.[9] This has only rarely happened, but the reversal of a verdict of acquittal by a High Court, and that too in a murder case, has no precedent. Not only did the major media channels make no mention of this, but none of them asked how such a verdict could be implemented after the convicted had been set free. Asghar Ali and one more of the accused could be made to serve out their sentences because they had been arrested in connection with another murder case and were being held in Vishakhapatnam jail in 2011. Three others who had been given five- and seven-year sentences had finished these before the Gujarat High Court acquitted them. A few of the accused were absconding and presumed to be in Pakistan. But what about the remaining four or five who had been set free in 2011? Surprisingly, no newspaper or television channel bothered to find out.

## Justice Was the Final Victim

One last clue about the case surfaced later. This was the call data records of Haren Pandya's cell phone for the month of March 2003. The police had recovered Pandya's cell phone from his car, but had shown an inexplicable reluctance to examine its contents. When *India Today* asked the service provider, Hutch (now Vodafone), to produce its manifests for March, it claimed that it could not do so because the data were too old, and had therefore been scrubbed. But it could provide the data for January and February. Hutch's explanation had sounded strange, for in its calendar, March seemed to have come before January and February.

However, *Tehelka* was able to obtain the records for March a short while later by means it did not care to disclose. These showed that there had been forty phone calls to Pandya from a female journalist in Ahmedabad during the twenty-five days before he was killed. No one knows who the journalist was, or what they spoke about, but apparently, for those to whom he posed a threat, the possibility that he had decided to go public could no longer be ignored.

With all avenues of inquiry now closed, we may never come to know who killed Pandya. But there can be little doubt about who gained the most from his death. That was the chief minister, Narendra Modi. As a powerful and popular home minister till only five months earlier, Pandya had any number of sources in the home ministry. He knew what Modi might have *suggested*, if not *instructed*, his police chiefs to do, at the February 27 meeting. And Modi would have known that Pandya had been speaking to the Concerned Citizens' Tribunal about it.

Pandya was also the only powerful politician in Gujarat who was completely outside Modi's control: whom he could neither persuade nor intimidate into 'forever holding his peace'. He therefore held Modi's future in his hands. That could have been why Modi's new deputy in the home ministry, Amit Shah, assigned the investigation of his murder to D.G. Vanzara, who had developed a bond with Mr Modi during his handling of the terrorist attack on the Akshardham Temple on September 24 of the previous year.

But unlike the question of his culpability for the Gujarat riots which was laid to rest by the Supreme Court in 2013, the Haren Pandya killing continues to haunt Modi till today. Pandya's family has repeatedly demanded a re-investigation as they believe the real culprits have never been caught. In March 2018, his wife, Jagruti Pandya managed to meet Asghar Ali, the principal accused, in Vishakhapatnam jail, where he was being held on a different murder charge. After the meeting, she told a correspondent from the *Hindu BusinessLine*, 'I had wanted to meet him ever since he had been here [Ahmedabad] at Sabarmati jail to find out the truth behind his role [in Pandya's murder]... My meeting with Ali lasted for two-and-a-half hours in which he narrated how, at the instance of CBI, he was framed in the case and how he was tortured to make a false confession.'

## Jagruti Pandya's Belief

Jagruti Pandya stated that she believed Ali when he said that he had no knowledge of her husband's murder until his arrest by CBI on April 20, 2003. After being acquitted by Gujarat High Court in the Pandya murder case, Ali had been arrested by the Andhra Pradesh police in connection with another murder. 'He told me that he had never visited Gujarat before April 2003, when a team of Gujarat police...brought him to the city [before his] arrest by CBI,' Jagruti said. At the state government's request, the CBI had taken over the probe into the case within two days of Pandya's murder. The central home minister then was L.K. Advani, who owed his Gandhinagar parliamentary seat to Modi's tireless campaigning on his behalf.

Elaborating on why she and her husband's family remained convinced that his had been a political murder, she pointed out that 'No leader from BJP, not even the Deputy Prime Minister L.K. Advani, helped us. I have been fighting a lone battle for justice.'

She also pointed out that Rajendra Kumar, the Intelligence Bureau officer who was responsible for generating intelligence inputs before Pandya's murder, was the same who had earlier generated intelligence that some terrorists were coming to Gujarat for an attack on a prominent BJP leader, which formed the basis for the Gujarat Police's stated belief that Ishrat Jahan and her three companions had been recruited by Pakistan to assassinate Modi. In short, she implied that Rajendra Kumar was an officer who had made a career out of concocting paranoia against Pakistan.[10]

On November 3, 2018, in yet another hearing of the Sohrabuddin case before a Mumbai court, Azam Khan, an associate in crime of Tulsiram Prajapati and Sohrabuddin, testified that the latter had told him while they were in jail that it was Vanzara who had ordered the killing of Pandya. Vanzara had given the *supari* (underworld term for contract) to three known hitmen, Naeem Khan, Shahid Rampuri and Sohrabuddin Sheikh. Sohrabuddin had passed the *supari* on to Tulsiram Prajapati who had done the actual killing with 'a boy'. Azam Khan told the court that Sohrabuddin had stated that the order for the execution had come from those holding high positions—'*upar se yeh kaam diya tha*' (the work was given from above).[11]

Khan also disclosed that way back in 2010 he had said the same thing to a CBI investigator, N.S. Raju, but was told not to create 'new confusion'. 'I had told the CBI officer that Haren Pandya's murder was done by Tulsiram Prajapati and one boy at the instance of Sohrabuddin. When I told him [Raju] about Haren Pandya, *unhone bola naye bakhede mey mat dalo* (don't create new problems for me),' Khan told the court.

A few years later, there was an attempt to assassinate him, in which his arm was badly damaged. Khan survived, but decided to stay underground till he turned himself in on October 12, 2018. Khan did so while the police put ever increasing pressure on his family to make him surface, appear in court and say what they wanted him to say.

Ajoy Ashirwad Mahaprashasta of *The Wire* spoke to Rizwana, Azam Khan's wife, and Akhilesh Mogra, the lawyer for Khan's family, in November. He reported:

> His wife and other relatives have complained that Khan is being tortured in jail and is gravely injured... According to his wife Rizwana and his lawyer, to ensure that he follows their directions, the police have allegedly opened nine new cases against him and have threatened that if Khan does not toe the line, he could also face murder charges.
>
> ... Khan's counsel Akhilesh Mogra, said, '... After his arrest on October 12 [2018] from New Delhi, he is continuously being beaten in jail. Khan fears he may be bumped off just like Sohrabuddin and his associate Tulsiram Prajapati.' ...

> In his testimony before the Mumbai trial court, Khan said that Prajapati had told him that he was tricked into giving information about Sohrabuddin to the police. The police had told Prajapati that there was 'political pressure' to arrest Sohrabuddin and that if Prajapati gave them the information they required, he would be released.
>
> ... Prajapati told Khan [that] Sohrabuddin and his wife Kausar Bi were killed in a farmhouse in Gujarat. Khan also told the court that Prajapati too was fearful of being eliminated and therefore lodged a complaint before an Ahmedabad court.
>
> 'I last met Tulsiram on December 23–24, 2006 [in Udaipur jail in Rajasthan], when I [had been] taken into custody for some old theft case pending against me. He was being to be taken to Ahmedabad for a court hearing. He had told me that either one [or the other] of us would be killed,' Khan said to the CBI trial court on November 3.[12]

In June 2018, as the CBI faced increasing pressure to bring Khan to testify, the police began to mount pressure on the family to make him surrender. According to a petition lodged by his mother Husaina Banu with the chief judicial magistrate of Udaipur on June 11, the Udaipur police did this by picking up her two other sons and a brother-in-law. In the petition, she said that when she met the police officials, they told her that the three would be released only if Khan said what the '*upar ke adhikari*' (higher officials) wanted him to say in front of the court in the Sohrabuddin and Prajapati encounter case.[13]

The petition further stated that the police officials wanted Khan to change his statement that Khan, Sohrabuddin and Prajapati were associates. They had picked up her sons on the orders of Sudhir Joshi, additional superintendent of police, Udaipur—who too was a witness in the Prajapati fake encounter case. She also told the Chief Judicial Magistrate that the police officials threatened her, telling her that if Khan did not stick to the tutored statement, he would also be killed in an encounter. 'The police is trying to send him off to Ajmer prison and he fears that he will be killed in an encounter during that journey,' Khan's wife Rizwana added.

The police released the three men they had arrested after a week, but only after the court had issued a search warrant. According to Akhilesh Mogra, the police was forced to release them as Khan's family was planning to move a *habeas corpus* petition against the illegal police action. He alleged that the police had forced the three to write a letter that they had gone to Ajmer on a pilgrimage to the Dargah without informing their families. 'You tell me—who goes to Ajmer Shareef without informing his family?' Mogra asked Mahaprashasta.

He also alleged that the court had to force the CBI officials even to produce Khan at the court: 'The court had finalized October 30 [as the date] when Khan had to be produced. But when the CBI did not produce him, the court had pretty strong words to say against the agency. It was only then that the police officials produced him at the Mumbai court.'

On August 12, 2018, Rizwana wrote a letter to the Chief Justice of India, the Chief Justices of Rajasthan and Maharashtra, the National Human Rights Commission, the President of India and even political leaders like Mamata Banerjee, Arvind Kejriwal, Rahul Gandhi. In the letter, she wrote:

> … I and my family have been receiving constant threats on the gestures of some of the top officials of Rajasthan police and the Gujarat police and the politicians. [M]y husband's statement is yet to be made in the fake Sohrabuddin and Tulsiram Prajapati encounter case. So I am being asked by some senior officials and politicians…tell your husband to make a statement according to us, otherwise police will [have to choose between getting] trapped up into a false case or 'encounter' you and your family members too [*sic*].

She added that one evening a few non-uniformed policemen accosted her on a 'black Pulsar' bike and asked her to meet one '*netaji* and *sahebji*'. When she refused, they forcibly took her with them. She said that she met a person in a 'white dress' who told her that if Khan did not give a tutored statement in court, he 'will not survive'.

She also said in the letter: 'A person in the car said that [the] government is theirs and CBI works according to them and all courts of India from CBI to Supreme Court have appointed our judges and no one says anything against us.' She could not recognize the person though.

Rizwana therefore pleaded before the court to provide security cover to her family. She told *The Wire* that Khan, who had always been accompanied by multiple security personnel in other cases, was being guarded by only two policemen this time around. That was the reason, she claimed, that Khan had requested the court that he be handcuffed during his transfers from jail to the court and vice-versa. 'At least that way the police will not be able to claim that he was trying to flee,' she said.[14]

Her simple, matter-of-fact statement said a lot about the case.

CHAPTER FOURTEEN

# The Maturing of Indian Fascism

When the BJP won 282 out of the Lok Sabha's 543 seats in 2014, it became the first political party to gain dominant party status in the Indian parliamentary system since Rajiv Gandhi's overwhelming victory after his mother's assassination, in December 1984.[1] This convinced the RSS that it had at last acquired the power needed to achieve its ninety-year-old goal of creating a Hindu Rashtra. But it did not take its leaders long to realize that the BJP that had come to power under Narendra Modi was a bird of a very different feather from the one it had been trying to hatch. For while the RSS' original goal may have been to create a Hindu nation united by a common *sanskriti*, what they have succeeded in hatching is an increasingly authoritarian state whose similarity with the Fascist states of twentieth-century Europe is becoming more and more striking with every passing year. The engine that is driving it is what Christophe Jaffrelot has labelled the 'Hindu Majoritarian Inferiority Complex'.[2] In Narendra Modi, it has found its perfect instrument.

From its birth in 1925, the goal of the RSS had been to make India the great *Hindu Nation* it had been during the thousand-year 'Golden Age' from the Maurya to the Gupta Empires. What it ignored was that the great religions of India—Hinduism, Buddhism and Jainism—were mystical, not prophetic. So, they did not lend themselves to the creation of a political, let alone military, national identity as Christianity or Islam did.

Hinduism's philosophical core was, and remains, the concept of '*Dharma*'. Over more than three millennia after the arrival of the first waves of nomads from the Iranian and Caucasian regions of Central Asia, this concept of Dharma was spread across the subcontinent not by crushing but by assimilating local faiths and traditions, gods and shrines into its larger cultural plurality. Dharma is the essence of Hinduism, but its observance does not require obeisance to any particular deity or belief system. The term is virtually synonymous with the secular concept of Duty. Over the past three or more millennia, it has been elaborated to include duty not only to the family, tribe, race or ruler, but to all living things, be they human, animal or vegetal, and to nature.

In the Golden Age of Hinduism that the Sangh Parivar wishes to revive, few if any of the subjects of the empires that straddled the Indo-Gangetic plain would have identified themselves as 'Hindus'. The term originated much earlier from the mixing of Old Persian and Sanskrit and may have been used by Persian traders and travellers to describe the people of the geographical area that lay beyond the 'Sindhu' river (the Indus) and its tributaries. The word 'Hindu', used to denote a race or a religion, probably came into general use less than a thousand years ago, when it became necessary to distinguish the followers of Dharma, the term that is common to all variants of the pre-Islamic religions of India, and the followers of Islam, the religion of the conquerors. Hindu Rashtra is not therefore an ancient concept but one of relatively recent origin.

Savarkar's three requirements for qualifying as a Hindu nation—a common political nationhood (*rashtra*), a common race (*jati*), and a common culture or civilization (*sanskriti*)—were sufficiently imprecise to remain subjects of debate within the Sangh Parivar itself. What emerged from their debates was a broad consensus that all those who believed that their identity was defined not by religion alone but even more powerfully by language and culture, and were rooted in the soil of the sub-continent, qualified as members of the Hindu Rashtra.

Savarkar wrote his defining thesis on Hindutva twenty-four years before Partition, when animosity between Hindus and Muslims had all but ceased to exist. Muhammad Ali Jinnah, the founder of Pakistan, had started his political life as a member of the Congress, which he joined after attending its twentieth annual meeting in Bombay in December 1904. Within the Congress, Jinnah was a member of the moderate group that favoured Hindu–Muslim unity in the quest for self-government, and was a follower of leaders such as Pheroze Shah Mehta, Dadabhai Naoroji and Gopal Krishna Gokhale. He left the Congress in 1920 not because of any communal issue but because he strongly opposed Mahatma Gandhi's call for Satyagraha which, he believed, would lead to chaos. He was Bal Gangadhar Tilak's lawyer when Tilak faced charges of treason.

Savarkar's own earlier career showed no signs of an anti-Muslim animus. The only time he attacked a mosque was along with other boys when he was twelve, after a local Hindu–Muslim riot. But his sojourn in London as a student of law from 1906 onwards turned him into a quintessential product of the era of the nation-state. Throughout the nineteenth century, across the whole of Europe and America, nation-states had been created through war. He could hardly have failed to be infected by his experiences any less than by Europe's history.

Among the several texts he wrote advocating violence to wrest independence from the British was *The Indian War of Independence*, his seminal contribution to the revival of Indian national pride when that was most needed. This was the book that correctly described the uprising in 1857, which the British were insisting had only been a mutiny, as a simultaneous uprising throughout the north and the south of the country against British rule. Nothing he had written, said or done till then, or after his release from jail in 1924, had smacked of an anti-Muslim bias, let alone the visceral hatred of them that the Sangh Parivar now lionizes him for. Even his strong opposition to the Congress' Quit India call in 1942 sprang from his belief, later proved correct, that this would only make the British recruit all the more heavily from the Muslims and the Sikhs. Joining the allies in the war against Germany would, on the other hand, teach lakhs of Hindus the art of modern warfare that they could use if necessary to drive the British away after the war was over. That was the political background against which Savarkar wrote his defining work *Essentials of Hindutva*, which was first published in 1923 and republished in 1928 as *Hindutva: Who is a Hindu*.

Most of the credit for the conversion of Savarkar's relatively benign concept of a Hindu Rashtra into the virulently anti-Islamic concept it became later needs to go to the RSS' second sarsanghchalak, Madhav Sadashivrao Golwalkar. Golwalkar was only thirty-four years old in 1940 when he became the head of the RSS, and only forty-one when India was partitioned in blood. His most formative years within the RSS therefore coincided with the build-up of Hindu–Muslim animosity, and riots and slaughter of Hindus in Calcutta (now Kolkata), Noakhali, the North West Frontier Province, Punjab, and elsewhere in 1946. He cannot therefore be blamed for being traumatized by these events and concluding that the only path ahead lay through the militarization of Hinduism itself. It was Golwalkar, therefore, and not Savarkar who gave the concept of Hindu Rashtra its messianic political edge. He expressed this over several years in innumerable speeches. The most important of these were collected and published in a book titled *A Bunch of Thoughts*, and in *We, Our Nationhood Defined*, a small book he wrote in 1938, which summed up his concept of the Hindu Rashtra. Both placed the boundaries of India across the Himalayas in the north and in the seas that surrounded the entire subcontinent including Sri Lanka—the Arabian Sea, the Bay of Bengal and the Indian Ocean. Golwalkar claimed that the entire land within these natural boundaries had been a single nation, *Bharatvarsha*, since the age when the *Ramayana* was written.

Far from resolving the problem of identity, Golwalkar's definition only made it more insoluble, even for his most devoted followers. For not only did it leave no place in this Hindu 'nation' for Muslims and Christians but also for the myriad other hybrid religious faiths that had developed out of differing historical and cultural interactions—such as the Christians of Goa who retained their Hindu caste identities for three or more centuries after being converted to Christianity, or followers of Kashmir's *Reshi* Islam, many of whose rituals, practices and even dietary proscriptions are incorporated in their entirety from Shaiva Hinduism. By Golwalkar's definition, even the Sikhs did not really qualify as a part of the Hindu Rashtra.

Far from recognizing that the caste system was the Achilles' heel of the Hindu community, Golwalkar did not even acknowledge its barbaric inequity. In his view, 'our old social order laid down a specific duty for each group and guided all the individuals and groups in their natural line of evolution just as the intellect directs the activities of the innumerable parts of the body'.[3] He readily conceded that 'Today, of course, the caste system has degenerated beyond all recognition', but then launched a tirade against those who sought to mitigate its impact through job and educational reservation:

> The feeling of inequality, of high and low, which has crept into the *Varna* system is comparatively of recent origin… [I] n its original form, the distinctions in that social order did not imply any discrimination of big or small, high or low, among its constituents. On the other hand, the *Gita* tells us that the individual who does his assigned duties in life in a spirit of selfless service only worships God through such performance.[4]

In Golwalkar's Hindu Rashtra, there was no room for the great Muslim *ustads* of Hindustani classical music who not only kept Vedic music alive but immeasurably enriched its content; no mention of the *Sufi-Bhakti* continuum of religious belief that created the *dargahs* of Ajmer Sharif in Ajmer, Nizamuddin in Delhi, Charar-e-Sharif in Kashmir and innumerable lesser known shrines all over the country, where Hindus and Muslims worshipped, and still worship, together; no place for the poetry of Kabir, or the ballads in praise of Krishna and Radha of Abdur Rahim Khan-i-Khanan who was not only a poet and philosopher, but a member of Emperor Akbar's *Ibadat Khana*—his inner circle of advisers. Needless to say, there is not even a mention of the Mughal emperor Akbar, or of the *Din-e Ilahi*, which was his attempt to bind the essence of India's many religions into a code of civil conduct for the entire nation.

By 2014, however, two generations after the holocaust of Partition, the RSS had moved a long way towards acknowledging, and even celebrating, the syncretism that exists in India. In a long disquisition on the meaning of Hindu Rashtra, written in September 2019, Seshadri Chari, former editor of the BJP's official news weekly, *The Organiser*, and a member of its National Executive, wrote:

> It may surprise many that the RSS prayer invokes 'Hindu Rashtra' only once. It says: '*vayam Hindu rashtraanga bhoota* (we are all part of "Hindu Rashtra")'. The RSS does not say we will *create* a new Hindu Rashtra... Nor does it say we will amend the Constitution of India and declare this country a Hindu Rashtra... The Sangh, in fact, believes that there is no need to create a *Hindu Rashtra* as India, that is Bharat, *is already one*... To ridicule and dismiss the idea of Hindu Rashtra as communal, divisive and *ultra vires* the Constitution, is as patently wrong as it would be to dismiss the 'Idea of India' as a mistaken identity...
>
> *In fact, on closer analysis, these ideas are seen to converge, with little or no difference between them*... [I]f the Idea of India is inclusive, so is the Idea of *Hindu Rashtra*; it encompasses each and every identity that constitutes the conglomeration called Hindu... In its essence, 'Hindu' refers to a society, a group of people with a distinct cultural and civilizational character, a core set of beliefs, traditions, practices, and yes, prejudices too. *In the Indian context, dharma forms the very basis of everyday life, it is about ethics, values and social mores, not religion*... Unlike the Western and Semitic religious traditions, *a single institution at the head of a command structure or a single holy book of doctrinal orders were the very antithesis of Hindu thought.*

> India, therefore, didn't need a Constitution to learn the virtues of secularism or coexistence, or to frame different rules for citizens and non-citizens. Our world view is guided by the mantra: '*vasudhaiva kutumbakam* (the world is but one family)...'
>
> *Low-level aberrations like vigilantism and lynching, abhorrent as they are, should not be laid at the door of Hinduism to score political brownie points... For the Sangh, the overarching unity of the Hindu fold respects the diversity of caste, class and religion but also transcends it. For the Sangh, the 'creation' of a Hindu Rashtra is only the anticipated dawn of an understanding that its embrace does not threaten diversity.*[5] (Emphases added)

Chari's concept of Hindu Rashtra was not a self-serving concoction designed to make the BJP more palatable to the still uncommitted voters of India's cosmopolitan, English-speaking middle class. For it tallied closely with the views that had been expressed two decades earlier by the late prime minister Atal Bihari Vajpayee. Starting with the year 2000, on New Year's Day of four of the five years of his second tenure as prime minister, Vajpayee penned a series of 'New Year Musings' on the state of the nation and its future. These were long, and very clearly the product of an unending dialogue within himself. Although released to the media, they were clearly not intended for the general public but for his own party, the RSS, and the rest of the Sangh Parivar.

The common theme of all four was a tireless reiteration that India draws its strength, and its unity, from its religious, ethnic and cultural diversity. That any attempt to impose cultural, social or religious uniformity upon it would weaken the bonds that bind the nation. His 'musing' from Goa, released on New Year's Day 2003, while the wounds inflicted by the Gujarat riots were still fresh in people's minds, could as easily have been written by Jawaharlal Nehru, Mahatma Gandhi, or Swami Vivekananda:

> Our diversity is as much a source of India's greatness—and of Indians' pride in their nation—as her antiquity. Foreigners have always wondered how we can embrace so much diversity

in religion, ethnicity, language and lifestyles, and yet remain a united nation. What they may not understand, and which we must never forget, is that living with diversity, and yet weaving a thread of unity and harmony through it, has been a way of life throughout India since time immemorial... From time to time, the theme of unity in diversity provokes intense debate, even controversies. I wish to comment on two distinct voices, which have become louder after the Gujarat elections. On the one hand, secularism is being pitted against Hindutva, under the belief that the two are antithetical to one another. This is incorrect and untenable. Secularism is a concept of the State, enjoining upon it the duty to show respect for all faiths and to practise no discrimination among citizens on the basis of their beliefs. In this sense, India has been secular since the beginning of her known history. We chose to remain wedded to secularism even when Pakistan was carved out on the basis of the spurious and communal Two-Nation Theory. This could not have been possible if the majority of Indians were not secular.

Gurudev Rabindranath Tagore has explained it very well. India has all along been trying experiments in evolving a social unity within which all the different peoples could be held together, while fully enjoying the freedom of maintaining their differences. The tie has been as loose as possible, yet as close as circumstances permitted. This has produced something like a United States of a social federation, whose common name is Hinduism.

Hinduism's acceptance of the diversity of faiths is the central feature of secularism in India. As Maharshi Aurobindo points out, Indian religion has always felt that since the minds, the temperaments and the intellectual affinities of men are unlimited in their variety, a perfect liberty of thought and of worship must be allowed to the individual in his approach to the Infinite.

On the other hand, Hindutva, which presents a *Viraat Darshan* [broad, all-encompassing view] of human life, is being projected by some people in a narrow, rigid and extremist manner: *an unfortunate and unacceptable interpretation that runs totally contrary to its true spirit.* Hindutva is an integral understanding of the entire Creation, showing the way both

> to the Here and the Hereafter. It emphasizes the inseparable relationship between the individual and society, as well as between man's material and spiritual needs. Hindutva is liberal, liberating and brooks no ill will, hatred or violence among different communities on any ground.
>
> We need to affirm and promote *that true understanding of Hindutva which is forward-looking, not one that seeks to take us back*; *that which makes us capable of meeting the challenges of the modern world, not one that is stuck in the grooves of the past; that which is reform-minded, and not one that protects obscurantism and injustice, against which all the reformers of the past have fought.* If understood and practised in this enlightened sense, which is how Swami Vivekananda and other great patriots propounded it, the current controversy over Hindutva will be seen as wholly unnecessary.
>
> There is no difference between such *Hindutva* and *Bharateeyata*, since both are expressions of the same '*chintan*' (thought). Both affirm that *India belongs to all, and all belong to India. It means that all Indians have equal rights and equal responsibilities. It entails recognition of our common national culture, which is enriched by all the diverse religious and non-religious traditions in India.* For centuries, both have synonymously pointed to our national identity... This *Indianness* is what we should all celebrate and further strengthen.[6] (Emphases added)

Chari's 2019 definition of Hindu Rashtra was therefore almost identical to Vajpayee's notion of *Bharatiyata*, the slogan of the Bharatiya Jana Sangh, the avatar of the BJP that Vajpayee had helped to found. This is not surprising, for Chari's father was a member of the Indian National Congress while his mother was an ardent supporter of the Sangh. Chari himself joined the RSS at the age of four, but his life and work in Mumbai (then Bombay) had brought him into close touch with Communist Party leaders such as Ahilya Rangnekar and B.T. Ranadive. One of his four uncles had been a close associate of the defence minister in the early 1960s, V.K. Krishna Menon.

Neither Chari nor Vajpayee had felt any discomfort with India's political heterogeneity because both were comfortable working within the framework of the 'unity in diversity' that was enshrined not only in the Indian Constitution but also the culture of India. In the eighties and nineties, the BJP was full of people who, like Chari, thought of Hindutva in purely cultural-nationalist terms. Luminaries like Nanaji Deshmukh and M.L. Sondhi spring readily to mind. The party itself was open to non-RSS members and attracted some of the best minds in the country, such as Vajpayee's foreign minister, Jaswant Singh, his finance minister, Yashwant Sinha, his National Security Adviser, Brijesh Mishra (the son of a former Congress chief minister of Madhya Pradesh), his media adviser, Sudheendra Kulkarni, and his minister for disinvestment, communication and information technology, Arun Shourie.[7]

A whole decade after Vajpayee's death, Mohan Bhagwat, the sarsanghchalak of the RSS who assumed this position in 2009, also explicitly rejected Golwalkar's concept of India. At an all-India meeting of RSS *prant pracharaks* (district leaders/guides) held at Somnath, Gujarat in July 2018, Bhagwat released an edited version of Golwalkar's book, from which the sections describing Muslims and Christians as internal enemies of the Hindu 'Nation', had been deleted.

In a televised interview that he gave in September 2018, he emphasized, 'We respect the Indian Constitution. A lot of thought has gone into making it. It was done through consensus. The Sangh has never gone against the Constitution.' At another point in the same interview, he said, '*Hindu Rashtra* does not mean it has no place for Muslims. The day it's said that Muslims are unwanted here, *the concept of Hindutva will cease to exist.*'[8]

Three years later, despite the Modi–Shah BJP's second mammoth victory in the 2019 elections, Bhagwat's views remained unchanged. On July 5, 2021, while presiding over the release of a book by Khwaja Iftikhar Ahmed titled *The Meeting of Minds* which was organized by the RSS' Muslim wing, the Muslim Rashtriya

Manch, Mohan Bhagwat again proclaimed that Hindus and Muslims shared the same DNA. 'It has been scientifically proven', he said, 'that we are all one.' Refuting claims that 'Hindus want Muslims to be wiped off the face of the Earth', Bhagwat reassured, and warned his audience, that '*Hindus who say such things are not Hindus at all...* We may have different interests, but society is the same. You can have differences over opinions. Islam came to India [through] attackers [but] since then attempts have been made to unite Hindus and Muslims.'

Bhagwat stressed this yet again in his annual speech on Vijay Dashami (October 24, 2023), a mere six months before the impending general election. Here is what he said:

> The permanent unity of society stems from a sense of belongingness, not from selfish pursuits. Ours is a very large society, with a remarkable breadth of diversity... Therefore, when we talk about unity, we must bear in mind that...if this unity is attained by force, it will get ruptured again and again. In today's environment, many people are naturally worried after seeing the efforts being made to spread discord in the society. We come across people who identify themselves as Hindus, and also those who are called Muslims and Christians because of their way of worship. They believe that leaving aside '*Fitna-Fasad* and *Kitan*' (discord and strife and violence)—it is best to pursue '*Sulah*, *Salamati* and *Aman*' (reconciliation, security and peace). An important thing to keep in mind in these discussions is that it is not about different communities coming together in one land by chance, and becoming one. *We are the descendants of common ancestors, children of one motherland, and inheritors of one culture, but have forgotten our mutual and inherent unity. We have to understand our inherent unity and get connected again on that basis.*[9] (Emphasis added)

And yet, for the economic and political reasons that have been described in preceding chapters, this syncretic view of Hindu Rashtra had been losing ground within the rank and file of the Sangh Parivar since 1985. It was finally overwhelmed when Atal

Bihari Vajpayee's National Democratic Alliance lost the 2004 general elections, despite having made peace with Pakistan and started a dialogue with it over the resolution of the Kashmir dispute, and, with interest rate and other reforms announced in the 2002 Budget, and the sale of 50 per cent of Maruti's shares to the parent company in Japan, triggered a stock market boom and the longest and most spectacular period of continuous economic growth that India has known (which began in 2003 and ended abruptly in 2011–12).

## The End of Bharatiyata and the Flowering of Indian Fascism

This golden period was severely marred by only one event: the pogrom in Gujarat that began on February 28, 2002 and lasted for almost a week in Ahmedabad and other cities, and did not come fully under control till the beginning of April. The unregretted and unpunished slaughter of more than 2,000 persons, all but a few of whom were Muslims, was the main cause of the National Democratic Alliance's defeat in the 2004 general elections. Ram Vilas Paswan, a former socialist student leader from Bihar, who served as a minister in Vajpayee's cabinet, as a member of the Janata Dal and then, from 2000, of his Lok Janshakti Party, resigned his office over the BJP's handling of the riots. Despite the NDA's many achievements—from making India a nuclear power in 1998 to winning the Kargil war against Pakistan in 1999, reviving rapid economic growth in 2003, and re-starting the dialogue with President Pervez Musharraf of Pakistan to end the debilitating five-decade-long conflict between the two countries—its share of the vote in 2004 fell 1.5 per cent below what it had been in 1999, and its share of seats from 182 to 137. This allowed the Congress party to emerge as the largest party in parliament, with 145 seats, and get the first shot at forming the next government.

Another key cause of the sharp fall in the NDA's strength in parliament was the debacle that Chandrababu Naidu, the leader of the Telugu Desam Party, a staunch ally of the BJP, suffered in Andhra Pradesh. The Telugu Desam lost twenty-four of the twenty-nine seats it had held in parliament earlier, for which Naidu blamed the communal holocaust in Gujarat. In the wake of the pogrom, Naidu had warned Vajpayee that he would leave the alliance if Modi was not ousted from the chief ministership of Gujarat. But Vajpayee had been talked out of doing so by Deputy Prime Minister L.K. Advani. The BJP paid the price for Vajpayee's indecision in 2004.

One can only surmise what would have happened in the next decade if the BJP had won in 2004. What is fairly certain is that by 2009 Advani would have taken over the reins of leadership from Vajpayee, whose health had begun to fail shortly after the 2004 election, and that the NDA would have gained the full political benefit of the six preceding years of 8 to 9 per cent growth that Vajpayee had triggered. In 2014, it would have been Advani, not Modi, who led the party into the Lok Sabha elections. A BJP victory would then have brought Advani and not Modi to power. That would have arrested, if not reversed the transition within the BJP from *Bharatiyata* to the Golwalkar version of *Hindutva* that actually took place.

The BJP's 2004 defeat changed everything. Modi came to power having made up his mind, possibly in 2002 itself, that he would punish everyone who had not supported him after the Gujarat pogrom. He did so by systematically excluding each and every one of Vajpayee's principal cabinet ministers and advisers, starting with his staunchest patron, Advani himself. He also vented his wrath on the former education minister, Murli Manohar Joshi, the former foreign minister, Jaswant Singh (who had already been shown the door before he had the accident that took him out of active life), and other highly competent ministers like Yashwant Sinha and Arun Shourie, who had held key portfolios in Vajpayee's government.

Any of these would have made an excellent finance minister. Sinha was the finance minister who had pulled India out of the 1997–2002 recession, and was more than qualified for the job. But for Modi, vengeance, and a complete destruction of any possible challenge to his power, mattered more than governance. And he was just the kind of ruthless leader that the huge, unqualified and unemployable *lumpenproletariat* of the Hindi belt were looking for when they flocked to the BJP and the RSS. In one of the more cruel ironies of history, therefore, Modi's cold-blooded politicization of the carnage in Gujarat in February–March 2002, and his systematic demonization of Pakistan and Muslims after his return to power in Gujarat in December that year, catapulted him to the prime ministership of India in 2014.

By 2019, therefore, when Chari wrote his essay for *India Today*, the world in which he had been so comfortable with colleagues of different political persuasions had passed into history. Under Modi, Amit Shah, and Yogi Adityanath in UP, the BJP had completed its internal transformation from a Hindu nationalist into a fascist party. Chari himself inadvertently revealed his awareness of how slim had become the ground on which he still stood when, in his 3,000-word defence of India's 'natural' secularism he did not, *even once*, use the word 'Muslim'.

CHAPTER FIFTEEN

# A Decade of Fascist Consolidation

Over the decade since Narendra Modi has been the prime minister of India, at the head of a BJP government supported by a few local allies in the states of northern India, he has worked diligently to complete the conversion of India into a fascist nation-state—a process that began during his tenure as chief minister of Gujarat in 2002.

The history of this transformation has been written in painstaking detail by scores of academics, journalists and defenders of civil rights and democracy, several of whom have been languishing in prison without bail, but also without having been charged with any specific crime, for years. How Modi has completed the journey to fascism is described in broad brush strokes below:

Modi took the first step towards dismantling the pluralist, ethnically diverse democracy that his predecessor, Atal Bihari Vajpayee, had taken so much pride in, within weeks of coming to power. His first step in this direction was seemingly innocuous: this was to instal TV cameras at the entrance to every ministry, and withdraw the PIB (Press Information Bureau) card which allowed special correspondents and other senior journalists to visit ministries and talk to civil servants without having to reveal their own, or their hosts', identity.

The PIB card had been created deliberately by India's first prime minister, Pandit Jawaharlal Nehru, to encourage public debate within an infant democracy by allowing senior journalists to explore different views on impending policy decisions within the government, at a time when there was virtually no opposition to the Congress in parliament. The Modi government destroyed this freedom barely a fortnight after it came to power. A further amendment during his second term, that required the officer to also come to the reception desk and sign his or her visitor in, ended all communication between government and the public except what Modi wanted the latter to hear.

Modi's second step towards the centralization of power was to create a system of monthly meetings between his departmental ministers and senior officers, and nominees of the BJP, in which the party would 'oversee' the functioning of the ministry. This transferred much of the decision-making power of government from the ministries to the party.

Modi's next target was the audio-visual media, which he tamed by using every instrument at his command, from the denial of advertisements to selected print and TV channels, to the framing of never-proved charges of tax evasion and money laundering against their promoters, under which it 'attached' (seized) their passports, and all their property till as long as the case lasted. Prannoy and Radhika Roy, the founders of NDTV, India's first commercial TV channel, were his first targets. Despite this, NDTV retained its independence till November 2022, but succumbed because by then all advertisers had deserted it, presumably under government pressure. Faced with imminent bankruptcy and the loss of the hundreds of jobs of its technical staff, the Roys resigned from the board of the company in November 2022, and allowed NDTV to be purchased by the Adani Group, Modi's principal financial supporters ever since his days in Gujarat. Since then, NDTV too has become a mouthpiece of Modi's budding fascist regime.

Modi's third target was the judiciary, which he corrupted through the offer of lucrative post-retirement appointments to High Court and Supreme Court judges. These ranged from the unprecedented appointment of a former chief justice of the Supreme Court of India, P. Sathasivam, to the governorship of Kerala, which we discussed in Chapter 12, to the appointment of former Supreme Court judge A.M. Khanwilkar to the post of India's Lokpal, its chief vigilance officer.[1] Other judges of the Supreme Court whom Modi similarly rewarded with post-retirement elevations and appointments are Chief Justices of the Supreme Court Ranjan Gogoi and Sharad Bobde, and Justice Arun Mishra.

Modi also made three other, more insidious and—over the long run—even more destructive moves, one deliberate and two defined by sustained avoidance. But all were expressly designed to undermine India's infinitely varied ethno-national, federal democracy. The first was that in all his years in power, Modi never held a single press conference. The second was that in those years, Modi also never held a meeting of the National Development Council, a council of state chief ministers that had become the main forum for coordinating central and state policies after the Congress lost its dominant party status in 1989. During Modi's decade, communication between the people and their government, and between the central and state governments on policy issues became strictly one-way.

But his most insidious assault on India's federal structure was his replacement of the Planning Commission with the NITI (National Institution for Transforming India) Aayog. On the face of it, nothing changed: NITI Aayog continued to work from the same building as the Planning Commission; none of its staff were dismissed and no new staff was added. The change of name therefore looked like no more than another, petty, manifestation of the BJP's obsession with 'Hinduizing' India.

Beneath that deceptively innocuous change, however, Modi took away the Planning Commission's most important function, and vested it in himself. This was the annual allocation of central Plan grants to the state governments. Till he came to power, this had been done by the Planning Commission on the basis of the oft-revised Gadgil formula for allocation based on factors like population, per capita income, and fiscal performance, aiming to promote balanced regional development, recommended five decades earlier by D.R. Gadgil, then deputy chairman of the Commission. Modi turned this allocation into his personal prerogative, and began lavishing the lion's share of these grants upon BJP-ruled state governments, at the expense of states in which the BJP had been unable to extend its influence.

**Warnings from Southern Indian States**

This provoked a succession of warnings from MPs and ruling state governments of the southern Indian states. In the first, delivered after the presentation of the railway budget in 2022, S. Kanimozhi, a Dravida Munnetra Kazhagam (DMK) member of the upper house of parliament, and daughter of the former DMK chief minister of Tamil Nadu, pointed out during the debate on the railway budget, that while the Union government had allotted Rs 59 crore for development to Southern railways, it had allocated Rs 13,200 crore to Northern railways. 'You keep talking about India being one nation,' she said. 'The railways also have to understand that it is one nation.'

Kanimozhi's warning did not fall on deaf ears. For both the 2023–24 and 2024–25 railway budgets contained large increases in the allocations for Southern railways. But Modi's discrimination against the southern states continued in other areas. This prompted the entire Karnataka state cabinet, led by the then chief minister Siddaramaiah, to land up at Jantar Mantar on February 7, 2024, raising objections to what its members described as the central government's 'biased fiscal policy'. They were followed the next day by Kerala's chief minister Pinarayi Vijayan, and by MPs of Tamil Nadu's ruling party, the DMK, who held a 'black shirt' demonstration for non-allocation of funds to the state. All had chosen Jantar Mantar, the site of a fourteenth-century observatory that has been the traditional venue for civic protest in Delhi since the first days of independence to highlight the political significance of the Modi government's act.

## Deepening Contempt for the Constitution

During his second term in office, Modi's disregard for the Constitution deepened into open contempt. He showed this by ordering BJP governors in opposition-ruled states to refuse to sign bills passed by their legislatures if these did not meet the centre's approval. Tamil Nadu accused Governor R.N. Ravi of toying with the citizens' mandate and causing a 'constitutional deadlock' by neither assenting to nor returning bills passed by them. The Aam Aadmi Party (AAP) government in Punjab complained, similarly, that seven of its bills were stuck with the Governor since June 2023, which threatened to bring the administration to a 'grinding halt'.

In a separate petition, in September 2023, the Kerala government protested against its governor's refusal to sign no fewer than eight laws passed by its legislative assembly. These bills had been awaiting the Governor's assent—something he is constitutionally required to give—for over two years! In a fourth opposition-ruled state, Telangana, the Supreme Court had to intervene in April 2023 to force the Governor to clear bills that had been awaiting assent since September 2022.

## A Growing Megalomania

Modi's need to dominate turned into megalomania in his second term in office, but it was evident even during his first. The most blatant manifestation of this was his government's audio-visual publicity of its policies and actions and its relentless portrayal of Modi on virtually each advertisement, poster and billboard throughout the country. According to one study published in 2018, the central government, under Prime Minister Atal Bihari Vajpayee, spent only Rs 9.3 crores a year on its own publicity. By contrast, in its first three full years in office, 2015 till 2018, Modi's government spent Rs 3,807 crores. Even after allowing for an average inflation rate of 10 per cent a year in the services sector of the economy, this amounts to a twenty-fold increase in real terms in 2017–18 over 2003–04.[2]

Another manifestation of his growing megalomania was his decision to build huge new houses of parliament to replace the Lutyens'-designed one in which free India had functioned effortlessly for seventy-five years, at a cost of Rs 1,250 crores (Rs 12.5 billion), a prime minister's residence at a cost of Rs 463 crores, and several more permanent residences for political VVIPs, as parts of a Rs 20,000-crore 'redevelopment' plan for the historic Central Vista lawns of New Delhi.

His decision to perform the opening ceremony for the new parliament building on May 28, 2023, all by himself, without asking the President of India, the Leader of the Opposition, the Chief Justice of India or a single leader of any other opposition party to participate in this historic event, was a broadcast to the country, and the world, of his belief in his unchallenged personal supremacy. To perform this ceremony, he ordered the royal sceptre of the Chola kings of Tamil Nadu to be retrieved from a museum in Allahabad, and entered the new building, holding it aloft, all alone, followed by a gaggle of unkempt head priests from a scattering of Hindu temples and holy places all over India. As if even that was not a strong enough message, a bare seven months later, he also took over the task of consecrating the idol of Ram Lalla—the infant Lord Rama of the Hindu epic, the *Ramayana*—in the *garbha griha* (sanctum sanctorum) of the newly-built Ayodhya mandir, from the Brahmin high priests whose function this normally is, over stiff objections and a boycott by the Shankaracharyas—the supreme head priests of the four Maths (religious centres) of Hinduism established by Adi Sankara, the sage who is credited with having restored the ascendancy of Hinduism over Buddhism in the eighth century AD.

## Destruction of the Bureaucracy's Independence

His actions could have been dismissed as theatre had their underlying purpose not been to destroy the safeguards against political interference that had been created by his predecessor governments for the four key central investigative agencies whose mandate covered the whole of India. These are the Central Bureau of Investigation; the Intelligence Bureau; the Enforcement Directorate (ED), created in 2002; and the more recent National Investigation Agency (NIA), created after the 2008 Pakistani terrorist attack on the city of Mumbai.

It was this independence that had allowed the BJP to come to power in the first place, for the CBI's findings, of corruption within the Manmohan Singh government, had become the political springboard for its successful vilification of the Congress. This proved easy because of three controversial issues that arose during the UPA's second term in office—the largely proven accusation of massive corruption in the award of contracts for the 2012 Commonwealth Games being held in Delhi, and the hugely exaggerated, and ultimately unfounded, allegations of a 'Coal block allocation scam' and a 2G spectrum mobile telephony 'scam' which, the BJP said, had both been run from the Prime Minister's secretariat.

The second and third charges gained near-total belief because they were levelled by no less respected a person than the Comptroller and Auditor-General of India, whose annual report for 2012 condemned the government for refusing to auction the 2G spectrum band in mobile telephony, and allotting them at the same rates as the 1G band had been sold at when mobile telephony first entered India. We have discussed this case in detail in previous chapters. The report made a similar accusation over the allocation of coal blocks at concessional rates (for which private companies were now allowed to bid), without holding a public auction.

The CAG estimated in its initial report that the allocation of coal blocks at fixed government prices had conferred a 'windfall gain' to the allottees, in terms of accessible reserves, of a mammoth Rs 10,673 billion (US $130 billion). After hearing the government's rebuttal, however, it had reduced this figure to $23 billion. But by that time 'Coalgate' had become as emotive a word in India as 'Watergate' had been in the US three decades earlier.[3]

Almost a decade later, in his memoirs titled *Who Moved My Interest Rate?*, Duvvuri Subbarao, who was the central government's finance secretary in 2007–08, and the Reserve Bank of India governor from 2008 till 2013, reflected that although he had favoured auctioning the 2G spectrum and coal blocks, he later saw that the decision the government finally took—that it would allow the 2G spectrum sale to be licensed on a first come, first served basis at fixed prices (as had been done in the original 1G spectrum sales), and would auction all future sales of bandwidth—had given India the cheapest mobile telephony rates in the world and resulted in a wildfire spread of mobile phones of which the poor, especially migrant workers, had been the main beneficiaries. Social benefits apart, this had also resulted in far greater government revenues than auctioning bands to the highest bidders would have yielded.[4]

All this was understood in hindsight. When the CAG's report was published, the Manmohan Singh government unhesitatingly handed over both cases to the CBI for investigation. But by the time it completed its work and exonerated the communications minister, A. Raja, 'Scamgate', 'Coalgate' and an abrupt drop in the growth of GDP and non-agricultural employment after 2011, had done their damage and brought the BJP to power.

## The Consolidation of Fascism I: How Modi–Shah Destroyed the Independence of the CBI

Modi was the prime beneficiary of the discrediting of the UPA, so he understood the immense damage that independent investigative agencies could do. He first tried, therefore, to tame the CBI by bringing in a director who would never allow the agency to train its guns on him or his government. His choice was Rakesh Asthana, a CBI officer whom he knew from Gujarat. Modi tried to replace the serving director, Alok Verma, with him but was unable to do so because, among the safeguards for the CBI's independence was a fixed two-year tenure for its director, with Verma having several months still to go. What is more, the appointment of a new director had to be made only after it had been approved by a high powered selection committee which, after an amendment in 2013, consisted of the prime minister, the leader of the opposition, and the Chief Justice of India or a nominee. So, he brought Asthana in as a 'Special Director', to be his eyes and ears in the CBI.

In 2018, Asthana, in an unprecedented act that reeked of conspiracy, accused Verma, his own senior in the CBI, of corruption, alleging that he had been interfering with Asthana's attempt to re-investigate Lalu Yadav's fodder scam in Bihar. Verma responded by pointing out that the charge was fabricated and that Asthana had levelled it because the CBI was even then investigating no fewer than six charges of corruption against him in Gujarat. The Modi government instantly sent both on leave. Verma went to the Supreme Court for redress; Asthana to the High Court.

The Supreme Court re-instated Verma after seventy-seven days with the caution that since he was only weeks away from retirement he should not take any major policy decision till the case had been decided. It also asked the Central Vigilance Commission to prepare a report, under the supervision of retired Supreme Court judge A.K. Patnaik. However, Verma did not heed the caution and brought back to Delhi ten CBI officers of his team who had been transferred by M. Nageshwar Rao, who was posted as interim chief in his absence. Of these, five had been investigating the extant charges of corruption against Asthana in Gujarat.

The Central Vigilance Commission gave a 1,000-page report alleging various irregularities by Verma in dealing with a case related to Lalu Yadav's fodder scam. The Supreme Court asked for the CVC's report. The Modi government complied but with a request that it be allowed to submit the report in a sealed envelope, i.e. it should be seen only by the judges and not the defence.[5] Since both this and the rejoinder from Verma were given to the Supreme Court in sealed envelopes, the contents never became public.[6] But after the verdict had been given, Justice Patnaik stated, in an interview to the *Indian Express*, that 'There was no evidence against Verma regarding corruption. The entire inquiry was held on Asthana's complaint. I have said in my report that none of the findings in the CVC's report are mine.' Justice Patnaik also made the following remark: 'The Central Vigilance Commission report, along with annexures ran to more than 1,000 pages. I am surprised the selection committee members could go through all the 1,000 pages in such a short period of time (a single day!), appreciate the evidence and take the decision that Verma should be shunted out from the CBI Director's post. It would have been better had the selection committee taken a little more time to appreciate the evidence and taken an informed decision.'

The ugly spat between Verma and Asthana did not, however, prevent Modi from continuing to use the CBI as a weapon for weakening and discrediting non-BJP governments in opposition-ruled states. He was able to do this because these agencies had been created under the umbrella of a Delhi Special Police Establishment Act passed even before Independence, in 1946, in anticipation of the turmoil that was likely to follow Partition. This Act had allowed the central government to create central investigative agencies, notably the CBI and the IB, to deal with crimes committed in, and with repercussions spread over, more than one state of the country. To make this possible under a Constitution that had made law and order a state subject, the state governments had signed a 'General Consent' that allowed central enforcement agencies to operate in their territory without their prior and specific permission.

Modi was quick to exploit this. During his first term in office, there were defections from the Trinamool Congress in West Bengal and the Congress party in Assam, presumably obtained by threatening key opposition leaders that the CBI would be turned loose to investigate the sources of their funds. This gave the BJP a measure of success, especially in Bengal. The scandal that he held over their heads was the collapse of the Saradha chit fund, a mammoth Ponzi scheme that had become one of the principal sources of revenue for scores of established and aspiring politicians in the state. The misery it inflicted on an estimated twenty million Bengalis allowed Modi to turn the CBI investigation that followed into a witch hunt for TMC leaders who had benefited from it. But the BJP created an escape hatch for them: defect to us and the criminal charges against you will disappear. Its two most important catches were Suvendu Adhikari, a senior minister in the Trinamool government, whom the BJP promptly made its leader in Bengal to act as a magnet for other defectors, and eight MLAs, six from the TMC and one each from the Congress and the Communist Party.

Adhikari almost certainly joined the BJP because not only he but his entire family had the most to lose. The son of a former Congress minister in the Union government of Dr Manmohan Singh, and himself a highly regarded member of the Trinamool Congress in Bengal, where he had already served as the minister for irrigation, water resources and transport between 2016 and 2020, he shifted his allegiance to the BJP solely, it seems, in order to avoid prosecution and imprisonment by the CBI on charges relating to the Saradha chit fund scandal. The moment he did so, the CBI dropped the charges, and the BJP made him its leader in Bengal.

A second important defector was Bengal's transport minister Mukul Roy, whom the CBI had caught in a similar manner, allowing the BJP to 'persuade' him to change sides. Proof of this surfaced in a conversation between him and the then BJP chief in Bengal, Kailash Vijayavargiya, which was caught on tape. In it he was heard asking to get two central government officers 'off his back'. The Modi government evidently complied, because Roy joined the BJP a short while later.

Modi's third, and the most fateful, success was the BJP's 'capture' of Himanta Biswa Sarma, the most powerful Congress politician in Assam, after Rahul Gandhi rejected his claim to chief ministership upon the death of the long standing Congress chief minister Tarun Gogoi. Sarma had also been ensnared by the chit fund scandals that were then rocking West Bengal. While he was summoned by the CBI and his home raided during the probe that began in 2014, he was not named in any charge sheet. By August 2015, however, Sarma had shifted his allegiance, followed by forty loyalists. This resulted in a loss of fifty-two seats to the Congress and a gain of fifty-five seats by the BJP, taking the latter to power in one swoop, from a paltry five seats in 2011 to a commanding sixty seats in the 126-member Assam Vidhan Sabha in 2016.

In November 2018, sensing that he might be next on the list, M. Chandrababu Naidu, the chief minister of Andhra Pradesh, took the fateful step of withdrawing his state's general consent given to the CBI under the Delhi Special Police Establishment Act, 1946. Soon after, the West Bengal government did the same. On January 10, 2019, the day Modi had sacked CBI Director Alok Verma for the second time, the newly-elected Chhattisgarh government also followed suit.[7] Modi reached the limit of his use of the CBI as an instrument of coercion when he sent a large team of its officers to arrest the police commissioner of Kolkata, Rajeev Kumar, and bring him to Delhi for interrogation in another chit fund scam. Not only did the Kolkata Police prevent the arrest, but it virtually imprisoned the CBI officials until New Delhi was forced to call in the Central Reserve Police Force to free them and bring them back, without their 'prisoner'.

This was the most spectacular of several high-handed attempts that the CBI under Modi had been making in other states. So, it rang a warning bell in all other state capitals. By December 2023, Punjab, Kerala, Rajasthan, Mizoram, Telangana, Meghalaya, and Tamil Nadu, i.e. virtually all the major states of the country not ruled by the BJP except for Odisha, had also withdrawn their general consent under the 1946 Act to allow central investigative agencies to function in their territories without their prior, explicit permission.[8]

## The Consolidation of Fascism II: Modi Unleashes the Enforcement Directorate

These developments perhaps made Modi realize that he could no longer use the CBI or the NIA as his attack dogs without creating a serious political rift in the country. But never having admitted that he had made a mistake and never having accepted defeat, he turned to the Enforcement Directorate, and laws enacted in 2004 to prevent 'money laundering' (now universally referred to as the PMLA), as his principal instruments for the destruction of his political rivals. He was able to do this because the Prevention of Money Laundering Act, 2002 originated in an Act passed only in 1957, and therefore did not fall under the Delhi Special Police Establishment Act. The Enforcement Directorate did not therefore need a state government's general consent to operate in its territory. Modi and his home minister, Amit Shah, knew this.

The purpose of the PMLA, as re-jigged by the Vajpayee government in 2004 had been to bring Indian foreign exchange laws in line with international practice. To enforce this it created an Enforcement Directorate. The ED took over this function in July 2005 after it got a nod from the new Congress-led UPA government headed by Dr Manmohan Singh.

But tracking illicit transactions made in 'black money', i.e. cash, particularly when a large part of it was immediately transferred abroad via 'Hawala' (clandestine) routes, was infinitely more difficult than tracking crimes that left a visible mark upon their victims. By 2012, the weaknesses in what had clearly been a hastily conceived enactment were apparent to the government. Dr Manmohan Singh nevertheless decided to retain the PMLA, but with substantial changes and safeguards. During the UPA's ten-year rule from 2004 till 2014, the Enforcement Directorate lodged only 112 cases. And it only did so after an equal number of searches had yielded some *prima facie* proof of financial irregularity.

Despite this lacklustre record, the Modi government turned to the PMLA. Ever since Mrs Indira Gandhi banned company donations to political parties in 1970, and doubled the cost of fighting elections by separating the central from the state elections in 1971, without creating any alternative, open and honest system for funding elections, there was no way left open for political parties to meet the skyrocketing cost of campaigning except by soliciting, and raising, funds in cash. From 1971 onwards, therefore, politics had become a criminal enterprise with parties left with little option but to break the law. Modi and his home minister, Amit Shah, were fully aware of this, as was the rest of the nation.

The ED was, therefore, the first agency that they tried to use. On December 19, 2016, Congress president Sonia Gandhi, vice president Rahul Gandhi, treasurer Motilal Vora, senior leader Oscar Fernandes, and two friends of the Gandhi family, Suman Dubey and Sam Pitroda, appeared before a judge of a Delhi district court to answer to the charge, levied against them by Subramaniam Swamy, a well-known political gun for hire, of having cheated the exchequer and misappropriated funds to the tune of Rs 902.5 million (to acquire the ownership of a defunct daily newspaper, the *National Herald*). In the media jamboree that followed, no one bothered to ask whether Swamy's petition should have been admitted by the district court, and the admission affirmed by the High Court, in the first place. When, after examining Swamy's charge for a full year, the Enforcement Directorate dismissed it on August 18, 2017, for want of substantive evidence, Modi not only dismissed its executive director, Rajan Katoch, but removed him from government service the very next day. Since then, no executive director of the Enforcement Directorate has dared to voice objections to his directives.

The Katoch episode appeared to have taught Modi and Shah a valuable lesson: the PMLA had to be drastically 're-modelled' if it was to be used as an instrument for the destruction of the opposition. Before this remodelling, however, on January 2, 2018, the Modi government first created anonymous electoral bonds that donors could legally buy and transfer to the party of their choice. Then it turned the ED loose upon its opponents in every state, to uncover the illegal ways in which they had been collecting money in the past. Knowing from the PMLA's conviction rate that proving cases of money laundering was not going to be easy, it also passed an amendment to the Act a month later that turned it into a weapon for defaming and imprisoning the leaders of rival political parties, without even having to frame a case against them, let alone provide *prima facie* proof of wrongdoing. A year later, in July 2019, it passed eight further amendments to it.

To make the arrest of political leaders even easier, these amendments hugely widened the ambit of 'suspicious transactions' that could be considered as money laundering, by adding a clause that brought 'terrorist financing' within its ambit, and widening the definition of the 'proceeds of crime' to include virtually everything that the suspect and even his or her relatives owned. The wording of the amendments that did so was a deliberate model of imprecision, designed to twist judges into a knot while trying to unravel their meaning: for instance, 'proceeds of crime' now 'include property not only derived or obtained from the scheduled offence but also *any* property which may directly or indirectly be derived or obtained as a result of *any* criminal activity relatable to the scheduled offence'. This is aside from (i.e. in addition to) the existing definition of money laundering, which states that 'Whosoever directly or indirectly attempts to indulge or knowingly assists or knowingly is a party or is actually involved in *any* process or activity connected with the proceeds of crime including its concealment, possession, acquisition or use and projecting or claiming it as untainted property shall be guilty of offence of money-laundering'.

As for the ED's power to attach private property before proving its origin, the amendments declared that a property will be considered as tainted if it relates to any offence on the basis of which a PMLA case has been initiated.

Taken together, these amendments allowed the Modi government to arrest anyone, and seize any property of the accused that he or she had not inherited from a parent or relative at an earlier time. But even these were not the most vicious clauses of the amendments. Two of the eight amendments widened the definition of money laundering to make it a 'continuous offence' that was indictable for as long as the indicted person continued to 'enjoy the proceeds of crime'. These 'proceeds' included every activity indulged in through the use of the indicted proceeds. As if that was not sufficiently vindictive, the 2018 amendment had reversed the burden of proof—a reversal that is repugnant to law because of the way in which it makes a mockery of justice, by making indicted persons prove their innocence, instead of the state having to prove their guilt. This provision, now effectively reinstated, had in fact been declared unconstitutional by the Supreme Court in 2017 in *Nikesh Tarachand Shah vs Union of India*.[9]

A reversal of the burden of proof is not entirely unknown in other democratic countries, but has been confined to a few very special circumstances, such as accusations of rape or sexual molestation. But Modi's amendment to the PMLA made this reversal routine, to the point where the accused have to prove their innocence even to obtain bail. And they have to do this when the ED has sequestered all their assets and made them virtually penniless. It is not surprising therefore that only a handful of those indicted since 2018 have been able to secure bail.

The amendments were immediately challenged by individuals and companies. These challenges reached the Supreme Court which it heard over twenty-three days during February and March 2022. The Court faced no fewer than 240 petitions against the powers of specialized agencies that deal with economic offences, of which eighty were aimed specifically against the PMLA. But in July, in one of the Court's most questionable judgements, a bench headed by A.M. Khanwilkar, a judge on the verge of retirement, rejected all 240 petitions. To do this, Khanwilkar felt no qualms about reversing the 2017 judgement—striking down the PMLA's placing of the burden of having to prove one's innocence on the accused—of the Supreme Court itself.[10]

### *The Strange Case of Justice Khanwilkar*

Why did this crucial case go to Justice Khanwilkar? And why did he give such a viscerally damaging judgement in his last weeks in office before retirement? This question begs an answer because in his earlier career he was one of the most liberal and far-sighted judges in the High Courts of Himachal Pradesh and Madhya Pradesh, before being elevated in 2016 to the Supreme Court.

He retained his liberal, human rights oriented stance even in the first four years of his six-year stint at the Supreme Court. Soon after his elevation, he was a part of the majority ruling by a five-judge bench that decided to decriminalize homosexuality. In 2018, he was part of another Constitution Bench decision, in which the Court held that the right to die with dignity formed an integral part of the right to life and liberty under Article 21, thus legalizing passive euthanasia for patients with terminal illnesses. And soon after that, in September 2018, he was again a member of the five-judge Constitution Bench in the landmark Sabarimala case in which the Court lifted a millennium old ban, and forced the famed Sabarimala Temple in Kerala to allow women of all ages to enter and pray in it. In 2021, he authored a three-judge bench judgement that established the protocol that state governments had to follow before reserving seats in local bodies.[11]

But something had changed him by 2020, for in that year he presided over a Supreme Court bench that upheld the Foreign Contribution (Regulation) Amendment Act (FCRA) that virtually cut off contributions to thousands of Indian NGOs working on rural diseases and other problems, and wholly or partly funded international human rights organizations working in India. Soon after this, worldwide advocates of human rights, such as Oxfam and Human Rights Watch, were forced to close down their work in India and leave the country.

As the date for his retirement drew nearer, Khanwilkar moved steadily further and further into Modi's political orbit. In June 2022, he was part of a Supreme Court bench that upheld the Special Investigation Team's 2012 clean chit to Modi, and his core team of advisers in government, of complicity through deliberate inaction, in the 2002 Gulberg Society massacre case, which had since then been challenged more than once by Begum Zakia

Jafri, the wife of slain ex-Congress member of parliament from Ahmedabad, Ehsan Jafri.

Not only did Khanwilkar's bench dismiss Begam Jafri's appeal peremptorily, but it directly accused Jafri, her co-petitioner Teesta Setalvad, and principal witness R.B. Sreekumar, ex-director of the Intelligence Bureau of Gujarat in 2002, of pursuing the proceedings to '*keep the pot boiling, obviously, for ulterior design*'. This was virtually an invitation to the government to indict them, so to no one's surprise, the Gujarat Police arrested Teesta Setalvad and Sreekumar on charges of fabricating evidence linked to the riots and sent them to prison pending applications for bail. Both spent more than three months in jail before being set provisionally free on terms that locked their political voices for the duration, at least, of the BJP's rule over India.

But even that was not the end of Khanwilkar's conversion. A month later, on July 27, 2022, just two days before his retirement, he delivered what will undoubtedly rank as one of the most infamous judgements in the Supreme Court's history. It upheld the constitutionality of the PMLA of 2002, and dismissed the petitions against the 2018 and 2019 amendments passed by the Modi government to the Act.

Data collected by the *Supreme Court Observer* confirm that some crucial change in him had genuinely taken place, which had converted him from being a pillar of individuals' rights in his pre-Modi years into their principal destroyer in his last two years in office. During his tenure at the Supreme Court, Khanwilkar wrote 226 judgements (only three judges wrote more), and was a part of 817 benches. Virtually all the damage he did to India's supreme judiciary and its Constitution took place in the last two of his six years.

The appellants challenging various provisions of and amendments to the PMLA had argued that the Act had given unchecked powers to the Enforcement Directorate to arrest, seize property, and force confessions out of them. These wide powers, along with the Act's narrow scope for bail, violated the fundamental right to liberty and a fair trial. These were serious concerns, but all of them fell on Khanwilkar's by then deaf ears.[12]

Modi 'rewarded' Khanwilkar a year later by appointing him the Lokpal, whose specific task is to ensure the probity of the government itself. His appointment as only the second Lokpal of India was not merely a routine reward to a sycophant for services rendered. The post itself had been created after a long struggle by Arvind Kejriwal and a fast unto death by Anna Hazare in 2011. The issue on which the government and the anti-corruption movement had not been able to agree was the inclusion of judges of the High Courts and Supreme Court under the Lokpal's purview. Kejriwal had eventually relented, and the Lokpal's mandate excluded judges of the High Courts and Supreme Court. As the chief vigilance officer, how little Khanwilkar is his own man may be judged not only from the fact that he took up a corruption case against a High Court judge while it was already being tried in a lower court, but that his action was defended by none other than the Modi government's chief prosecutor in all sensitive cases, Solicitor General Tushar Mehta.

How ruthlessly the Modi government used the PMLA amendments—appeals against which were dismissed by A.M. Khanwilkar—to break political parties and crush the political opposition in the country can be judged from the fact that against a total of 112 cases that the ED launched between 2005 and 2014, it launched 5,310 cases between June 2014 and the end of March 2022, conducted 3,086 searches, attached Rs 104,702 crore (1.04 trillion) worth of assets, calling these the 'proceeds of crime' (when they had not even framed charges against the victims), and filed 880 charge sheets. How little these arrests have had to do with upholding the law of the land is revealed by the fact that *in this entire time the ED was able to secure only twenty-three convictions*. That is less than four in every thousand indictments![13]

The amendments, however, served Modi's real purpose, which was to break up one state government after the other in opposition-ruled states through a combination of threat and inducement to its leaders. The threat has been of imprisonment for a virtually unlimited period of time at the government's will, now made fatally easy by the amendments to the PMLA. The inducement has been that all will be forgiven and the cases being prepared against him or her will vanish if the politician under attack breaks away from his or her party and joins the BJP.

### The Consolidation of Fascism III: The Electoral Bonds Scheme

In January 2, 2018, the Modi government introduced the system of making entirely anonymous donations to political parties through the purchase of electoral bonds from the State Bank of India, the authorized sellers of these. Until the Supreme Court declared the scheme illegal in 2024, it had created a sufficiently strong inducement not only to corrupt business corporations but also individual politicians to pay their way out of prosecution.

The scheme was an immediate success. Between March 2018 and January 2024, the 'public' of one of the poorest countries in the world purchased a colossal Rs 16,518 crores ($1.95 billion) worth of electoral bonds, of which the BJP received Rs 8,251.8 crores. The Congress came a distant second with Rs 1,952 crores, and the Trinamool Congress third with Rs 1,705 crores.

Despite the huge discrepancy in receipts, if the bonds had been truly anonymous, they would have filled the lacuna that the Constitution-makers had left in the Constitution and Prime Minister Indira Gandhi had sealed. This was the absence of a legal system of election financing. Had the Modi government administered the electoral bonds scheme with scrupulous honesty, it might have provided a good, though still not the best, solution to the problem of election finance. But the cleansing of politics was the very last thing on Prime Minister Modi and Home Minister Amit Shah's minds when they enacted this so-called reform. For the electoral bonds were never truly anonymous—all of them had to be purchased through just one bank, the State Bank of India, which is wholly owned by the government, and could not, therefore, refuse to answer its questions.

Keeping anonymity in mind, the State Bank kept no official record of who had purchased the bonds, and whom these had ultimately gone to. But it did create a concealed master list of the bonds sold that enabled the government to know from moment to moment who was purchasing the bonds, and to whom the buyer was donating them. It did this by numbering every bond sold sequentially in invisible ink.

The existence of this secret numbering system was discovered by Poonam Agarwal, a journalist working for *The Quint*, a highly regarded online journal that is one of a dozen or so online media channels that have escaped joining the '*Godi*' (government's 'lap') media in the past decade. To test the anonymity of the electoral bonds, she bought two Rs 1,000 bonds at different times, and found a different number stamped on each in the top right hand corner, in invisible ink.[14]

After a Supreme Court judgement declared the scheme to be unconstitutional, and compelled the Election Commission to publish the complete list of bond purchasers and recipients, these numbers made it possible for investigative journalists to identify not only the firms that had bought the bonds, but also the political parties to which they had given them.

Correlating the list of donors with a list of companies that had been raided by the Enforcement Directorate in the days before, or in some cases after, their donations, revealed the true extent to which the BJP had used extortion to garner funds for itself. A first exercise, published by *The Hindu* on March 21, 2024, showed that forty-one companies, which had donated Rs 2,592 crores ($305 million) to the BJP and were among its top donors had been raided by the Enforcement Directorate, among other agencies, fifty-six times. Of this amount, Rs 1,853 crores had been donated *after the raids against them*. These sums amounted to 43 and 30 per cent, respectively, of the total donations that the BJP received during these years.[15] The data also showed how the BJP had showered companies that had made large donations to it with large contracts: thirty-eight corporate groups received 179 government contracts for projects worth Rs 3.8 lakh crores ($46 billion) after donating electoral bonds to the BJP.

The Pandora's Box of the BJP's financial dealings with the corporate world did not close even after these sensational revelations. On April 4, 2024, *The Hindu* dropped another bombshell: companies that had reported net losses or zero net profits between 2016–17 and 2022–23, had contributed a total of Rs 576.2 crore in electoral bonds, of which Rs 434.2 crore was encashed by the BJP in those same years.[16] Another six had donated sums that exceeded their net profits, and another three had given donations that exceeded the taxes they paid to the exchequer.

The largest donor to political parties via the electoral bond route was a company named Future Gaming and Hotel Services PR.[17] Its founder was Santiago Martin, a well-known lottery king who resides in Chennai. Between April 2018 and February 2024, Martin purchased Rs 1,349 crores worth of electoral bonds. But within this period, till April 2022, he contributed funds only to the dominant political parties in the states where he had the largest gaming operations. These were Bengal, where the Trinamool Congress received Rs 542 crores, and Tamil Nadu, where the DMK got Rs 503 crores.

Martin's desire to stay on the right side of the governments of states where he had the maximum business was understandable. But no one has asked why he contributed such vast sums. The possibility that he did so in order to forestall state government inquiries into an industry that is notoriously corrupt because it runs entirely on cash cannot be ruled out. From the data released by the Election Commission, it seems that initially Martin did not contribute anything to the BJP, which had no power and little support in either Bengal or Tamil Nadu. On April 2, 2022, however, the Enforcement Directorate attached movable assets belonging to the company and its subsidiaries, worth Rs 410 crore, under the PMLA on the charge that it was running a lottery scam. Just five days later, on April 7, 2022, the company purchased electoral bonds worth Rs 100 crore. This was the company's largest purchase on a single day. Coincidentally, this was the exact amount that Martin's companies contributed to the BJP.[18]

## The Consolidation of Fascism IV: Turning the Penal Code into a Reign of Terror

Even this huge increase in the government's power to persecute those it considers its enemies did not fully assuage the paranoia with which Modi had been living ever since the communal slaughter of 2002 in Ahmedabad. On July 1, 2024, in a move that completely overhauled the criminal justice system in the country, Home Minister Amit Shah introduced three new criminal laws that came into immediate effect. These were given abstruse Sanskrit names—the Bharatiya Nyaya Sanhita (BNS), the Bharatiya Nagrik Suraksha Sanhita (BNSS) and the Bharatiya Sakshya Adhiniyam (BSA)—that nine out of ten Indians did not even understand, let alone comprehend the implications of. The pretext for the reform was an urgent need to replace the Indian Penal Code (IPC), 1860, the Criminal Procedure Code (CrPC), 1973, and the Indian Evidence Act, 1872, respectively.

The need to modernize these archaic laws had been obvious for decades, and had been the subject of innumerable reports by the Law Commission, the Commonwealth Human Rights Initiative and independent analysts. As has been described in Chapter 4, the powers given to the police by the imperial laws of the Code of Criminal Procedure had not only not been curtailed but increased, till the police had acquired a virtual *carte blanche* to arrest, incarcerate and even kill suspects with impunity. What is more, a century and a half of technological change in crime detection and investigation had turned these laws into an impenetrable jungle in which the dispensation of law itself had stalled. This had created a situation in which the judiciary had a colossal backlog of cases.

Data collected by the National Judicial Data Grid (NJDG) in May 2022 showed that there were 41.4 million cases pending in the Indian judiciary. Three quarters of these were criminal cases that were being appealed in court after court, state after state, and on every possible pretext that lawyers could concoct. The degree to which the judiciary had accommodated these is astonishing, for 5.2 million of these cases had been 'pending' for five to ten years, 408,000 had been 'pending' for twenty to thirty years, and more than 73,000 had not been decided even after thirty years of litigation.

A root-and-branch reform of the entire civil and criminal procedure of the country was therefore essential. The Bharatiya Nagrik Suraksha Sanhita and the Bharatiya Sakshya Adhiniyam were therefore carefully crafted to eliminate many of these flaws. It was only when the draft was submitted to the executive that their perversion into an instrument of terror began. To achieve this, the government slipped in new laws and clauses that further drastically reduced civil liberties and further increased the arbitrary powers of the police. A total of twenty new crimes were added to the criminal code bill, and the imprisonment sentence was increased for thirty-three of the existing list.

More disturbingly, the Bharatiya Nyaya Sanhita introduces provisions related to terrorism and acts endangering the sovereignty, unity and integrity of India. Under the BNS and BNSS, the definition of subversive or separatist activities includes *any act* threatening the sovereignty or unity and integrity of India. But there is no attempt to spell out the conditions these actions must fulfil to qualify as a threat to India's sovereignty and unity. Inevitably, therefore, the determination is left to local police officials and their political bosses, thereby greatly increasing their right to persecute citizens without having to bother with such democratic obstacles as bail and *habeas corpus*.

To further shore up this right of politically guided persecution, the two new acts have vastly extended and legitimized the unfettered right of virtually any police officer to arrest and incarcerate a citizen on suspicion, entirely on his or her own cognizance. The original Criminal Code (CrPC), taken from the Government of India Act of 1935 and enshrined in the 1950 Constitution, had allowed the police to hold a suspect for a few days at most for interrogation, before producing him or her for a hearing before a magistrate. The magistrate would then decide whether the suspect merited being given bail, or sent into judicial custody and therefore out of reach of further punitive police interrogation designed to force a confession out of him or her. Over the ensuing decades, as the Indian political class became more and more corrupt and criminalized, state governments increased the period allowed in police custody from a few days to a maximum of two weeks. But once the suspect was handed over to the magistracy and went into judicial custody, the police lost the right to bring him back for further custodial interrogation and had to rely on investigation alone to build its case. The Bharatiya Nagrik Suraksha Sanhita and the Bharatiya Sakshya Adhiniyam have removed this limitation on the powers of the police. They now allow the police to bring the suspect back from judicial to police custody repeatedly within the ninety-day period of judicial custody for further coercive interrogation in order to obtain a confession, thus codifying into law what was previously merely the general practice.

Although these laws have come into force only recently, and their full consequences are yet to unfold, there is little ambiguity about the direction in which they are designed to steer the country—and it is one that should alarm every thinking citizen. *Pari passu* with the Prevention of Money Laundering Act these Acts have turned India's criminal justice system into a reign of terror within which there appears to be little hope of reprieve.

CHAPTER SIXTEEN

# A Glimpse of India's Electoral Autocracy

In the years he has been prime minister, Modi has made less and less effort to hide the lengths to which he is prepared to go to get his way on whatever issue confronts his government. He began within days of coming to power with a sustained attack on the Aam Aadmi Party and its chief, Arvind Kejriwal, whom he could not forgive for sweeping the Delhi Vidhan Sabha elections in 2015 by winning sixty-seven out of its seventy seats. The loophole he was able to use is Delhi's peculiar status as a state with its own elected legislature but which is also a Union territory because it is the capital of India. This is reflected in the structure of Article 295AA of the Constitution, which leaves the ownership of land, the maintenance of law and order, and the police in the hands of the central government.

Kejriwal never contested this so Modi could not find a pretext for picking a fight with him over issues arising in these areas. But there was another loophole that he exploited to the hilt: this was the ambivalent position in which a conflict between the central and the Delhi governments leaves Delhi's bureaucracy, whose officers are drawn from the Indian Administrative Service or DANICS (a Union Territories cadre created to provide the day-to-day administration of Delhi, Andaman & Nicobar, Lakshadweep, Daman and Diu, and Dadra and Nagar Haveli). Both of these cadres are controlled by the Union home ministry. This enabled Home Minister Shah, and through him the Prime Minster, evidently to use the home ministry's control over their careers to keep themselves fully informed about everything the AAP was planning or executing, and then, using the power of veto of the Lieutenant-Governor (also left intact by Article 295AA of the Constitution), block whatever initiatives they felt threatened by. The number of occasions on which the home ministry sabotaged Kejriwal's plans are too numerous to recount.[1] Modi eventually got a ruling from Justice Ashok Bhushan, a complaisant judge of the Supreme Court, endorsing every action that his government had taken to hamstring the Delhi government. It took Kejriwal more than two years to get this decision reversed by a Constitution Bench of the Supreme Court. Two months after he retired, on October 29, 2021, Bhushan was 'rewarded' (as Supreme Court Chief Justice P. Sathasivam had been 'rewarded' for his judgement exonerating Modi of any complicity in the Gujarat pogrom of Muslims in 2002) by being appointed the head of the National Company Law Appellate Tribunal (NCLAT).

Modi followed this with a sustained attack on Bihar's chief minister, Nitish Kumar. Kumar took the safer option and succumbed to the BJP's blandishments without putting up a fight because Modi, it was widely believed, had discovered the source of the funds Kumar had used to fight successive elections, and was about to turn the Enforcement Directorate against his financial backer.

As has already been described, another of Modi's attacks was on Mamata Banerjee and the Trinamool Congress in Bengal. But it was after A.M. Khanwilkar's 2022 judgement in *Vijay Madanlal Choudhary vs Union of India*, rejecting all eighty petitions against Modi's eight 2019 amendments to the PMLA, that he threw all caution to the winds in an attempt to destroy every remaining shred of opposition in the country. Within months of the judgement, action was taken against leaders of the elected Shiv Sena–Nationalist Congress Party coalition government in Maharashtra. Anil Deshmukh, the home minister, in custody facing money-laundering charges by the ED since November 2021 was arrested by the CBI in another corruption case in April 2022. Sanjay Raut, the deputy chief minister and 'strongman' of the ousted government, too, was arrested in August under the PMLA. To give a semblance of legality to their arrests, in view of the public and a by then utterly docile media, their offices, homes and known properties and bank accounts were searched for evidence of undeclared income or assets for days before they were taken to prison.

The charge against Raut was that he had made vast sums of 'black money' when he piloted the modernization of a slum in central Mumbai. When, after searching his premises diligently for days, the Enforcement Directorate found Rs 1.075 million ($13,000) in cash in his home, its officers waved their find triumphantly before the eyes the audio-visual media as proof that Raut had been hoarding 'black money'. Not one of the assembled journalists pointed out that, in 2022, this would have been his household expenditure needs for at most a month, and was the extant value of only 1.8 square metres of land in that part of Mumbai. It was therefore hardly a sum that could qualify as concealed income.

Raut and Deshmukh were kept in jail for more than three months (100 days) and thirteen months, respectively, before the Bombay High Court refused repeated pleas by the ED (and in Deshmukh's case both the ED and CBI) to extend the time given to them to present their case against the grant of bail, and released them in November and December 2022, respectively.[2] One and a half years later, when the country again went to the polls to select a new national government, the Enforcement Directorate had still not been able to frame a case that would bring them to trial. But by this time the entire print and audio-visual media of the country had been so thoroughly tamed that few of them made more than a passing mention of their release.

As the 2024 Lok Sabha elections approached and Modi's paranoia increased,[3] he began to use the ED and the PMLA with greater and greater abandon. He reached the end of this road when he arrested and imprisoned two reigning chief ministers, Hemant Soren, the chief minister of Jharkhand, on January 31, 2023, and Arvind Kejriwal, chief minister of Delhi, on March 21, 2024, less than one month before the start of the voting in the 2024 elections.

## The Defamation of Arvind Kejriwal and Destruction of the AAP in Delhi

The ED made the same kind of accusations against both that it had made against Raut and Deshmukh in Maharashtra. Hemant Soren was accused of having illegally sold reserved tribal land in Jharkhand to builders for vast sums of money paid in cash. Kejriwal was accused of—through his new liquor policy introduced in November 2021—privatizing liquor sales, which had been a government monopoly since the 1970s, in exchange for hefty bribes from a group of private distillers and wine-makers from South India, whom the commercial media had labelled the 'South Group'.

The accusation against AAP was so meticulously crafted that even the *Indian Express*, Delhi's most respected newspaper, published it in detail without any attempt, to the best of this writer's knowledge, to cross-check it with the AAP's leaders.[4] Here are the key details of the case the ED built against them:

The so-called South Group, investigators told the newspaper, which allegedly included K. Kavitha, the daughter of Telangana Chief Minister K. Chandrashekar Rao, and Magunta Sreenivasulu Reddy, a Lok Sabha MP from the (then Congress-backed) Yuvajana Sramika Rythu Congress Party (YSRCP), paid kickbacks to the tune of Rs 100 crore ($115,000) to AAP leaders. According to the ED, members of the South Group paid bribes to exploit loopholes in the excise policy that would secure their uninhibited access to various wholesale businesses and retail zones in violation of the rules. It alleged that the kickbacks were 'paid in advance to the AAP leaders through Vijay Nair [AAP's communication-in-charge] by the South Group as a part of agreement between the South Group and the AAP leaders', and that the South Group 'secured uninhibited access, undue favours, attained stakes in established wholesale businesses and multiple retail zones [over and above what was allowed in the policy]'.

The complaint stated that to 'recover the kickbacks given by the South Group, partners of the "south group" were given 65 per cent stake in M/s Indo Spirits [*sic*]' in collusion with the owner of this liquor distribution company, Sameer Mahendru, who was also an accused in this case. The ED claimed that the formation of the partnership was 'directed by Nair on the assurance of giving the wholesale business of Pernod Ricard to Indo Spirits'. Pernod Ricard is a well-known French wine and spirits company which owns many popular brands. The ED also claimed that Kavitha spoke to Mahendru in September 2021 on Facetime, 'congratulated Sameer for Delhi business', and was 'happy that they have partnered up'. As per the *Indian Express* report, the complaint 'relied almost entirely upon the statement of Mahendru to allege that he was approached by members of the South Group who expressed interest in his company'. It also notes that Mahendru told the ED that when he was told by Nair that the South Group 'was keen on investing in Delhi business, that this group had deep pockets, political connections and [were] friends of Arvind Kejriwal', he had initially not wanted to join the partnership, because he felt that the South Group wanted to own stake in his company without making much investment.

The ED also stated that 'the partners belonging to this group were allowed to withdraw from the profits of Indo Spirits. There is evidence to show that this withdrawal can be linked to the money that was paid to Vijay Nair. That, in order to create a device for continuous payment of kickbacks to Sh Vijay Nair, an unheard of margin of 12% was provided to the private wholesalers…contrary to the recommendations of the Expert Committee'. According to the agency, the loss to the government exchequer was to the tune of Rs 581 crore, which 'got illegally diverted into ostentatious profits to the wholesalers including the accused M/s Indo Spirits, which was used to recoup the kickbacks paid in advance by the South Group'.

What was even more surprising than the fact that no newspaper cross-checked these allegations with any of AAP's senior members was that no newspaper or political commentator asked the first question that should have come up in his or her mind: When both the choice of liquor wholesalers and retailers was being done through public auctions, how was it possible to pre-determine who the winners would be?

In pursuit of evidence, the ED arrested no fewer than four AAP leaders: first, Satyendra Jain, the minister for home and industries among other portfolios, in May 2022; then the deputy chief minister, Manish Sisodia, in February 2023; then Sanjay Singh, another AAP leader and Rajya Sabha member, in October 2023; and finally Chief Minister Kejriwal himself. All of the arrests were based upon ten sequential statements made by a single employee of the South Group, Dinesh Arora, who was arrested and then turned a police witness (approver) to obtain his freedom.

Jain was arrested in May 2022 for 'allegedly misusing his position as minister from February 2015 to May 2017 to acquire disproportionate assets'.[5] Almost two years later, during which he had been behind bars with only brief periods of interim bail granted on medical grounds, the ED, after sparing no effort to unearth some or all of the proceeds of Jain's alleged crime, told the Supreme Court while opposing yet another plea for bail from Jain, that it had attached as presumptively illegal gains Rs 4.60 crores ($560,000) worth of Jain's property. In 2022, this would have been barely sufficient to pay for a three-bedroom apartment in the outer suburbs of Delhi, ten to fifteen kilometres from the city centre. It is an amount that perhaps half of the city's middle-class families possess, or can raise. But after Modi's amendments to the PMLA, and Justice Khanwilkar's peremptory dismissal of all the eighty petitions against them, the Supreme Court was left with no option but to reject the plea.

Since then, the ED has hunted high and low for evidence against Sisodia and Sanjay Singh but failed to find any that will enable it to bring the case to trial. On April 3, 2024, the Supreme

Court ran out of patience and granted bail to Sanjay Singh, stating that it was doing so because Mr Singh had been behind bars for six months with 'no headway made in recovering the proceeds of the alleged crime or any trace of the money trail leading to him'.[6]

But that was ten days after the ED had arrested Arvind Kejriwal. By then, the procession of arrests, and denials of bail in what the media had been calling the 'Liquor Scam' for more than two years, had achieved their purpose: nearly everyone in the city had come to believe that where there was so much smoke there had to be at least a small fire. Few if any residents of the city remembered the rampant corruption that had existed within the government in the choice of wholesale suppliers of alcohol, and of shops that would be its retail sale points.

None of the mainline print or TV channels pointed out that (i) by awarding supply contracts to liquor wholesalers by a public auction, (ii) predetermining the retail vend points where the liquor would be sold, (iii) spreading these evenly across the city for easy access to rich and poor alike, and (iv) awarding these contracts also only via public auctions, the AAP had actually *eliminated all possibility of corruption in the sale of liquor within the state, for every transaction it made was now open to investigation under the Right to Information Act that Dr Manmohan Singh's Congress-led government had passed, two decades earlier, in 2005*. So great was the change in the liquor trade that, in the ten months it was in place, Delhi's excise revenues from liquor sales doubled—before a diktat from the Lt Governor to civil servants belonging to Delhi's excise department killed the reform itself.

The success of this policy was confirmed when the AAP came to power in Punjab and implemented the same policy there. Punjab's revenues from excise duties rose from Rs 6,254.74 crore in 2021–22 to Rs 8,841.4 crores, a record growth of 41.41 per cent, in 2022–23.[7] They went up further to Rs 10,743.72 crore in 2024–25.[8]

So, what was the reason for the Kejriwal government to have abandoned it in Delhi after only ten months? The lack of any explanation from his government played into the BJP's hands because it sowed the seeds of suspicion in the public that the AAP was, in the final analysis, no better than any of the other political parties that had ruled the state. It is not surprising therefore that this was the main explanation seized upon by commentators to explain the AAP's surprise defeat in 2025.

The real explanation for AAP's abandonment of the policy was fairly straightforward and entirely different. It was a sudden pen-down strike by the officers in the state's excise department, who simply refused to sign any documents on liquor purchases and sales. The orders for this, and the threat to those who did not comply, came from the Union home ministry. Kejriwal was therefore left with no option but to abandon the new policy altogether.[9]

Four years later, on February 25, 2025, the Comptroller and Auditor-General of India issued a report that estimated the loss from AAP's change of policy to have been Rs 2,002.68 crores during the ten months of its existence. The BJP's propaganda machine promptly cited this to be clinching proof that the AAP had changed the old liquor policy with ulterior motives. But by then the same policy had been yielding a bonanza to the exchequer in Punjab, so the CAG's report also needs to be taken with a pinch of salt.

At the time, Kejriwal's decision was understandable, but it turned out to be a serious political mistake, for with no journalist daring to cross-check a sensational story for fear of falling foul of the central government, his side of the story never became public. The decision to stay silent also weakened support for AAP among the poor despite the party having devoted all its energy to improving their lot.[10] It was indeed a new type of political party—uninterested in caste and communal differences and determined to use political power not to enrich its members and financiers but improve the lives of the poor through better education, improved health facilities, access to social services, denied by its predecessors to those who lived in the so-called unauthorized slum colonies, and to more humane conditions of work, especially for the female working poor of the city. The alleged liquor scam, the arrests by the ED of AAP's top leaders, and the incessant repetition of the ED's accusations by the 'Godi' media in print and on the TV screen, without any journalist even trying to present AAP's account, made many people believe that it too had been corrupted by its incessant need for 'black' money to finance a nationwide election every few years.

The fact that a small new party had been able to defeat the entire clientelist network created and established in Delhi by the ban on company donations in 1970, and the criminalization of politics and governance that followed, and genuinely considered its duty to be to work in the interests of the poor, became a mighty threat not only to the ruling BJP but to all other parties in the country.

For Modi and Shah, who still faced a possible revival of criminal charges related to the Ahmedabad riots of 2002 and the faked encounters that followed, winning the parliamentary elections of April and May 2024 was important for not only ideological but personal reasons as well. For them, therefore, the sudden rise of AAP, with its radically opposed philosophy, was a dire, personal threat. The need to destroy it, at any cost, and thereby discredit even the possibility of a moral rejuvenation of India's secular democracy remained a matter of the utmost personal importance.

Since the BJP's share of the vote in the two general elections of 2019 and 2024 has stalled at 38 and 37 per cent, respectively, whether they succeed or not will be decided by the short-sightedness and internal bickering within the Congress, and among its coalition partners. While all the leaders of the INDIA (Indian National Developmental Inclusive Alliance) bloc, formed in July 2023, understood this, the realization remained weak within their second rank, local and state leaders, even after surprising defeat of the Congress in Haryana in October 2024, brought about by the party's state leader Bhupinder Singh Hooda's point blank refusal to partner with the AAP. It was only after the Alliance's abject defeat at the hands of a motley crowd of defectors from it in the Maharashtra state elections in November 2024 that the Congress began to realize that it could no longer either go it alone or even as the undisputed leader of the INDIA bloc. The clinching realization, however, came with the AAP's unexpected, razor-thin defeat in the Delhi state assembly elections next year.

## How BJP Stole the Delhi Vidhan Sabha Election

In February 2025, BJP won the Delhi assembly elections. Coming after the many unexplained anomalies in the December 2024 Maharashtra state assembly elections, it has been difficult not to suspect that Amit Shah, the BJP's master strategist on the electoral battlefield, may have found a method of gerrymandering the results of elections in India,[11] to perpetuate their hold on power and create, by admittedly less brutal means, the one-party national state to last for 'a thousand years' that Hitler, Goering and their closest confidants had come close to creating in 1943.

Indeed, the only party which has managed to increase its vote share slowly over the years in Delhi is the BJP. In 2013, when the BJP won thirty-two seats, its vote share was 33.07 per cent. In 2015, the vote share was more or less in the same bracket, at 32.19 per cent, but its seats dropped to three. In 2020, there was an increase of around six percentage points in the BJP's vote share but its seats tally rose only to eight.

Everything changed dramatically in the 2025 state assembly elections. In the sharpest political shift seen in India in seventeen elections held separately in over twenty-eight states and eight union territories, even though the BJP's vote share jumped by only 7.1 percentage points—from 38.51 to 45.61 per cent—it gained forty more seats in Delhi, dislodging the AAP after ten years. What is more, it was able to do this with only a 1.9 per cent edge in its share of the vote.

The AAP's vote share in the 2013 elections, when it jumped out of anonymity and bagged twenty-eight seats, had been 29.49

per cent. In 2015, it saw a sharp increase in its vote share to an unprecedented 54.34 per cent votes and won sixty-seven out of the assembly's seventy seats. AAP did this yet again in the 2020 elections when it again secured 53.57 per cent of the vote share and sixty-two seats.

Based on these figures, however, there appears to be a glaring anomaly when one compares the results of the last two Vidhan Sabha (2015 and 2020) and Lok Sabha (2019 and 2024) elections in Delhi, one that had never been seen in previous elections to the Lok Sabha and the Vidhan Sabha in the ten sets of elections held from 1971–72 onwards, when Mrs Gandhi separated the central from the state elections. In the Lok Sabha elections that followed the spectacular Vidhan Sabha victories of 2015 and 2020, the AAP's share of the vote fell to 18.2 per cent and 24.1 per cent in 2019 and 2024, respectively. The drop of its vote share between consecutive Vidhan Sabha and Lok Sabha elections was therefore *66 and 55 per cent.*[12]

A substantial part of this drop can be explained by the AAP having fought in only four out of Delhi's seven parliamentary seats in both 2019 and 2024. But even if it had not left the remaining three seats to the Congress, and been able to retain a similar share of the vote in them, its share would at most have been 30–31 per cent in 2019, and at most 42 per cent in 2024. That would still have left a 35 per cent drop in support in 2019 and an almost 12 per cent drop in 2024 unexplained, which, while still surprising, would not have lifted too many eyebrows.

A part of the latter figure of a 12 per cent drop could be attributed to the sustained three-year campaign by the BJP to discredit AAP's moral credentials by accusing its leaders of the so-called liquor scam, and then imprisoning its principal leaders, including Arvind Kejriwal himself, without bail for periods of up to two years despite not having, according to the Supreme Court, 'a shred of proof'.

The BJP's propaganda machine understood the Indian electorate only too well and knew that mere incarceration would do its intended damage. Not entirely surprisingly, none of this ruthlessly planned smear campaign was questioned by the mainstream media. But what is surprising is that the significance of this anomaly did not dawn upon our most respected political analysts either, even after it happened twice in a row. This was the main reason why nearly all placed the blame for AAP's defeat on the moral decline of the party in the fourteen years since it was born. *None of them even raised the possibility that the elections might have been stolen.*

There was this lack of scrutiny in spite of the mounting evidence from the Maharashtra Vidhan Sabha elections that these had been gerrymandered to ensure the BJP's victory, most probably through the misuse of Form 7 of the Election Commission—a seemingly innocuous form that simply allows residents of a constituency to inform the Commission of deaths and changes of residence within their localities since the previous election.

A damning allegation in this regard was made by Rahul Gandhi at a press conference on February 7. A day before the Delhi Vidhan Sabha election results were announced, he informed the media that two discrepancies he had pointed out to the Election Commission about the Maharashtra Vidhan Sabha elections had never been responded to. The first was: 'Between the 2019 Assembly elections and the 2024 Lok Sabha election, 32 lakh voters were added to Maharashtra's electoral rolls over five years. However, between the 2024 Lok Sabha elections and the 2024 Assembly elections, 39 lakh new voters were added in just five months.' The second was how there happened to be more names in the voters' list in the Maharashtra Vidhan Sabha elections than the entire adult population of the state.

This was not the first accusation of such manipulation to reach the Election Commission. The first had come as long ago as on March 8, 2019, and had been filed by no less significant a person than G.K. Dwivedi, who was the chief electoral officer for the state of Andhra Pradesh during the assembly elections that year. This was not an unofficial but an official complaint to the

CDAC (Centre for Development of Advanced Computing), which operates under the central government's Ministry of Electronics and Information Technology, and it asked for all the Form 7s to be sent to him for vetting. Dwivedi was ignored.[13]

In October 2024, Kejriwal had also accused the BJP of falsely reporting thousands of voters as having either relocated to different addresses or died. Citing the Shahadara constituency as a specific example, he claimed that BJP workers led by Vishal Bhardwaj, a media co-ordinator for the BJP in Shahadara, had signed *11,018 Form 7 applications* to delete voters' names in this constituency. Kejriwal claimed that an examination of 500 randomly selected deletions had shown that 70 per cent of the deleted voters were alive and resident in Shahadara, and were therefore eligible to vote. But this was a single accusation, and by then the world seemed to have moved on from elections, so neither the Election Commission nor the BJP responded to his accusation.[14] Instead, the district magistrate of Shahadara was made to deny the report. Since he belonged to a central government service he could hardly have done anything else.

Whether this indeed happened or not, there can be little doubt that by the 2024 Lok Sabha and 2025 Vidhan Sabha elections, Form 7 had become a major weapon in the BJP's armoury of tactics for winning elections. Coming after the two questions that Rahul Gandhi asked the Election Commission, and received no answer, someone should have raised the matter along with the obviously quixotic results of the Maharashtra election, which the former had highlighted in parliament and press conferences with the mainstream media.

But no one did. After the Delhi results were announced, no one even asked the obvious question that if the AAP lost 10 per cent of the total vote, amounting to a fifth of its entire support base, why did all of it go only to the BJP?

By February 8, Kejriwal's October 2024 analysis of the alterations in the Shahadara voting list had been forgotten, but a thorough though perhaps still incomplete post-poll analysis of voters' lists by the AAP showed just how far the BJP took the misuse of Form 7, and with what utter contempt for the political opposition.

Sanjay Singh, one of the AAP's main party organizers, disclosed a small part of its findings on Kapil Sibal's YouTube programme, *Dil Se* ('From the heart'). Singh, who was among those arrested on PMLA charges, gave a detailed account of the number of deletions that had taken place in several constituencies, during the 2025 Vidhan Sabha elections, before Sibal stopped him, saying that he had made his point. These were: Janakpuri: 6,247; Sangam Vihar: 5,862; Palam: 4,031; Dwarka: 4,013; RK Puram: 4,287; Tughlaqabad: 4,987; Okhla: 4,933; Karawal Nagar: 2,957; Laxmi Nagar: 2,147.

In Shahadara, Sanjay Singh confirmed, *a single BJP karyakarta* (party worker), possibly the same Vishal Bhardwaj, had asked for 11,000 deletions! In the Janakpuri Vidhan Sabha constituency, twenty-four karyakartas had applied for a total of 4,874 deletions. At Tughlaqabad, fifteen party workers had applied for a total of 4,235 deletions. At booth number 117 in this same constituency, which had a voter list of 1,337 persons, *two BJP party workers had applied for a total of 554 deletions*! At Palam, the site of the Delhi airport, nine BJP karyakartas had applied for a total of 1,641 deletions; at Harinagar, four had applied for the deletion of 637 voters from the electoral rolls; at Rajouri Garden, a middle-class neighbourhood in outer Delhi, BJP's workers had applied for 571 deletions, and so on.

These added up to 69,330 voter deletions in just over one-fifth of Delhi's assembly constituencies. If we assume similar deletions having taken place in all constituencies, it means that just over three lakhs of voters may have been disfranchised. That amounts to only 3 per cent of all the votes cast in the election. But for vote stealing, that would have been enough, for the BJP emerged victorious in forty-eight seats against the AAP's wins in twenty-two constituencies, with slivers of a majority that added up to 1.9 per cent of the vote share percentage.

A 1.9 per cent advantage averages less than four in a thousand deletions of voters via Form 7 submissions. The total voter turnout in the 2025 Delhi elections was 9.488 million across seventy constituencies, or an average of approximately 135,000 per constituency. It would therefore require only 1.9 per cent of this number—2,565 Form 7 deletions per constituency—to get Delhi's result. This turns the possibility that there could have been extensive vote stealing in Delhi, as in Maharashtra, into a probability.

So far, neither the Chief Election Commissioner nor his deputies have made even a token attempt to explain these glaring discrepancies. In a farewell televised statement in early 2025, Rajiv Kumar, the outgoing chief election commissioner, gave a detailed description of the balloting process. He also sought to allay the doubts being expressed with increasing frequency about the sanctity of the electronic voting machines. But what he did not say a word on was how the Commission had dealt with the deluge of Form 6s, demanding additions to, and Form 7s, demanding deletions from the voters' lists.

It is apparent that the Modi government had begun to look for ways to 'influence' the results of the Lok Sabha and Vidhan Sabha elections at least as far back as 2020. The Form 7 was intended to allow residents of a constituency to inform the Election Commission that a voter on the list had died or moved out of the constituency and others had taken his or her place. There is good reason to believe that the BJP has made a wholesale abuse of this privilege granted to voters to, in essence, steal the elections.

None of this could have happened had there been a truly independent Election Commission. Messrs Modi and Shah seem to have understood this well enough and set their sights on it. The first signal came in 2020, when Ashok Lavasa, an election commissioner since 2018, who had been tipped to become the next chief election commissioner in April 2021, only a year later, suddenly resigned from the Commission and took up a job with the Asian Development Bank. Arun Goel, the second election commissioner, lasted longer, but also resigned equally suddenly in March 2024, stating categorically that he was doing this because of irreconcilable differences with the CEC, who by then was none other than Rajiv Kumar.

By then Modi had found the loophole in the law through which to take over the election system, and thus complete his conversion of a democratic nation into a one-party state. This was to comply with the Supreme Court's *Baranwal* directive (in *Anoop Baranwal vs Union of India*, 2023) to pass a law sanctifying the existing method of choosing the chief election commissioner—putting in place a three-member selection committee comprising the chief justice, the prime minister and the leader of the opposition—but with only one small change that the opposition was too weak to prevent: the replacement of the chief justice of India with a minister of the prime minister's choosing. The passage of the Chief Election Commissioner and Other Election Commissioners (Appointment, Conditions of Service and Term of Office) Act in December 2023 gave his government, and any future government, a permanent majority of two to one in the choice of the chief election commissioner and his two deputies.

Seen in hindsight, the chain of events—from the weaponization of the PMLA and the systematic targeting of opposition leaders, to the calculated misuse of Form 7 and the quiet reshaping of the Election Commission—reveals a strategy that is designed not to promote electoral competition, but cement electoral control. What has taken place is not merely the manipulation of isolated elections, but the deliberate engineering of a political system to give one, and only one, result—the return of the ruling party to power. In this architecture of dominance, the illusion of choice is preserved, but the machinery of power is no longer answerable to the people.

If there is a lesson to be drawn from the rapid descent of Indian democracy into an electoral autocracy, it is that no constitution, however meticulously crafted, and no institution, however firmly rooted in tradition, can withstand the sustained corrosion of power unchecked. The transformation of constitutional provisions into instruments of suppression, the weaponization of investigating agencies, the capture of the media, and now the hollowing out of the Election Commission itself, reveal not just a political strategy but a coldly planned, systemic demolition of democracy from within, brick by brick. That this could have happened in the land of Gandhi and Ambedkar, in full view of an increasingly silent public and a pliant political class, should haunt the conscience of every Indian. The road back from this precipice will be long and hard, but it begins with recognizing that what has happened is not an aberration that can be set right by the BJP's opponents winning one election. Democracy can be saved only if there remains a people still willing to reclaim the republic that was once theirs. At present, the confusion, infighting and jostling for the fruits of office among the members of the opposition alliance gives little hope of there being a change of heart within in it, despite the dire peril that the country is in today.

# Epilogue

## *Can Democracy Still Be Saved?*

The answer to this question is short and dismal. Indian democracy is on its last legs. Every one of its four pillars—the legislature, the executive, the judiciary and the media—so carefully and lovingly constructed by the Constitution and fostered by Pandit Jawaharlal Nehru, is now a hollow shell, still standing, still with a semblance of shape, but with its core eaten into wormy dust by an all-pervasive greed for money and power that knows no end.

But even that remnant is now in imminent danger of being extinguished by two recent decisions of the Narendra Modi government. The first is its determination to push through a fresh delimitation of parliamentary constituencies in 2026, over stiff protests from all the southern states. The second is its disempowerment of the Muslim Waqf Board on April 5, 2025, by pushing a bill through parliament, again in the face of stiff opposition, that will take away the Board's autonomy in deciding the ownership and control over Waqf properties. Not only has this power been given to a member of the executive branch of government, the district magistrate of the concerned area, but Waqf Boards are required now to include non-Muslims, specifically Hindus, on them. Each of these decisions contains the potential to set off a general conflagration in the country.

If the delimitation were to take place, the number of seats in parliament will rise from the present 543 to 848. But the five southern states will lose more than twenty seats. The chief gainer will be Uttar Pradesh whose runaway increase in population will add another sixty to its present eighty seats. Modi wishes to ram this through because it will make the impoverished, jobless Uttar Pradesh the virtual master of the country. This is the cannon fodder that Modi needs to complete his transformation of democratic India into a 'Hindu' Fascist India.

It is not surprising therefore that delimitation has become the banner around which southern India, now joined by Odisha and almost certain to be joined by West Bengal and Punjab, is gearing up for a confrontation with the Modi government. Should this go out of hand, it could plunge the country into a civil war that will end in the disintegration of India. This disintegration will be painful but sudden, swift and complete.

There is a simple reason for this: the Indian armed forces are recruited locally from every district of India. As a result, as every army, navy and air force chief has made clear to various prime ministers on more than one occasion, the army will not open fire upon its own people. It is possible that Modi will perceive this danger and push back the next delimitation to 2056, as the opposition wants. But nothing that he has done in twelve years in Gujarat and eleven in New Delhi shows that he is capable of admitting a mistake, let alone conceding defeat. On the contrary, twenty-two years of public life in the glare of uncritical adoration and visceral criticism has inured him to any reaction from a public that he holds in utter contempt.

Were Modi to insist upon going through with a fresh delimitation of constituencies, history will repeat itself in India. When Aurangzeb alienated the Rajput nobility upon whose shoulders the Mughal Empire had rested, and prospered, for two hundred years, he was forced to fight campaigns incessantly for the last thirty-five of his forty-nine-year reign, which left the Mughal Empire a bankrupt shambles for the likes of Ahmad Shah Abdali, Nadir Shah and the British, to pillage at will—till India was reduced from being the richest nation in the world to the poorest. This tragic history will be repeated if Modi continues down the road upon which he is now travelling.

## Why Has Opposition Unity Remained a Will-o'-the-wisp?

Contrary to the vociferous assertions of Congress party leaders and cadres, it has been apparent to every student of politics for more than two decades that the days of Congress dominance are irrevocably over. That position has been usurped by the BJP, whose vote has jumped from 19 per cent in 2009 to 31 per cent in 2014, 37.8 per cent in 2019 and stabilised at 36.9 per cent in 2024, while the Congress' vote has fallen from 28 per cent in 2009 to 19.3 per cent in 2014 and 19.5 per cent in 2019, though it rose marginally to 22.3 per cent in 2024.

The next development in Indian politics should therefore have been a coming together of like-minded parties that were opposed to the BJP's project to convert India into a theoretically 'Hindu' but in actual fact an upper-caste-dominated nation by ironing out their differences and creating a second coalition large enough to make the simple majority voting system work in their favour. In India, this has not happened despite the palpably growing danger that Modi represents to all of them, because of two hurdles that the opposition parties have not been able to overcome.

The first is a shift of decision-making power within each national party, except the cadre-based Communists and Jana Sangh (now BJP), from its known and respected central command to anonymous syndicates of local financiers. From known leaders whom the voters could hold accountable, power thus shifted to anonymous local financiers whom the public did not know, or feared, and consequently could not. This was the result of the blocking of all legal ways to meet the cost of running political parties and that of elections without either restricting the franchise, as the British had done and some members of the Constituent Assembly had suggested, or creating a system of state funding for recognized national and state parties.

The second hurdle to the formation of a durable coalition of democratic parties to fight the BJP was the unanticipated impact of the splitting of the Congress party in 1969 upon its internal structure. From its formation in 1885 till 1969, the

Congress had been a coalition of powerful state leaders fighting for independence who had joined Mahatma Gandhi's campaign based on *ahimsa* (non-violence) to wrest power back from the British. After 1947, this essentially federal structure within the Congress had persisted in the shape of 'the Syndicate'. The split in 1969 destroyed the Syndicate, to the benefit of Indira Gandhi. But this victory proved in the long run to be a pyrrhic one. For it turned the central Congress from a federal party—a federation of elders that mimicked the ethnic federation of the nation—into a unitary party with a single supremo at its head. This radically changed its internal structure from a democratic to an autocratic one. Even as power passed out of the hands of known party leaders to anonymous financiers, nominal leadership within the Congress also, simultaneously, became dynastic—concentrated in the hands of first Mrs Indira Gandhi, then Rajiv Gandhi, then Sonia Gandhi and finally Rahul Gandhi. The multi-tiered structure of the party—from district to *pradesh* to the all-India committees—remained but sapped of its decision-making power, an empty shell.

These developments within the Congress, in particular, have acted as hindrances to the creation of an effective opposition to Modi's BJP, and were therefore the cause of the stillborn nature of INDIA (Indian National Developmental Inclusive Alliance). They snatched defeat from the jaws of victory by creating a set of circumstances in which Nitish Kumar, leader of the Janata Dal (United), decided to place his trust upon the BJP rather than upon the Congress-centred Alliance in the 2024 elections.

*

Like other nations with simple majority voting systems, India will not become a stable democracy till it has a two-party democracy. Nitish Kumar was the first to recognize this. He made his first exploratory move towards opposition unity within weeks of his party's victory in the Bihar state assembly polls of 2017, by proposing to the Congress that the opposition should field a common candidate for the presidency of India. The name he proposed was that of Gopal Gandhi, the grandson of Mahatma Gandhi, who after a distinguished career in the Civil Service, had been appointed the Governor of Bengal by Dr Manmohan Singh's government.

With the BJP and its allies holding more than 300 seats in the Lok Sabha, Kumar knew that Gandhi had no chance of being elected, but uniting behind a candidate with such a powerfully symbolic name and an irreproachable reputation would have set the ball rolling towards opposition unity. Kumar's proposal reportedly got immediate support within the Congress and the entire opposition but was then met by seventeen days of unexplained silence by the then Congress president, Rahul Gandhi. This gave Modi the chance to propose an alternate candidate, and he skilfully chose Ram Nath Kovind, a skilled and principled Supreme Court lawyer and former governor of Bihar with whom Kumar had enjoyed excellent relations from 2015 till 2017, and whom he therefore could not refuse to support. That was the end of Kumar's first effort. A year later, for reasons that still remain obscure, Nitish Kumar broke his ruling alliance with the Rashtriya Janata Dal in Bihar, and joined the BJP, thus bringing that party to power in Bihar for the first time.

Modi's second, thundering victory in 2019 should have brought home to the opposition the folly of internecine competition over petty issues, but it did not. Bickering, mutual recrimination and name calling continued unabated among the rank and file, effectively isolating the few in each party, such as the Congress' group of twenty-three intellectuals and former ministers, who still continued to emphasize the need for opposition unity around key issues of governance, such as the rapidly rising numbers of educated unemployed and rising despair among the rural poor that was making millions of them drop out of the labour force altogether.[1]

In spite of the vilification he had suffered after his *volte-face* in 2017, Nitish Kumar made his second attempt at opposition unity in 2023 by calling a 'grand conclave' in Patna on June 23. That meeting created the framework for the 'grand coalition of opposition parties' to challenge the rule of the BJP that became the INDIA bloc.

The next logical step would have been to form an all-party committee to select candidates for each parliamentary seat. The obvious choice in each constituency should have been the party that had fielded a winner or the first runner-up in the constituency in the 2019 elections. But the Alliance was unable to go the extra mile because of a silent revolt against its very formation by the state, district and constituency level managers of the Congress, and to a less visible extent, of every other party in the Alliance.

The reason for this is that by 2019 India had completed its transformation from a popular democracy into a clientelist democracy, in which groups of local moneybags in each constituency met the election expenses of candidates in the hope of getting licenses, permits and land grants if their candidate won. If the party had a candidate in the election, there was a chance, however slim, that he or she might win. If that happened, those who financed the victor would get the cream of the contracts that would flow from the victory, under the MPLADS and other developmental schemes. This was the lure that the local cadres of the non-ideological political parties used to raise funds for the party and for themselves at election time.

All this would disappear if their party ceded their constituency to an ally. For cadres of the parties without a candidate in the fray, therefore, preventing such a coalition became a matter of life and death. Since the ban on company donations had made the central command in every political party dependent upon local clientelist financing to meet the cost of the elections, not having a candidate in the fray was the kiss of death to its entire client group in the constituency.

The Congress government's failure to create an honest, state-funded and Election Commission-audited system for state financing of elections, combined with the doubling of these expenses after the 1971 separation of the Lok Sabha and Vidhan Sabha elections, had shifted decision-making power from the officially recognized party leaders in Delhi, Lucknow and other state capitals to their largely anonymous clientelist financiers in the constituencies and rural townships.

This created clientelist democracy in its most poisonous form. It is this poison that has, drip by drip, turned the Gandhi family into powerless icons to be brought out on festival days, and then stowed away in lockers till the next time the need to produce them arises. It is the reason why, despite being members of the same so-called Grand Alliance against the BJP, Delhi state Congress party chiefs like Sandip Dikshit and Ajay Maken did not speak a word against the arrest of a single AAP leader—be it Satyendra Jain, Manish Sisodia, Sanjay Singh or Chief Minister Arvind Kejriwal—on charges of running a liquor scam, and their incarceration for periods ranging from four months to two years without 'a shred of evidence'.

It is the reason why the Congress' spokesperson Supriya Shrinate peremptorily dismissed Kashmir Chief Minister Omar Abdullah's caustic comment on the INDIA bloc, '*Aur lado sab aapas me*' (go ahead and keep fighting with each other), when he saw the purely destructive role that the Congress had played in engineering the defeat of the AAP in Delhi. Shrinate's retort was revealing: 'The onus of making AAP win is not on the Congress… [W]e will look for fertile political bastions and try to win these over, and Delhi is a place where we have been in the government for 15 years.'[2] With such enemies, the BJP has no need for friends.

### State Funding of Elections: The First Essential for the Survival of Democracy

If democracy is to be saved from the pit that Modi is digging for it, the first requirement is for decision-making power to be restored to the recognized leaders of the democratic political parties in the country. This will only happen if financial power in all political parties is taken back from local clientelist syndicates and concentrated once more in the hands of the central leaders of recognized political parties. Only state funding of elections can do this.

Political parties had recognized this need at least as far back as in 1998. This was revealed by the answer given to an unstarred question asked in parliament on July 23, 2009.[3] Following the initial question asked in 1998, the parliament had set up a committee consisting of some of the most eminent MPs in the country to study the issue and submit recommendations. These were Indrajit Gupta, chairman; Somnath Chatterjee, Dr Manmohan Singh, V.K. Malhotra, Madhukar Sarpotdar, R. Muthiah, Digvijay Singh, and Prof Ram Gopal Yadav.

The committee submitted its report in December 1998 and recommended the setting up of an 'election fund' of Rs 1,200 crores a year with contributions of Rs 600 crores from the central government and the remaining Rs 600 crores by the state governments. In addition to the above, on the advice of the Election Commission of India, it recommended a substantial amount of help in kind. This included free party premises, free telephone calls and up to 3,750 litres of free gasoline or diesel to cover candidates' travel costs.

Rs 1,200 crores a year meant Rs 6,000 crores every five years, half for the central and half for the state elections. Had this been pegged to the cost of living, it would have quadrupled to Rs 24,000 crores per quinquennium by 2025. If the Lok Sabha and Vidhan Sabha elections had remained united, as they were before 1971, even this relatively paltry amount would have empowered the central leaders of recognized parties and enabled them to choose a substantial number of candidates on the grounds of merit alone, to alter the level and tenor of debate in parliament and the state assemblies.

Since then there have been three more reports on state funding: a Law Commission report on *Reform of the Electoral Laws* (1999); another by the National Commission to review the working of the Constitution (2001); and by the Second Administrative Reforms

Commission (2008). All have recommended state funding, but election costs have soared well beyond the limits estimated by all of them.

The 2024 Lok Sabha elections were the most expensive ever held in India. According to a report in *India Today*, the combined expense of all political parties amounted to Rs 1.35 trillion ($160 billion), thus, considerably exceeding the sum of Rs 1.2 trillion spent on the US 2020 presidential election.[4] A similar amount will have to be spent on Vidhan Sabha elections over the next five years. The figure looks huge but is in fact only 0.47 per cent of India's GDP of 286 trillion rupees in 2023–24. Divided over five years this is less than 0.1 per cent of the GDP per year. This can easily be funded through a small additional cess on the income or corporate tax collected every year.

Generous state funding of elections is therefore entirely within the capacity of any future government. If it is limited to only recognized political parties, it will end the participation of the vast numbers of unrecognized parties and individuals that presently clog the work of the Election Commission and inflate the cost of holding elections. But even the above sum can, and indeed should, be further halved by reuniting the Lok Sabha and Vidhan Sabha elections as they were before 1971. For the INDIA bloc, or any future combination of opposition parties, this would be a boon, because it would remove the single main hurdle to opposition unity that they face today—the sudden redundancy of party cadres in a constituency that has been allocated to another party.

As in the European democracies, recognition should require a political party to obtain a minimum share of the vote in the previous election. The most frequently used threshold in Europe is 5 per cent. The criteria being used by the Election Commission today—which requires a party to secure 6 per cent of the total votes polled in four states in the last Lok Sabha or assembly elections, and in addition, have four of its members elected to the Lok Sabha, or win 2 per cent of seats in it from at least three different states—are far too severe and complicated to be of practical use as a yardstick for the apportionment of state funds to recognized political parties.

The most important, and necessary, effect of state funding of elections will be to restore the control over the party to its recognized central and state leaders. It will allow them to enrol the most politically committed of the youth in small towns and villages who wish to enter politics, by offering them a degree of financial security, and a career to look forward to. Above all, it will remove the barrier that has made every politically sensitive, intelligent and ambitious young person shun politics, which is that to become a politician, you need to become a criminal first.

Since state funding will severely weaken the clientelist networks that create what passes for policy in the central and state governments, long-term planning for the common good will become easier. It is unlikely to end corruption in the making and execution of policy, but will limit it by reducing, if not eliminating, the compulsion to get in bed with criminal syndicates in order to raise the money to fight an election.

## Re-learning Our Own History: Instilling Syncretism Through Education

Replacing the present clientelist democracy with a genuinely popular democracy in which the poor have an equal say with the rich is the first, immediate, challenge before a democratic opposition to the BJP. But the second, greater challenge is to root out the communal animosity, especially towards Muslims, that the BJP is relentlessly instilling in the minds of school children and the new Hindu middle class, through a relentless barrage of propaganda through the social media, and increasingly through incendiary, hate-inspired films.

To understand how the BJP's, or more specifically Modi's, relentless targeting of the Muslim community has damaged the global reputation of Hinduism, it's important to first recognize how highly Hinduism—along with Buddhism—was regarded by scholars and students of comparative religion before it began to be corrupted by politics. Here is an excerpt from the inaugural address given by the late Prof Friedrich Heiler, professor of Comparative Religion at the University of Marburg, at the 9th International Congress for the History of Religions held in Tokyo and Kyoto, Japan, from August 27 to September 9, 1958. Heiler opened his address with a question:

> 'Have we not all one father? Has not one God created us? Why then are we faithless to one another?' These words of the prophet Malachi (2, 10) were repeated several decades ago by a Jewish rabbi as he extended his congratulations to a Catholic bishop on the occasion of his consecration. The belief in one God should indeed awaken in the faithful among all the high religions the consciousness of belonging together in one family and their obligation to stand together fraternally. But thus it has been in the history of religions. The faithful among the higher religions have opposed one another again and again, indeed if not engaging in bloody persecution, then despising the followers of other religions as deplorably ignorant who must be led with all possible speed to the true church and religion.
>
> How many human beings have become the victims of religious wars? How frequent was the oppression of other religious consciences, how numerous were the martyrdoms suffered in courageous confession of individual faith! Although in more modern times religious persecution has passed from the hands of religious to totalitarian political powers, the deeply irrational contempt for other religions is still widespread. Indeed in Western Christianity to-day it has in certain respects become more widespread than in the eras of Enlightenment, Classicism, and Romanticism. If we ask why the sense of unity should be most hindered from that quarter where it ought be most vitally fostered, we will find the reason for this paradox in the sense of absoluteness characteristic of *one segment of the higher religions*.
>
> In *An Historian's Approach To Religion* (the best theological book of the last ten years, though not written by a theologian), Arnold Toynbee suggests that those three religions of revelation which spring from a common historical root, Judaism, Islam,

> and Christianity, have a tendency toward exclusivism and intolerance. They ascribe to themselves an ultimate validity. While the faithful among the Indian and Far Eastern religions recognize the other religions in-so-far as they discern in them another manifestation of the essentials of their own religion, the three religions mentioned above are so exclusive that their followers often enough look upon other religions as the outgrowth of error and sin. Thereby they transfer the absoluteness which is an attribute alone of the divine and eternal to their own system of faith without seeing that this divine absolute can also be comprehended in entirely different forms of thought and devotion. There is indeed something essentially true in Toynbee's objection. *The Indian religions are a bulwark of more than two thousand years of tolerance.* Two hundred fifty years before Christ, King Asoka, one of the noblest figures in world history and the great promulgator of Buddhism, proclaimed to his subjects not only tolerance but also love for other religions. He states in one of his famous edicts carved in rock: The divinely favored King Piyadasi honors all sects, both the ascetic as well as the local. He honors them with gifts and tributes of all kinds. But the divinely favored one does not lay so much weight upon gifts and tributes, but rather that in all religions there might be a growth in essence. The reason for this is that no praise for one's own religion or reproach of other religions should take place on unsuitable occasions. On the contrary, every opportunity ought to be taken to honour other religions. If one proceeds in this way, he furthers his own religion and renders good to other religions. Otherwise he does harm to his own religion and reproaches other religions, and all of this out of admiration for his own religion. When he would magnify his own cause, he rather does all the more harm to his own religion. (Emphases added)

It is against these profound observations that the lies that the BJP is spreading about India's history, culture, religion, and about the Muslim onslaught upon the Hindu identity, need to be measured. Fortunately, this task has been made much easier by the emergence of artificial intelligence tools such as Grok, but an in depth study of religion, especially of the difference between mystical religions such as Hinduism, Buddhism, Sikhism, and Zoroastrianism, and the three Messianic religions—Judaism, Christianity and Islam—needs to be an essential part of every school curriculum in the country today.

The Constituent Assembly discussed whether India should describe itself as a secular state in clause 1 of Article 1 of the Constitution at great length. After extended debate, it decided not to do so. This was because of a recognition, voiced by many of its members, that India was not only a deeply religious state but also one in which almost every religion in the world, ranging from Judaism through Zoroastrianism, and many versions of Islam and Christianity, had found comfortable acceptance alongside Hinduism. In such a nation, the role of the state had to be one of acceptance and support, not denial of religious identity.[5]

It was not till 1976 that Indira Gandhi added the word secular to clause 1 of Article 1. She did so because by then India was in the middle of the Emergency which, her government knew, had been stoked by the BJS which was anything but a secular party.

As recent experience has proved, Indira Gandhi's fears were well founded, so her addition of the word was timely. But in the decades that have followed, the repeated description of India as 'secular' by Indian as well as foreign students of India's politics has obscured the real nature of the relationship between the state and religion in today's republic.

## The Guiding Philosophy of India Is Not Secularism but Dharma

The guiding philosophy that has underpinned not only the modern Indian state but all major empires in India's history, and from which India's comfort with ethnic and religious diversity springs, is not secularism, but *religious syncretism*. This springs from the philosophy and practice of '*Dharma*'.

Dharma is the original faith of Vedic India. There is no

reference in the Vedas, the oldest texts of the Indo-Aryan civilization, to a Hindu dharma, because the word 'Hindu' was coined by the Persians 3,000 years ago to describe the land beyond the Sindhu (i.e. Indus) river. It was brought to India from Persia more than two millennia later by the first Muslim invaders who came through Afghanistan and Persia.

Dharma was not a religion in the modern, exclusivist, sense of the word, because the messianic religions that are now the subject of most discourses on religion had not even been born when the word was coined. Dharma prescribed the right way of living: it dwelt at length on how people needed to relate to each other and to the wider world and the cosmos that surrounded them.

The *Rig Veda* differentiates between different forms of *dharma*, such as *Prathama Dharma* (the first duty), *Raj Dharma* (the duties of the king to his subjects) and *Swadharma* (our duty to ourselves). But every one of these centres around the concept of human duty, which is 'to uphold, to support, to nourish'.

Dharma ('*Dhamma*' in Pali) was the word Gautama Buddha used to describe his sermons on the four noble truths and the eight-fold path. Some Western students of comparative religion have done Buddhism a disservice by presenting it as another exclusivist religion similar to the three messianic religions.

Buddha's use of the Vedic term suggests that he considered himself to be a social reformer and not a religious prophet. What he had rebelled against was the corruption of Dharma, and the growth of *Adharma* (a dereliction of duty and therefore a sin). It was caused by self-absorption, avarice, expensive and impoverishing ritual, and Brahminical control of the temples of India. Buddhism was therefore the first great recorded rebellion against a still nascent organized religion in human history.

Describing Buddhism as one of several prophetic religions, as most students of comparative religion in the West habitually do, has obscured a critical difference between Hinduism, Buddhism and other mystical religions, on the one hand, and the messianic ones, on the other. Messianic religions have to be professed.

Belonging to one of them requires a profession of faith in it and a repudiation of other faiths. It is a surrender of oneself to the 'true' God, and its reward is the possibility of gaining absolution for one's sins through repentance, in *this* life.

Mystical faiths have to be lived. Only virtue in this life can gain the soul freedom from the chain of rebirth. Dharma requires no profession of faith, no submission to a single prophet. And it offers no easy absolution from sin. It is the Hindu way of referring to Buddhism, as *Bauddha Dharma*, or the remark that Hindus frequently make even today, '*Yeh mera dharma hai*' (This is my duty), that capture its essence.

The idea of religion as a set of beliefs that have to be practised and not merely professed is not limited to Hinduism and Buddhism, but has carved out a niche in Islam and Christianity as well. In the eleventh and twelfth centuries, it found a home in a Christian sect called the Cathars (or Albigenses) in southern France and Spain, and in some branches of Shia Islam such as the Alawis of Syria, Iraq and Turkey.

Not surprisingly, both sects have been treated as heretical apostates by the clergy of orthodox Christianity and Islam. In AD 1200, Pope Innocent III launched a little known Fourth Crusade against the Cathars, and instructed the knights and barons who joined it to kill everyone, women and babies included, without mercy and leave it to God to sort out the heretics from the true believers. As for the Alawis, the most recent of innumerable attacks upon them in Syria has just been re-ignited by none other than that paragon of democracy, the USA.

But in the sharpest possible contrast, the encounter between Dharma and Islam in India has been almost entirely peaceful. Dharma's first encounter with Islam occurred when Arab traders came to Gujarat and built mosques there in the eighth and ninth centuries. Not only did this not spark religious conflict but, as contemporary Jain texts recorded two centuries later, when an Afghan invader, Mahmud of Ghazni, attacked the famed Somnath Temple ('Temple of the Moon God') in Gujarat, the

Arabs who had by then been living there for generations,[6] joined in the defence of the temple and died to protect it.[7] The fact that Somnath was a Hindu temple did not matter to them. It had to be defended because the raiders were foreigners bent upon plunder and destruction, and stopping them was important for themselves and the Hindus among whom they lived.

The second, more prolonged, interaction between Dharma and Islam occurred after the establishment of the Delhi Sultanate by another Afghan invader, Muhammad Ghori, in 1193 AD. The period that followed is the one that the RSS would like to erase from Indian memory, if not from history, for it was a period in which there was an unprecedented flowering of art, music and literature. It was the time of Amir Khusro, among the first Indian poets who wrote in Persian. It was the time when Indian and Persian music and dance fused to create a distinct new genre, the *khayal gayaki* and the kathak dance. It was the period during which the delicate penmanship of Persian miniature painting fused with the vivid colours of Hindu art to create a profusion of Mughal, Rajput, Kangra, Basohli and other schools of miniature painting in India. It was the time when the Indo-Islamic architecture that has given the world wonders like the Taj Mahal and Humayun's Tomb was born.

### *Hindutva's Selective Memory*

The ideologues of Hindutva ignore all this and prefer to dwell on the defeat of the Rajputs, the destruction of temples and the conversion of large numbers of Hindus to Islam during this period. This is a manufactured litany of defeat, that they use to fan hyper-nationalism, Hindu religiosity and hatred of the Muslims.

Not surprisingly, therefore, their 'memory' is selective and distorted. The Rajputs, who then ruled most of north India were, admittedly, driven into the wilds of southern Rajasthan and Gujarat. But their defeat arose from the superior military technology of the invaders—such as the superiority of cavalry over elephants, and of archers over infantry—and not from any innate superiority of the (Muslim) fighters. On the contrary, the conquerors recognized the valour of the Kshatriyas and other martial classes in which India abounded, and quickly inducted them into their armies.

The votaries of Hindutva harp endlessly on the damage the Muslim invaders did to the Hindu polity and society, but they again choose to ignore the fact that the same Muslim dynasties saved India from the greatest scourge of medieval times—the Mongol invasions that ravaged Europe. Like other impoverished groups from the Asian steppes, the Mongols first tried to invade India. Their first foray, in 1243, took the Delhi Sultanate by surprise and the Mongols were able to come all the way till Lahore, now Pakistan's most beautiful city, and sack it at their leisure.

But that was the last time they were able to enter the plains of India. Ghiyasuddin Balban, the ruler in Delhi at the time, created a standing army—India's and the world's first—built a string of forts along the foothills of the Hindu Kush mountains, and prevented all subsequent invaders from getting far into the plains of Hindustan. After his death, another warrior king of the Delhi Sultanate, Alauddin Khilji, inflicted two successive defeats on them in 1304 and 1305, with such great slaughter that they turned towards Europe and never returned.

Temples were admittedly destroyed, and precious art, sculpture and architecture irretrievably lost, but the motive of the invaders, like that of invaders everywhere else in history, was pillage, not forced conversion to Islam. All but a fraction of the conversions that took place in the next 400 years were voluntary. The converts came from the lower Hindu castes. They converted because Islam offered an escape from the iniquities of caste—in much the same way as Buddhism had done two thousand years earlier, and as the Bhakti ('devotion') anti-Brahmin movement in southern India had been doing since the seventh century, well before the arrival of the Muslims. Far from being a blot on the conquerors, these conversions were an impeachment of the Brahminical, temple-centred Hinduism from which the lower castes had been systematically excluded.

### *Sulh-i-Kul*—the Reconciliation Between Hinduism and Islam

In northern India, the encounter between Islam and Hinduism proved beneficial to both in important ways that the Sangh Parivar prefers not to remember. In Hinduism, it weakened the link between religion and the state by cutting off the single most important source of patronage to the temples. As state patronage dwindled, Brahmins, who had previously flocked to the *peeths* and *maths* were forced to remain in their villages and tend to the spiritual needs of the villagers. The emphasis in their functions, therefore, shifted from presiding over elaborate temple rites to providing guidance on the issues the villagers faced in their everyday lives. The importance of ritual in Hinduism therefore declined and that of Dharma increased.

Hinduism met the challenge from Sufi Islam by disseminating the core ideas of Dharma, already espoused and rejuvenated by the Bhakti movement, through the literature, poetry and song of Tulsidas, Surdas, Kabir, Rahim, Mira Bai, Tukaram, Chokhamela and a host of lesser-known poets, bards and singers. The interaction between the two made Hinduism accessible and mellowed Islam further, to the point where except for scripture, little remained of what had divided the one from the other. No couplet I know captures this more succinctly than one by Kabir that children learn at school and this writer, personally, has never forgotten:

> *moko kahaan dhoone bande, mai to tere paas me*
> *na mai mandir, na mai masjid, na kaaba kailash me*
> (Where dost thou seek me, oh devotee, for I am right beside thee; not in a temple, nor in a mosque, not at the Kaaba, nor on Mount Kailash, shalt thou find me)

The profound reconciliation between Hinduism and Sufi Islam is perhaps best reflected in the writings of Guru Nanak and the other gurus of Sikhism. And it was not confined to the villages. It was codified by no less august a person than Emperor Akbar as the Din-e Ilahi, the religion of the enlightened, at the height of the Mughal Empire. Some British historians have hailed it as an attempt at founding a new religion based on universal tolerance. Others have dismissed it as a religion that never had more than nineteen followers.

In fact, Akbar had no such intention. The Din-e Ilahi was no more than a distillation of what today's corporate world would call 'current best practices' of the heterodox population of India. It propagated *sulh-i-kul*—universal peace—and urged ten virtues upon the realm. Among these were: liberality and beneficence; forbearance from bad actions; repulsion of anger with mildness; abstinence from worldly desires; frequent meditation on the consequences of one's actions; and 'good society with brothers so that *their will may have precedence over one's own*'—in short, putting the well-being of one's fellows ahead of one's own.

Akbar's goal was not proselytization. Unlike the great Mauryan emperor Ashoka's Buddhist edicts of 1,800 years earlier, Akbar issued no edicts. Nor did he create a religious police to oversee their observance.

The significance of the Din-e Ilahi lies in what it did *not* prescribe: It did not ascribe primacy to Islam, and it did not give a special place to Muslim clergy within the structure of the state. Instead, it declared emphatically that 'he [the emperor, i.e. the state] would recognize no difference between [religions], his object being to unite all men in a common bond of peace'. It was, therefore, a restatement of Dharma in a contemporary form. If any 'religion' can claim to have emerged the victor in the grand ideological battle that ensued after the arrival of Islam in India, it is not Islam, nor is it Hinduism. It is Dharma.

Among Hindus, the practice of Dharma has been—and remains—sullied by its endorsement of the notion of ritual purity and pollution that is associated with caste. But its core idea, that true religion is not what we preach but what we practise, has remained the driving force behind all movements for religious reform from the Buddha to the present day. Dharma was the concept with which Swami Vivekananda electrified the Parliament of the World's Religions in Chicago in 1893, by explaining that Hinduism does not merely *tolerate*, but *accepts*, all the great religions of the world because they are like different paths up the same mountain, or different rivers that flow into the same sea.

Even the blood-soaked partition of India and Pakistan in 1947 did not kill off the syncretic impulse in Islam. It has led to a sustained study of the writings of Dara Shikoh, Shah Jahan's eldest son and heir apparent, even in Pakistan. Dara Shikoh was a scholar of Sanskrit and translator of the *Bhagavad Gita*, one of Hinduism's holiest texts. He had made no secret of his fascination with Din-e Ilahi, and of his intention to propagate it throughout his realm, before his life was cut short by his younger brother, Aurangzeb.

In 2010, the noted Pakistani playwright, Shahid Nadeem, wrote a play, *Dara*, that highlighted his syncretism, as a protest against the rampant Islamic sectarianism that Partition had unleashed upon Pakistan and was, even then, tearing it apart.

Three years later, two Pakistani historians from GC University, Faisalabad, published a peer-reviewed paper in the *International Journal of History and Research* titled, 'Dara Shikoh: Mystical and Philosophical Discourse', which highlighted his belief that 'the mystical traditions of both Hinduism and Islam spoke of the same truth'.

This is the awe-inspiring durability of religious syncretism in the land of Dharma. It is what made Indian Muslims virtually immune to the lure of the Islamic State in Syria and Iraq in 2014. It is the bone-deep syncretism of India that the votaries of Hindutva and Hindu Rashtra are bent upon destroying.

Hindutva is therefore the complete antithesis—a hideous parody—of Dharma. The profound truths of Dharma cannot be absorbed by the intellect alone. They need to be felt and to become a part of our unconscious perception of ourselves and our friends. Children of all faiths in all countries gravitate naturally to this understanding as they make friends and find playmates. It is their parents, and other adults who make them self-conscious and begin to question their natural reactions. Children therefore need to be exposed to the fundamental idea of syncretism, so eloquently expressed by Swami Vivekananda 130 years ago, that all the great religions of the world teach us the same code of morality, and that far from being a late comer to this idea, India is the civilization in which it was born.

This is best done in elementary school. But those are the schools that have been most neglected throughout northern India, with the result that the vast majority of the unemployed under the age of thirty are concentrated in its five large states. On the other side of the coin, the RSS has been concentrating precisely upon this age group to proselytize them into its version of Hinduism. In fairness to the RSS, these schools do not discriminate between Hindu and Muslim students. In 2020, the Vidya Bharati schools in Uttar Pradesh had 12,000 Muslim and Christian students and had recruited Muslim teachers to teach at their schools.[8] As the RSS supremo Mohan Bhagwat's speeches and Prime Minister Vajpayee's musings, described in Chapter 14, show, the syncretic impulse has not completely died out even within the RSS.

# Appendix

## 'New Evidence Establishes that Narendra Modi was Directly Monitoring Tulsi Prajapati Fake Encounter', by Mukul Sinha

*This article was posted on the online resource, Truth of Gujarat, on October 8, 2013. The website is now defunct, and the URL of this article (http://www.truthofgujarat.com/new-evidence-establishes-narendra-modi-directly-monitoring-tulsi-prajapati-fake-encounter/), last accessed by the author on June 3, 2021, showed a 404, or page not found error, when the attempt was made to access it before this book went to press.*

*The full text of the article is reproduced below:*

While researching the conspiracy behind Modi's IT story, we also looked at the antecedents of Narendra Modi's own website 'narendramodi.in'. We discovered that the registrant of Modi's website is a gentleman named Parag Shah (paragjshah@yahoo.com). While researching Parag's background, we found his LinkedIn profile…

What caught our attention in it was his appointment as the 'Officer on Special Duty (OSD) to the Gujarat Chief Minister for the period 2003 to 2008' and another fact stated by him: 'Associated with cyber cell of Anti-terrorist Squad'. This accidental finding led us to the missing link of the Sohrabuddin–Tulsi Prajapati fake encounter!

Thereafter, we looked at the supplementary charge sheet filed by CBI in the Tulsi Prajapati case, specially where the CBI has elaborately dealt with the Call Data Records (CDR) of Amit Shah and Rajkumar Pandian, who were in constant touch with each other while monitoring the movements of Tulsi Prajapati between Udaipur (where he was jailed) and Ahmedabad (where he was being brought to attend a criminal case). We reproduce the extract of the CBI charge related to the month of December, 2006 (Tulsi Prajapati was murdered on 28th December early morning near Ambaji, Rajasthan–Gujarat border):

> **6.21.** On 11.12.2006, an escort party from the Reserve Police Line, Udaipur, headed by Sub-Inspector Shyam Singh accompanied Tulsiram Prajapati and Mohd. Azam for Ahmedabad by train. On this date also, the mother and wife of Mohd. Azam had accompanied them to Ahmedabad. After reaching Ahmedabad on *12.12.2006*, both Mohd. Azam and Tulsiram Prajapati were taken to the Sabarmati Jail, Ahmedabad, from there they were produced via video conferencing before the competent Court instead of being physically produced in the Court. The next date of hearing was fixed for 26.12.2006. The escort party while leaving for Udaipur in the night of *12.12.2006* at the Ahmedabad Railway Station made efforts in furtherance of the criminal conspiracy to separate the mother and wife of Mohd. Azam from Tulsiram Prajapati and his co-prisoner Mohd. Azam, but were prevented by the unexpected vociferous and vigorous protest by the mother and wife of Mohd. Azam that resulted in a large gathering of bystanders that deterred the police from succeeding in their objective of isolating Tulsiram Prajapati, a necessary preparatory stage for his murder in a planned fake encounter.

We are also reproducing in here the Call Data Record (CDR) from the CBI charge sheet for the relevant period:

The [CRD] fully establishes the contact between Rajkumar Pandian, the SP of Anti-Terrorist Squad, the Home Minister Amit Shah, and less [*sic*] in the murder of Tulsi Prajapati and both of them have been charge-sheeted as the main accused in the case. In fact, Rajkumar Pandian who was the SP of the ATS played a vital role in abduction of Sohrabuddin and Kauserbi and killing them both on 26th and 29th November, 2005 at Ahmedabad. In that case as well, both Amit Shah and Rajkumar Pandian are charged as accused.

As we had the CDRs of the accused officer Rajkumar Pandian, we searched within Pandian's CDR for Parag Shah's number after coming to know that he was appointed as the Officer on Special Duty for the Anti-Terrorist Squad. This appointment attains special significance since the Chief Minister's office had declared their 'No Tolerance' policy towards terrorism 'and it was Mr Parag Shah as the OSD to CM who was to monitor the functions of ATS and report to the CM'. To our surprise *we found a large number of phone calls between Pandian and Parag Shah* inter-spaced with phone calls of Amit Shah and Pandian (Call Records reproduced at the bottom of the post). In light of the call records, it becomes abundantly clear that Mr *Parag Shah was in constant touch with Rajkumar Pandyan IPS*, the man who planned and executed the murder of Tulsiram Prajapati, *and in turn Parag Shah was reporting to CM.*

This piece of vital information read with the fact that Mr Parag Shah was working as the Officer on Special Duty for Narendra Modi, CM, [makes it] obvious as daylight that the CM was fully aware of the Tulsi fake encounter which was carried out entirely by the police officers working in Anti-Terrorist-Squad led by DIG Vanzara. In light of this irrefutable evidence, we can now interpret the statement made by D.G. Vanzara in his resignation letter recently tendered to the Government of Gujarat. His statement reads as under:

> We, being field officers, have simply implemented the conscious policy of this government which was inspiring, guiding and monitoring our actions from the very close quarters.

Would the CBI now care to explain to the nation why it has failed to investigate Parag Shah's phone calls when they had the entire CDR with them? Was it to obfuscate the role of Narendra Modi?

[Relevant entries from the CRDs of Rajkumar Pandian between December 1 and 31, 2006:]

| ***Calling Party*** | ***Name*** | ***Called party*** | ***Name*** | ***Duration*** | ***Date/time*** |
|---|---|---|---|---|---|
| 9427306077 | Pandian | 919427306014 | Parag | 109 | 12/1/2006 13:01 |
| 9427306077 | Pandian | 919824010090 | Amit Shah | 13 | 12/2/2006 8:14 |
| 919824010090 | Amit Shah | 9427306077 | Pandian | 12 | 12/2/2006 9:36 |
| 919824010090 | Amit Shah | 9427306077 | Pandian | 53 | 12/4/2006 19:10 |
| 919427306014 | Parag | 9427306077 | Pandian | 158 | 12/5/2006 18:39 |
| 919824010090 | Amit Shah | 9427306077 | Pandian | 12 | 12/5/2006 20:55 |
| 919824010090 | Amit Shah | 9427306077 | Pandian | 8 | 12/6/2006 8:23 |
| 9427306077 | Pandian | 919824010090 | Amit Shah | 25 | 12/7/2006 10:21 |
| 919824010090 | Amit Shah | 9427306077 | Pandian | 39 | 12/7/2006 17:12 |
| 919824010090 | Amit Shah | 9427306077 | Pandian | 20 | 12/7/2006 18:05 |
| 427306077 | Pandian | 919824010090 | Amit Shah | 10 | 12/8/2006 21:32 |
| 919824010090 | Amit Shah | 9427306077 | Pandian | 70 | 12/9/2006 11:59 |

| *Calling Party* | *Name* | *Called party* | *Name* | *Duration* | *Date/time* |
|---|---|---|---|---|---|
| 919824010090 | Amit Shah | 9427306077 | Pandian | 39 | 12/9/2006 14:03 |
| 9427306077 | Pandian | 919427306014 | Parag | 36 | 12/10/2006 15:30 |
| 9427306077 | Pandian | 919824010090 | Amit Shah | 18 | 12/11/2006 8:26 |
| 919824010090 | Amit Shah | 9427306077 | Pandian | 8 | 12/11/2006 11:57 |
| 919824010090 | Amit Shah | 9427306077 | Pandian | 6 | 12/11/2006 11:58 |
| 919824010090 | Amit Shah | 9427306077 | Pandian | 59 | 12/11/2006 22:08 |
| 9427306077 | Pandian | 919427306014 | Parag | 32 | 12/12/2006 11:54 |
| 919427306014 | Parag | 9427306077 | Pandian | 7 | 12/12/2006 16:52 |
| 919427306014 | Parag | 9427306077 | Pandian | 25 | 12/12/2006 21:48 |
| 919427306014 | Parag | 9427306077 | Pandian | 34 | 12/13/2006 15:56 |
| 919427306014 | Parag | 9427306077 | Pandian | 24 | 12/14/2006 11:37 |
| 9427306077 | Pandian | 919427306014 | Parag | 175 | 12/14/2006 13:35 |
| 919824010090 | Amit Shah | 9427306077 | Pandian | 31 | 12/18/2006 10:16 |

| *Calling Party* | *Name* | *Called party* | *Name* | *Duration* | *Date/time* |
|---|---|---|---|---|---|
| 919824010090 | Amit Shah | 9427306077 | Pandian | 23 | 12/18/2006 12:05 |
| 919824010090 | Amit Shah | 9427306077 | Pandian | 88 | 12/19/2006 22:07 |
| 919824010090 | Amit Shah | 9427306077 | Pandian | 81 | 12/21/2006 18:01 |
| 9427306077 | Pandian | 919824010090 | Amit Shah | 22 | 12/22/2006 18:46 |
| 9427306077 | Pandian | 919824010090 | Amit Shah | 7 | 12/23/2006 17:19 |
| 9427306077 | Pandian | 919824010090 | Amit Shah | 133 | 12/23/2006 17:19 |
| 919824010090 | Amit Shah | 9427306077 | Pandian | 66 | 12/24/2006 19:58 |
| 9427306077 | Pandian | 919824010090 | Amit Shah | 21 | 12/24/2006 21:19 |
| 9427306077 | Pandian | 919824010090 | Amit Shah | 23 | 12/25/2006 8:51 |
| 919824010090 | Amit Shah | 9427306077 | Pandian | 18 | 12/25/2006 14:36 |
| 919824010090 | Amit Shah | 9427306077 | Pandian | 42 | 12/25/2006 21:00 |
| 9427306077 | Pandian | 919824010090 | Amit Shah | 3 | 12/26/2006 18:31 |
| 9427306077 | Pandian | 919824010090 | Amit Shah | 178 | 12/26/2006 19:17 |

| *Calling Party* | *Name* | *Called party* | *Name* | *Duration* | *Date/time* |
|---|---|---|---|---|---|
| 919824010090 | Amit Shah | 9427306077 | Pandian | 79 | 12/27/2006 12:50 |
| 9427306077 | Pandian | 919427306014 | Parag | 48 | 12/30/2006 14:14 |
| 9427306077 | Pandian | 919824010090 | Amit Shah | 47 | 12/30/2006 19:08 |
| 9427306077 | Pandian | 919824010090 | Amit Shah | 101 | 12/30/2006 19:23 |
| 9427306077 | Pandian | 919824010090 | Amit Shah | 19 | 12/31/2006 12:47 |
| 9427306077 | Pandian | 919824010090 | Amit Shah | 24 | 12/31/2006 12:55 |
| 919824010090 | Amit Shah | 9427306077 | Pandian | 4 | 12/31/2006 13:40 |

# Notes

## 1. A Brief Note on Representative Democracy

1 Perhaps the best description of this change is to be found in Karl Polanyi, *The Great Transformation: The Political and Economic Origins of Our Time*, Beacon Press, 2001.

2 R.M. Hartwell, 'The Rising Standard of Living in England, 1800–1850', *Economic History Review*, vol. 13 (3) (1961), pp. 397–416.

## 2. India's Unique Achievement

1 The author was present at the press conference. Its video recording is available at https://www.youtube.com/watch?v=ZajqHfledvY&ab_channel=PoliticsDude (accessed April 5, 2025).

2 Nadir Shah carried away the Peacock Throne and the Koh-i-noor diamond, and Ahmad Shah changed his name to Durrani and founded the Kingdom of Afghanistan.

3 Romila Thapar, *Asoka and the Decline of the Mauryas*, 3rd ed., Oxford University Press, 1997.

4 Ashley Kirk, 'Iraq and Syria: How many foreign fighters are fighting for ISIL?', *The Telegraph*, March 24, 2016 (https://www.telegraph.co.uk/news/2016/03/29/iraq-and-syria-how-many-foreign-fighters-are-fighting-for-isil/, accessed April 5, 2025).

5 'Over 40,000 foreign militants from 100 countries fighting in Syria—US State Department', *RT*, June 3, 2016 (https://www.rt.com/usa/345269-40000-foreign-terrorists-syria/, accessed April 5, 2025).

6 U.C. Jha 'Growing presence of ISIS poses security concerns for India', DNA, September 2, 2018 (http://www.dnaindia.com/analysis/column-growing-presence-of-isis-poses-security-concerns-for-india-2600085, accessed April 5, 2025).

## 3. Where Did Disenchantment Begin?

1 Shubham Pandey and Uday Shankar, 'Issue of Rising Arrears and Pendency in Indian Judiciary: A Consequence of Non-Adherence to Policy Recommendation and Uninformed Policymaking', SCC Online, February 7, 2023 (https://www.scconline.com/blog/post/2023/02/07/issue-of-rising-arrears-and-pendency-in-indian-judiciary-a-consequence-of-non-adherence-to-policy-recommendation-and-uninformed-policymaking/https://www.scconline.com/blog/post/2023/02/07/issue-of-rising-arrears-and-pendency-in-indian-judiciary-a-consequence-of-non-adherence-to-policy-recommendation-and-uninformed-policymaking/, accessed April 5, 2025).

2 *Statistics on Industrial Disputes, Closures, Retrenchments and Lay-Offs in India During the Year, 2015*, Government of India: Ministry of Labour and Employment, Labour Bureau, Shimla. 2015) (available online: https://labourbureau.gov.in/uploads/pdf/IDA_2015.pdf, accessed April 5, 2025).

3 'World's most polluted cities', IQAir (website) (https://www.iqair.com/in-en/world-most-polluted-cities, accessed April 5, 2025).

4 For details, see Prem Shankar Jha, 'Forty Two Years After the Emergency, India's Democracy is Once Again in Danger', *The Wire*, June 25, 2017 (https://thewire.in/politics/forty-two-years-emergency-indias-democracy-danger, accessed April 5, 2025).

## 4. Where Did India Take the Wrong Road?

1 Proceedings of the Constituent Assembly, November 29, 1948 (available online: https://www.constitutionofindia.net/debates/29-nov-1948/, accessed April 5, 2025).

2 The limit, however, has increased from Rs 25,000 in the 1951–52 Lok Sabha elections to, as per the revision in January 2022, Rs 95 lakh for parliamentary and Rs 40 lakh for assembly constituencies; for small state and Union Territories, the cap is Rs 75 lakhs and Rs 28 lakhs, respectively. See the Election Commission's press note dated January 6, 2022 (https://old.eci.gov.in/files/file/13928-limits-of-candidate%E2%80%99s-expenses-enhanced/, accessed April 5, 2025). An estimate by the Association for Democratic Rights showed

that in the six-year period from 2016 till 2022, the total donations received by the 31 political parties was Rs 16,437.6 crores (164,376 million rupees). If we assume that half of this was spent on the Lok Sabha elections, and that there were on an average three serious candidates in each constituency, who together spent 80 per cent of this money, the expenditure on each of them would have would have averaged Rs 80.6 million. See 'Analysis of Donations to Registered Recognised Political Parties, FY 2016–17 to FY 2021–22', ADR, July 11, 2023 (https://adrindia.org/sites/default/files/Analysis_of_Donations_to_Registered_Recognised_Political_Parties_FY_2016-17_to_21-22_English.pdf, accessed April 5, 2025).

3 This provision can also be traced back to British constitutional practice, albeit a highly contested one. As the British Crown is the source of legitimacy for all law in Britain it is, of necessity, above the law. But the Crown operates through its servants. Does this mean that they too are above law when carrying out the sovereign's orders? This immunity was contested by the British Parliament with increasing vigour for nearly a hundred years from the rule of William and Mary at the end of the 17th century till that of George III a century later and ended with a typical messy British compromise. While individuals cannot bring charges against the state in a court of law, they can do so against civil servants in their personal capacity for the manner in which they perform the duties given to them by the State.

4 This would have completely pre-empted a 2006 judgement of the Supreme Court in which it held that Section 19 of the Prevention of Corruption Act, 1988, did not protect former public servants. See G.P. Joshi and Maja Daruwala, 'The web of corruption: Centre must take the bull by its horns', *The Tribune*, January 16, 2011 (https://www.tribuneindia.com/2011/20110116/edit.htm#2, accessed April 5, 2025).

5 *Broken System: Dysfunction, Abuse, and Impunity in the Indian Police*, Human Rights Watch, August 2009 (https://www.hrw.org/report/2009/08/04/broken-system/dysfunction-abuse-and-impunity-indian-police, accessed April 5, 2025).

## 5. How Did India Criminalize Its Democracy?

1 Jagdish Bhagwati and Padma Desai, *India: Planning for Industrialization and Trade Policies Since 1951*, Oxford University Press, 1970.

2 The term was coined by Colin Leys, who had made a lifelong study of the evolution and decline of democracy in Kenya. See Colin Leys, *Underdevelopment in Kenya*, East African Publishers, 1975.

3 Excerpt from Patrick French's *India: A Portrait*, published in *Outlook*, January 11, 2011. French describes how the constituency clientelist network mobilized a tidal wave of support for the son of Andhra Chief Minister Y.S. Rajasekhara Reddy, when he died in a helicopter crash: '[W]hen the chief minister of Andhra Pradesh, Y.S. Rajasekhara Reddy, died in an accident, the local Congress party said 462 people had died of shock or committed suicide in grief. The purpose of this implausible piece of news was to force the national party to appoint his fabulously rich son, Jaganmohan Reddy, in his place. The move failed, and an investigation showed that families of people who had died in different ways were paid Rs 5,000 by local Congress leaders for "funeral expenses", and persuaded to say they were victims of the mass grief.'

4 Patrick French, 'India in Transition: The Political Alienation of India's New Middle Class', Center for the Advanced Study of India, June 6, 2011 (http://casi.sas.upenn.edu/iit/french, accessed April 5, 2025).

5 It may have been Congress party treasurer Atulya Ghosh's moan of complaint in December 1966 that the party had till then received only a third as much in donations as five years earlier, that triggered the ban on company donations!

6 National Election Watch newsletter, May 16, 2011. See the Association for Democratic Rights website (adrindia.org).

7 Rahul M., 'Lok Sabha Election Results 2024: Almost Half Of Newly-Elected MPs Face Criminal Cases, Reveals ADR Analysis', *Free Press Journal*, June 7, 2024 (https://www.freepressjournal.in/india/almost-half-of-newly-elected-mps-face-criminal-cases-reveals-adr-analysis, accessed April 5, 2025).

8 This figure has been drastically reduced by more careful analysis in subsequent years, which has showed that this estimate of the loss

incurred by not auctioning the 2G telecom bands by the Manmohan Singh government had been hugely overestimated. See later in book.

9 In Tamil Nadu, for instance, a decision taken by the AIADMK government headed by J. Jayalalithaa, after it came to power in 1991, not to refund the ten per cent 'earnest money' that it took from prospective investors, led to a sharp fall in the rate of private investment in the state between 1991 and 1996. The indignation this caused as Tamil Nadu slipped rapidly back in the industrialization race was partly responsible for the AIADMK's resounding defeat in 1996.

10 This came spectacularly to light about a decade ago when an aspirant to the position of the chairman of the Vishakhapatnam Port Authority, who got the job of a deputy, insisted on returning the money he had borrowed and got caught while trying to raise it.

11 *Broken System*, Human Rights Watch.

12 *Crime in India 2007*, National Crime Records Bureau, Ministry of Home Affairs (http://ncrb.nic.in/cii2007/home.htm, accessed March 28, 2009). Quoted in the HRW report cited above.

13 Sachi Satapathy, 'When police stations turn crime scenes', *Deccan Herald*, September 27, 2024 (https://www.deccanherald.com/opinion/when-police-stations-turn-crime-scenes-3244090, accessed April 5, 2025).

14 Maja Daruwala, 'We need a root and branch repair of police, guardian agencies to keep them lawful, *The Indian Express*, July 13, 2020 (https://indianexpress.com/article/opinion/columns/vikas-dubey-encounter-tamil-nadu-custodial-deaths-police-brutality-6502596/, accessed April 5, 2025).

15 'Police Brutality and the Question of Human Rights: A Critical Analysis', Juris Centre, August 9, 2023 (https://juriscentre.com/2023/08/19/police-brutality-and-the-question-of-human-rights-a-critical-analysis/, accessed April 5, 2025).

16 Mohammad Ali, 'Why did they have to burn me, asked dying scribe', *The Hindu*, June 13, 2015 (https://www.thehindu.com/news/national/other-states/Why-did-they-have-to-burn-me-asked-dying-Uttar-Pradesh-scribe/article60326458.ece, accessed April 5, 2025).

17 'Journalist burnt to death; UP minister booked', *The Hindu*, June 9, 2015 (https://www.thehindu.com/news/national/other-states/

UP-minister-booked-in-journalist-killing-case/article60325434.ece, accessed April 5, 2025).

18 *Dr Subramanian Swamy vs Union of India and Others*, WP (Civil) No. 10 of 2011, judgment of G.S. Singhvi, Delhi High Court (available online: https://www.thehindu.com/migration_catalog/article13287900.ece/BINARY/Supreme%20Court%20verdict%20on%202G%20spectrum%20allocation, accessed April 5, 2025).

19 '2G scam case: Anil Ambani denies that Swan Telecom was a front for his company; CBI says he's retracting', *The Economic Times*, August 23, 2013 (https://economictimes.indiatimes.com/industry/telecom/2g-scam-case-anil-ambani-denies-that-swan-telecom-was-a-front-for-his-company-cbi-says-hes-retracting/articleshow/21988400.cms?utm, accessed April 5, 2025).

20 Arvind Subramanian and Josh Felman, 'India's Great Slowdown: What Happened? What's the Way Out?', CID Faculty Working Paper No. 370, December 2019, Harvard Center for International Development (https://www.hks.harvard.edu/centers/cid/publications/faculty-working-papers/india-great-slowdown, accessed April 5, 2025).

## 6. What Is Fascism?: *A Necessary Digression*

1 See Chapter 1: 'The Origins of Fascism', in Nathanael Greene (ed), *Fascism, An Anthology*, Thomas Y. Crowell Co., 1968, p. 1.

2 S.J. Woolf (ed), *The Nature of Fascism*, Random House, 1968, p. 9.

3 H.R. Trevor-Roper, 'The Phenomenon of Fascism', in *Fascism in Europe*, edited by S.J. Woolf, Routledge, 2020.

4 Stanley G. Payne, *Fascism. Comparison and Definition*, University of Wisconsin Press, 1990, pp. 204–6.

5 Trevor-Roper, 'The Phenomenon of Fascism'.

6 Gino Germani, 'Fascism and Class', in Woolf, *The Nature of Fascism*, pp. 73–77. See also Erich Fromm's *Escape from Freedom*, and Harold D. Lasswell's *The Analysis of Political Behaviour*, pp. 235–45.

7 A.F.K. Organski, 'Fascism and Modernisation', Woolf, *The Nature of Fascism*, pp. 19–31.

8 Gino Germani highlights the dual nature of the threat when he says, '[I]n Italy and Germany, [the lower middle] classes were threatened both by the rising proletariat and the increasing power and the wealth

of the bourgeoisie.' C. Seton-Watson points out that the Poujadisme in Vichy and post-war France and the Uomo Qualqunque in post-war Europe drew most of their strength from the obsolescent small business and shopkeeper class and from regions and towns that were in decline. About half of the support for the National Democratic Party of Germany (NPD) has also come from this class. Germani, op. cit., p.74, and Seton-Watson, 'Fascism in Contemporary Europe', in Woolf, *Fascism in Europe*, pp. 364–5.

9 Dani Rodrik, 'Premature Deindustrialization', Working Paper 20935, February 2015, National Bureau of Economic Research (http://www.nber.org/papers/w20935, accessed April 5, 2025).

10 John D. Stempel, *Inside the Iranian Revolution*, The Clark Group, 1981.

11 Ibid., p. 13.

12 Jahangir Amuzegar, *The Dynamics of the Iranian Revolution: The Pahlavis' Triumph and Tragedy*, State University of New York Press, 1991, chapter 2, and Misagh Parsa, *The Social Origins of the Iranian Revolution*, Rutgers University Press, 1989, chapter 1, p. 1–10.

13 Official statistics quoted by Amuzegar and Parsa.

14 Amuzegar, op. cit., pp. 26–30.

15 Parsa, op. cit., chapters 1, 3 and 4.

16 Calculated from figures given by Parsa from official statistics, op. cit., p. 65.

17 Ibid., p. 129.

18 Organski, op. cit.

19 Parsa, op. cit., p. 69.

20 Compiled from statistics given by Parsa. Ibid., pp. 68–70, 92, 107.

21 Ibid., p. 73.

22 OPEC was formed in Baghdad in 1960 but did not come together around a common oil pricing policy until 1973.

23 Ibid., p. 72.

24 Ibid., p. 71.

25 Ibid., pp. 71-72.

26 Ibid., p. 75.

27 Ibid., p. 90–93. Mohammad Mosaddeq was the first and only democratically elected of Iran, whom the British and the Americans conspired to have removed in 1953.

28 Ibid., p. 92.

29 The White Revolution consisted of 19 reforms that were introduced over a period of 16 years, with the first six introduced on January 9, 1963, and put to a national referendum on January 26, 1963. They included a land reforms programme and the abolishing of feudalism, nationalization of forests and pasturelands, the privatization of the government owned enterprises, profit sharing for industrial workers in private sector enterprises, extending the right to vote to women, the formation of the Literacy Corps, so that those who had a high school diploma and were required to serve their country as soldiers could do so by fighting illiteracy in the villages, etc.

30 Parsa, op. cit., p. 50.

31 Amuzegar, op. cit., and Parsa, op. cit., p. 83. Inflation jumped from an average of 15 per cent in the sixties to over 25 per cent in the seventies.

32 Parsa, op. cit., p. 142.

33 Ibid., p. 103.

34 Ibid., p. 104.

35 Ibid., p. 102.

36 Amuzegar, op. cit.

37 Parsa, op. cit., p. 252.

## 7. India's Journey from Hindu Nationalism to Fascism

1 It was a logical decision for the Congress, but it put the Muslisms of northern India in an invidious position, for the language of government and of the courts had, till then, been Persian. Thus, any sudden shift to English would put the Muslims of India at a severe disadvantage in relation to the Hindus and other minorities such as the Christians and Parsis (Zoroastrians, followers of one of the great mystical (as against prophetic) religions who had fled from Iran to India in the eighth to tenth centuries, under the onslaught of Islam.) In a succession of letters, Sir Syed Ahmed beseeched the Congress to at least postpone the decision on language to give time for a generation of Muslims to be educated in English, in addition to Urdu and Persian. He pointed out that at the time of his writing Muslims about occupied 30 per cent of posts in the administration and the army. They would immediately be reduced to 10 per cent or less if this reform was rushed though in a single move. But,

possibly afraid of triggering a spate of similar demands from India's many major linguistic groups, the Congress did not heed Sir Syed's warning. He was therefore left with no option but to start educating Muslims in the English language. This was the genesis of the Aligarh Muslim University, which has consistently remained one of the finest universities in the country.

2 A.K. Bhagwat and G.P. Pradhan, *Lokmanya Tilak: A Biography*, Jaico, 2015, p. 226.

3 Pavan Kulkarni, 'History Shows How Patriotic the RSS Really Is', *The Wire*, first published on April 17, 2017 (https://thewire.in/history/rss-hindutva-nationalism).

4 See *Letters for a Nation: From Jawaharlal Nehru to his Chief Ministers, 1947–1963*, Penguin, 2014, p. 33.

5 Christophe Jaffrelot, *Hindu Nationalism: A Reader*, Princeton University Press, 2007, pp. 175–79.

6 The difference between Hindutva and Bharatiyata is that Bharatiyata accepted the religious plurality of India and sought to protect it by giving it a syncretic identity. One reason why it was frequently confused or equated with Hindu chauvinism was that the '50s and '60s saw a very large number of ugly communal riots, especially in Bengal, Bihar and UP, which Hindu rioters justified as communal self-righteousness.

7 Jaffrelot, *Hindu Nationalism*.

8 Various reports in *The Hindu* and the *Times of India* from December 7, 1992, to January 13 1993.

9 Sushil Srivastava, *The Disputed Mosque: A Historical Inquiry*, Vistaar Publications, 1991, p. 51.

10 Ibid.

11 Zoya Hasan, 'Representation and Redistribution: The New Lower-Caste Politics of North India', in *Transforming India: Social and Political Dynamics of Democracy*, edited by Francine R. Frankel, Zoya Hasan, Rajeev Bhargava and Balveer Arora, OUP, 2000, p. 150. See also Sushil Srivastava, op. cit.

12 Quoted to the *Times of India* on December 21, 1992, by Maulana Syed Abul Hasan Ali Nadwi. The Maulana was known as Ali Mian and was widely revered in India for his erudition.

13 See Isaiah Berlin, 'Nationalism: Past Neglect and Present Power', in *Against the Current: Essays in the History of Ideas*, 1979.

14 For details of this period, and the events leading to the fall of the National Front government see Prem Shankar Jha, *In the Eye of the Storm*, Viking Press, 1993, Chapter 9.

## 8. The Economic Roots of Fascism in India

1 Report of the Santhanam Committee. Quoted in Bhagwati and Desai, op. cit.

2 The rise of an intermediate class of capitalists in Indonesia has been described by Michal Kalecki, and in Turkey by Anne Kruger. Its rise in India was first noted by K.N. Raj, 'The Politics and Economics of Intermediate Regimes', *Economic and Political Weekly*, July 7, 1973. It is described in detail by Prem Shankar Jha in *India: A Political Economy of Stagnation*, Oxford University Press, 1980.

3 Data taken from censuses of small scale industries in India—1987–88 till 2006–07. See 'Essay on Micro, Small and Medium Enterprises (MSMEs) in India', India Essays (website) (https://www.indiaessays.com/essays/india/enterprises/essay-on-micro-small-and-medium-enterprises-msmes-in-india/1162, accessed April 5, 2025).

4 Albert Speer, Hitler's architect and later Minister for War, described this in his memoirs, *Inside the Third Reich*. And Misagh Parsa, op. cit., described it for Iran. The way in which the intermediate class gave its support first to the opposition and then was wooed by the Congress is given in greater detail in Prem Shankar Jha, *In the Eye of the Storm*, chapters 5 and 6.

5 *Basic Statistics Relating to the Indian Economy, August 1994*, Centre for Monitoring the Indian Economy, 1994, Table 8.1.

6 Since there has been considerable controversy around the estimates of GDP in 2011–12 prices, this is in 2004–05 prices. Source: Ministry of Programme Implementation, Government of India (http://www.mospi.nic.in/sites/default/files/press_releases_statements/statement12_27mar15.xls, accessed April 5, 2025). See also 'It is official: Unemployment rate in rural, urban India highest in 47 years', *Down to Earth*, June 4, 2019 (https://www.downtoearth.org.in/economy/it-is-official-unemployment-rate-in-rural-urban-india-highest-in-47-years-64902, accessed April 5, 2025).

7 '25 percent of Punjab, Haryana SME's near Closure', *The Indian Express*, October 25, 2012 (https://indianexpress.com/article/news-

archive/web/25-punjab-haryana-smes-near-closure/, accessed April 5, 2025).

8 Leela Visaria, 'The Continuing Fertility Transition', in Tim Dyson, Robert Cassen and Leela Visaria, *Twenty-First Century India: Population, Economy, Human Development, and the Environment*, Oxford University Press, 2004, p. 67.

9 Astha Savyasachi, 'Communal Textbooks, Teachers Who Brought Down Babri: How RSS Schools Create Hindutva Foot Soldiers', *The Wire*, May 22, 2023 (https://thewire.in/communalism/communal-textbooks-teachers-who-brought-down-babri-how-rss-schools-create-hindutva-foot-soldiers, accessed April 5, 2025).

10 'Teach Hate Young: RSS Leader's School Gets Kids to Re-Enact Babri Demolition', *The Wire*, December 16, 2019 (https://thewire.in/communalism/rss-run-school-makes-children-re-enact-babri-masjid-demolition, accessed April 5, 2025).

11 Astha Savyasachi, 'Communal Textbooks, Teachers Who Brought Down Babri'.

12 Sobhana K. Nair, 'Reverse migration to villages has set economy back by 15 years, says JNU professor', *The Hindu*, December 4, 2021 (https://www.thehindu.com/business/Economy/reverse-migration-to-villages-has-set-economy-back-by-15-years-says-jnu-professor/article61652893.ece, accessed April 5, 2025).

13 Edward Anderson and Christophe Jaffrelot, 'Hindu nationalism and the "saffronisation of the public sphere": An interview with Christophe Jaffrelot, *Contemporary South Asia*, December 4, 2018 (https://www.tandfonline.com/doi/abs/10.1080/09584935.2018.1545009).

## 9. Gujarat—the Laboratory Where Indian Fascism was Created

1 Niccolao Manucci, *Storia do Mogor*, translated by William Irvine, 1965.

2 For the full report of the Concerned Citizens' Tribunal (CCT)—Gujarat 2002, visit http://www.sabrang.com/tribunal/ (accessed April 5, 2025).

3 The Additional DG of Intelligence at the time, R.B Sreekumar, reported to the Additional Secretary (Law and Order) and the Chief Election Commissioner in August 2002 that communal

incidents had taken place in 993 villages and 151 towns covering 284 police stations out of a total of 464 and were spread over 153 assembly constituencies out of a total of 182. By August 2002 (as recorded in the Report of the Women's Parliamentary Committee) as many as 132,532 persons had been displaced/forced to leave their houses and were living in 121 riot relief camps of which 58 were in Ahmedabad city. By August 2002, the government itself had recorded those 185 cases of attacks on women of which 100 were in Ahmedabad city; that there had been 57 attacks on children of which 33 were in Ahmedabad and that 225 women and 65 children killed. The government had also recorded 11 cases of rape of women: 3 cases from Dahod, 1 from Anand, 4 in the Panchmahals and 3 in Ahmedabad. In fact the rape/molestation of women were far more pervasive. Many of the victims were killed and burnt beyond recognition. Others were too terrified to record complaints. (Extract from the protest petition in the court of the 11th metropolitan magistrate, Ahmedabad)

4 Pandya was the first among several persons who figured in a *Tehelka*–Aaj Tak sting operation relating to the 2002 Gujarat riots to acknowledge that the camera had not lied. But when the Gujarat government filed cases against him, he claimed that he had uttered those words under the impression that he was rehearsing for a television serial. He maintained that the correspondent of Aaj Tak, Dhimant Purohit, had offered him a role in a serial the channel was purportedly producing. 'I have known Purohit for many years. He told me his channel was making a reality show on the riots and they wanted real-life persons to act,' he said. See Rathin Das, 'Gujarat lawyer says he read out "script"', *Hindustan Times*, October 28, 2007 (https://www.hindustantimes.com/india/gujarat-lawyer-says-he-read-out-script/story-kPcCiW6icX9qxGcrK1OgyI.html, accessed April 5, 2025).

5 Vinod K. Jose, 'The Emperor Uncrowned: The Rise of Narendra Modi', *The Caravan*, March 2012 (https://caravanmagazine.in/reportage/emperor-uncrowned-narendra-modi-profile, accessed April 5, 2025).

6 Concerned Citizens' Tribunal, 'History of Communal Violence in Gujarat', *Crime Against Humanity: An Inquiry into the Carnage in Gujarat*, Volume I.

7 Jose, 'The Emperor Uncrowned'.
8 'Hindu Rashtra in two years: Togadia', PTI, December 15, 2002 (https://www.rediff.com/election/2002/dec/15guj13.htm, accessed April 5, 2025).

### 10. Fire in the Sabarmati Express: *Accident or Conspiracy?*

1 So complete is the hold of this version of events on the public mind that to this day Wikipedia has the following description of the origins of the fire: 'The train was attacked by a mob of around 2,000 people. After some stone-pelting, four train coaches were set on fire, trapping many people inside. Fifty-nine people, including 27 women and 10 children were burnt to death, and 48 others were injured. J. Mahapatra, Additional Director General of the Gujarat Police, stated that "miscreants had kept the petrol-soaked rags ready for use much before the train had arrived at Godhra"'. The passage does, however, begin with '[a]ccording to one narrative'. See the 'Godhra train burning' page on Wikipedia (https://en.wikipedia.org/wiki/Godhra_train_burning, accessed April 5, 2025).
2 'The Godhra Fire', Saaf Baat (website), September 8, 2016 (https://saafbaat.com/gujarat-genocide/godhra-fire, accessed April 5, 2025).
3 See 'Modi's Lies to the SIT', Saaf Baat (website), July 27, 2016 (https://saafbaat.com/gujarat-genocide/question-marks-on-sit/modis-lies-sit, accessed April 5, 2025).
4 '"A Cold-Blooded and Clear-Cut Conspiracy": Text of press release put out by the Trustees of the Citizens for Justice and Peace on the protest petition filed by Mrs Zakia Jafri', *Outlook*, January 27, 2022 (https://www.outlookindia.com/website/story/a-cold-blooded-and-clear-cut-conspiracy/284941, accessed April 5, 2025).
5 'If the Gujarat Government's theory of Godhra being a pre-planned conspiracy was indeed the truth, why did their lead investigator need to resort to bribing the witnesses? Why couldn't they create a foolproof case, with more reliable witnesses? Why did they have to change their own charge-sheet after the forensic reports?' Many such pertinent questions are raised in this write-up online. 'The Godhra Fire', Saaf Baat, September 8, 2016.
6 R. Ramachandran, 'More light on the Godhra fire', *Frontline*, February 11, 2005 (https://frontline.thehindu.com/the-nation/

article30203493.ece, accessed April 5, 2025). This was described to the author in detail by IIT professor Dinesh Mohan, who was one of the members of the experts' team.

7 The railways did, in fact, make flame retardant furnishings mandatory in all its carriages after the Godhra tragedy.

8 CCT, *Crime Against Humanity*, Volume III.

9 Report of the Forensic Science Laboratory, Ahmedabad, included in its entirety in ibid.

10 CCT, *Crime Against Humanity*, Volume III, pp. 57–8.

11 See Asghar Ali Engineer, 'Godhra Train Burning Incident And Banerjee Report', *Secular Perspective*, February 1–15, 2004 (https://communalism.blogspot.com/2005/02/godhra-train-burning-incident-and.html, accessed April 5, 2025), and 'Passenger aboard S-6 disputes official line', *The Times of India*, September 10, 2003 (https://timesofindia.indiatimes.com/city/ahmedabad/passenger-aboard-s-6-disputes-official-line/articleshow/176001.cms, accessed April 5, 2025).

12 Publicized by the *Times of India* in July 2002. CCT, *Crime Against Humanity*, Volume III, p. 55.

13 'According to the sequence of events as found by the police, all was not well in coach S-6 of the Ahmedabad-bound Sabarmati Express on that day. A group of unruly Ram sevaks had boarded the train at Lucknow without reservations and had put to discomfort the 66 genuine passengers of the coach. Some of the ticket-paying passengers had to sleep on the floor; so overcrowded had the compartment become that the ticket collector who came aboard the train at Ratlam (two stations before Godhra) was not allowed to enter the coach.' CCT, *Crime Against Humanity*, Volume II, para 3.2.

14 'In all probability, as the fire broke out, there was extreme panic and, the compartment being over-packed, many of the able-bodied persons managed to escape through the vestibules to the other coaches, leaving mostly women and children behind, who must have succumbed to the smoke and suffocation and fallen down in a pile, one over the other. The evidence also suggests that the passengers had stacked their belongings against the doors and it was just not possible for anyone to escape from or enter the coach.' CCT, *Crime Against Humanity*, Volume II, para 2.2.

15 Letter to the SIT examining the Gujarat riots, from Jaspal Singh, a former Gujrat Police chief and cabinet minister in the state government, written on September 7, 2009 (https://www.countercurrents.org/jaspalsingh080909.htm, accessed April 5, 2025).

16 The Special Investigating Team appointed by the Supreme Court six years later, in 2008, accepted VHP leader Jaideep Patel's claim that he had rushed from Ahmedabad to Godhra because of a call he had received on his mobile from a kar sevak travelling in the ill-fated train. But call data records cited by Begum Zakia Jafri's lawyer, showed that Patel had received a call from one of Modi's personal assistants. This evidence indicated that Modi himself had asked Patel to go to Godhra with him. Possibly on his instructions, the police allowed Patel and his followers to enter the gutted coach and take out the bodies. More significantly, after Modi's visit, the Godhra administration issued a letter to Patel authorizing him to take possession of 54 bodies.

17 The Gujarati newspaper *Sandesh* carried the following headlines, among others, the next day: (1) 'THE DISTRICT COLLECTOR [of Godhra] SAID ONLY ONE THING: THIS IS THE HANDIWORK OF ANTI SOCIAL ELEMENTS. THIS IS THE SORRY STATE OF THE ADMINISTRATION'; (2) 'THE DEAD ARE NOT MERE RAM SEVAKS, THEY ARE THE HEIRS OF RANA PRATAP, GURU GOVIND SINGH.' CCT, *Crime Against Humanity*, Volume III, Annexure 36.

18 CCT, *Crime Against Humanity*, Volume II, p. 75.

19 Media reports, downloaded from the Gujarat Police website in 2002.

20 CCT, *Crime Against Humanity*, Volume I.

21 The sequence of events at the Prime Minister's office was described to the author by a senior member of the office on condition of anonymity.

22 'My govt is being defamed, says Modi', *The Tribune*, March 9, 2002 (https://www.tribuneindia.com/2002/20020310/main4.htm, accessed April 5, 2025).

23 '"Who Started The Fire?"', published in English translation in *Outlook*, April 20, 2002 (https://www.outlookindia.com/website/story/who-started-the-fire/215254, accessed April 5, 2025).

## 11. Gujarat, 2002 to 2014: *The Birth of an Authoritarian State*

1 Jose, 'The Emperor Uncrowned'.

2 Ibid.

3 M. Saleem Pandit, 'Case "solved" twice in three days', *The Times of India*, September 1, 2003 (https://timesofindia.indiatimes.com/india/Case-solved-twice-in-three-days/articleshow/156036.cms, accessed April 5, 2025).

4 The Gujarat High Court also upheld the sentence in 2010, but in 2014 the Supreme Court reversed its judgement and acquitted all the six accused saying, 'We intend to express our anguish about the incompetence with which the investigating agencies conducted the investigation of the case of such a grievous nature, involving the integrity and security of the nation. Instead of booking the real culprits responsible for taking so many precious lives, police caught innocent people and got imposed the grievous charges against them which resulted in their conviction and subsequent sentencing… On the basis of the issues, we have already answered the facts and evidence on record, and on the basis of the legal principles laid down by this court, we are convinced that accused persons are innocent with respect to the charges levelled against them. As a result no one was punished for the killing and injuring of more than a hundred innocent civilians.' 'SC acquits Akshardham terror strike convicts, slams Gujarat Police probe', *Business Standard*, May 16, 2014 (https://www.business-standard.com/article/news-ians/sc-acquits-akshardham-terror-strike-convicts-slams-gujarat-police-probe-114051601843_1.html, accessed April 5, 2025).

5 Erda was later accused of 'criminal negligence' but acquitted by the special court set up after the Supreme Court mandated SIT filed charges against him. He did, however, send several messages from his post describing the attack on the Gulberg Society, but no police came to the rescue till past 4.30 in the evening.

6 Vinay Menon, 'Cops admit killing more Muslims', *Hindustan Times*, May 3, 2002.

7 Rupak Sanyal, 'Indian police reports say governing party official and Hindu nationalist leaders led mobs', Associated Press, March 5, 2002.

8 '"We Have No Orders To Save You": State Participation and

Complicity in Communal Violence in Gujarat', Human Rights Watch report, April 30, 2002 (https://www.hrw.org/report/2002/04/30/we-have-no-orders-save-you/state-participation-and-complicity-communal-violence, accessed April 5, 2025).

9 Dionne Bunsha, *Scarred: Experiments with Violence in Gujarat*, Penguin, 2006.

10 https://indialawyers.wordpress.com/2009/05/18/a-bold-and-fearless-judge/

11 *Zahira Habibulla H. Sheikh and Anr vs State of Gujarat and Ors*, Appeal (Crl) 446–449 of 2004 (available online: https://api.sci.gov.in/jonew/judis/26084.pdf, accessed April 5, 2025).

12 Jose, 'The Emperor Uncrowned'.

13 Ibid.

14 Sadiq Naqvi, 'Modi's Revenge on Good Cops', Hardnews, May 16, 2011 (https://web.archive.org/web/20190907075338/http://www.hardnewsmedia.com/2011/05/3968, accessed April 5, 2025).

15 Ibid.

16 Neena Vyas, 'Geetha Johri Report speaks of "Collusion of State Government"', *The Hindu*, May 5, 2007 (https://www.thehindu.com/todays-paper/Geetha-Johri-report-speaks-of-ampquotcollusion-of-State-governmentampquot/article14759360.ece, accessed April 5, 2025).

17 'Geeta Johri's career graph: From Latif to Sohrabuddin', *The Times of India*, January 21, 2010 (https://timesofindia.indiatimes.com/city/ahmedabad/Geeta-Johris-career-graph-From-Latif-to-Sohrabuddin/articleshow/5482793.cms, accessed April 5, 2025).

18 Harsh Mander, 'To Sanjiv Bhatt, a Man Who Displayed the Highest Courage', *The Wire*, June 12, 2019 (https://thewire.in/rights/sanjiv-bhatt-sentenced-narendra-modi-gujarat-riots, accessed April 5, 2025).

19 'Gujarat police officer implicates Modi in riots', *The Hindu* (http://www.thehindu.com/news/national/Gujarat-police-officer-implicates-Modi-in-riots/article10321755.ece, accessed April 5, 2025).

20 'Proceed against Modi for Gujarat riots: amicus', *The Hindu*, October 18, 2016 (https://www.thehindu.com/news/national/Proceed-against-Modi-for-Gujarat-riots-amicus/article12828442.ece, accessed April 5, 2025).

21 Rana Ayyub, *The Gujarat Files: Anatomy of a Cover Up*, 2016, p. 159.
22 'Gujarat police officer implicates Modi in riots', *The Hindu*.
23 'Acute kidney injury', Mayo Clinic website (https://www.mayoclinic.org/diseases-conditions/kidney-failure/symptoms-causes/syc-20369048, accessed April 5, 2025).
24 'Gujarat Cops in Modi's line of fire', *India Today*, August 12, 2011 (http://indiatoday.intoday.in/story/gujarat-in-modi-government-line-of-fire/1/147826.html, accessed April 5, 2025).
25 This case was eventually suspended by the Supreme Court in 2012. Bhatt maintained that the arrest had been driven by 'political vendetta'. See 'India court stays trial of Gujarat riots policeman', BBC, April 20, 2012 (https://www.bbc.com/news/world-asia-india-17781286, accessed April 5, 2025).
26 '"Modi-phobia" has gripped Gujarat police: Ex-DGP RB Sreekumar', *The Times of India*, October 3, 2011 (https://archive.ph/20131106152100/http://articles.timesofindia.indiatimes.com/2011-10-03/india/30238039_1_role-in-gujarat-riots-gujarat-police-narendra-modi#selection-563.1-563.62, accessed April 5, 2025).
27 Rana Ayyub, 'Dead Man Talking', *Tehelka*, vol. 8, issue no. 48, December 3, 2011 (https://web.archive.org/web/20140221160825/http://archive.tehelka.com/story_main51.asp?filename=Ne031211Coverstory.asp, accessed April 5, 2025).
28 Ibid.
29 Krishnadas Rajagopal, 'Probe all 22 fake encounters between 2002 and 2006, SC tells Gujarat panel', *The Indian Express*, January 25, 2012 (http://archive.indianexpress.com/news/probe-all-22-fake-encounters-between-2002-and-2006-sc-tells-gujarat-panel/903979/2, accessed April 5, 2025).
30 Krishnadas Rajagopal, 'Gujarat encounters: Supreme Court takes up plea for SIT probe', *The Hindu*, December 3, 2018 (https://www.thehindu.com/news/national/gujarat-encounters-sc-gives-time-for-state-govt-to-respond/article25653334.ece, accessed April 5, 2025).
31 '3 Gujarat Encounters Fake, Says Probe Panel; 9 Police Officials Indicted', NDTV, January 12, 2019 (https://www.ndtv.com/india-news/justice-hs-bedi-panel-finds-3-out-of-17-gujarat-encounters-fake-recommends-action-against-9-cops-1976615, accessed April 5, 2025).

32 'India: Gujarat Chief Minister Endorses Unlawful Killings', Human Rights Watch, December 7, 2007 (https://www.hrw.org/news/2007/12/07/india-gujarat-chief-minister-endorses-unlawful-killings?utm, accessed April 5, 2025).

## 12. Faked Encounters: *A Foretaste of India's Lawless Future*

1 Quoted in extenso by S.P. Tamang in his report, available online: https://cjp.org.in/s-p-tamangs-report-on-police-encounters-in-gujarat/ (accessed April 5, 2025).

2 Ibid.

3 Satish Jha, 'CBI finds common link in Haren Pandya murder, Ishrat encounter', *The Indian Express*, August 15, 2013 (http://archive.indianexpress.com/news/cbi-finds-common-link-in-haren-pandya-murder-ishrat-encounter/1155698/, accessed April 5, 2025).

4 Manas Dasgupta, 'Ishrat Jahan killing also a fake encounter: probe report', *The Hindu*, December 4, 2021 (http://www.thehindu.com/news/national/ishrat-jahan-killing-also-a-fake-encounter-probe-report/article16559.ece, accessed April 5, 2025).

5 'A senior police officer in Gandhinagar told rediff.com that the plan suggests a list of things that every policeman from the constable level upwards must do to keep the police force abreast of the situation at the ground level and one step ahead of the terrorists. One of them is to keep tabs on meetings at masjids and sermons made by members of the Tablighi Jamaat in the state. "The plan is going to be a trend-setter in India with respect to tackling terrorist activities," a source in the state's home ministry said, adding, "After the communal riots in 2002, Gujarat has become vulnerable. [Gujarat Chief Minister] Narendra Modi faces the biggest threat from Islamic terrorists. We have taken the challenge seriously."' This appeared in the online journal *Rediff.com* on July 15, 2004, exactly a month after Ishrat Jahan and her companions were killed. Sheela Bhatt, 'How Gujarat plans to counter terrorists', *Rediff.com* (https://web.archive.org/web/20210314171744/http://us.rediff.com/news/2004/jul/15sb.htm?headline=How~Gujarat~plans~to~counter~terrorists, accessed April 5, 2025).

6 Its members were the additional director general of police (ADGP) of the Central Industrial Security Force, R.R. Verma, ADGP of

Gujarat Police, Mohan Jha, and inspector general of Gujarat police, Satish Verma.

7 'The journalist who cracked Gujarat fake encounter case', *Rediff.com*, April 25, 2007 (https://web.archive.org/web/20250314101209/https://www.rediff.com/news/2007/apr/25spec.htm Rediff.com/news/2007/April/25spec.htm, accessed April 5, 2025).

8 'Fake encounter: How Sohrabuddin Sheikh was killed', *Hindustan Times*, May 5, 2007 (https://www.hindustantimes.com/india/fake-encounter-how-sohrabuddin-sheikh-was-killed/story-qIH4v5v4g0LTyhhSlz59AN.html, accessed April 5, 2025).

9 Julio Ribeiro is a famed, almost legendary former chief of police who was later appointed to this post in Punjab during the height of the Khalistan rebellion. He was shot and almost killed by the terrorists.

10 'Modi boots out Godhra collector', *The Times of India*, July 5, 2002 (https://timesofindia.indiatimes.com/city/ahmedabad/modi-boots-out-godhra-collector/articleshow/15065046.cms, accessed April 5, 2025).

11 See 'Is SIT hiding proof in Gujarat riots case?', *The Times of India*, July 18, 2013 (https://timesofindia.indiatimes.com/india/is-sit-hiding-proof-in-gujarat-riots-case/articleshow/21132148.cms, accessed April 5, 2025).

12 'Read DG Vanzara's letter', *The Times of India*, September 3, 2013 (http://timesofindia.indiatimes.com/india/Read-DG-Vanzaras-letter/articleshow/22262722.cms, accessed April 5, 2025).

13 See 'State Complicity, Government of Gujarat, 2002, Role of Chief Minister', Sabrang India, November 30, 2002 (https://sabrangindia.in/state-complicity-government-gujarat-2002-role-chief-minister/, accessed April 5, 2025).

## 13. The Mystery of Haren Pandya's Murder

1 Jose, 'The Emperor Uncrowned'.

2 See Kingshuk Nag, 'Who killed Haren Pandya?', *The Times of India*, September 12, 2011 (https://blogs.timesofindia.indiatimes.com/masala-noodles/who-killed-haren-pandya/, accessed April 5, 2025).

3 Jose, 'The Emperor Uncrowned'.

4 Sankarshan Thakur, 'Who Killed Haren Pandya?', first published in *Tehelka*, August 19, 2006 (https://sankarshanthakur.in/2012/12/02/who-killed-haren-pandya/, accessed April 5, 2025).

5 Ibid.

6 'A Midnight Meeting On Feb 27 And A Murdered Minister', *Outlook*, November 12, 2007 (https://www.outlookindia.com/national/a-midnight-meeting-on-feb-27-and-a-murdered-minister-news-235982, accessed April 5, 2025).

7 Sankarshan Thakur, 'Who Killed Haren Pandya?'.

8 Aparna Chandra, William H.J. Hubbard, and Sital Kalantry, 'The Supreme Court of India: An Empirical Overview of the Institution', University of Chicago, Public Law Working Paper No. 660, August 31, 2018 (https://papers.ssrn.com/sol3/papers.cfm?abstract_id=3154597, accessed April 5, 2025).

9 Srishti Ojha, '"Reversal Of Acquittal Is Permissible Only If Trial Court's View Is Not Only Erroneous But Also Unreliable & Perverse" Supreme Court Reiterates, *LiveLaw*, December 22, 2021 (https://www.livelaw.in/top-stories/supreme-court-acquittal-order-reversal-trial-court-erroneous-unreliable-perverse-188187, accessed April 5, 2025).

10 'Jagruti Pandya meets man acquitted in Haren Pandya murder case', *Hindu BusinessLine*, March 12, 2018 (https://www.thehindubusinessline.com/news/jagruti-pandya-meets-man-acquitted-in-haren-pandya-murder-case/article20623567.ece, accessed April 5, 2025). He was not the only one: Ajit Doval, whom Modi had selected to be his National Security Adviser, was another.

11 Sadaf Modak, 'Sohrabuddin encounter case: Ex-IPS officer gave contract to kill Haren Pandya, says witness', *The Indian Express*, November 4, 2018 (https://indianexpress.com/article/india/sohrabuddin-encounter-case-ex-ips-officer-gave-contract-to-kill-haren-pandya-says-witness-5433145/, accessed April 5, 2025).

12 Ajoy Ashirwad Mahaprashasta, 'The Story of Azam Khan, Endangered Keeper of Deadly Secrets from Haren Pandya to Sohrabuddin', The Wire, November 15, 2018 (https://southasiajournal.net/the-story-of-azam-khan-endangered-keeper-of-deadly-secrets-from-haren-pandya-to-sohrabuddin/, accessed April 5, 2025). See also 'Mystery over Haren Pandya Killing Deepens After Witness Says Top Gujarat Cop Gave Order', *The Wire*, November 5, 2018 (https://thewire.in/rights/mystery-over-haren-pandya-killing-deepens-after-witness-says-top-gujarat-cop-gave-order, accessed April 5, 2025).

13 Mahaprashasta, 'The Story of Azam Khan'.

14 Ibid.

## 14. The Maturing of Indian Fascism

1 The Congress won 404 seats out of 543, based on 49.1 per cent of the votes polled.

2 See Christophe Jaffrelot, *Modi's India: Hindu Nationalism and the Rise of Ethnic Democracy*, Princeton University Press, 2021.

3 *A Bunch of Thoughts*, Vikrama Prakashan, first published February 1966, p. 100.

4 Ibid., p. 107.

5 Seshadri Chari, 'Decoding "Hindu Rashtra"', *India Today*, November 8, 2019 (https://www.indiatoday.in/magazine/cover-story/story/20191118-decoding-hindu-rashtra-1616717-2019-11-08, accessed April 5, 2025).

6 'Prime Minister Shri Atal Bihari Vajpayee's Musings from Goa: Let Us Celebrate—and Strengthen—Our Indianness', December 13, 2002, archived page of the PMO website (https://archivepmo.nic.in/abv/speech-details.php?nodeid=9133, accessed April 5, 2025).

7 Vajpayee's governor of the strategically important Andaman and Nicobar Islands, N.N. Jha, was also a similar inductee. He was the author's brother.

8 Karan Thapar, 'Has the RSS ground shifted?', The Indian Express, September 21, 2018 (https://indianexpress.com/article/opinion/columns/mohan-bhagwat-rss-event-hindutva-congress-5367217/, accessed April 5, 2025).

9 'Param Poojaniya Sarsanghchalak Dr. Mohan Bhagwat Ji's Full Speech on the occasion of Shri Vijayadashami Utsav 2023', RSS' official website, October 24, 2023 (https://www.rss.org/Encyc/2023/10/24/VijayaDashami-2023-Speech.html, accessed April 5, 2025).

## 15. A Decade of Fascist Consolidation

1 Khanwilkar had also headed a bench a few months earlier that had taken the unprecedented step of recommending the imprisonment of Teesta Setalvad, two noted civil rights activists, and former director of Gujarat's Intelligence Bureau, R.B. Sreekumar, for having had the temerity to bring Begum Zakia Jafri's case against the murder of her husband, Ehsan Jafri, during the 2002 Ahmedabad riots, back to the Supreme Court after Sathasivam had 'returned' it to the Gujarat High Court more than a decade earlier.

2 See 'The Central Government spent close to Rs 10000 crore on Publicity in the last 16 years', Factly, May 4, 2018 (https://factly.in/the-central-government-spent-10000-crore-on-publicity-in-the-last-16-years/, accessed April 5, 2025).

3 *Draft Performance Audit: Allocation of Coal Blocks and Augmentation of Coal Production by Coal India Limited*, report of the Comptroller and Auditor-General of India, available online: https://www.sourcewatch.org/images/4/40/Draft_CAG_report_Pt_1.pdf (accessed April 5, 2025).

4 'Ex-RBI Governor D Subbarao on 2G scam: "CAG's Rs 1.76 lakh crore 'presumptive loss' contestable"', *Business Today*, May 1, 2024 (https://www.businesstoday.in/india/story/ex-rbi-governor-d-subbarao-on-2g-scam-cags-rs-176-lakh-crore-presumptive-loss-contestable-427772-2024-05-01, accessed April 5, 2025).

5 'Sealed Cover Procedure Fundamentally Against Judicial Process: Supreme Court [VIDEO]', *LiveLaw*, March 21, 2023 (https://www.livelaw.in/videos/sealed-cover-procedure-fundamentally-against-judicial-process-supreme-court-224346, accessed April 5, 2025).

6 The submission of evidence in a sealed envelop only to the judges, which continues till this day, is an extremely retrograde practice, because it does not permit the lawyers of the defendant to question the verity of the statements it contains. The practice of accepting such evidence goes back to British law passed in 1872, within fifteen years of the Indian uprising of 1857, which very nearly ended British rule in India. It was therefore an intentionally retrograde permission deliberately intended to allow a post-colonial regime to retain every shred of the arbitrary power when they were the masters and not the servants of the people.

7 'States Barring CBI Investigation', PIB press release, March 24, 2021 (https://pib.gov.in/Pressreleaseshare.aspx?PRID=1707269, accessed April 5, 2025).

8 '10 states withdraw general consent to CBI to investigate cases', *Economic Times*, December 20, 2023 (https://economictimes.indiatimes.com/news/india/10-states-withdraw-general-consent-to-cbi-to-investigate-cases-centre/articleshow/106151348.cms?from=mdr, accessed April 5, 2025).

9 'Section 45 of the Act…takes away the presumption of innocence usually afforded to accused persons under criminal law. To be

granted bail, the accused must prove prima facie that they were not guilty, and satisfy the Court that they will not commit any further offence. These "twin bail conditions" under PMLA [were central to *Vijay Madanlal Choudhary vs Union of India*, 2022]. Interestingly, the SC declared this provision unconstitutional in *Nikesh Tarachand Shah vs Union of India* (2017). The Union government then amended the provision in 2018. The ED claimed that this amendment brought the provision in line with *Nikesh Tarachand Shah*. The petitioners argued that the amendment undermined the Judgment, and re-established the original twin conditions.' See 'Challenges to the Prevention of Money Laundering Act', Supreme Court Observer (https://www.scobserver.in/cases/challenges-to-the-prevention-of-money-laundering-act-vijay-madanlal-choudhary-union-india-case-background/, accessed April 5, 2025).

10 See *Vijay Madanlal Choudhary vs Union of India*, July 27, 2022 (https://indiankanoon.org/doc/14485072/), and *Nikesh Tarachand Shah vs Union of India*, WP (Criminal) No. 67 of 2017 (https://indiankanoon.org/doc/117859307/).

11 Ajoy Sinha Karpuram, 'Justice AM Khanwilkar: Aadhaar to UAPA to PMLA, he authored many crucial orders', *The Indian Express*, February 28, 2024 (https://indianexpress.com/article/india/justice-a-m-khanwilkar-aadhaar-to-uapa-to-pmla-he-authored-many-crucial-orders-9185026/, accessed April 5, 2025).

12 Ayushi Saraogi, 'Months from Retirement, Justice Khanwilkar Reserves Three Critical Judgments', *The Supreme Court Observer*, March 23, 2022 (https://www.scobserver.in/journal/months-from-retirement-justice-khanwilkar-reserves-three-critical-judgments-2/, accessed April 5, 2025).

13 'Of 5,422 money laundering cases, 98% filed in past 8 years', *The Tribune*, June 14, 2022 (https://www.tribuneindia.com/news/nation/of-5-422-pmla-cases-98-filed-in-past-8-years-403614/).

14 'Book the Guilty: Quint Journalist Who Found Alphanumeric Code on Electoral Bonds', *The Quint*, March 20, 2024 (https://www.thequint.com/news/india/electoral-bonds-hidden-alphanumeric-numbers-data-the-quint-journalist-poonam-agarwal-first-discovered-investigation-what-to-expect, accessed April 5, 2025).

15 Statement made by Congress General Secretary Priyanka Vadra, on March 24, 2024, based upon *The Hindu*'s analysis. See 'Electoral

bonds full data | Complete list of donors, parties and unique numbers', *The Hindu*, March 21, 2024 (https://www.thehindu.com/data/electoral-bond-full-data-complete-list-of-donors-parties-and-unique-numbers/article67976056.ece, accessed April 5, 2025). See also 'Priyanka Gandhi's big charge on electoral bonds: 41 companies under ED, CBI, IT radar donated Rs 2,592 cr to BJP', *Business Today*, March 24, 2024 (https://www.businesstoday.in/india/story/priyanka-gandhis-big-charge-on-electoral-bonds-41-companies-under-ed-cbi-it-radar-donated-rs-2592-cr-to-bjp-422705-2024-03-24?onetap=true, accessed April 5, 2025).

16 Prasenjit Bose,The Hindu Data Team, '33 loss-making firms donated electoral bonds worth ₹582 crore, 75% went to BJP | Data', *The Hindu*, April 4, 2024 (https://www.thehindu.com/data/thirty-three-loss-making-firms-donated-electoral-bonds-worth-582-crore-75-went-to-bjp-data/article68025625.ece, accessed April 5, 2025).

17 'Santiago Martin aka Lottery King | The business tycoon who topped the list of electoral bond donors', *The Hindu*, March 15, 2024 (https://www.thehindu.com/news/national/tamil-nadu/santiago-martin-aka-lottery-king-the-business-tycoon-who-topped-the-list-of-electoral-bond-donors/article67953870.ece, accessed April 5, 2025). Source of data: the Election Commission of India.

18 Ibid.

## 16. A Glimpse of India's Electoral Autocracy

1 See Prem Shankar Jha, 'Narendra Modi's War on Arvind Kejriwal Will Have Repercussions Beyond Delhi', *The Wire*, October 8, 2016 (https://thewire.in/politics/narendra-modis-war-arvind-kejriwal-will-repercussions-beyond-delhi-2, accessed April 5, 2025), and 'Narendra Modi's War on Arvind Kejriwal Will Have Repercussions Beyond Delhi', *The Wire*, August 8, 2016 (https://thewire.in/politics/57117, accessed April 5, 2025).

2 For a detailed description of the ED's delaying tactics, see 'Former Maharashtra home minister Anil Deshmukh walks out of jail: A timeline of the events that led to his release', *The Indian Express*, January 5, 2023 (https://indianexpress.com/article/cities/mumbai/former-maharashtra-home-minister-anil-deshmukh-jail-timeline-8349145/, accessed April 5, 2025).

3 Ibid.
4 Anand Mohan J., 'Who are the so-called 'South Group', accused by ED in the Delhi Excise Policy case?', *The Indian Express*, February 28, 2023 (https://indianexpress.com/article/explained/delhi-excise-policy-case-south-group-ed-explained-8471901/, accessed April 5, 2025).
5 'SC dismisses ex-Delhi minister Satyendra Jain's bail plea, asks him to surrender', *Hindustan Times*, March 18, 2024 (https://www.hindustantimes.com/india-news/sc-dismisses-ex-delhi-minister-satyendra-jain-s-bail-plea-asks-him-to-surrender-101710740743925.html, accessed April 5, 2025).
6 Statement of Justice Khanna on April 1, 2024. See 'AAP's Sanjay Singh granted bail in Delhi Excise policy case as ED concedes', *The Hindu*, April 4, 2024 (https://www.thehindu.com/news/cities/Delhi/aaps-sanjay-singh-gets-bail-after-six-months-in-delhi-excise-policy-case/article68019306.ece, accessed April 5, 2025).
7 'Punjab's excise revenue up by 41.4% in 2022-2023', The Hindu, April 7, 2023 (https://www.thehindu.com/news/national/other-states/punjabs-excise-revenue-up-by-44-in-2022-2023/article66707494.ece, accessed April 5, 2025).
8 'Punjab collected record excise revenue this year: Harpal Cheema', *The Tribune*, April 1, 2025 (https://www.tribuneindia.com/news/punjab/punjab-collects-record-excise-revenue-this-year-harpal-cheema/, accessed April 5, 2025).
9 Explained to the author by Arvind Kejriwal after his release from prison on bail in February 2025. Till then no journalist had asked him this question.
10 For a detailed description of the transformation that the party has brought to the lives of the working class in Delhi state, see chapters 1, 2, 3, 6 and 7 of *The Delhi Model* by Jasmine Shah (Penguin Business, 2024). Shah is a member of the AAP. The data cited in his book have not been challenged.
11 It would not have been the first time that elections had been rigged. For it had been a regular practice of the Jammu and Kashmir National Conference in the decades between the imprisonment of Sheikh Abdullah, in 1953, and his final reconciliation with Delhi and return to power in 1977. In those years, the disqualification of a few non-National Conference aspirants in the Kashmir valley

to ensure an absolute majority for the JKNC over the whole of Jammu and Kashmir, had been a routine practice. It was the long brewing revolt against this, and not a revolt against 'Hindu' India that led to the eruption of insurgency in 1987. When state assembly elections were finally held in 1996 after the nine-year insurgency in the state had died down, many Kashmiris had complained that this practice had been resumed by the National Conference to register a thumping win. The clamour that this would happen again rose in the state again before the 2002 elections. But this time there was an exceptionally strong chief election commissioner in Delhi, James Michael Lyngdoh, from India's Northeast. Lyngdoh resolved this doubt by decreeing that instead of all the four polling officers who manned each polling station being drawn from within the state's bureaucracy, two out of the four would have to be inducted from other states. The result was a thumping win for the Peoples' Democratic Party (PDP) that gave Kashmir the six best governed years in its history. Lyngdoh received the Ramon Magsaysay Award for Government Service in 2003 'for the important role he played in ensuring free and fair State Assembly elections in Jammu & Kashmir and Gujarat in 2002 despite the prevailing unfavourable circumstances in the states'. But Lyngdoh retired in 2002, and the solution that he had applied in Kashmir was not replicated in the rest of the country in any of the elections that followed.

12 From 54.3 to 18.2 between the state assembly election of 2015 and parliamentary election in 2019, and from 53.6 percent to 24.1 percent between the former in 2020 and the latter in 2024. See also Prem Shankar Jha, 'Why Is Defeating the AAP So Important for Modi?', *The Wire*, February 7, 2025 (https://thewire.in/politics/why-defeating-aap-important-for-modi, accessed April 5, 2025).

13 '"Form-7 can be filed for deletion of bogus votes"', *The Times of India*, March 8, 2019 (https://timesofindia.indiatimes.com/city/amaravati/form-7-can-be-filed-for-deletion-of-bogus-votes/articleshow/68314111.cms, accessed April 5, 2025).

14 Saumya Shubham Jha, 'Names of AAP voters being deleted from electoral roll, Arvind Kejriwal claims', *India Today*, December 6, 2024 (https://www.indiatoday.in/elections/assembly/story/delhi-elections-arvind-kejriwal-claims-name-of-aam-aadmi-party-voters-being-deleted-electoral-roll-2645966-2024-12-06, accessed April 5, 2025).

## Epilogue: Can Democracy Still Be Saved?

1 Sobhana K. Nair, 'G-23 should answer why they didn't stand by me, says Shashi Tharoor', *The Hindu*, October 22, 2022 (https://www.thehindu.com/news/national/shashi-tharoor-says-congress-g-23-should-answer-why-they-didnt-stand-by-him/article66032143.ece, accessed April 5, 2025).

2 '"Not Our Responsibility…": Congress Shrugs Off INDIA Ally AAP's Delhi Rout', NDTV, February 8, 2024 (https://www.ndtv.com/video/not-our-responsibility-congress-shrugs-off-india-ally-aap-s-delhi-rout-899732, accessed April 5, 2025).

3 Unstarred Question No: 2657, Lok Sabha (available online: https://eparlib.nic.in/bitstream/123456789/618748/1/75702.pdf, accessed March 26, 2025).

4 'State Funding of Elections', PRS website (https://prsindia.org/theprsblog/state-funding-of-elections?page=9&per-page=1, accessed March 26, 2025).

5 Adrija Roychowdhury, 'Secularism: Why Nehru dropped and Indira inserted the S-word in the Constitution', *The Indian Express*, December 27, 2017 (https://indianexpress.com/article/research/anant-kumar-hegde-secularism-constitution-india-bjp-jawaharlal-nehru-indira-gandhi-5001085/, accessed March 26, 2025).

6 See Mehrdad Shokoohy, 'The Legacy of Islam in Somnath', *Bulletin of the School of Oriental and African Studies*, vol. 75, no. 2 (2012), pp. 297–335 (http://www.jstor.org/stable/23259581).

7 Romila Thapar, 'Somanatha and Mahmud', *Frontline*, April 10-23, 1999 (https://franpritchett.com/00islamlinks/txt_thapar_somnath.html, accessed April 5, 2025).

8 Kapil Dixit, 'Muslim students in UP's RSS schools rise 30% in 3 years', *The Times of India*, February 21, 2020 (https://timesofindia.indiatimes.com/city/allahabad/muslim-students-in-ups-rss-schools-rise-30-in-3-years/articleshow/74234292.cms, accessed April 5, 2025).